Baedeker
Denmark

GW00729196

Baedeker's

DENMARK

Imprint

123 colour photographs, 38 maps and plans, 1 large map at end of book

Original German text: Reinhold Dey, Norbert Ney, Bettina P. Oesten, Axel Patitz, Dr Eckart Pott

Editorial work (German edition): Baedeker, Redaktion (Andrea Wurth)
(English edition): Margaret Court

Cartography: Gert Oberländer, Munich; Mairs Geographischer Verlag, GmbH & Co., Ostfildern-Kemnat (large map)

General direction (German edition): Dr Peter Baumgarten, Baedeker
(English edition): Alec Court

English translation: Wendy Bell, David Cocking, Alec Court, Brenda Ferris

Source of illustrations: Aalborg Turistbureau (3); Dr Madeleine Cabos (9); Danish Tourist Bureau (53); Ebeltoft Glass Museum (1); Esbjerg Museum (1); Udo Haafke (6); Historia-Photo (4); Hans Klüche (7); Korsør Turistbureau (1); Kubel Foto (1); Helga Lade (5); Legoland A/S (2); Uwe Lochstampfer (3); Louisiana Museum (3); Manesse Verlag, Zurich (1); Wolfgang Müller (4); Peter M. Nahm (1); Odense Bys Museer (2); Pedersen (1); Dr Eckart Pott (5); Silkeborg Art Museum (2); Storebælt Billedarkiv (1); Süddeutscher Verlag Bilderdienst (2); Jörg Trobitzsch (1); ZEFA (1)

Following the tradition established by Karl Baedeker in 1844, sights of particular interest and hotels and restaurants of particular quality are distinguished by either one or two asterisks.

To make it easier to locate the various places listed in the "A to Z" section of the Guide, their co-ordinates on the large country map are shown at the head of each entry.

Only a selection of hotels, restaurants and shops can be given; no reflection is implied therefore on establishments not included.
In a time of rapid change it is difficult to ensure that all the information given is entirely accurate and up-to-date, and the possibility of error can never be entirely eliminated. Although the publishers can accept no responsibility for inaccuracies and omissions, they are always grateful for corrections and suggestions for improvement.

2nd English edition 1994

© Baedeker Stuttgart Original German edition

© 1994 Jarrold and Sons Ltd English language edition worldwide

© 1994 The Automobile Association United Kingdom and Ireland

Distributed in the United Kingdom by the Publishing Division of The Automobile Association, Fanum House, Basingstoke, Hampshire, RG21 2EA

The name *Baedeker* is a registered trademark
A CIP catalogue record for this book is available from the British Library.

Licensed user: Mairs Geographischer Verlag GmbH & Co., Ostfildern-Kemnat bei Stuttgart

Reproductions: Golz Repro-Service GmbH, Ludwigsburg; Filderset Offsetreproduktionen GmbH, Ostfildern-Kemnat

Printed in Italy by G. Canale & C. S.p.A – Borgaro T.se – Turin

Published in the United States by:
Macmillan Travel
A Prentice Hall Macmillan Company
15 Columbus Circle, New York, NY 10023

Macmillan is a registered trademark of Macmillan Inc.

ISBN 0–671–89688–1 US and Canada
        0–7495–0884–1 UK

Contents

Principal Sights at a Glance

N.B. The places listed above are, merely a selection of the principal places of tourist interest in Denmark, the Faroes and Greenland which are worth visiting for themselves or for attractions in the surrounding area. There are in addition many other interesting sights indicated by stars in the individual entries.

Preface

This guide to Denmark is one of the new generation of Baedeker guides.

These guides, illustrated throughout in colour, are designed to meet the needs of the modern traveller. They are quick and easy to consult, with the principal places of interest described in alphabetical order, and the information is presented in a format that is both attractive and easy to follow.

The subject of this guide is Denmark, that is the Jutland peninsula and the Danish islands, including Bornholm. Also included is brief information about the Faroe Islands and Greenland, the largest island in the world, both lying in the north of the Atlantic.

The guide is in three parts. The first part gives a general account of the country, its landscape, climate, flora and fauna, protected areas, population, government and administration, economy and communications, history, famous people, and art history. A selection of quotations and a number of suggested itineraries provide a transition to the second part, in which the country's places and features of tourist interest – towns, villages, islands and scenery – are described. The third part contains a variety of practical information. Both the sights and the practical information are listed in alphabetical order.

The new Baedeker guides are noted for their concentration on essentials and their convenience of use. They contain numerous specially drawn plans and colour illustrations; and at the end of the book is a large map making it easy to locate the various places described in the "A to Z" section of the guide with the help of the co-ordinates given at the head of each entry.

Facts and Figures

General

Denmark, which consists of the peninsula of Jutland and numerous islands, also has external possessions, in particular the Faroe Islands and Greenland. Entries on both are included in the A–Z section of this guide.

N.B.

Denmark (Danish "Danmark") is situated in northern Europe between latitudes 54°34′ and 57°45′N, longitudes 8°5′ and 12°35′E (Bornholm Island 15°12′E). In the south it has a common border with Germany, but elsewhere is surrounded entirely by water. The long German frontier, running obliquely across the Jutland peninsula, stretches for some 68km/42 miles; the coastline is about 7400km/4598 miles in length. To the west, Denmark is bordered by the North Sea, but a large part of its territory lies in the Baltic. Two narrow straits, the Kattegat and Skagerrak (east and north-west of Jutland respectively), separate the Baltic, an inland sea, from the North Sea and the Atlantic Ocean beyond. Owing to its position, Denmark has always acted as a stepping-stone between Central Europe and the countries of the Scandinavian peninsula (there is a plan to build a bridge across the Øresund to connect Denmark with Sweden).

Situation

Denmark

© Baedeker

It is difficult to put a precise figure on Denmark's size since its area is constantly changing owing to the action of the sea and the recovery of new stretches of land. In coastal areas subject to tides the line of the coast can vary considerably between high and low water, a phenomenon particularly noticeable on the west coast of southern Jutland. Ignoring the many lakes and watercourses as well as the fjords and bays with open access to the sea, Denmark's boundaries enclose an area totalling some 43,092sq.km/16,633sq.miles. Of this the largest portion comprises the Jutland peninsula (Jylland), covering 29,647sq.km/11,444sq.miles; the 406 islands, of which 92 are inhabited, together make up a further 13,309sq.km/5137sq.miles. The largest island is Zealand (Sjælland) with an area of 7517sq.km/2901sq.miles, followed by Funen (Fyn; 2984sq.km/1152sq.miles), Lolland (1234sq.km/476sq.miles), Bornholm (588sq.km/227sq.miles) and Falster (514sq.km/198sq.miles).

Size

Topography

Denmark is a low-lying country, the highest point being Yding Skovhøj, with an altitude of only 173m/568ft, in East Jutland south of Skanderborg. The landscape is characterised by low hills, forests, lakes, little rivers and beaches, often excellent for bathing.
Geologically the Jutland peninsula and the Danish islands are made up of layers of chalk, which appear as outcrops around the Limfjord and on

◄ *Old Lighthouse near Rubjerg (North Jutland)*

Countryside near Hornbæk

certain of the islands. The island of Bornholm, however, is composed of ancient granites.

Like the whole of northern Europe, Denmark was covered for thousands of years by huge expanses of ice. After the melting of the Ice Age glaciers about 10,000 years ago, diluvial moraine was left in many places, a mixture of granite and detritus which has become consolidated with the rock of the substrata.

Throughout the Ice Age, periods of relative warmth alternated with those in which much colder conditions prevailed. Mean annual temperature on land ranged between 4° and 12°C/7° and 22°F below those of today, sea surface temperatures being between 4° and 7°C/7° and 13°F lower. Worldwide the snow-line dropped by some 700–1000m/2300–3300ft (and by as much as 1500m/4900ft in the Alps). During the most recent Ice Age period, known in Northern Europe as the Vistula icing, the outer edge of the covering ice-sheet bisected the Jutland peninsula not far from the Limfjord from north to south. Consequently the western side of Jutland is characterised mainly by infertile sandy deposits from the earlier phases of the Ice Age, while the eastern side of the peninsula and the islands are covered by fertile deposits from the terminal and base moraines of the most recent glacial period.

The retreat of the ice was followed by a rise in the level of both the sea and the land. Since the land rose less than the sea however, parts of the original land mass were flooded. The land bridges between Sweden and Denmark and also between the Danish islands and the mainland disappeared, creating the various sounds – or "bælts" as they are called – including the Store Bælt (Great Belt) and Lille Bælt (Little Belt).

About one tenth of the entire surface area of Denmark, principally in the northern part of Jutland, consists of coastal plains. These are made up of marine deposits laid down during the so-called Yoldia phase (from the Yoldia Sea which covered the area in the Late Ice Age). In the west the Jutland coast is girded by an almost unbroken line of dunes, among which is Denmark's last remaining shifting dune, the Råbjerg Mile in Skagen, moving eastwards at a rate of 8–10m/9–11yd a year. Many of what were once bays on the west coast of Jutland have today become lagoons, closed off by narrow spits of land; as a result there are few harbours apart from the Limfjord, 180km/112 miles in length and the longest fjord in Denmark. The majority of fjords, especially on the east coast of Jutland, are glacial valleys flooded by the sea. The protection afforded by these inlets has given rise to several ports.

The majority of the islands have flat coastlines, the exceptions being the eastern sides of Falster and Møn and the south-eastern coasts of Zealand, where chalk cliffs can be seen. In the north of the island of Bornholm a narrow horst of primeval rock protrudes through more recent deposits. Here erosion and glaciation have carved long deep valleys in the ancient granites.

Climate

Situated on the edge of the Central European climatic zone and surrounded on all sides by water (apart from the land frontier between South Jutland and Germany), Denmark has a cool temperate maritime climate similar to that of Scotland and the northern half of England. Lying on the western side of the Euro-Asian land mass and bordering the Atlantic Ocean, it is influenced by the Gulf Stream bringing warmth from more southerly latitudes. Winds throughout the year are predominantly westerly in direction, and the Gulf Stream exercises a moderating influence on temperatures during the winter. Average temperatures during the coldest months at Hvide Sande (Jutland) and Helsingør (Zealand) for example, are some 12°C/22°F higher than those experienced at the same latitude (56°N) in other parts of the world.

Standing between Denmark and the main land mass of Eastern Europe, the waters of the Baltic also serve to insulate the country from the extremes of

Climatic Table Copenhagen					
	Temperature in °C				
	Air				
Month	Average maximum	Average minimum	Sunshine Hours per day	Days of Rain	Rainfall in mm
I	2.0	−2.0	1.2	17	49
II	2.1	−2.5	2.2	13	39
III	5.0	−0.8	3.8	12	32
IV	10.4	3.1	5.4	13	38
V	16.1	7.5	7.9	11	43
VI	19.4	11.2	8.2	13	47
VII	21.8	13.6	7.7	14	71
VIII	21.2	13.5	6.7	14	66
IX	17.5	10.5	5.2	15	62
X	12.1	6.7	2.8	16	59
XI	7.3	3.3	1.1	16	48
XII	4.2	0.7	0.6	17	49
Year	11.6	5.4	4.7/1703	171	603

continental climate in most years. In exceptionally severe winters however, the Sund and the Bælts do sometimes freeze. On the rare occasions when the Baltic is iced up, so cutting off the water's normal store of warmth, cold air masses from the east penetrate into Denmark, producing considerable cold spells. In summer on the other hand, warm air from the east can greatly reduce the effect of westerly winds coming off the sea and lead to a heat wave.

The Danish climate is also much affected by frontal systems resulting from the meeting of heavy cold Arctic air and relatively warm moist air from the Atlantic. These fronts, marking the boundaries between different types of weather, move across the country throughout the year, creating a characteristic pattern of changeability.

Temperature

Since the country is relatively small in area, temperatures in Denmark vary little from place to place. The annual average ranges from 7.2°C/45°F at Rugbjerg (north-east of Tønder) to 7.9°C/46.2°F at Odense. The February temperature varies from −1.2°C/29.8°F at Copenhagen to 1.4°C/34.5°F at Skagen, the July average from 15.5°C/59.9°F at Tønder and Rugbjerg to 17.2°C/63°F at Copenhagen. The average of the coldest month (February) is 0.3°C/32.5°F, of the warmest month (July) 17°C/63°F. The annual range varies from between 14.5°C/58°F at Tønder to 18.4°C/65.1°F at Copenhagen. On the coast the frost-free period lasts for more than 200 days and in northern Jutland about 150 days.

Precipitation

The average annual rainfall in Denmark is 550–650mm/21.5–25.5in. (Copenhagen 603mm/23.7in., Odense 621mm/24.4in., Alborg 611mm/24.1in., Rønne 559mm/22in.). On some of the eastern islands it falls below 500mm/20in. (at Christiansø 419mm/16.5in.), while further west in Jutland amounts above the average are recorded (particularly in the north of Schleswig, at Åbenrå 762mm/30in. and Tønder 750mm/29.5in.). The rainiest month is almost invariably August (Copenhagen 71mm/2.8in., Tønder 98mm/3.9in., Christiansø 52mm/2in.), the driest February (Copenhagen 39mm/1.5in., Tønder 41mm/1.6in., Christiansø 22mm/0.9in.).

The number of days with precipitation is between 120 and 200 per year. In general there is good weather from April to July; August to October on the other hand experience spells of rainy weather.

Snow falls on an average of 6–9 days during the months of January to March.

Storms

Westerly winds predominate, especially when storms are approaching. Storm damage is most frequent in western Jutland. In the spring months, when precipitation is generally low, strong winds can cause severe soil erosion with destruction of the humus layer.

Flora and Fauna · Nature Conservation

Vegetation

General

Denmark with its maritime climate experiences neither excessively cold winters nor excessively hot summers. Mean annual temperatures and rainfall are only slightly lower than those of Germany, and the flora and fauna are the same as in Central Europe. With the exception of Bornholm, Denmark also belongs to Central Europe from a geological point of view. On all these counts the country is more continental than Scandinavian, in keeping with which the woodland in the southern part of Denmark is largely deciduous (i.e. consisting mainly of trees which shed their leaves in autumn). The natural vegetation of the outwash areas of West Jutland includes oak and birch forest (common oak, weeping birch). Intensive forestry, however, has tended to replace the native stock with coniferous

*Common heather (*calluna vulgaris*)*

forest, predominantly spruce and pine. The wildwood area of oak and birch ceases at the southern end of the Limfjord.

The large areas in northern and eastern Denmark covered by moraine are natural beech (red beech) country. In the north many have been planted with coniferous forest, but in eastern Denmark the Forestry Commission has managed to preserve a relatively natural combination of tree species. The red beech is a valuable source of timber and it is seldom more profitable to replace beech woods with conifers.

Beech forest

In Denmark, as in other parts of Europe, human cultivation has considerably reduced the extent of natural forest. Today only about 10% of the land is wooded, and even this is mostly due to re-afforestation. Natural decidous forest survives in only a few places. One of these is the island of Møn where beautiful beech forests are still found, supporting a wide variety of other flora and providing a glimpse of what the primeval Danish beech forest must have been like. The woods are particularly lovely in spring when the wood-anemone, yellow anemone, liverwort, wild garlic and daphne are in bloom. Birds which breed in these calcareous beech forests include the spotted and black woodpeckers, stock-doves, tits and jackdaws. The natural beech forest belt continues in southern Sweden.

Vegetation on Møn

The dunes, heaths and wetlands which account for about 8% of the Danish landscape (principally in Jutland) also retain much of their natural vegetation. The sandy beaches and belt of dunes fringing the western coast of Jutland are among the most intriguing of these areas. Sea rocket, sea lyme grass, marram grass, sea sandwort, storksbill, sea pea and spear thistle are all present in abundance. A range of plants found nowhere else inhabit the mud flats and salt marshes of the tidal shallows, including varieties of glasswort, sea lavender and sea asters.

Dunes and wetlands

Flora and Fauna · Nature Conservation

Heathland

Although the typical Danish heathland may appear entirely "natural" to the eye, such areas are in fact the product of human interference, having taken over after the ancient forests were cut down. During the 19th c. much of the heathland (and also the moorland) came under cultivation and was turned into farmland. Statistics show that about 1 million ha/2½ million acres of heath in Jutland were transformed within a few decades into 700,000ha/1¾ million acres of agricultural land; a further 200,000ha/½ million acres were afforested. Here as elsewhere therefore, only the barest vestiges of the former landscape survive.

Plant communities on the Limfjord

The area around the Limfjord in North Jutland is a particular naturalists' paradise, supporting a wide variety of plant communities. Here the sea penetrates far inland, meeting heathland, meadows and fields. Brackish and freshwater ecosystems mark the boundary and determine the character of the vegetation growing near the fjord. Further away there are extensive areas of heath where moorland plants (sphagnum moss, cotton grass, sundew, etc.) are well-established in some of the hollows. In order to stabilise the dunes the Danes began introducing trees in about 1800, with plantations mainly of blue and forest pine. Today these are strung like chains along the north Danish coast, in some places extending south almost as far as the fjord.

Flora on Bornholm

The island of Bornholm differs in its flora from the rest of Denmark, supporting a variety of plants either not found at all or found in greater numbers here than elsewhere in the country. The main reason is the nature of the subsoil, formed largely from primary rock. Woodland, moorland, heath, rocky coasts and sandy beaches follow one another with a correspondingly wide range of vegetation.

Fauna

N.B.

The margin entries in this section refer to the animals' habitats.

Deciduous forest

Both in terms of species and population size Denmark's native fauna have been greatly affected by high density human settlement and extensive cultivation of the land. The wildlife of the deciduous forests is very similar to that found in Central Europe generally, including roe and red deer, foxes and badgers. Fallow deer are also widely dispersed and common in Denmark. Woodpeckers, song thrushes, robins, tits, chaffinches and other birds typical of Central Europe are to be seen everywhere.

Wetlands

Many of Denmark's wetlands still survive in a natural state, offering nature lovers and birdwatchers in particular excellent opportunities. The Limfjord (see above), the many-armed inlet of the sea in North Jutland where sea-, brackish and freshwater ecosystems exist side by side in a small area, is especially notable in this respect. Several conservation areas have been established, including some delightful bird sanctuaries where various species of sea-birds breed (e.g. avocets and a number of terns – Sandwich terns, common terns, Arctic terns and little terns). The extensive reedbeds of the freshwater wetlands are home to the red-necked grebe, black-necked grebe, bittern, greylag goose, marsh harriers, ruffs and warblers. As the entire area forms a gateway to and from the North, many other species stop off in the course of their migration (e.g. the Bewick swan, brent-goose, wigeon, bar-tailed godwit, golden plover and dunlin).

Salt-marshes

The fauna inhabiting the Danish coast and marshlands are much the same as can be seen along the North Sea coasts of Britain and Germany. Birds include lapwings, redshanks, black-tailed godwits, oystercatchers, black-headed gulls, herring gulls and several kinds of tern. Seals also live around these coasts – even the occasional grey seal can be spotted, though their numbers have drastically decreased. Seals should never be disturbed while basking.

Sea pea

Coastal tern

Oystercatcher

Sea sandwort

Rocky coasts

Rocky coasts, which in Denmark are confined almost entirely to Bornholm, are particularly varied habitats with plenty to interest the naturalist. Several species of macro-algae (seaweed) cling to the rocks at the base of the cliffs – green sea lettuce and Enteromorpha, the brown varieties bladder-wrack and sea-tangle, and the red Delesseria sanguinea and carrageen. Various kinds of invertebrates, for example worms, the moss-like polyzoa, snails, crabs, starfish, sea-urchins and sea-squirts, settle on the rocks and in the seaweed. Anyone walking along the shore in Denmark will have little trouble in spotting the difference between the sand, mud and rock plant and animal communities.

North-east of Bornholm lies a small group of islands called the Ertholmene ("Pea Islands"). Here, or more precisely on the uninhabited island of Græsholm, is the only site in Denmark where typical cliff-nesting birds such as the guillemot and razorbill breed. Eider duck and black-backed gulls also still nest on Græsholm.

Tidal shallows

Many places on the Danish coast, especially the tidal flats along the North Sea, are of particular ornithological interest, not only in the nesting season but also during the migratory period and in winter when large numbers of many different kinds of birds can be observed. Among them are waders such as golden plover, red- and greenshank, green sandpiper, dunlin, knot, etc., as well as ducks and geese. The birds which pass through or over-winter here have their breeding grounds further north. Altogether there are more than 300 species of birds in Denmark, of which 160 species breed there. Waterfowl and shore birds are especially numerous.

Marine life (aquariums)

A glimpse of life under the sea can be obtained by visiting one of Denmark's aquariums, such as those at Esbjerg or Hirtshals. Catches from fishing boats and displays in fishmongers' shops offer further insight into the marine life of the North Sea and Baltic.

Nature conservancy

Some 156,000ha/385,476 acres across Denmark, representing 3.5% of its area, have been designated sites of special importance, to be preserved on account of their great natural beauty or other unique features. However, the density of the population and intensiveness of agriculture practised throughout most of the country, severely restricts the work of the nature conservancy authorities. Creating a protected area in Denmark seldom involves preservation of a tract of wilderness; more often than not areas so designated remain in agricultural use at least in part. Indeed in some places cultivation is deliberately maintained, having been responsible in the first place for the plant and animal communities now to be preserved.

Protected areas

The character of protected areas in Denmark varies widely. The Rebild National Park in North Jutland (established in 1912) does not, for example, meet the international standard, and many of the areas are quite small. They include the diverse coastal landscapes of the islands, such as the chalk cliffs of Møn, the Helligdom cliffs of Bornholm and the steep Vodrup Klint (chalk cliffs) on the west coast of Ærø. In Jutland a section of the military road ("hærvej"), with an old bridge and some stretches of heath are protected, as are part of the island of Fur (Limfjord), the hills of Mols (east coast) and the shifting dunes of Råbjerg Mile near Skagen at the northernmost tip of Denmark.

North Sea sands
Nature reserve

The tidal sands off the west coast of Jutland are a particularly important nature reserve. Together with the similarly protected shallow waters along the North Sea coasts of Germany and the Netherlands, they represent one of the world's most valuable wetland areas.

Nature conser-
vancy regulations

Specific regulations apply to each of the protected areas and must be observed by anyone visiting them.

Nature Reserves in Denmark

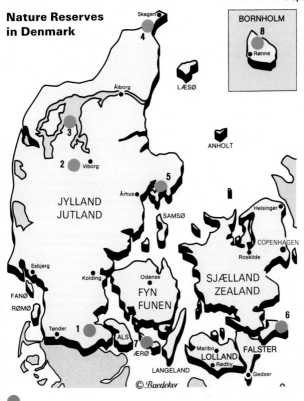

1 Hærvejen (military road/drove road)
2 Den jyske Hede (heathland in Jutland)
3 Fur Island
4 Råbjerg Mile
5 Mols Bjerge (hills of Mols)
6 Møns Klint (chalk cliffs)
7 Vodrup Klint (steep coast)
8 Helligdomsklipperne (rocky cliffs)

Some of the reserves offer guided walks in the company of a biologist expertly informed about the plants and animals.

Population and State

Population

Denmark, culturally and historically one of the five Scandinavian countries, has a population of 5.2 million, which at present is increasing at a rate of less than 1% a year. Population density is in the region of 120 per sq.km/ 311 per sq.mile, but lower in Jutland and the smaller islands. Funen and Zealand are the more heavily settled parts of the country, the latter including the Copenhagen conurbation where about a quarter of the total population live. There is a German minority (1.7%) in northern Schleswig and also a number of ethnic Swedes (0.4%).

General

17

Population and State

Denmark has a tradition of religious freedom. The principal church is the Evangelical Lutheran Church to which some 88% of the population belong. Minority religious groups include Catholics (about 30,000) and Jews (6500), as well as Baptists and Methodists. In Copenhagen there are Anglican, Russian, Norwegian and Swedish congregations. The hitherto small numbers of people leaving the Church now show some sign of increasing.

Schooling is compulsory throughout Denmark for children aged from seven to sixteen. Ten years of primary education are followed, in the case of 15–18% of pupils, by a further three years at grammar school, concentrating either on languages or mathematics. School-leaving examinations provide entrance qualifications for university or other forms of higher education. A law passed in 1976 gave parents more say in the running of schools. Education in State schools is free, in addition to which the State provides loans and bursaries. There are also private schools.

Denmark's most significant contribution to education has been the introduction of the adult education centre, a type of educational establishment which has spread to other European countries and, in a modified form, into countries outside Europe.

The idea of founding a new kind of educational institution originated with the poet and theologian Bishop Nikolai Fredrik Severin Grundtvig (1783–1872) who, when political democracy began to take root in Denmark, sought to counter the lack of knowledge in great parts of the population. The first ever adult educational centre was built in Rødding, South Jutland, in 1844; others followed. Having in the 19th c. served principally to further the education of the rural population, such centres gained additional impetus by catering for all classes of society after the Second World War. The age of most participants in Denmark is between 18 and 35.

Women in local costume (Fanø island)

18

State

The Kingdom of Denmark ("Kongeriget Danmark") is a parliamentary democracy and constitutional monarchy. Its territory comprises the Jutland peninsula and the numerous Danish islands, also the Faroe Islands and Greenland. The Faroes are an autonomous country under the Danish Crown. Greenland was granted regional autonomy in 1985.

Constitution and territory

The Danish national flag, known as the "Danebrog" (Danish broge = colourful cloth), consists of a white cross on a red ground. According to legend the flag was acquired in the course of Waldemar II's conquest of Estonia. A decisive battle was fought on June 15th 1219, during which the Danes were threatened with heavy losses. Climbing a nearby hill, the Bishop of Denmark sought God's help, promising to erect churches throughout heathen Estonia in the event of a Danish victory. While he was at prayer a red cloth with a white cross fluttered to the ground from Heaven and the Danes, given new heart, went on to defeat the Estonians.

Danish national flag

The State coat of arms, which probably goes back to the time of King Waldemar I, is emblazoned with three blue lions and nine red "hearts"; Waldemar II added crowns to the lions' heads as symbols of his victory. Dispute surrounds the exact origin of the lion emblem, one theory being that the lions represent the three arms of the Baltic Sea which enter Danish territory.

State coat of arms

For administrative purposes Denmark is divided into 14 districts (amtskommuner) and 275 parishes (primaerkommuner), each under the control of a democratically elected council. The capital, Copenhagen, is an exception to the rule. It has a civic legislative assembly (Borgerrepraesentationen) and separate municipal authority (Magistraten).

Administrative structure

Folketing

Since the abolition of the Landsting in 1953, the Danish parliament has consisted of a single chamber, the Folketing, with 175 members and two representatives each from Greenland and the Faroes. Everyone over the age of 18 is entitled to vote. There have always been numerous political parties in Denmark, often resulting in minority governments. Among the more recent parties to emerge are the Schleswig party, founded in 1970 by the German minority in North Schleswig, and the environmentalist Green Party (De Grønne) which came into being in 1983. In 1953 a parliamentary "Ombudsman" on the Swedish model was introduced, to follow up complaints from the public. The Folketing is the legislative body. Executive power, formally vested in the Crown, is wielded by a cabinet the members of which are elected by parliament. The government is led by the Prime Minister.

Denmark's Head of State is the monarch (since 1972 Queen Margrethe II) whose principal role is to represent the country on official occasions – such as receiving foreign politicians, or abroad. Queen Margrethe, daughter of King Frederik IX, was born in Copenhagen on April 16th 1940. She attended State schools, afterwards going on to study at the universities of Copenhagen and Århus. She has been married since 1967 to Prince Henrik, Henri de Laborde de Monpezat, a Frenchman.

Head of State

The Crown is inherited through the House of Schleswig-Holstein-Sonderburg-Glücksburg. The monarch must be Lutheran. Female succession was incorporated into the Danish constitution in 1953. When, following the death of her father, Margrethe acceded to the throne on January 14th 1972, she became the first woman to rule Denmark for 600 years.

Denmark has been a member of NATO since 1949 (though it has always refused deployment of nuclear weapons). Together with Norway and Schleswig-Holstein it forms NATO's North European sector. In 1988 Denmark was the first NATO country to allow women to serve in front-line

Membership of international organisations

Denmark

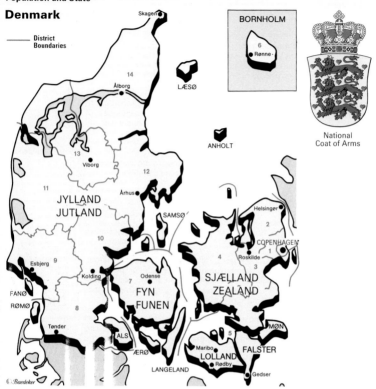

--- District Boundaries

BORNHOLM

National Coat of Arms

The Danish Administrative Districts

District (amt)	Area sq.	Area sq.miles	Population	District (amt)	Area sq.km	Area sq.miles	Population
1 Københavns amt		240	1,154,000	10 Vejle amt	2997	1157	334,000
2 Frederiksborg amt	1:	520	345,000	11 Ringkøbing amt	4853	1873	269,000
3 Roskilde amt	8	344	221,000	12 Århus amt	4561	1761	607,000
4 Vestersjællands amt	29	1152	286,000	13 Viborg amt	4122	1591	230,000
5 Storstrøms amt	33	1311	257,000	14 Nordjyllands amt	6173	2382	486,000
6 Bornholms amt	5	227	45,000				
7 Fyns amt	34:	1346	464,000	**Denmark**	43,082	16,633	5,170,000
8 Sønderjyllands amt	39:	1520	251,000	(excluding Faroes			
9 Ribe amt	31:	1210	221,000	and Greenland)			

units. I also belongs to the Nordic Council, the Council of Europe and the European Union.

Economy and Transport

Agriculture

Made fertile by moraine-derived soil and marl, East Jutland and the Danish Islands are a region of intensive cultivation. Overall about 70% of the

Windmills on a jetty near Ebeltoft

Bridges across the Little Belt near Middelfart

Bridges in Denmark

Large bridges have a fascination which defies explanation, quite unaccounted for by their economic function or the time they save. In addition they are often aesthetically very pleasing and – with the exception of those permanently rust-scarred constructions of the steel era which made expansion of the railways possible – a joy to behold.

Tunnels by comparison lack any sort of character, disappearing anonymously beneath the landscape to emerge with equal anonymity somewhere miles away. Nothing can be done to beautify them – they are, after all, just holes in the ground.

Yet tunnels have advantages which are increasingly becoming recognised. They leave the ecological system on land or seabed largely undisturbed, and building a tunnel seldom has any lasting effect on the quality of ground-water.

Ideology not ecology however has been the driving force behind recent Danish decisions to build a succession of important new transport links in the form of of a bridge and tunnel combined. Politically speaking rail tunnels are favoured by the left-wing, road bridges by the right. With major projects such as these in the pipeline for as long as 20 to 30 years, during which time governments change and various coalition partners have their say, it is little wonder that compromise, in the shape of part bridge, part tunnel, should eventually result.

The latest link over (and under) the Store Bælt between Funen and Zealand is a case in point. From Funen in the west to the little island of Sprogø there is now a 6.6km/4 mile road and rail bridge; from Sprogø to Zealand further to the east there is soon to be a 7.4km/4½ mile rail-only tunnel. Road traffic arriving on Sprogø will, for the time being, have only one option – all change – until a projected 6.8km/4¼ mile road bridge between Sprogø and Zealand is completed at a later date.

On the evidence of events so far, a contemporary chronicler might be forgiven for doubting the words of the Danish Minister of Transport who in 1993, gazing presumably into a crystal ball, predicted completion of the rail link in 1996 and the road link in 1998. Hope, it seems, will once more be shown to have triumphed over experience!

The merits or otherwise of the Store Bælt crossing have been vigorously debated ever since the project was first mooted. Even greater controversy surrounds the proposal, already announced but not yet properly underway, to bridge the Öresund between Malmö in Sweden and the Copenhagen suburb of Kastrup, location of the international airport.

If for every word uttered about the Øresund link just one öre (10 öre = roughly 1p) was placed in a big pot, the costs of the project (variously put at £3 billion or £5 billion depending on whose estimate is believed, that of the politicians or of the environmentalists) would easily be covered.

The technical challenge of such a project holds no terrors for the engineers; from the Golden Gate and Bosporus bridges to the Store Bælt bridge, and from tunnels in Japan and Norway to the Channel Tunnel (Eurotunnel), a wealth of design and construction experience is already available.

Any ecological problems that might arise, however, are less clear-cut and obviously manageable. The most recent Ice Age bequeathed to mankind, in the form of the Baltic, an ill-understood and particularly sensitive marine ecosystem.

The Baltic relies crucially upon drawing salt and oxygen from the North Sea. If these supplies were to be cut off, or reduced to even a small degree, the inland sea could well become a vast murky puddle, its surface littered with dead and dying seals, fish and eels deprived of life-sustaining air.

The main lung of the Baltic is the Øresund. No-one knows to what extent its currents could withstand interference before causing the Baltic's ecological collapse. All the claims and counter-claims, all the models, each one backed up by so-called calculations, are pure conjecture, nothing more. Probably the environmentalists' warnings have more substance than the assurances of the pro-bridge lobby. The balance of the Baltic is so sensitive that even minimal interference might well, in the longer term, cause irreversible damage.

This, of course, cannot be proved. Even so, the Danes and the Swedes would do well to heed the Swedish saying "Make haste slowly". Other countries bordering the Baltic are becoming increasingly concerned (Germany has already made cautionary noises and, in keeping with their growing self-confidence, the Baltic States as well as Poland and Russia will soon be making their opinions heard). As attitudes crystallise, Denmark and Sweden could well find themselves having to call a halt in mid-project sometime towards the turn of the millennium.

Surface and underground engineers are also already drawing up plans for both a bridge *and* a tunnel spanning the Fehmarn Bælt between Puttgarden (Germany) and Rødby Havn (Lolland). No great technical problems arise, but the project does raise the question – more urgently perhaps than even a combined bridge-and-tunnel scheme – of whether everything technically feasible should on that account be done.

Great Belt: western bridge (Fünen–Sprogge)

country is in agricultural use. Although livestock – cattle, pigs, poultry – play a principal role, wheat and sugarbeet as well as barley, oats and other cereals are widely cultivated. Flower and vegetable growing has also increased considerably in recent years. In addition there are some 2500 mink farms, mostly run as adjuncts to agricultural businesses. To ensure high quality in its finished products, Danish agriculture organised itself on a co-operative basis from an early stage. Heavy rationalisation and mechanisation has meant that today only 5.7% of the workforce is engaged in this sector of the economy.

Fishing is also of considerable importance to the country's economy. As Danish coastal waters have became over-fished, an increasing number of vessels have extended their operations further afield in the North Sea and Baltic. The most important catches are herring, cod, plaice, mackerel, eel and flat-fish. The largest fishing port is Esbjerg on the west coast of Jutland.

Industry

Largely in response to changing export opportunities and demand in world markets, Denmark has in recent years completed its conversion from a typical agrarian economy to a modern industrial State. Industry, employing 27.7% of the workforce, is now second in importance in the Danish economy after the service sector (66.6%).

Since Denmark has few minerals, almost all industrial raw materials must be imported from abroad (though in 1989 considerable deposits of mineral sand containing titanium and other elements were discovered in the northwest of Jutland). Both chemicals and engineering contribute substantially to industrial production. In the early 1940s a steel and rolling mill, chiefly processing scrap metal, opened at Frederiksværk on Roskilde Fjord in Zealand, providing material for shipyards in Copenhagen, Helsingør, Odense, Ålborg and elsewhere. Ships are built not only for Danish firms but also foreign orders.

Food processing is Denmark's major industry, with meat preparation and canning playing a leading role. Milk is turned into butter and cheese. Alcoholic drinks, including aquavit and beer, are also produced. More than 250,000 people a year visit the two largest Danish breweries, Carlsberg and Tuborg in Copenhagen.

In Jutland the textile industry, formerly based on sheep-rearing, still has a presence in some of the smaller towns. Other manufactures include furniture, carpets and ceramics.

Energy

Essential to any industrial expansion is an increase in energy resources, for which in the 1970s Denmark was still almost entirely dependent on imports. Since then supplies of natural gas and oil have been developed which, combined with other sources, are sufficient to supply more than 50% of energy requirements (1990). The Stigsnæs electricity generating station on the coast of Zealand is a prime example of modern energy production in Denmark (with an oil refinery built close by).

In recent years alternative forms of energy have assumed increasing importance in Denmark; these include solar collectors and heating installations making use of wind power or straw as fuel. The Danes have been especially successful in harnessing the wind for electricity generation. The wind energy converters (windmills) are generally grouped together in windmill parks rather than erected as single units, the largest of the parks so far built being near Ebeltoft in Jutland. Small and medium-sized factories turn out wind machines for the home market as well as for export (many of the windmills find their way to California for example).

Export markets

Denmark's principal export markets are Germany, Sweden, Great Britain, the USA and France, followed by the Netherlands, Norway, Italy and Japan.

Machinery and vehicles, food and livestock, chemicals and pharmaceutical products, mineral fuels and other commodities make up the exports. In 1990 a balance of trade surplus was recorded for the first time since 1964, a development which was maintained in 1991 and 1992. It was achieved by renouncing growth in public and private consumption alike (taxes and social security contributions absorb about half the nation's income).

Denmark, which in addition to Jutland consists of a multitude of islands, relies heavily on efficient transportation. All parts of the country are served by a comprehensive network of railways and well-engineered roads. There is generous provision of major traffic arteries – highways, motorways, and main roads of motorway standard.

Transport

Ferry services and bridges are especially important for a country made up of a peninsula and islands and occupying a position between continental Europe and Scandinavia. Danish State Railways (DSB) run ferries between the mainland and larger islands, and also between Denmark, Sweden and Germany.

Strategically placed bridges span the waterways, crucial links in an uninterrupted route from Central Europe to Denmark and the Scandinavian countries beyond. A major bridge and tunnel project at present under construction will connect the islands of Funen and Zealand across the Store Bælt. The initial section, a 6.6km/4 mile-long road and rail bridge from Funen to the little island of Sprogø, was completed early in 1994.

Tourism makes an important contribution to the Danish economy, representing an expanding source of income. A major component is the renting of holiday homes, hotel bookings being of less consequence. At one time the tourist trade was almost entirely concentrated on the Copenhagen area and the nearby resorts. Even today the resorts on the north-east coast of Zealand are still the most popular, the beaches on the west coast of Jutland north as far as Skagen, and the small seaside towns and villages on the north-east coast of Jutland and on Funan, being less heavily frequented. The island of Bornholm with its beautiful beaches and footpaths is a big favourite with holidaymakers. Denmark also has a number of sanatoriums with the climatic advantage of being situated on the coast.

Tourism

Holidaymakers with an interest in sport can enjoy facilities provided by the Danish Tourist Bureau as well as by local tourist offices. These include fishing holidays, surfing courses and cycling tours. Whether visited on an outing or for a longer stay, Denmark's ancient towns and cities, such as Roskilde, Odense or Ålborg, have much to offer in the way of culture and the arts, with fine old buildings, museums and alleyways to be explored. Highpoints are Copenhagen itself and also the famous Louisiana arts centre between Copenhagen and Helsingør, with its beautiful sculpture park.

History

10,000–8000 B.C.	End of the Ice Age. Man arrives in the area of present-day Denmark. Forest cover and animal numbers increase.
Stone Age: 7000–1800	The rising and sinking of various parts of the land mass cause the Jutland peninsula and large and small islands to be formed. In the New Stone Age the transition to agriculture and stock-breeding is complete; settlements appear.
Bronze Age: 1800–500	Burials make use of coffins of oak, the greater durability of which later results in important grave finds including woollen garments (clothes of the "Egtved girl"; today in the National Museum in Copenhagen).
Iron Age: 500 B.C. to A.D. 800	Traces of villages of this period can be detected, as well as of the so-called prehistoric fields (fields in the form of a depression surrounded by an earth rampart). Important clues to Iron Age life are provided by the bog corpses, among them the corpse of the Tollund man.
7th and 8th c.	Towards the end of the Iron Age, Scandinavian Danes occupy southern Sweden, the islands and the Jutland peninsula, driving the West Germanic Heruli, Angles, Saxons and Jutes from their ancestral homelands.
Emergence of the Danish state and the Viking era: 800–1060	Start of the documentary period of Danish history. The 9th c. is marked by the migration of peoples. A Danish state begins to emerge. The Vikings appear on the scene.
9th and 10th c.	King Godfred (804–810) constructs a rampart, the Danewerk, in southern Jutland, marking the boundary between his kingdom and Charlemagne's empire. Hedeby (Haithabu) is founded on the Schlei. The conversion of the population to Christianity begins in the 9th c. Gorm the Old (900–940) and Harald Bluetooth (940–985) weld the different parts of the country into one Danish nation, doing battle with the chieftains of the various regions Traversing the coasts in their small but seaworthy craft, the West Vikings (Danes and Norwegians), mostly still known as the Norsemen, extend their conquests into north-western, western and southern Europe. They also venture further afield, founding settlements in Iceland from 874 and Greenland from 983; around 1000 they even reach America. In 911 the Viking chieftain Rollo is made Duke of Normandy (called Robert I) by the Carolingian King Charles of France.
1000–42	Sven Forkbeard (985–1014) and Knud (Canute) the Great (1018–35) subjugate Norway and Britain. After 1042, however, the Viking kingdom splits into three separate states once again.
Transition period: 1060–1157	Following the disintegration of the great North Sea kingdom, Zealand under Svend II (1047–74) becomes the heart of the kingdom of Denmark and Roskild its ecclesiastical centre. These are times of political unrest.
Age of the Valdemars: 1157–1375	Under the Valdemars, the kingdom of Denmark grows in strength at home and becomes a power to be reckoned with abroad. Civic culture develops.
12th c.	A period of civil war, during which the Germanic Wends invade the country several times, ends when Valdemar I (1157–82), known as "Valdemar the Great", restores unity, also taking possession of the Wendish island of Rügen.

At the beginning of the century Valdemar II (1202–41) wrests the Baltic lands from the Germanic Wends. | 13th c.

Valdemar II conquers part of Estonia. The Danes found Reval. Later Estonia is sold to the German Order. | 1219

At the Battle of Bornhöved Valdemar II is defeated by the North German princes and forced to give up his Baltic possessions. | 1227

Following a period of internal strife, Valdemar IV (1340–75) restores the power and financial strength of the Crown, regaining alienated Danish provinces. | 14th c.

The King sacks Visby (Gotland), an ally of Lübeck. | 1361

Defeat by the German Hanseatic League forces Valdemar IV ("Atterdag") to acknowledge the League's supremacy in the Baltic region. | 1367–70

For almost 150 years the three Nordic kingdoms – Denmark, Norway and Sweden – are united in Danish hands. The power of the nobility increases. | The Union 1375–1523

Margarethe, daughter of Valdemar IV, who in 1363 had married King Håkon VI Magnusson of Norway, becomes regent for her son Olaf in Denmark. When he dies in 1387 she is elected Queen by the Danish estates. – In 1380 she succeeds her husband in Norway and from 1389 also rules Sweden. The three Nordic kingdoms are thus united in Danish hands. | 1375

The "Kalmar Union" (June 20th). Meeting in Kalmar the nobility of all three nations proclaim the inseparable union of Denmark, Norway and Sweden. Each kingdom is to retain its identity and rights but in times of war will assist the others.
Margarethe's great nephew, Erik of Pomerania, is crowned king. Thereafter Norway and Denmark remain united until 1814. | 1397

Death of Margarethe, in whose hands *de facto* power has hitherto rested. | 1412

Erik of Pomerania (1412–39) establishes himself in Copenhagen, until then in the possession of the Bishop of Roskilde. It becomes the country's capital. | 1417

In Sweden strong opposition develops to Danish supremacy. The peasants rise up against their foreign rulers; Engelbrecht Engelbrechtsson, a native of Dalarna, becomes their leader. In due course the Swedes break away from the Union. | 1433–1523

After the death of the childless King Christoph, Christian I of Oldenburg becomes King of Denmark and Norway (until 1481), marrying his predecessor's widow, Dorothea of Brandenburg. | 1448

The estates of Schleswig-Holstein elect Christian I Duke of Schleswig and Count of Holstein. This union of the two Duchies with Denmark through the person of Christian is destined to lead eventually to conflict (1848–64). | 1460

Christian II (1513–23) attempts to re-impose the Kalmar Union. | 16th c.

The Danish king defeats Sten Sture the Younger of Sweden. Opposition among the Swedish nobility is cruelly crushed ("Stockholm Blood Bath"). Christian is crowned King of Sweden. | 1520

Gustavus Vasa (b. 1496) leads a new Swedish rebellion. With the aid of Lübeck the Danish governor is driven from the country. | 1521

The election of Gustavus Vasa as regent and two years later to the Swedish throne marks the end of Swedish union with Denmark. | 1523

History

Struggle for regional supremacy: 1523–1660	The Reformation reaches the countries of northern Europe. Denmark vies for supremacy in the Baltic region but in the end has to give up territory there.
1534–36	Early in the reign of Christian III (1534-59) Denmark and Sweden unite to end Lübeck's commercial domination of the Baltic. In the "Counts' War" Lübeck is defeated.
1536	By a decision of the Rigsdag Denmark officially embraces the Reformation. Church property is secularised. Among those active in the creation of the new Danish Church is the North German reformer Johannes Bugenhagen (1485–1558).
1563–70	During the reign of Frederik II (1559–88), war against Sweden (Nordic Seven Years War) leads to bitter fighting but no territorial changes (Peace of Stettin). Sweden is, however, compelled to accept Denmark's right to levy dues on shipping in the Øresund.
1576–97	Under Frederik II's patronage Tycho Brahe achieves vastly greater accuracy in astronomical observations from his observatory on the island of Ven (in the Øresund).
1588	Accession to the throne of Christian IV, best loved of Danish kings (reigned until 1648), commemorated in the popular song "King Christian stood on the Topmost Mast" composed in 1778. Inspired by the example of countries in western Europe he encourages economic activity and founds and rebuilds towns.
1611–13	Successful campaign against Sweden (Kalmar War): Denmark imposes its hegemony over the Lapp marches of the North Cape.
1625–29	Christian IV intervenes in Germany during the Thirty Years' War. His defeat by Tilly at Lutter seriously weakens Denmark.
1643–45	The Swedish-Danish War results in a shift in the balance of power in the Baltic. By the Peace of Brömsebro (1645) Denmark is forced to cede to Sweden the Norwegian provinces of Jämtland and Harjedalen, the islands of Gotland and Ösel, and Halland (on the Swedish side of the Kattegat).
1657–60	Under Frederik III (1648–70) Denmark embarks upon two further wars against Sweden. Charles X of Sweden suddenly invades Denmark. After a heroic defence of Copenhagen and a victory at Nyborg, Denmark is defeated and has to yield its territory in southern Sweden – Schonen, Blekinge and Bohuslän – as well as the Norwegian town of Trondheim and the island of Bornholm (treaty signed in Roskilde on February 26th 1658). The Peace of Copenhagen (1660) returns Trondheim and Bornholm to Denmark.
The Age of Absolutism: 1660–1848	Denmark becomes a hereditary monarchy and enjoys a period of relative stability. Fundamental reforms are introduced, among them the right of ordinary citizens to hold public office. In the 19th c. Norway becomes independent.
1660	Under Frederik III Denmark ceases to be an electoral kingdom and becomes a hereditary monarchy following a decree of the Rigsdag in which the clergy and the bourgeoisie are the decisive factor and the nobility acquiesces.
1661	Promulgation by the King of the "Acts of Hereditary Absolution", not only creating a hereditary monarchy but also bestowing absolute power on the monarch. These acts are endorsed by Norway, Iceland and the Faroes.

Despite opposition from the nobility, the Rigsdag, convened by Frederik III, grants the King absolutist powers; the "Lex Regia", destined to remain in force until 1849, is unique in Europe. The "Augsburg Confession" (Lutheranism) becomes the official State religion.   1665

Christian V (1670–99) establishes a Court and "bureaucratic nobility".   1671

Under Christian V and Frederik IV (1699–1730), both of whom attempt to recover the territory lost to Sweden, the Danish fleet enjoys several naval victories: 1677 in Køge Bay under Niels Juel, in 1715 at Rügen and 1719 at Marstrand under Tordenskjold.
The end of the Nordic War (1700–20) ushers in a lengthy period of peace for Denmark in which the country experiences an economic and intellectual revival.   1675–1720

Under Frederik V (1746–66) Count Johann Hartwig Ernst Bernstorff becomes chief minister.   1751

In his role as minister, Count Andreas Peter Bernstorff, a nephew of Count Johann Hartwig Ernst Bernstorff, introduces measures leading to the emancipation of the Danish peasantry.   1788

Napoleon forces Denmark to join the Continental Blockade prohibiting the import of English goods into continental ports.   1806

To prevent closure of access to the Baltic, the British bombard Copenhagen and destroy the Danish fleet.   1807

Following the British attack in the previous year, under Frederik VI (1808–39), regent for his mentally ill father, Christian VII, Denmark allies itself with France and so becomes involved in the Napoleonic Wars.   1808

By the Treaty of Kiel Denmark loses Norway, which a year later enters into special union with Sweden. Helgoland (Heligoland) passes to the British.   1814

Denmark becomes a constitutional monarchy and after the Second World War joins international defence and economic alliances.   Denmark from 1848 to the present

Extreme tension between the Danish and German nationalist movements in Schleswig-Holstein results in the Danish-German War.   1848

Under Frederik VII (1848–63) a new constitution is introduced; Denmark becomes a constitutional monarchy.   1849

Having defeated the Schleswig-Holsteiners at Idstedt, the Danes occupy Schleswig. Pressure from Prussia and Austria extracts from Denmark a solemn undertaking not to annex Schleswig.   1850

Denmark finally renounces its right to levy dues on shipping in Øresund.   1857

Christian IX (1863–1906) re-affirms the constitution which, in contradiction to the undertaking given, envisages the incorporation of Schleswig into Denmark.   1863

When Denmark persists in its position, Prussian and Austrian troops march into Schleswig. Following decisive German victories Denmark has to cede the dukedoms of Schleswig, Holstein and Lauenburg to Prussia and Austria (Treaty of Vienna).   1864

History

1866	A two chamber parliament is introduced, the Landsting representing the voice of the wealthy landowners and the Folketing that of the popular parties. In the following decades struggles between the Conservative government and the Liberal-radical majority in the Folketing characterise Danish internal politics, reaching a climax under the Conservative Cabinet of Estrup (1875–94). It is only in 1901 that a Liberal government comes to power led by Johann Heinrich Deuntzer.
1903	Iceland, which in 1814 had remained with Denmark, gains constitutional autonomy.
1912	Christian X (b. 1870) becomes King of Denmark.
1914	Outbreak of the First World War. Denmark remains neutral.
1915	A new Danish constitution grants women the right to vote in local and Folketing elections. Elections to both chambers of the Danish parliament are henceforth by universal suffrage.
1917	Denmark is forced to sell its possessions in the West Indies (Virgin Islands) together with the port of St Thomas to the United States of America
1918	First World War ends. Iceland becomes an independent country in personal union with Denmark.
1920	As provided for in the Treaty of Versailles, a plebiscite is held in the northern Danish-speaking part of Schleswig; 75% vote in favour of incorporation into Denmark, which thereby acquires an area of some 4000sq.km/1534sq.miles and more than 160,000 new inhabitants, about 25% of whom are German.
1924	Led by Thorvald Stauning, a Social Democratic government comes to power in Denmark for the first time. In the decades which follow the reins of government are held variously by the Social Democrats, the Liberals and coalitions in which the Conservatives are partners.
1939	Outbreak of the Second World War; Germany and Denmark conclude a non-aggression pact (May 31st).
1940	Occupation of Denmark by German troops (April); a nationalist movement takes root among the population. British forces occupy the Faroes (although government remains in the hands of the islanders).
1944	Iceland withdraws from union with Denmark, becoming a republic.
1945	End of the Second World War. In the final months vast numbers of refugees pour into Denmark (Jutland). – A coalition government of all parties is formed with Knud Kristensen as Prime Minister.
1947	Christian X dies; Frederik IX becomes King.
1948	The Faroe Islands are granted independence in all internal matters, the Danish Parliament, in which the Faroes are represented by two members, retaining responsibility for foreign policy and defence (March 23rd).
1949	To protect its territorial integrity Denmark abandons its traditional neutrality and joins the North Atlantic Pact (NATO).
1952	Denmark becomes a member of the Nordic Council, an inter-parliamentary advisory body to which Finland, Iceland, Norway and Sweden also belong.

Constitutional reforms abolish the Landsting and establish a single-chamber parliament (Folketing); a measure is also introduced allowing female succession to the throne.
Greenland becomes a fully-fledged part of the kingdom, with two representatives in the Folketing.
1953

Formation of a passport and customs union with Norway, Sweden, Finland, Denmark and Iceland as members.
1958

Denmark becomes a founder member of the European Free Trade Area (EFTA), designed to further the commercial interests of countries outside the EEC.
1960

Death of King Frederik IX; Crown Princess Margarethe accedes to the throne as Margarethe II.
1972

On January 1st Denmark enters the EEC; its membership of EFTA lapses in consequence.
1973

After the return of a Social Democrat and Liberal coalition government (September) new elections bring further small gains for the Social Democrats. They form a minority government (October) led by Anker Jørgensen, already Prime Minister.
Following a plebiscite Greenland is granted autonomy over internal affairs.
1979

In the Faroes (an autonomous country under the Danish Crown), the Social Democrats suffer electoral defeat (November).
1980

Fresh elections to the Danish Folketing in December result in losses for the Social Democrats. Jørgensen forms another Social Democratic minority government.
1981

In Greenland about 52% of the electorate vote to leave the EEC (February 2nd).
Unable to resolve the country's economic problems, Jørgensen's government resigns (October 1st). Conservative leader Poul Schlüter forms a four-party minority coalition government.
1982

Mogens Glistrup, lawyer and Chairman of the Progressive Party, is sentenced to prison and fined for tax evasion (June 22nd).
A border dispute with Sweden, prompted by Danish test borings on the Kattegat island of Hesselø, is settled by the signing of an agreement establishing maritime boundaries in the Skagerrak, Kattegat and Øresund.
The Folketing votes 87 to 75 against deployment in Denmark of a new generation of US medium-range rockets (December 1st).
Prime Minister Poul Schlüter resigns (December 16th).
1983

In the parliamentary elections (January 10th) Schlüter's KFP (Det Konservative Folkepartei) makes further gains; the government can now count on the support of 90 of the 179 members of the new chamber. The SPD (Det socialdemokratiske parti) remains the strongest party however. The Faroes declare themselves a nuclear weapons free zone (February 28th). Abstention on the part of the governing coalition results in the Folketing approving an SPD proposal for the creation of a nuclear weapons free zone in northern Europe (May 3rd).
In parliamentary elections in the Faroes the Social Democrats, then in opposition, make gains; together with the People's Party they form the new government.
1984

Greenland formally withdraws from the EEC (February 1st), being accorded the special status of "overseas country or territory". It agrees to
1985

preserve a balance in fishing rights in respect of the waters off its coast, in return for which it will receive annual recompense from the EEC budget. Denmark lays claim to a sea area in the Atlantic south of the Faroes where oil is believed to exist; other countries (Great Britain, Ireland) have already asserted their interests in this region.

The Danish Government acts to reduce internal demand and therefore imports in an attempt to cut the foreign trade deficit.

1986 After an initial refusal to endorse extension of the European Economic Community – a measure designed to broaden the internal market in Europe – a referendum is held. The Danes vote 56% in favour of the agreement (February).

1987 In May Parliament approves the construction of a bridge and tunnel across the Store Bælt between Nyborg and Halsskov, the aim being to improve road and rail access to the island of Zealand.

In elections brought forward to September the ruling coalition led by Prime Minister Poul Schlüter loses votes, further impeding the work of the minority government.

1988 At the parliamentary election in May the Social Democrats maintain their position as the strongest party. Poul Schlüter forms another minority government (June). – Alarming increase in mortality among seals in the North Sea and Baltic.

1989 Bundes President Weizsäcker visits Denmark (April).

1990 A fire aboard the Danish ferry "Scandinavian Star" leaves 158 dead. – After parliamentary elections in December another minority government takes office led by Poul Schlüter.

1991 Following further elections – called because of disagreements over taxation – Prime Minister Schlüter forms yet another minority government (December 18th) in which only the Conservative and Liberal Parties are represented.

1992 A referendum on June 2nd fails to endorse the Maastricht Treaty, seen by many as the first step towards political union among EC countries.

1993 In January Prime Minister Poul Schlüter resigns, accused of withholding from Parliament in 1989 information about the illegal suspension of immigration involving the families of Tamil separatists seeking political asylum. Poul Nyrup Rasmussen, a Social Democrat, becomes Prime Minister (January 25th).

In a new referendum on the Maastricht Treaty 56.8% vote "Yes". Though Prime Minister Rasmussen welcomes the result it leads to rowdy scenes in Copenhagen. On November 1st the Treaty comes into force.

1994 Prime Minister Rasmussen reshuffles his Cabinet (January 28th) after growing criticism from two smaller partners about a lack of consensus within the four-party governing coalition. At the end of February the former Minister of Social Services, who resigned from office on February 11th, leaves the Centre Democratic Party. As a result the coalition government loses its narrow majority in Parliament.

In March Queen Magarethe II and her husband, Prince Henrik, make an official visit to Germany.

Famous People

Hans Christian Andersen, son of a cobbler, was born in Odense on the island of Funen. From 1819 he lived in Copenhagen where he trained for the theatre, gaining, until his voice broke, the occasional small part in the chorus or as an extra in a play.

Hans Christian Andersen (1805–75)

Andersen possessed great natural literary talent. In 1838, on the strength of his first publications, which included "The Improviser" (1835), a character development novel, he was granted a pension by the King. Between 1831 and 1871 he made numerous trips abroad, especially to Germany where his autobiography "The Story of my Life" first appeared (1845–46; Danish edition 1855). His "Eventyr" (fairy-tales) brought him international fame. Among the best known are "The Little Match Girl", "The Snow Queen", "Tom Thumb", "The Tinder-Box", "The Nightingale" and "The Little Mermaid". In them he created a world full of humour and ironic wit, tempered by a calm resignation. Many of these tales have a "deeper" meaning and are addressed to adults as much as to children – the Little Mermaid yearns for an immortal soul, but can gain one only by winning the love of a human being. Andersen's special talent was his ability to see insignificant things in an unexpected light.

His novels, which were not well known outside Denmark, laid the foundations of modern realistic Danish prose writing. He also wrote poems, diaries and letters. He died in Copenhagen in 1875 and was buried in the Assistens Kirkegård (cemetery). (See also Baedeker Special pp. 182–183.)

Martin Andersen Nexø was born in Copenhagen but spent the greater part of his youth as a shepherd boy and cobbler's apprentice on the island of Bornholm. After attending various adult education courses he worked first as a teacher before becoming a writer. He joined the Communist Party after the First World War and from 1951 until his death in 1954 lived in Dresden (East Germany).

Martin Andersen Nexø (1869–1954)

Social criticism and solidarity with the poor and alienated are the main themes of his work. His partly autobiographical novel "Pelle the Conqueror" (1906–10; four volumes) focuses on the lives of farmers, fishermen and workers and the objectives of the workers' movement around the turn of the century. His second novel cycle, "Ditte, Daughter of Man" (1917–21; five volumes), more pessimistic in tone, revolves around the story of a lower class woman unable to escape the life she finds so unsatisfactory. Nexø also produced first-class short stories, travel sketches and reminiscences.

Niels Bohr (full name Niels Hendrik David Bohr), Denmark's greatest physicist, was born in Copenhagen, becoming Professor of Theoretical Physics in 1916. In 1913, building on Ernest Rutherford's work on the atom, he had developed the Bohr atomic model and discovered the principle of correspondence between classical and quantum physics. He was awarded the Nobel Prize for Physics in 1922. In 1943, when Denmark was occupied by German troops, Bohr was smuggled out of the country disguised as a fisherman, making his way to the United States via Sweden and Britain. In America he was involved in the development of the atomic bomb, although concerned about its implications. After the Second World War he returned to Copenhagen, continuing his work at the Institute of Theoretical Physics. In 1947 he received the Order of the Elephant, Denmark's highest honour. His son Niels Aage Bohr, also a physicist, was awarded the Nobel Prize in 1975.

Niels Bohr (1885–1962)

Tycho Brahe was born at Knudstrup in southern Sweden in 1546. He first studied law, later turning to astronomy. In 1572 he discovered a new star in

Tycho Brahe (1546–1601)

Famous People

Martin Andersen-Nexø

Niels Bohr

Tycho Brahe

the northern hemisphere constellation of Cassiopeia, naming it Nova Cassiopeia. After travelling in Europe Brahe lectured in Copenhagen; in 1576 he received from King Frederik II an endowment and the offer of the island of Ven in the Sound where he built the observatory of Uranienborg and continued his researches.

Following the death of Frederik II in 1588 the astronomer found himself in difficult circumstances and in 1599 he left Denmark and went to Prague. There he became Astronomer Royal to the Emperor Rudolf II. He died in Prague in 1601 and was buried in the Tyn Church. His tombstone (near the fourth pillar on the right) is always bedecked with the Danish flag (Danebrog).

Brahe was the most important astronomical observer prior to the discovery of the telescope. The observations he made of the positions of the planets, especially those of Mars, laid the foundations for Kepler's work on planetary motion. Brahe developed the "Tychonic System", named after him, according to which the sun and moon circle the earth, still positioned at the centre of the universe, while the other planets circle the sun. One of his achievements was to prove that comets are not phenomena of the earth's atmosphere, as Aristotle had held.

King Christian IV (1577–1648)

Christian IV, who was still a child when his father died, acceded to the throne in 1588. He became the most popular of Danish kings.

Having shown considerable artistic gifts while young, he was later responsible for the construction of numerous Renaissance buildings, including Rosenborg Castle in Copenhagen and Frederiksborg Castle near Helsingør. The seafarers' houses in Nyboder were built on his initiative, as also the Christianhavn district (both in Copenhagen).

Politically however Christian IV was less successful. From 1625 he allowed the Danish army to become embroiled in the Thirty Years' War, suffering heavy defeats. The King died in Copenhagen in 1648, unhappy and disillusioned.

Niels Ryberg Finsen (1860–1904)

Born at Tórshavn in the Faroes, the physician Niels Ryberg Finsen founded in 1896 in Copenhagen an institute for light-therapy. He invented the method of treating tuberculosis of the skin with the "Finsen Lamp", a carbon-arc lamp with cooled light rich in ultra-violet rays. Treatment of smallpox with infra-red light was another of his fields of research. Finsen received the Nobel Prize for medicine in 1903.

Johannes Vilhelm Jensen (1873–1950)

Jensen, born in Farsø in Jutland, ranks as one of Denmark's greatest writers. He began by studying medicine; then from 1896 he spent a lengthy period in the United States before embarking upon several assignments as

Søren Kirkegaard   *Asta Nielsen*   *Bertel Thorvaldsen*

a newspaper correspondent to France, Spain and the Far East. In 1944 his novels and stories won him the Nobel Prize for Literature. His latter years were spent in Copenhagen, where he died in 1950.

Jensen's writing is characterised by his strong attachment to his homeland and love of Danish folklore. One of his major works, the six-part novel cycle "The Long Journey" (Den lange rejse, 1908–22), recounts the history of the Nordic people from their earliest beginnings to the discovery of America by Christopher Columbus. Jensen's great regard for his homeland is also manifest in his "Himmerland Stories" (Himmerlandstorier, 1898–1910), a collection of myths, legends and folk tales.

Søren Kierkegaard was born on May 5th 1813 in Copenhagen, the seventh child of a prosperous wool merchant. He studied theology and philosophy at Copenhagen University from 1830 to 1840. In 1840 he became engaged to the 17-year-old Regine Olsen, the engagement being broken off a year later. Thereafter he lived as a freelance writer, supporting himself with the help of money he had inherited.

Søren
Kierkegaard
(1813–55)

Kierkegaard published most of his books under pseudonyms. In imitation of Socrates many of his works are in dialogue form. In his writing the concepts of "angst" and "existence" play a fundamental role, those of freedom and decision being subordinate to them. His thought leads to the conclusion that only by the grace of God can doubt and despair be overcome. As a religious theorist, Kierkegaard adopted a thoroughly subjective standpoint, so came into conflict with the Danish Lutheran Church of his time, finally being led to renounce entirely a Church which professed a closed system of objective truth. His works of religious philosophy had a profound influence on many 20th c. thinkers, the ideas expressed in them forming much of the basis of dialectical theology and existentialism.

Among his important works are: "Either-Or" (1843), "Fear and Trembling" (1843), "The Concept of Fear" (1844), "Sickness unto Death" (1849) and "Practice in Christianity" (1850). Kierkegaard died in 1856 in Copenhagen, where he was interred in the Assistens Kirkegård.

The Danish actress Asta Nielsen first gained recognition in films directed by Urban Gad, who became her second husband. From 1911 until 1914, and again from 1919, she worked in Berlin, playing tragic roles on the silent screen. Among her best-known films are "Afgrunden" (Precipices; 1910), "Die Arme Jenny" (Poor Jenny, 1911), "Rausch" (Smoke, 1919), "Hamlet" (1920), "Fräulein Julie" (1922), "Vanina Vanini" (1922), "Die Freudlose Gasse" (The Cheerless Street, 1925), "Dirnentragödie" and "Unmögliche Liebe" (Impossible Love, 1932).

Asta Nielsen
(1885–1972)

Famous People

Count Johann
Frederik Struensee
(1737–72)

Having qualified as a physician at the age of 20, in 1769 Struensee became personal physician to the degenerate King Christian VII, in which capacity he accompanied the monarch to Copenhagen. A liaison soon developed between Struensee and Queen Caroline Mathilde. With the Queen's connivance Struensee's influence over the King mounted, until in 1771 he was appointed Private Secretary, taking the title of Count. For sixteen months he was in virtual control of the Court and country, the liberal reforms he introduced anticipating developments in later centuries.

Struensee's increasing high-handedness, and revelation of his affair with the Queen, led to the formation of an opposing faction at Court, loyal to the King. They succeeded in having a warrant issued against him. On January 17th 1772 he was arrested and, on April 28th, the punishment laid down by law was duly carried out: "His right hand will . . . be cut off his living body and then his head; the body will be cut into pieces and placed on a stake and wheel, but the head and hand will be put on poles." Some 3000 citizens of Copenhagen attended this gruesome spectacle.

The English-born Queen was banished from the country.

Bertel
Thorvaldsen
(1770–1844)

Bertel Thorvaldsen (Thorwaldsen) was born in Copenhagen, the son of an Icelandic carver. While still a pupil at Copenhagen's Academy of Art he showed great promise, winning the Great Gold Medal in 1793. With the aid of a Travel Scholarship from the Academy in 1797 he was able to go to Rome, where he settled and began creating sculptures in marble. In Rome he discovered the classical style which is so typical of his work. He sculpted youthful figures, busts, reliefs, monuments and memorials. In 1838, by which time he had achieved a European-wide reputation, Thorvaldson returned to Copenhagen, making a gift of his works to his native city. Between 1839 and 1847 a museum, designed by Gottlieb Bindesboll, was erected on Porthusgade to accommodate the collection. On his death Thorvaldson was interred there. Among his best-known masterpieces are the freestanding reliefs "Day" and "Night" (1815), the "Dying Lion" (Lucerne, 1818, commemorating the Swiss killed in Paris in 1792) and "Christ" (begun 1821, in Copenhagen's Vor Frue Kirke). Several copies were made of most of his works, some being studio repeats, others produced after his death. A number of monuments designed by Thorvaldsen can be seen in Germany, including the equestrian statue of the Prince Elector Maximilian I in Munich's Wittlesbacher Platz. Unveiled in 1839 it reflected a new source of inspiration for the sculptor in the form of medieval-Romantic ideals of style. The Schiller Memorial in Stuttgart is also by Thorvaldsen. Raised up on a plinth it was unveiled on May 8th 1839 in the presence of Schiller's grandson. Another commission took the sculptor to Warsaw where he designed a memorial to Nicholas Copernicus.

Bjørn Wiinblad
(b. 1919)

Bjørn Wiinblad was born in Copenhagen, where he studied painting and illustration at the Academy of Art. As well as book illustration he designed posters, stage sets and costumes for the theatre. However, he soon became interested in other materials and techniques, designing wallpaper, tapestries and ceramic pieces. It was the latter which brought him his first real success at exhibitions in Copenhagen, Sweden and Norway. In 1954 he exhibited in New York. Among a remarkably varied output his ceramic work stands out. His shapes and decoration have an attractive and satisfying effect. Wiinblad made designs for dinner-services, glassware, vases and decorative wall-plates, sometimes being responsible for both the shape and the decoration, at other times for only one or the other. His surfaces are covered with ornamentation, painted figures or scenes from fictional tales (e.g. "A Thousand and One Nights"). While showing a predilection for black and white, he also works in colour. Bjørn Wiinblad has for many years designed for Rosenthal, a company noted for its porcelain and ceramic ware and which has its head offices in Bavaria.

Art History

Denmark is a rich treasury of creative art, ranging from finds from prehistoric times to Romanesque church architecture, works of the Renaissance and Neo-Classical periods and the most modern buildings and sculpture of today.

Among the relics of prehistory the numerous megalithic graves of the New Stone Age (c. 3000–1800 B.C.) are of particular interest. Dolmens of unhewn granite blocks and funeral mounds concealing burial chambers or stone coffers are features of the Danish landscape in many places. Flint tools and earthenware pots have also been found, many of the latter bearing scratch decoration. Nothing has survived, however, of the houses in which the people lived.

Stone Age

The dawning of the Bronze Age (1800-500 B.C.) brought new scope for technological and artistic development, particularly in the form of bronze vessels, tools, weapons (for example swords with bronze blades) and ornaments (e.g. womens' jewellery). Decoration tended to be strictly lineal – concentric circles and wavy lines. Also characteristic of the period are the wind instruments known as lurs and the many relics of sun worship (principally representations of the sun's disc, as in the Trundholm "sun chariot", a 60cm/2ft-long cart which today can be seen in the National Museum in Copenhagen).

Bronze Age

In the Iron Age, which began about the middle of the first millennium B.C. (500 B.C.–A.D. 800), iron took the place of the much softer bronze in the manufacture of a variety of items such as sword blades. At the same time, writing made its first appearance in the form of runic script. Few ornamental objects were made during this period. The magnificent silver Gundestrup Cauldron, discovered in a bog near Ålborg in North Jutland, has been identified as a cult object of Celtic origin, the half-length figures of gods on the outside and scenes of sacrifices on the inside testifying to its origin (now in the National Museum in Copenhagen).

Iron Age

There are very many finds from the Viking era (A.D. 800–1060). The rise of the Vikings was made possible by their keeled long-ships which, with bottoms strengthened to support a mast and keel, proved far superior to oar-driven craft. The Viking Ship Hall at Roskilde contains several reconstructed examples of such boats, these particular ones having been sunk between 1000 and 1050 in Roskilde Fjord in order to form a dam. Insight into Viking building techniques is provided by the Viking camp of Trelleborg near Slagelse, the remains of the Viking fortress at Fyrkat near Hobro, and the excavated settlement on the Lindholm Høje (Lindholm Hill) north of Ålborg where there is also a large number of graves marked by stones, including stones in the shape of ships from the Viking period.

Viking era

Among the most important relics of this period are the Jelling Stones, runic stones engraved with figures as well as characters. The large runestone of Harald Bluetooth (c. 985) is considered the finest surviving example of Viking sculpture. While older stones tend to be carved with animals, this one has, in addition to a lion devouring a snake, a figure of Christ. The inscriptions and images on stones such as these are thought to have been picked out in colour (the National Museum in Copenhagen has a copy of the Harald Bluetooth stone painted in typical colours used in Viking times).

Danish farmhouses, which first made their appearance in the early Middle Ages, were built principally of wood. In the period 1060–1265 stone, and

Romanesque

Silver basin from Gundestrup (detail)

later also brick, was used as a building material. Large Romanesque cathedrals were constructed during the reign of Valdemar the Great (1157–82), including those at Ribe and Viborg which were influenced by the cathedrals of the Lower Rhine; both are stately, three-aisled basilicas with two west towers. Also noteworthy are the west section of Århus Cathedral, the church at Ringsted, the church at Sorø, which belonged to a Cistercian monastery, and the five-towered Vor Frue Kirke at Kalundborg.

This period also saw the building of several churches, circular in plan, doubling as both church and stronghold. Their sturdy form made them similar to rural fortresses. Four of the seven round churches in Denmark are situated on Bornholm. As a rule they have a number of storeys linked by a staircase.

Among the principal examples of Romanesque stone sculpture are the arched windows in the cathedral at Ribe incorporating an impressive "Descent from the Cross". Denmark also has an unequalled store of 12th and 13th c. altarpieces in beaten and gilded copper. – Copenhagen's museums contain numerous treasures of this kind.

Gothic

Gothic (1265–1525/50), which originated in France in about 1140 and is characterised particularly by its pointed arches, came to influence Danish architecture in the 13th c. With numerous churches having been built earlier, in the 12th c., however, the legacy of the Gothic period in Denmark is relatively small. Begun in about 1170 the cathedral at Roskilde, where most of the Danish kings lie buried, was completed in the Gothic style. Other examples include the churches of St Mary and St Olaf in Helsingør and St Knud in Odense, with their elegant interiors, also Århus Cathedral and St Peter's Church in Næstved, all of which are indebted to the Brick Gothic tradition in Germany.

Tombs in Roskilde Cathedral

Gothic sculpture is represented chiefly by examples in wood and ivory. Late Gothic sculpture in Denmark was heavily influenced by Germany, reaching its zenith in the work of Bernt Notke (*c.* 1440–1509), the master of the winged altar in Århus Cathedral, and Claus Berg (*c.* 1470–1532), the creator of the great altar-screen in St Knud's Church at Odense.

In the Middle Ages many country churches were embellished with frescoes portraying scenes from Biblical history or other Christian themes. Those by the Elmelunde Master, whose work can be seen in several churches including Fanefjord Church on the island of Møn (*c.* 1500), are of particular note.

The Renaissance style, Italian in origin, came to Denmark from the Netherlands, flourishing between 1550 and 1650/60 during which time the Reformation, adopted here in 1536, also had a major influence on architecture. Window arches became flatter and squared openings gradually came into being. Great numbers of secular buildings were erected during this period, especially mansions and manor houses. | Renaissance
The architecture of the Dutch Renaissance was the preferred style of both Frederik II (1559–88) and Christian IV (1588–1648). Its principal exponents were Anthonis van Opbergen of Mechelen and Hans van Steenwinkel the Elder from Antwerp, together with their sons Lourens and Hans. Frederik II had Kronborg Castle (1574–84) erected at Helsingør, while between 1602 and 1620 the van Steenwinkels built Frederiksborg Castle in Hillerød for Christian IV. The little Rosenborg Castle (1610–26) in Copenhagen, also commissioned by Christian IV, remains a particularly fine example of the Danish Renaissance style.

Among the finest of the manor houses are Rosenholm and Gammel Estrup in East Jutland, Holckenhavn on Funen and Holsteinborg in South Zealand. In addition there are picturesque moated mansions at Egeskov and Rygård on Funen.

As regards sculpture, the Renaissance era produced numerous impressive funeral monuments, perhaps the most striking of which is the tomb of Christian III (1575) in Roskilde Cathedral's Chapel of the Three Kings; it takes the form of a temple made of marble and alabaster with rich decoration and statues.

Baroque and Rococo

Although originating in Italy, Baroque reached Denmark by way of Holland (1660–1750/60), during which time French and South German influences also made themselves felt. Symmetry in the use of space became an important feature. A period of intensive building began in Copenhagen. One of the first Baroque buildings was Charlottenburg Palace, which since 1754 has housed the Danish Royal Academy of Art. In the 18th c. Christiansborg Palace was built in the Viennese Baroque style on the site of an old fortress; having burned down in 1794 it was later rebuilt by the architect Christian Frederik Hansen.

About 1750 a start was made on remodelling "Frederiksstad", an area of some 2sq.km/1sq.mile around the present Amalienborg Palace. The success of this exercise in 18th c. town planning was in large measure due to Niels Nikolai Eigtved (1701–54), an architect who was also responsible for the Rococo Amalienborg Palace, one of the principal works of the century. Following the destruction of Christiansborg Palace (see above), Amalienborg Palace became and remains the royal residence. Eigtved also designed the Prince's Palace which, built in Rococo style on the model of the Hotel de Ville in Paris, is now the Danish National Museum.

In the field of sculpture the most important works during the Baroque period were equestrian statues, two fine examples of which are the statue (1688) of Christian V by Abraham César L'Amoureux of Lyons, in Copenhagen's Kongens Nytorv, and the statue of Frederik V by Jacques François Saly of Valenciennes, erected in 1768 in Amalienborg Palace Square.

Classicism

The Louis XVI style, known as Classicism, another French development, manifested itself in Denmark as a continuation of Rococo, remaining in fashion for only a few decades (1760–1825/35). The most important architect of this period was Christian Frederik Hansen (1756–1845) who was responsible for Copenhagen's Vor Frue Kirke and the Courthouse on Nytorv. Together with his teacher Kaspar Frederik Harsdorff (1735–99) Hansen also created the connecting courtyards between the Amalienborg Palaces (from 1794).

In sculpture the classical ideal was developed in its purest form by Bertel Thorvaldsen (1770–1844; see Famous People), the most important of Danish sculptors despite becoming addicted to certain weaknesses of style. From 1819 he worked on the interior of the Vor Frue Kirke in Copenhagen, creating large statues of the Apostles, relief friezes on the life of Christ and, as his *pièce de résistance*, the great statue of the Blessed Redeemer. Thorvaldsen bequeathed a collection of his own and foreign works to his native Copenhagen; these can be seen today in the Thorvaldsen Museum. Other Danish sculptors of note in this period were Vilhelm Bissen (1798–1868) and Jens Adolph Jerichau (1816–83).

From 1815 onwards painting, especially landscape painting, assumed a new importance. Among the artists of the classical tradition were Jens Juel (1745–1802), Nicolai Abraham Abildgaard (1743–1809) and Christoffer Wilhelm Eckersberg (1783–1853), the latter in particular influencing painters of the following generation. Around the turn of the century the Copenhagen Academy attracted many German artists, including the Romantic painter Caspar David Friedrich.

Historicism

The advent of Romanticism in architecture led to the imitation of medieval styles. Several important buildings, especially in Copenhagen, date from this era of Historicism (1835–1915): Martin Nyrop (1849–1921) built the City

Asger Jorn: "Fishermen from Silkeborg"

Hall, Michael Gottlieb Bindesbøll (1800–56) the Thorvaldsen Museum. The massive Grundtvigskirken in West Copenhagen, designed by Peter Vilhelm Jensen Klint (1853–1930), displays Historicist elements while at the same time anticipating the transition to modern architecture.

In painting, Christian Købke (1810–48), in his scenes of Italy and Copenhagen and also in his portraits, carried on the example of C. W. Eckersberg, Professor at the Copenhagen Academy of Art. Købke and other pupils of the distinguished landscape- and portrait-painter were the chief source of artistic inspiration during the "Golden Age" of Danish painting, characterised by balance of composition and colour.

In the second half of the 19th c. there emerged in Skagen (North Jutland) a group of painters who, deliberately seeking to free themselves from academic constraints, took to painting out of doors; among them were Peter Severin Krøyer (1851–1909), Anna Ancher (1859–1935) and Viggo Johansen (1851–1935). Their example was followed by artists on the island of Funen, including Johannes Larsen (1867–1961). For both groups light was the dominant element in painting.

Scandinavia has often been at the forefront of innovation in 20th c. architecture. In the 1920s and 1930s a modest functionalism became the vogue, an example being the terrace houses of the Bakkehusene development by the Danish architect Ivar Bentsen (1876–1943). Leaders in the modern

20th century

Danish Design

Because designer products are usually branded goods, often costly to produce and something of an extravagance, design has come to be associated with the luxury end of the market.

In fact nothing could be further from the truth. Design means standards, applied unobtrusively but as a matter of course, to any process and any product. Manufacturing costs are kept down and style becomes affordable to the less affluent consumer. This in turn leads to even greater economies of scale, lowering costs and prices still further and bringing goods within the reach of an ever widening public.

Design also means consumer protection. – At least in Denmark it does, and has for hundreds of years.

The very first – and very famous – Danish designer product was neither mass produced nor cheap. "Flora Danica", a dinner service decorated with pictures of the entire Danish flora, was commissioned in 1788 by Crown Prince Frederik, who intended it as a gift for Catherine the Great of Russia. She however died in 1796, seven years before the service was finished; Frederik, who by this time had acceded to the Danish throne, kept it for his Court.

The "Flora Danica" design is still available – but hardly at bargain prices. Anyone intent on purchasing all 2600 pieces would pay a great deal of money!

Even earlier, in 1777, the Crown had founded a royal furniture emporium with the object of bringing "good taste in furniture manufacture to a wider public". Craftsmen were commissioned to reproduce sample pieces, the best being rewarded with a certificate of quality of workmanship and the opportunity to display their wares for sale in the royal showrooms.

What was in effect a Crown consumer service brought advantages to more than its customers. Imported furniture from France and England was no longer considered *ne plus ultra*, and beautifully crafted Danish handiwork came to be highly valued abroad – much to the benefit of Denmark's chronic trade deficit.

Nowadays Denmark exports far fewer designer articles than pig carcasses or ham, but its reputation for design remains as high as ever. Throughout the world the Danes are regarded as having few equals and quality of design provides a glowing advertisement for Danish industry.

Danish design would be nothing, however, without the pride of the Danish craftsman. Shoddy workmanship is unknown. Danes are as happy as anyone to break off for a beer, but when they set to, they produce excellent work. The entrepreneurial spirit is today taking them further afield (if only as yet into North Germany). Their skills are always in great demand, particularly in the building trade, whether engaged on minor house repairs or working on larger contracts. These are not manual labourers assigned to menial tasks, but dependable highly skilled craftsmen, partners in trade.

The Danish concept of design extends also to architecture, as Jørn Utzon's world-famous Sydney Opera House amply testifies. This extraordinary building, destined to become an increasingly familiar sight as the Olympic 2000 Games draw near, was completed at incredible cost in 1973. Time and again estimates were exceeded, until eventually a lottery was set up to bring much needed relief to the over-burdened tax-payer and straining public purse. The moans and grumbles however have long since been forgotten and the Opera House, with its distinctive roof of overlapping sails and its opera theatre, concert hall, drama theatre, play-house-cum-cinema and exhibition and conference areas, played its part in Sydney's successful bid to host the Games.

No one better exemplifies the synthesis of architecture and design than Arne Jacobsen (d. 1971), responsible for a whole range of buildings and residential complexes in Denmark, England (St Catherine's College, Oxford) and North Germany (the Concert Hall in Hannover). Not even the SAS building opposite Copenhagen's main railway station, euphemistically described as Bauhaus-Eclectic, has tarnished Jacobsen's world-wide reputation. Like the Finnish architect Alvar Aalto, Jacobsen also went on to design furniture and other household items such as thermos flasks, ash-trays and cutlery.

The dream of all Danish designers is to be given the task of creating what in the USA and Western Europe is called "corporate identity". Such a commission ranks as a real feather in the cap – Danes also have business acumen and designers like authors are usually paid by output. Small wonder then that to be put in charge of every aspect of design for a bus company or even the State railway – everything from railcars to tickets – should be seen as the pinnacle of success.

Danish designers strive for function as well as effect, and are thus better known for leisure clothing than *haute couture*. Skirts slit to the hip and busts concealed by nothing more substantial than gossamer are not their forte at all.

Whether the eye is caught by furniture, clothing or household items, a stroll around any Danish town, with its plentiful opportunities for window shopping, leaves no doubt whatever about the excellence of Danish design.

architectural revolution included Erik Møller and Arne Jacobsen to whose prize-winning plans the new City Hall in Århus was built, in reinforced concrete, between 1938 and 1942. Arne Jacobsen (1902–71), whose buildings excel in clarity of design and technical execution, is probably the internationally best known Danish architect.

Among several notable sculptors of the modern period are Kai Nielsen (1882–1924), creator of a new monumental style, and Robert Jacobsen (b. 1912) who worked in metal; also Gunnar Westmann (b. 1915), Svend H. Hansen (b. 1922), Bengt Sørensen (b. 1923), Jørgen Haugen Sørensen (b. 1934) and Hein Heinsen (b. 1935).

Well-known 20th c. Danish artists include Richard Mortensen (b. 1910), Ejler Bille (b. 1910), Else Alfelt (1910–1974), Carl-Henning Pedersen (b. 1913), Asger Jorn (1914–73), Stig Brøgger (b. 1941) and Anders Kierkegaard (b. 1946). In 1937–38, in a climate dominated by the growing threat of war, Egill Jacobsen (b. 1910) painted his "Ophobning" (Accumulation), considered the first Abstract-Expressionist work in Danish art. After the war Richard Mortensen likewise turned to abstract painting, articulating space in his pictures (e.g. "Evisa", 1960; Louisiana) by a rhythmic arrangement of coloured surfaces and lines. Mortensen is also known for his murals and carpet designs.

In 1948 the modernist painter Asger Jorn founded a group which also included Dutch and Belgian artists. Known as COBRA (short for Copenhagen-Brussels-Amsterdam), its members aspired to a folk art based on popular imagery and realised through an informal blending of Expressionism, Surrealism and Abstractionism. The group, whose influence spread to Germany, Italy and Spain, was disbanded in 1951.

In the 1960s another circle formed among Danish artists associated with Den Eksperimenterende Kunstskole (School of Experimental Art), a private institution founded in protest against the teaching of the Danish Academy. Its members included Per Kirkeby (b. 1938), Richard Winter (b. 1926), Paul Gernes (b. 1925) and Bjørn Nørgaard (b. 1947; "Spirale", 1980, Louisiana). – Per Kirkeby, artist and theoretician, known especially for his architectonic sculptures, was among those whose work was seen at the Kassel "documenta" in 1982.

Relatively few works by members of this circle, or by other important Danish artists of the day, find their way into museums or private collections. The National Art Fund, set up to encourage and support Danish art, does however commission work from contemporary artists, principally for the embellishment of public buildings. Asger Jorn carried out one of the Fund's first projects, a ceramic relief (1959) for the State Grammar School in Århus. The Fund gives talented young artists the opportunity to express themselves on a more monumental scale.

It is not only in art in the narrower sense that Danish design has achieved international acclaim. This is true in particular of furniture, porcelain, ceramics, silverware and stainless steel, the design of which in recent times has tended chiefly towards functionalism in both form and decoration.

Quotations

Denmarke, lying neere the Artick circle, must needs be subject to great cold, howsoever the mistie aire, caused by the frequent Iles, doth in some sort mitigate the extremity thereof.
From "An Itinerary", 1617

Fynes Moryson (1566–c. 1617)

Elsinore and Cronenburg Castle

This is a poore village, but much frequented by sea-faring men, by reason of the straight sea, called the Sownd; where the King of Denmark hath laid so great imposition upon ships and goods comming out of the Balticke sea, or brought into the same, as this sole profit passeth all the revenues of his Kingdome. . . . In respect of the Danes scrupulous and jealous nature, I did with great difficulty, (putting on a Merchants habite, and giving a greater reward then the favour deserved,) obtaine to enter Croneburg Castle, which was built foure square, and hath only one gate on the East side, where it lies upon the straight. Above this gate is a chamber in which the King useth to eat, and two chambers wherein the King and Queene lie apart. Under the fortification of the Castle round about, are stables for horses, and some roomes for like purposes. On the South-side towards the Baltich sea, is the largest roade for ships. And upon this side is the prison, and above it a short gallery. On the West side towards the village is the Church of the Castle, & above it a very faire gallery, in which the King useth to feast at solemne times. On the North side is the prospect partly upon the Iland, and partly upon the Narrow sea, which reacheth twenty foure miles to the German Ocean. And because great store of ships passe this way in great Fleets, of a hundreth more or lesse together: this prospect is most pleasant to all men, but most of all to the King, seeing so many shippes, whereof not one shall passe, without adding somewhat to his treasure.
From "An Itinerary", 1617

A Region which is the very reverse of Paradise. The seasons here are all of them unpleasant, and the Country quite destitute of Rural Charms. I have not heard a bird sing, nor a Brook murmur, nor a Breeze whisper, neither have I been blest with the sight of a Flowry Meadow, these two Years. Every wind here is a Tempest, and every Water a turbulent Ocean.
From "Spectator," No. 393, May 31st 1712

Ambrose Philips (?) (1675–1749)

Zealand

Nor is Zealand of sufficient magnitude, to take away altogether the odious idea of restraint and confinement. In England, or Ireland, we wholly forget that we are in an island. Even in Sicily or Sardinia, that impression might rarely occur to the mind. But Zealand, were I compelled to reside in it, I should consider only as an agreeable prison, the bars of which are not far enough removed from the eye, or the imagination, to enable an inhabitant to divest himself completely of recollection allied to captivity. Such at least, have been my feelings and reflections, on this capital and island.
From "A Tour Round the Baltic", 1775 (1807 edn)

Sir N. W. Wraxall (1751–1831)

Copenhagen

Copenhagen is the best-built city of the north; for although St Petersburg excels it in superb edifices, yet as it contains no wooden houses, it does not display that striking contrast of meanness and magnificence, but in general exhibits a more equable and uniform appearance. The town is surrounded towards the land with regular ramparts and bastions, a broad ditch full of

William Coxe (1747–1828)

45

water, and a few outworks: its circumference measures between four and five miles. The streets are well-paved, with a foot-way on each side, but too narrow and inconvenient for general use. The greatest part of the buildings are of brick; and a few of free-stone brought from Germany. The houses of the nobility are in general splendid, and constructed in the Italian style of architecture. The royal palace is a magnificent pile of building of hewn stone, the wings and stables of brick stuccoed. . . .

The busy spirit of commerce is visible in Copenhagen. The haven is always crowded with merchant-ships; and the streets are intersected by broad canals, which bring the merchandise close to the warehouses that line the quays. The city owes its principal beauty to a dreadful fire in 1728, that destroyed five churches and sixty-seven streets, which have since been rebuilt in the modern style. The new part of the town, raised by the late king Frederic V is extremely beautiful: it consists of an octagon, containing four uniform and elegant buildings of hewn stone, and of four broad streets leading to it in opposite directions.

From "Travels into Poland, Russia and Sweden, etc.", 4th edn, 1792

Edward Daniel Clarke (1769–1822)

Our French companions complained of the bad taste by which everything in Copenhagen is characterised. To our eyes, it seemed, indeed, that a journey from London to Copenhagen might exhibit the retrogression of a century; every thing being found, in the latter city, as it existed in the former a hundred years before. . . .

From "Travels in Various Countries", 1824

Hans Christian Andersen (1805–75)

Summer Visit to Jutland and Funen (1830)

August 4th
Went to St Jørgensgaard, broken cross. Garden in front of Bregninge Church. Could see the ferry landing. In the water there was a stake, some sort of mark. An old women sat under the apple tree reading her hymnal. St Jørgens convent was founded by Gustav Vasa's aunt Anna Rønnow, who lived in Hvidkilde. The extremity of the convent garden is the southernmost point of the town. Looking towards Svendborg you can see ships seemingly floating on land. It is beyond a branch of the Thorseng, where there are golden fields of corn. Right on the far shore lies the fishing village of Strandhuse with its red chimneys. Iholm is a small islet in mid Sound; people hunted there in olden times. Ærø is also within view. Fishing nets spread out. – The convent houses both women and men. The lord of Hvidkilde decides who goes there. In the belfry is a bell with St George on it, shown thrusting his spear into the dragon's throat; a Madonna too. Pulpit raised on a great stone. Also visited Mahgaard (unwell).

From "The Diaries of Hans Christian Andersen, 1825–75"

Arnold Bennett (1837–1931)

What strikes me now most as regards Denmark is the charm, beauty, and independence of the women. They go about freely, sit in cafés together, smoke without self-consciousness. They seem decidedly more independent than Englishwomen. The men have charm of manner, especially of voice and tone. The race is evidently receptive, and it must be beneficially influenced by the attractiveness of its women. On the other hand, Denmark struck both Rickards and me as being an unimportant and dull little country. Its villages were simply naught. They had nothing, except a material sufficiency – no beauty, no evidence of ancient traditions. The landscape also was practically everywhere negligible.

From "Journal", August 29th 1913

Hans Christian Branner (1903–66)

My father never had any luck in life. . . . In his youth he wanted to be a sailor, but after a few years at sea his father summoned him home, getting him a job in the customs service. When he married my mother, she and her family took him out of the customs and put money into a business for him. It was a marine provisioning business. He had a warehouse by the harbour. When ships arrived from foreign parts he would go out to them in a small boat and take orders. That is how it was during my childhood.

At that time we lived in Havnegade, in a big apartment with long white lace curtains at the windows and old mahogany furniture from my mother's home. My father kept a lookout for ships and studied the shipping lists; news of arrivals came by telephone – I can always picture him in my mind's eye, donning his uniform before going out to them. It wasn't a real captain's uniform because he wasn't a captain; but with its brass "anchor" buttons on the navy blue cloth, and its cap and badge, it looked just like one. He came and went in his uniform, made entries in his ledgers and busied himself with his endless lists and tables.

From "The Ship", 1944

Suggested Itineraries

N.B. In what follows, places with entries in the "A to Z" section of this Guide are highlighted in **bold** type.
While the itineraries suggested take in many of Denmark's principal sights, others lie at varying distances off these well-beaten tracks. The excursions necessary to visit them can be planned with the help of the map provided. All the places mentioned here are listed in the Index.

Marguerite Route Named after Denmark's Queen, the "Marguerite Route" is a 3540km/2200 mile-long tourist route drawn up by the Danish Tourist Board. Marked by special brown, white and yellow signs with a daisy motif, it takes visitors through the country's most scenic areas, avoiding wherever possible the busier roads. Although designed as a holiday route covering the whole of Denmark, it is divided for convenience into five sections (brochure available from the Danish Tourist Board).

Getting there See Practical Information.

1. Flensburg to Århus, Ålborg and Skagen

Main route The road from Flensburg to Kupfermühle on the German–Danish frontier (for border crossing points see Practical Information) runs parallel to the head of the Flensburger Förde (Flensburg Fjord). Once across the frontier it joins the E 45 at Kruså, from where it follows the route of the old A 10 all the way north to Frederikshavn. Just over the border is an intersection with the A 8 to **Tønder** (west) and **Nyborg** (east). Beyond Kruså the E 45 makes its way through the low hills of south-east **Jutland**, passing close to the west of **Åbenrå** on the Åbenrå Fjord and **Haderslev** on the Haderslev Fjord. North of Haderslev it skirts the town of Christiansfeld, founded by the Moravian Brethren.

Detour A few kilometres further north a road to the right leads via Taps to Skamlingsbanken (113m/370ft), a popular vantage point from where there are fine views over the Lille Bælt. Crowning the heights is a column made from 25 granite blocks, erected in the 19th c. to commemorate eighteen champions of the South Jutland cause.

Main route The E 45 continues to **Kolding** at the head of Kolding Fjord (ruins of Koldinghus Castle) and on to **Vejle** on Vejle Fjord.

Detour From Vejle the A 18 can be followed north-west to Jelling; the Jelling Stones, dating from the 10th c., are among the most impressive relics of the pre-Christian era in Denmark. West of Vejle (A 28 via Bredsten) is **Billund**, home of Legoland, the famous pleasure park with its Lego models of buildings, etc. from around the world.

Main route North of Vejle the E 45 swings north-eastwards to **Horsens**, a sizeable industrial town on Horsens Fjord, and then Skanderborg on Skanderborg Sø (lake).

Detour **Himmelbjerget**, the second highest point in Denmark, with lovely views, lies a few kilometres north-west of Skanderborg. Take the 445 to Ry where the road turns left and then bends sharply left again across the railway line.

Main route From Skanderborg the E 45 continues north-eastwards to Århus, Denmark's second largest city with its fine cathedral, delightful open-air museum (Den Gamle By = The Old Town) and amusement park.

Silkeborg, attractively situated in the lake district west of Århus (A 15) boasts two museums neither of which should be missed (the Tollund Man; paintings by Asger Jorn). | Detour

Beyond Århus there is a choice of routes. The more direct (E 45) heads inland through an area of hills to **Randers**. | Main route
The other follows the A 15 east along the Djursland peninsula to **Grenå** on the Kattegat coast from where the A 16 leads back to Randers via Auning. Near Auning is a Renaissance castle, Gammel Estrup, home of the Jutland Manor House Museum.

From Randers the A 16 makes its way further west to **Viborg**, one of Denmark's oldest towns, surrounded by woods and heaths. Huge frescoes adorn its handsome cathedral. | Detour

Leaving Randers the E 45 proceeds to **Hobro** on the Mariager Fjord. Near by are the remains of Fyrkat, a fortified Viking settlement. Thereafter the route cuts through the Rebild National Park to **Ålborg** on the southern shores of the **Limfjord**. Among the attractions of this delightful town is Jens Bangs Stenhus, a splendid Renaissance merchant's house. Near Nørresundby on the north side of the Limfjord lies Lindholm Høje with graves dating from the Iron Age and the Viking period. | Main route
Beyond the Limfjord the E 45 veers north-east again to Sæby on North Jutland's eastern coast, then north to the port of **Frederikshavn** (ferry services to Sweden and Norway). From Frederikshavn the A 40 follows the wide sweep of Albaek Bay to **Skagen** on the northern tip of the Jutland peninsula, a landscape dominated by water and dunes.

Although the route just described keeps mainly to the E 45, much of it can be followed making use of country roads (see map). | N.B.

2. Frederikshavn to Holstebro, Esbjerg and Tønder

From **Frederikshavn** take the A 35 west across northern **Jutland** to **Hjørring**, chief town of Vendsyssel. Then head south-west on the A 55 to Løkken, a small resort with superb beaches on the long and gently curving Jammer Bay. | Main route

Just before Løkken a road branches left towards Børglum Kloster, a medieval monastery converted into a Baroque mansion. | Detour

Follow the A 55 south from Løkken to join the A 11 at Åbybro, turning west towards Fjerritslev (brewery museum); from here both Jammer Bay and the Limfjord are within easy reach. Beyond Fjerritslev the A 11 makes its way south-west to Thisted (Thy Peninsula) on one of the Limfjord's many bays, afterwards continuing south. | Main route

South of Thisted the Sundby road branches off left across the Vilsund Bridge to the exceptionally attractive island of Mors. The island's "capital", Nykøbing Mors, boasts an unusual museum of local history housed in a restored wing of the former Dueholm Monastery. | Detour

Beyond the Sundby turn-off the A 11 makes its way south to Struer on Venø Bay (local history museum with collection of model ships). | Main route

From Struer a road leads east to Vinderup and then Skive (on the fjord of that name) which has a Romanesque church (frescoes) and museum (amber). 17km/10½ miles north-west of Skive, through Sønder Balling, stands Spøttrup, a beautifully restored medieval moated castle with | Detour

49

knights' hall, etc. Hjerl Hede (heath) south-west of Skive is a conservation area with an interesting open-air museum (history of the Danish village).

Main route

The A 11 continues south from Struer to the north-west Jutland market town of **Holstebro**, its streets and squares enlivened with sculptures.

Detour

30km/18½ miles or so beyond Holstebro the A 11 meets the east–west-bound A 15. Turn west for **Ringkøbing** on Ringkøbing Fjord and east for **Herning**, centre of the Danish textile industry.

Main route

Heading almost due south the A 11 next proceeds via Skjern to Varde. Just south of Varde the A 12 branches off on the right to **Esbjerg**, Denmark's principal North Sea port (museum of fishing and the sea). On leaving Esbjerg follow the A 24 south-east to rejoin the A 11 near Gredstedbro, soon arriving at **Ribe**, a town with a great many old half-timbered houses and a fine Romanesque cathedral. Beyond Ribe the A 11 continues south.

Detour

Shortly before reaching Bredebro a road leads off left to Løgumkloster. Several buildings survive from the Cistercian monastery, including the lovely brick-built church (winged altar, choir stalls, etc.).

Main route

11km/7 miles south of Bredebro the A 11 arrives at **Tønder**. Situated close to the Danish–German border the town once boasted a considerable bobbin-lace industry.

About a kilometre beyond Tønder the A 8 starts on its way eastwards across the peninsula to Kruså (for Kupfermühle and Flensburg).

The frontier crossing at Saed (Danish passport and customs control) and Böglum (German passport and customs control) is then only a short distance from the junction.

3. Flensburg to Kolding (or Fåborg), Nyborg and Copenhagen

N.B.

From the frontier crossing at Kupfermühle (near Flensburg) Nyborg can be reached either by motorway (E 45/E 20 north and then east via Kolding: Route A) or the A 8 (north-east via Fåborg: Route B). Both routes are described below. Beyond Nyborg the two coincide.

Main route A

For details of the route from Kupfermühle (Flensburg) to **Kolding** see Route 1 above.
A few kilometres north of Kolding the main north–south and east–west traffic arteries (E 45, E 20) intersect. Follow the E 20 eastwards towards the Lille Bælt.

Detour

18km/11 miles beyond Kolding a country road branches left to **Fredericia**, just to the north. The town dates from the 17th c. and was originally a fortress.

Main route A

A kilometre-long suspension bridge carries the E 20 over the Lille Bælt to the island of **Funen**. To the right, on the shores of the Bælt south of the motorway, lies **Middelfart**, a thriving port. From there the route traverses the interior of the island to **Odense**, the largest town on Funen and birthplace of Hans Christian Andersen.

Detour

Leave the E 20 east of Odense and drive north to visit Ladbyskibet, site of a Viking ship burial near the village of Ladby.

Main route A

The E 20 continues to **Nyborg**, another busy port, on Funen's east coast (Store Bælt bridge under construction).

Cross the German–Danish frontier at Kupfermühle (Flensburg) and join the | Main route B
A 8 east-bound at Kruså, following it north-eastwards via Rinkenæs to
Gråsten on the Flensburger Förde (Flensburg Fjord). Gråsten Palace is the
summer residence of Queen Ingrid, widow of Frederik IX. Beyond Gråsten,
as the road skirts Nybøl Nor, a bay on the fjord, the historic Dybbøl Mølle
(mill) comes into view on the right. A little further on a bridge spans the Als
Sund to the island of **Als**, which the road then crosses to Fynshav on the
east coast. Having taken the ferry over the Lille Bælt to Bøjden on the island
of **Funen**, follow the A 8 once more to **Fåborg**, a pleasant town lying on a
bay; Fåborg Museum boasts a particularly fine collection of paintings by
Funen artists. Leaving Fåborg continue north-east on the A 8.

Shortly before reaching Kværndrup a road branches off left to Egeskov | Detour
Slot, a magnificent Renaissance manor house set on an island in a lake.
One of the outbuildings houses a veteran car and aircraft museum.

From Kværndrup the A 8 makes its way north-eastwards to **Nyborg**. | Main route B

Arriving at Nyborg take the ferry across the Store Bælt to Korsør on the | Main route
south-west coast of **Zealand**. From Korsør the E 20 crosses the centre of the
island to **Køge** on the east coast.

13km/8 miles beyond Korsør a side road leads left off the E 20 to the Viking | Detour
fortified encampment at Trelleborg.

Continue on the E 20 via **Slagelse** to Sorø and **Ringsted**, two small towns | Main route
with Romanesque churches. At Ringsted leave the E 20 and drive north-
east on the A 14 to **Roskilde** with its lovely cathedral (royal tombs) and
Viking Ship Museum.

A motorway (21) connects Roskilde with **Copenhagen**. Among the Danish
capital's many attractions for visitors are its port, the pedestrianised Strøget (main shopping area), the numerous palaces and museums and vast
range of amusements (e.g. at the Tivoli).

4. Copenhagen to Hillerød and Helsingør

Take the motorway (Lyngbyvej) north out of **Copenhagen**, stopping in the | Main route
northern suburb of Lyngby to visit Sorgenfri Palace (park) and the Frilandsmuseet (open-air museum with traditional buildings from all over Denmark). Continue north-westwards on the 201 via Birkerød to **Hillerød** where
Frederiksborg, Christian IV's magnificent Renaissance castle, now the Danish Museum of National History, stands surrounded by its lake. After
Hillerød follow the A 6 through the southern part of Gribskov forest,
bounded on the east side by Esrum Sø (lake), to Fredensborg and Fredensborg Palace, summer residence of the Danish royal family.

Beyond Fredensborg the A 6 proceeds east to **Helsingør** from where ferry
services run to Helsingborg (Sweden) and where the famous Kronborg
Castle occupies a peninsula overlooking the Sund.

An alternative route from Copenhagen follows the 152 as it makes its way | **N.B.**
along the coast – known as the "Danish Riviera" – to Helsingør. As well as
the lovely scenery bordering the shores of the Øresund, the attractions
of the route include Louisiana, the internationally renowned museum of
modern art at Humlebaek.

5. Copenhagen to Rødbyhavn

Main route | Leave **Copenhagen** heading south-west along Gammel Køge Landevej to join the E 47 motorway. Beyond Vordingborg the road follows the old A 2 south down the east side of **Zealand**.

Detour | Near Ølby a side road branches off left to **Køge** on the bay of that name, along the shores of which there are several beach resorts. A short distance south of Køge stands Vallø Castle, a fine Renaissance building set in a magnificent park. South-east of Køge (via the 261 to Store Heddinge) are the extensive limestone cliffs known as Stevns Klint, with splendid views over the sea.

Main route | The E 47 continues south towards Rønnede. Between Algestrup and Rønnede roads lead off right to Bregentved Manor and Gisselfeld (lovely park).

Detour | From Rønnede take the A 54 west to **Næstved**, an industrial port. On the nearby island of Gavnø (causeway) stands Gavnø Castle housing one of the largest private collections of paintings in Denmark.

Main route | Beyond Rønnede the E 47 makes its way through south-east Zealand, the coast of which is heavily indented with numerous bays and headlands.

Detour | At the junction of the E 47 and the 265 from Næstved, turn off east and drive via Præstø to Kalvehave on the coast; here there is a bridge over the Ulvsund to the island of **Møn**.

Main route | Approaching **Vordingborg** the E 47 veers south-east to cross to the island of **Falster** by the Farø Bridges. The island can also be reached from Vordingborg by way of the Storstrøm Bridge.

Detour | Beyond the Farø Bridges the E 55 branches off southwards to Nykøbing Falster (museum in the old "Czarens Hus").

Main route | From the Storstrøm Bridge the 153 crosses the north-west tip of Falster to the island of **Lolland** (bridge over the Guldborg Sund). Once on Lolland it makes its way via Sakskøbing, Maribo and Rødby (by-passed) to the ferry terminal at **Rødbyhavn** in the south of the island. Maribo, which straddles two lakes, has a fine cathedral and interesting open-air museum.

The ferry service from Rødbyhavn to Puttgarden across the Fehmarn Bælt is the shortest of the ferry crossings between Denmark and Germany.

6. Rostock (Warnemünde) to Copenhagen via Gedser

Main route | Disembarking from the Rostock (Warnemünde) ferry at Gedser (2hr crossing), take the E 55 north to Nykøbing F, the largest town on the island of **Falster**. Beyond Nykøbing the E 55 merges with the E 47 coming from the west, afterwards heading north-east to cross the Storstrøm, the channel separating Falster and **Zealand**, by the Farø Bridges. On its way through south-east Zealand the motorway passes close to the little village of Udby, birth-place of the educationalist N. F. S. Grundtvig (on the left, just before Junction 40).

Alternative route | Instead of following the E 47/E 55, turn west off the motorway before reaching the Farø Bridges and proceed via Nørre Alslev and along the Storstrøm coast, crossing to Zealand by the Storstrøm Bridge. **Vordingborg**, at the north end of the bridge, on the Zealand coast, boasts an interesting landmark, the "Goose Tower". From Vordingborg head north-east again to rejoin the motorway.

Beyond Udby the E 47/E 55 continues north in an almost straight line, skirting Køge Bay before arriving at the Danish capital. Worthwhile detours can be made to the port of **Køge** and to **Roskilde** where the cathedral contains the tombs of Danish royalty. From there the next stop is **Copenhagen** itself.

Main route

From Copenhagen there is a ferry to Bornholm.

N.B.

Historic Military and Drove Roads

In the period of pre- and early history and also in the Middle Ages, so-called military roads (hærvejen) followed the ridge of higher ground through Jutland and into Schleswig-Holstein, now part of Germany. At first these tracks took their course from the lie of the land, circumnavigating difficult terrain; later they carved out a more direct line.

The roads not only provided passage for armies in times of war but were also used as trade routes and pilgrims' paths. Apart from the network of regional tracks they formed the sole north–south link on the Danish peninsula. An important medieval military road led from Viborg southwards towards North Germany. Burial sites, memorial tablets and old travellers' rests are found in many places along the route of the earlier roads.

From the late Middle Ages onwards drove roads also made their appearance throughout Europe. Cattle were driven from the areas where they were raised to the towns whose inhabitants required meat. From Jutland animals were driven as far as Hamburg and Lübeck. Sheep and pigs as well as cattle were taken for sale to the centres of population. The eastern drove road led from Hobro via Vejle to Haderslev, while the central one began in Skive and, following an old military road, went first via Pårup and Kongeå near Foldingbro to Tønder. There it joined the western drove road leading from Holstebro via Varde and Tønder southwards to Husum (in Germany). Later there was a cattle-track to Itzehoe (also in Germany).

In the 15th and 16th c. the trade in cattle increased in volume. It was at this time that the inns called "kroer" (jugs) were set up along the route to provide accommodation and food for the drovers. The animals, too, were given fodder. With the coming of rail transport in the 19th c., the drove roads lost their importance for the movement of cattle, and when modern roads began to be built they were often laid along stretches of the ancient ways. Sections of the military and drove roads have survived however, still in something like their original state; some are now protected features of the landscape.

Particularly beautiful stretches of the old military roads can be found between Nørre Snede and Kollemorten (north-west of Vejle; part of the military road from Viborg) and in South Jutland near Haderslev. In the latter case the road follows the high ridge of Jutland and for considerable distances runs parallel to the main road. As a result it is much used today by walkers.

Near the German–Danish frontier there are many boundary posts and waymarks bearing the names of the families and communities responsible for the upkeep of the roads. The arms of Bov, a little place to the west of Kruså, include an echo of this by-gone age in the form of two oxen and a boundary post.

Near the border town of Padborg, in the area of the old roads, there are several places of interest, among them the Bov Museum "Oldemorstoft", an ancient farm building housing relics of the military road. Other exhibits – documents, maps, battle scenes and weaponry – recall the momentous events of April 9th 1848 when one of the first battles between the Danes and Schleswig-Holsteiners was fought at Bov, ending in a Danish victory. The redrawing of the frontier in 1920 had a profound effect on the development of Bov and the neighbouring small towns and villages.

More recent history still is commemorated by the Frøslevlejren Museum set up in the former Second World War internment camp at Frøslev. Among the exhibits are the white buses with red cross markings in which Scandinavian survivors were brought back from the concentration camps in Germany in 1945. That operation was master-minded by Count Folke Bernadotte, whose statue in Kruså is a further reminder of events at the end of the Second World War.

Denmark from A to Z

Åbenrå

Jutland
District: Sønderjyllands amt
Population: 22,000

The Baltic resort of Åbenrå lies surrounded by forests in the south-east of Jutland, on the west bank of the fjord of the same name. — Situation

In the year 1935 Åbenrå, the town with the largest harbour in South Jutland, was granted trading rights. In the 17th and 18th c. ships sailed from here to South America and the Far East. Many fine residences date from this period when the populace enjoyed considerable prosperity. — History

In addition to shipping and fishing, trade in cereals, cattle and timber is of importance. Industries include engineering and the production of animal foodstuffs. Organs are also built in Åbenrå. — Economy

Sights

The town centre lies to the west of the harbour area (Gammelhavn, Nyhavn, etc.). Near the pedestrian precinct stands the Church of St Nicholas, originally a Late Romanesque single-aisled brick building which was restored in 1949–56. The interior is notable for its Romanesque font, a magnificent Baroque reredos of 1642 and a canopied pulpit. — Church of St Nicholas

The Town Hall on the main market square is a two-storeyed building of yellow stone with a hipped roof; it was built between 1828 and 1830 by Christian Frederik Hansen, who was then the leading Danish architect. In the hall can be seen a collection of portraits of Danish kings and queens, including that of Caroline Mathilde, the wife of Christian VII, painted by the Danish artist Jens Juel. — Town Hall

Some 18th c. residences, several with beautiful gables, survive in Slotsgade (Castle Street), in the south of the town. Of these the most attractive are No. 14 (1767), No. 15 (1713), No. 28 (1797) and No. 29 (1770). No. 20 Søndergade boasts a pretty Rococo façade. Dominating the Vægterpladsen is a statue of a night-watchman. — Slotsgade

The town's seafaring tradition is documented in the Åbenrå Museum at H. P. Hanssens Gade 33B. Owners and captains often had pictures painted of their ships, and the shipping section of the museum exhibits a collection of about 200 such paintings as well as ships in bottles. There is also an interesting collection of souvenirs brought back by sailors from all over the world.
Other departments are concerned with pre- and early history, ethnology (especially objects from China) and Danish painting of the 19th and 20th c. (open: June 1st–Aug. 31st Tue.–Sun. 10am–4pm, Sept. 1st–May 31st Tue.–Sun. 1–4pm). In front of the museum stands a sculpture "Seated Youth" (Siddende Dreng), by Astrid Noack. Jacob-Michelsen-Gård, an old courtyard with a house dating from 1704, forms a part of the museum. — Åbenrå Museum

◀ *A windmill on Mandø island*

| Brundland Castle | To the south of the town stands Brundland Castle (12th c.), which was rebuilt in 1411 under Queen Margarethe I and considerably restored between 1805 and 1807. It is surrounded by a moat. |

Surroundings

Gråsten	South-east of Åbenrå, on the Forth of Flensburg, lies the pleasant town of Gråsten, with its lively harbour. In the middle of the town stands the 16th c. castle, which was rebuilt after a fire in 1759. Today it is the summer residence of Queen Ingrid, the widow of Frederik IX, and can be visited when she is not in residence. It is surrounded by a magnificent park.
Broager	Broager, a little town on the Broagerland Peninsula in South Jutland, between the Bay of Sonderborg and the Flensburg Inlet, has a 12th c. church with twin spires. The interior contains 13th and 16th c. wall-paintings and some beautiful 16th c. wood-carving. In the cemetery stands Denmark's tallest bell-tower (1650); war graves of 1848 and 1864 are reminders of the struggle for Schleswig.
Løjt Church	The pretty north coast of the Åbenrå Fjord is reached along by-roads. Among the Løjtland hills, 6km/2½ miles north of Åbenrå, stands the Romanesque Løjt Church, with its notable Gothic winged altar and frescoes of around 1530 on the ceiling of the choir, with arabesques and busts; note also the carved Late Gothic altar, painted over by Jes Jessen.

Ærø   C 4

District: Fyns amt
Area: 88sq.km/sq.miles
Population: 9000

| Situation | The island of Ærø is situated south of Funen and west of Langeland, at the entrance to the Little Belt. The coast is generally steep, particularly in the north-western part but there is good bathing, especially along the north and east coasts. Inland among green hills nestle pretty little villages and many relics of the past, such as dolmens and passage graves. |
| | Although the coast on the west of the island runs in a straight line, the northern part has more spits of land and bays, and it is here that the larger towns are situated. Car ferries ply between Ærøskøbing and Svendborg (Funen), Marstal and Rudkøbing (Langeland), Søby and Fåborg (Funen), and between Søby and Mommark (Als). |

Places of interest on Ærø

*Ærøskøbing	Ærøskøbing, an attractive old market town, lies on a promontory of the north coast. The town received its trading charter in 1398, grew in importance as a result of its trade with South Jutland and provides an example of a well-preserved merchants' township of the 17th and 18th centuries, with half-timbered houses lining narrow cobbled streets. There are 36 houses under preservation orders, including Denmark's oldest post office (1749) and the Kjøbinghus (1645). Hammerich's House (c. 1700; note the furniture and glazed tiles), formerly the residence of the sculptor Hammerich, and Hans Billedhugger's House are furnished as museums.
Ærø Museum	Objects of local history, including costumes, are exhibited in the Ærø Museum.
Bottle-ship collection	A visit is also recommended to this Museum at Flaskeskibssamlingen, Smedegade 22, which boasts several hundred examples of model ships.

Ærø Island: huts on the beach

At the eastern end of the island lies the little fishing port of Marstal, which was one of the most important ports in Denmark in years gone by. Model ships can be seen hanging in the medieval church, which also has some beautiful wall-paintings, including a portrait of a bishop. The gallery of the church was once known as the "Captain's Bridge", because ships' captains used to sit up there.
Visitors should note the Romanesque font, which was originally in the church at Tranderup.

Marstal

In Marstal's Maritime Museum on Prinsengade there are numerous model ships, paintings of ships' captains and figureheads on display, as well as objects brought home by sailors from their voyages – jewellery, weapons, stuffed animals, etc.

Maritime Museum

Søby, at the north-western tip of Ærø, is also worth a visit. Here can be seen a country house, the Søbygård, built on the foundations of a massive medieval fortress. One of the cellars once served as a prison; leg-irons and chains which were used can be seen in the Ærø Museum.

Søby

In the north-west of the island several windmills have been preserved, including the Vitsø Mølle and the Vester Mølle.

Windmills

Ålborg/Aalborg

B/C 1

Jutland
District: Nordjyllands amt
Population: 157,000

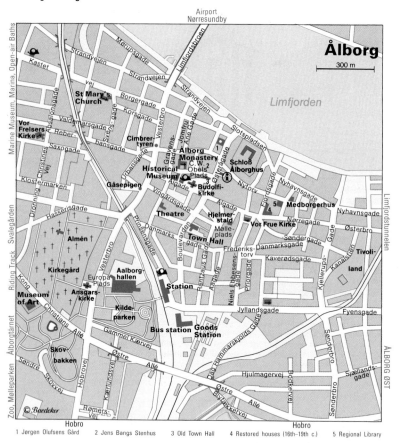

Airport
Nørresundby

Ålborg

300 m

Limfjorden

1 Jørgen Olufsens Gård 2 Jens Bangs Stenhus 3 Old Town Hall 4 Restored houses (16th–19th c.) 5 Regional Library

| Situation | Ålborg or Aalborg (the latter spelling is preferred by the inhabitants), the fourth largest town in Denmark, is situated on the south bank of the Limfjord, which links the North Sea with the Kattegat and is particularly narrow at this point. A road and rail bridge and a six-lane motorway tunnel lead to Nørresundby, on the north side of the ford, which forms part of Greater Ålborg. The popular beaches along the North Sea are within easy reach. |

History

Ålborg is mentioned about 1070 by Adam of Bremen as a "well-known seafaring town". In 1342 the existing Viking settlement was granted its town charter. During the Middle Ages there was a close link with Norway. The town enjoyed considerable commercial importance and in 1534 it became the seat of an Evangelical bishop. Until the early 16th c. Ålborg was a prosperous trading centre but from 1625, largely as a result of the quartering of foreign troops during the Thirty Years' War against Sweden, it entered a period of decline. Only towards the end of the 18th c. did it recover, and from 1850 onwards various industries became established. The deepening of the Limfjord was of benefit to the town, because it could

now be reached by larger ships. During the Second World War enemy
aerial attacks and bombardments caused great damage.

Today trade and industry have put their stamp on the economic life of the
town. Among the most important branches of industry are shipbuilding
and cement, paper and metal, glass and timber, tobacco and the production of Ålborg aquavit, a Danish version of schnapps. The modern port is
the place from which Danish trade with Greenland is conducted. There are
regular flights from Ålborg to the capital Copenhagen (see entry) and to
Norway. (See Travel Discounts.)

Economy and
Transport

Ålborg is also a centre of education and training and has been a university
town since 1973. Tourists can glean much about the region's culture by
visiting museums such as the Museum of Modern Art and the Historical
Museum, as well as concerts and theatrical performances. In August the
Ålborg Festival of concerts is held.

Culture

To the south of the place where the Limfjord Bridge (Limfjordsbroen)
crosses from Nørresundby lies the old part of Ålborg, with its beautiful
buildings and restored houses. In the newer parts, which adjoin on the west
and east, can be found well-tended parks, such as Møllepark, from the
highest point of which there is a view of the greater part of the town.

Town area

Old Town

In the centre of the Old Town lies Budolfi Square (Budolfi Plads), to the
north of which in Algade stands St Botolph's Church (Sankt Budolfi Kirke),
named after a British seafaring saint. The Gothic building, which has been
altered on several occasions, was erected about 1430 when the remains
of an old Romanesque church were incorporated into the new edifice.
The dome of the tower (c. 1780) of this whitewashed brick church retains
the Baroque style, and the spire has been adopted as the town's symbol.
The church was rebuilt in the first half of the 20th c. The carillon plays on
the hour every hour between 9am and 10pm. In the vestibule of the church,
formerly a Catholic chapel, can be seen some excellent frescoes. In the
interior itself visitors can admire an impressive reredos and a carved pulpit
(1689–92, by Laurids Jensen), a marble font and – in the northern aisle – a
Renaissance gallery with illustrations of the Ten Commandments. In the
south aisle are representations of the Way of the Cross and inscriptions
with the names of men who held important positions in Ålborg in 1650.

*St Botolph's
Church

Not far north-west of St Botolph's Church in Algade (house No. 48) stands
the Ålborg Historical Museum (Aalborg Historiske Museum). Its collections
include interesting items from prehistoric times, an illustrated history of
the town with emphasis on commerce and levels of society, as well as a
beautiful collection of North Jutland glass. The Ålborg Room of 1602 with
its Renaissance interior is of special interest (open: Tue.–Sun. 10am–5pm).

Historical
Museum

North of the museum lies C. W. Obels Plads where the C. W. Obel tobacco
factory stood until 1896. At the north-east corner of the square will be found
the former Monastery of the Holy Ghost (Heiligåndsklosteret), founded in
1431 as the House of the Holy Spirit and later designated a monastery. The
purpose of the monastery was and is to care for the old and the sick. It is
Denmark's oldest social foundation; today it is a care centre, and guided
tours are available. In the excellently preserved buildings will be seen
frescoes dating from 1500 and some beautiful stepped gables. The frescoes depict a mermaid, the Crucifixion, an angel with a trumpet, a monk
and a bishop. On the square in front of the building stands a fountain
(Dragon Fountain).

Ålborg Monastery

Gravensgade, to the west of the Ålborg Monastery, forms part of the busy
pedestrian zone, with its stores, banks and boutiques.

Gravensgade

Ålborg/Aalborg

Gammel Torv

North of St Botolph's Church lies Gammel Torv, the market square on which the Old Town Hall (1762) stands. The name "Gammel Torv" indicates that this is the oldest market-place in the town. At one time the town was governed from here, and there were gallows and stocks to prove it! The granite obelisk on the square is still the point from which the lengths of roads leading out of Ålborg are measured.

**Jens Bangs Stenhus

On Østergade can be seen one of the town's most impressive buildings, known as Jens Bangs Stenhus, a beautiful mansion built in 1624 by the prosperous merchant Jens Bang, a lover of ostentation and grandeur. With its five storeys it is the largest Renaissance mansion in Northern Europe. Built of brick, it has a roof with curved gables. The whole building is covered with sandstone ornamentation which shows a Dutch Renaissance influence. Although he was the richest man in Ålborg, Jens Bang was never elected on to the town council. This rankled, and so he had a stone figure of himself built on the gable of the house with its tongue sticking out at the town hall.

Jørgen Olufsens Gård

A few yards from Jen Bangs Stenhus on Østergade stands Jørgen Olufsens Gård, a well-preserved half-timbered property with a gabled stone front (1616). It, too, was formerly owned by a merchant.

Ålborghus

Near the harbour stands the former Ålborghus Castle, built in 1539 and now occupied by various authorities. The castle courtyard and parts of the ramparts and dungeons are open to visitors in summer (from 8am to sunset).

Church of Our Lady

The Church of Our Lady (Vor Frue Kirke), one of the oldest churches in the town stands at Niels Ebbesengade. Built about 1100 in granite blocks as a monastery church, it was completely rebuilt in Romanesque style in 1878. In the course of the rebuilding the original north door with its granite relief was placed at the main west entrance. In the tympanum can be seen two scenes from the Childhood of Christ surrounding a Majestas Domini (Christ in Majesty).

Northern Renaissance: Jens Bang's Stenhus

Inside the church, the 17th and 18th c. monuments, font, pulpit and a Late Gothic crucifix are all worthy of note.

There are a number of old houses near the church, and an historic pottery in Hjelmerstald Lane. In Geviert, which is bordered by Nørregade and Fjordgade, nine houses 150 to 400 years old from various parts of the town have been re-erected and restored.

Near the Church of Our Lady at Peder Barkesgade 5 can be found the Danish Emigrant Archive, where a collection of books, letters and photographs on the subject of Danish emigrants can be seen (open: Mon.–Thur. 9am–4pm, Fri. 9am–2pm).

Danish Emigrant Archive

The Medborgerhus, a town house at Nytorv 26, now houses the North Jutland Regional Library, which boasts a large collection of Danish and foreign books as well as a children's library. The building also contains a council chamber, conference rooms and a cafeteria.

North Jutland Regional Library

On the south-eastern periphery of the Old Town lies Tivoliland, an amusement park with beautiful gardens, fountains and flowers. Its 80 or so attractions include a loop-the-loop switchback, a ghost train and a China Town. On the open-air revolving stage, musical shows with international artistes (open: April to mid-September). There are also restaurants and picnic sites.

Tivoliland

West and South-west

Vesterbro, running north to south, forms the western boundary of the Old Town. In this street are two notable sculptures: at the end of Bispegade is the "Cimbrian Bull" (Cimbrertyren, 1937) by A. J. Bundgård with a poem by the Nobel Prizewinner Johannes V. Jensen (1873–1950) on the plinth. Further south is the statue of "The Goose Girl" (Gåsepigen) by Gerhard Henning (1937). On Vesterbro, too, stands St Ansgar's Church. Opposite lies Kilde Park, Ålborg's oldest park (1802), with a number of sculptures including "The Three Graces" by Thorvaldsen and "Child of Bacchus" by Anne Marie Carl Nielsen. Also to be found here are the Ålborg Halls.

Vesterbro

Ålborg Halls is a complex of two large buildings, Ålborg Hall and Europa Hall, inaugurated in 1953 and 1959 respectively, and forming one of the largest function centres in Scandanavia. They are used for theatrical performances and concerts, exhibitions and conferences. There is a restaurant ("Papegøjehaven") and a bowling alley.

Ålborg Halls

At Kong Christians Allé 50 stands the impressive building of the North Jutland Museum of Art (Nordjyllands Kunstmuseet), built in 1968–72 to plans by the Finnish architects Elissa and Alva Aalto and the Dane Jean Jaques Baruël. The museum consists of a complex of various shapes and includes an amphitheatre, a sculpture park and function rooms, including a concert hall. The principal exhibits comprise post-1890 Danish paintings and 20th c. foreign art. The main emphasis is on the works of the COBRA group, founded in 1948 and named after the initial letters of the towns Copenhagen, Brussels and Amsterdam. The group was made up of Danish, Dutch and Belgian painters, including Asgar Jorn and Karl Appel (open: Tue.–Sun. 10am–5pm; also Mon. during July and Aug.).

** North Jutland Museum of Art

To the south of the museum rises a wooded hill known as Skovbakken, with an open-air theatre and the Ålborgtarnet observation tower, which stands 55m/180ft high.

Skovbakken (observation tower)

The Møllepark, some 1·5km/1 mile to the south-west, is a large park offering an extensive view of Ålborg and the island of Egholm (Limfjord). In the park is the sculpture "Noah's Ark", by Roda Reilinger. Ålborg's Zoological Gardens within the park is the home of 800 animals from all

Møllepark; Zoological Garden

The North Jutland Art Museum in Ålborg

over the world, including African elephants, monkeys, Rothschild giraffes and South American marsh beavers. There is also a sea-lion and penguin area in which the animals can be observed under water through a viewing window. (Open: all the year 9am–6pm.)

Svalegården West of the great park area, in the suburb of Hasseris, stands the Svalegården, a merchant's residence which was built about 1600. It was moved here during the modernisation of the old part of the town in 1952.

Technical Museum At Riihimäkivej 6, in the Hasseris district of the town, is an interesting Technical Museum (Danmarks Tekniske Museum). It offers permanent and temporary natural science and technology exhibitions (open: daily 10am–5pm).

Ålborg Øst

Urania Observatory The Urania Observatory (Urania Observatoriet), at Borgmester Jørgensensvej 13, in the south-east of Ålborg is worth a visit. It houses Denmark's second largest telescope, through which visitors can observe the various heavenly bodies in detail.
(Open: Sept. 1st –Apr. 4th Wed. 7.30pm–10pm, or by prior arrangement by telephone.)

Hans Egedes Church Mention should also be made of Hans Egedes Kirke, on Grønlands Torv. It was designed by several architects – Dam and Dirckinck Holmfeld, Hoff and Winding – and built in yellow brick between 1966 and 1982.

Southern Suroundings

On the southern edge of the town lies "Vandland Ålborg", a bather's paradise with a sub-tropical atmosphere, offering relaxation and diversion in the form of swimming pools, waterchutes, swirl canals, saunas, etc.

Vandland Ålborg

27km/17 miles south of Ålborg on the E 3 road in an area of heathland lie the charming Rebild Hills (Rebild Bakker), declared a National Park at the request of Danish Americans; celebrations are held here annually on July 4th to mark American Independence Day. At the entrance to the park are a restaurant and a local history and minstrel museum. In the park can be seen a replica of Lincoln's Log Cabin, built in 1934 with logs from America, which is now a Museum of Emigration.
On a hill to the north-east stands the Cimbrerstenen, a rock with the carved figure of a bull and the inscription "Cimbrerne drog ut fra disse egne" ("The Cimbri set out from this area").

*Rebild National Park

Near the park lies the village of Rebild, and a little way west along the A 10 is the Thingbaek Limestone Quarry (Kalkminer), in the great subterranean workings of which will be found a museum with sculptures by Bundgård and Bonnesen (open: daily May–Aug. 10am–5pm; Sept.–Oct. Sat. and Sun.).

Thingbaek Limestone Quarry

To the south of Rebild stretches one the largest and most unspoiled forest areas in Denmark, the Forest of Rold (Rold Skov), covering an area of 6400ha/16,000 acres, with many rare trees. Particularly noteworthy is the "Bewitched Wood" of stunted beech trees (250–300 years old). There are also bogs, lakes and heathlands. In the village of Rold the rebuilt ring of the Miehe circus family has been turned into a circus museum. Old equipment, pictures and other objects are souvenirs of the halcyon days of the circus in the first half of the 20th c.

Forest of Rold

North of the town

The Marine Museum (Ålborg Marinemuseum) is on the Limfjord, to the north-west of the town centre. The museum's exhibits portray the development of the Danish merchant fleet particularly over the last 200 years. The navy is also featured. The museum's main attraction is the last submarine to be built in Denmark, the "Springeren", which is exhibited on dry land and open fore and aft so that visitors can walk right through (open: March–Apr. and Sept.–Dec. 10am–4pm, May–Aug. daily 10am–6pm; closed Jan. and Feb.).

*Marine Museum

Egholm Island, in the Limfjord, is accessible all the year round by ferry. It boasts a museum with some 20 farms (Egholm Museet), which is equipped with agricultural machinery and tools as well as domestic items. It is open every weekday and has a restaurant.

Egholm Island

On the far side of the Limfjord lies Nørresundby. In the market-place, the Nørresund Torv, stands the "Stone Dog" sculpture by Henrik Starcke. In the pedestrian zone can be seen other works of art, including some by Edgar Funch, Jørgen Brynjolf and Kaj Nielsen. The Sundby Samlingerne at Gl. Østergade 8 displays a collection of pictures which portray the town's history, some dredgers, etc (open: Wed.–Fri. 2–4pm, Sat. 10am–noon). To the west of Nørresundby is Ålborg Airport, from which sightseeing trips can be made.

Nørresundby

North of Nørresundby lies Lindholm Høje, with nearly 700 graves dating from the Iron Age and the Viking era. Most of the graves which have been excavated contained ashes; the dead were burned, together with their

*Lindholm Høje

Stones marking ancient graves on the Lindholm Høje

burial objects, and then interred in a grave marked with a stone. The old gravestones are triangular, the later ones round or oval. Upright stones in the form of ships date from the Viking period.

To the north of the cemetery lies a settlement which has also been investigated. Paths paved with wood, postholes of houses, wells and cooking-pits have been uncovered. Here and there the postholes have been filled with cement so that the visitor can obtain an impression of the size of the houses. The settlement was abandoned in 1100, as it was subject to frequent sandstorms. Many interesting finds from the region are displayed in the "Lindholm Høje Museet" (open: June–Aug. daily 10am–7pm, the rest of the year 10am–4 or 5pm; closed mid-Oct.–Easter Mon.).

Brønderslev

20km/13 miles north of Ålborg the E3 leads to the important commercial and industrial town of Brønderslev. The Romanesque church (*c.* 1150) is now used only for funerals. In Øster (East) Brønderslev, at Hallundvej 137, the Vendelboernes Egnsmuseum, with its exhibits of regional customs is worth a visit. In the vicinity can be seen some 600 burial barrows.

Als

B/C 3/4

District: Sønderjyllands amt
Area: 315sq.km/122sq.miles
Population: 53,000

Situation

The island of Als lies at the southern end of the Little Belt, between the Jutland Peninsula and the island of Funen. Although the coastline facing the Belt has few bays many will be found on the landward side. Its beautiful beaches make it a popular place for vacations, and old churches (Lysabild) and mills render the towns most attractive.

Sønderborg Castle

Places of interest on Als

The chief place on the island is the old town of Sønderborg (pop. approximately 30,000), which is situated at the southern end of the island and has spread on to the promontory on the opposite side of the Als Sund. The two towns are linked by a bridge over the narrow Sound to the west of the island. To the south-east of the town on Sønderborg Bay is a wood of old trees. — Sønderborg

The medieval castle, a building with four wings, was where King Christian II was imprisoned between 1532 and 1539. Note the Renaissance chapel of 1571. The castle is now a museum with collections of historical material and art.

In St Mary's Church, built in 1625 and restored in this century, can be seen 17th c. wood carvings, a 1625 altar and a pulpit dating from 1559. Sønderborg also has a modern church, Christian Church; built in 1957 by the architects Esben and Kåre Klint in a Gothic style, it can be compared with Grundtvig Church in Copenhagen. The church's pride and joy is a small 14th c. crucifix.

A number of modern sculptures can be found in Sønderborg including: in Town Hall Square, "Alspigen" by Adam Fischer, a symbol of the island's fertility (1951); in the pedestrian precinct, "Gateway to the Mind" by Jørgen Haugen Sørenson (1979); in the garden of the chemist's shop, "The Largest Vase in the World" by Aksel Krog and other artists (1989 Guinness Book of Records); on the promenade, "Young Lady Seated" by Victor Kvedéris (1962). To the south of the town centre stands the modern College of Sport, worth seeing for its mosaics and sculptures by Danish artists.

7km/4½ miles north-east of Sønderborg lies the town of Augustenborg. In a large park stands a palace built in 1776 in the Rococo style, now a psychiatric hospital. — Augustenborg

Note the palace chapel with its beautiful stucco work by the Italian Michelangelo Taddei; the font was a gift from the Russian Czar Alexander I.

Another interesting palace, Nordborg, lies in the north of the island. Originally a castle, it was built in the 12th c. as defence against the Wends, destroyed during the wars against Sweden and rebuilt between 1665 and 1670. In the early 20th c. it was further converted and now houses a college of further education. — Nordborg

Road No. 8 passes through the centre of Als and on to Fynshav, a village on the Little Belt, from where a ferry plys to the island of Funen. — Fynshav

Surroundings

*Dybbøl Mølle

On the mainland of Jutland south-west of Sønderborg lies the little township of Dybbøl, the name of which is closely associated with the events of the year 1864. On April 18th of that year, at the Dybbøl Trenches (Dybbøl Banke), a natural hill near the windmill (Dybbøl Mølle), German forces overcame the numerically inferior Danes who had retreated from Danewerk, and so Denmark lost the whole of Schleswig to Prussia.
The windmill, reconstructed after a fire, and the cannon are now a monument. The mill contains a museum displaying arms, uniforms, etc.

Dybbøl Banke
History centre

Since 1992 there has been an ultra-modern History Centre ("Historiecenter Dybbøl Banke") opposite the windmill. With the aid of multivision and other modern aids it graphically portrays the highlights of the retreat from Danewerk and the Battle of the Dybbøl Trenches. A model of the entrenchments to the scale of 1:10 illustrates the basic tactics employed and is currently the largest and most detailed model of its kind in Denmark (open: mid-Apr.–May, Sept.–Oct. 10am–5pm; June–Aug. 10am–6pm).

Anholt   D 2

District: Århus amt
Area: 22sq.km/8½sq.miles
Population: 160

Situation

The little island of Anholt lies in the Kattegat about half-way between northern Denmark and Sweden. The island can be reached by ferry from Grenå in about two and a half hours.

Nature reserve

The island is mainly heathland and dunes, with just the occasional tree. The area of drifting sand, the Ørkenen (Desert), produced by wind and waves, is unique in Denmark and can be observed from the chain of hills in the west, the Sønderbjerg. In the north-west of the island lies a lagoon with a bird sanctuary (Flakket). "Totten", the dune hill in the east of Anholt, is a seal reserve. The lighthouse is a protected building.

Århus   C 2

Jutland
District: Århus amt
Population: 264,000

Situation

Århus, Denmark's second largest city, lies on the east coast of Jutland where the river "Århus Å" flows into Århus Bay, in the Kattegat. In the vicinity of the town are parks and woods and along the coast beaches extend for several miles.

History

The settlement was first mentioned in 928 as the see of a bishop, and it received its municipal charter in 1441. During the Middle Ages commerce, seafaring and fishing were of considerable importance to Århus. For a time the town played a part in the great herring markets in Falsterbro on Schonen, to which people came from the whole of northern Europe. In the 16th and early 17th c. Århus enjoyed its heyday, with agriculture making a major contribution. Trade spread to Germany, Holland and Norway and merchants from other countries also settled here. A number of well-preserved Renaissance buildings are evidence of the town's prosperity during this period.

From 1627 Århus had to suffer occupation by troops during the Thirty Years' War and the wars against Sweden. After the town had recovered from the effects of the wars, various industries became established here towards the end of the 18th c. In the battles for Schleswig (1848 and 1864) Århus was occupied by German troops. In 1902 the Crown Prince of Denmark, later King Christian X and his consort, were presented with Marselisborg Castle by the city.

The town has various industries. Beer, textiles, machines, iron and steel, food processing and locomotives, etc. are produced here. Århus has the biggest container terminal in Denmark.

Economy

Århus, which boasts a university, technical college and conservatoire, is the cultural and educational hub of Central Jutland. Periodic exhibitions are mounted in the Art Gallery. The musical scene embraces folk, jazz, chamber concerts, operatic performances and church concerts. The Århus festival takes place annually in September and includes open-air events.

Culture

The centre of the city is the port. Protected by breakwaters, it has five harbour basins (the quay being 9·5km/6 miles in length) and a fishing harbour. There is a ferry service to Kalundborg (Zealand). Some streets in the inner city – Søndergade, etc. – form a pedestrian zone. In the north of Århus are the educational establishments and in the south the popular amusement park, "Tivoli Friheden".

Topography

Inner City

The Inner City consists of a semicircle enclosed by a ring road (Ringgade), its heart being the Great Market Square (Store Torv), in which stands the Cathedral (Sankt Clemens Kirke), dedicated to St Clement. The first church was a Romanesque basilica built between 1200 and 1500. Romanesque features are still to be found in the external walls of the nave and transepts; the chapels on the east side of the transepts also date from this time.
After 1400 the church was converted to a Gothic cathedral, Bishop Jens Iversen Lange (15th c.) being the driving force behind the venture. The façade was replaced by a front with a single tower which bears an anchor, the symbol attributed to St Clement.
Features of the interior include the 1497 winged altar, with its rich array of figures of St Anne, John the Baptist, St Clement and the Apostles by the Lübeck master Bernt Notke, the beautifully carved 16th c. pulpit by Mikkel van Gröningen, two organs and the font. The vault paintings date from the 15th c. and portray St Clement as the patron saint of the church and Christ sitting in judgment. Also of interest are the coats of arms, including those of Jens Iverson Lange; in the choir are some medieval crucifixion scenes. As well as religious services, church concerts are also held here. In front of the cathedral stands a monument to King Christian X (1955).

*Cathedral

Near the cathedral, at No. 6 St Clemens Torv in the basement of a merchant bank, is the Viking Museum (Vikingemuseet). When excavating for the foundations of the present bank in the 1960s, builders stumbled on remains of ramparts with which the Vikings had surrounded their little settlement a thousand years earlier. In the museum a reconstruction of the ramparts, a typical house of the Viking period and tools used by these first inhabitants of Århus can be seen (open: Mon., Tue., Wed. and Fri. 9.30am–4pm, Thur. 9.30am–6pm).

Viking Museum

The Danish Women's Museum (Det danske Kvindemuseum) in Domkirkeplads (No. 5) offers a rare opportunity of obtaining information on women's living conditions. The main emphasis of the exhibition is on

Danish Women's Museum

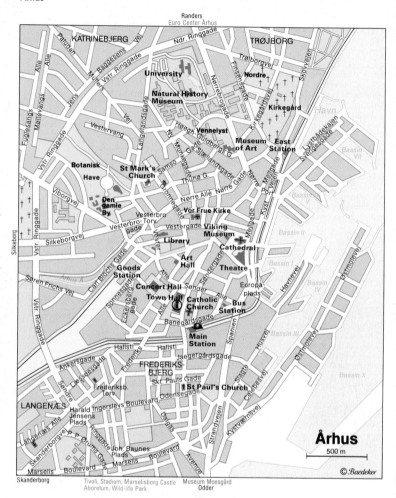

Randers
Euro Center Århus

KATRINEBJERG

TRØJBORG

University

Nordre

Natural History
Museum

Kirkegård

Vennelyst

Museum
of Art

East
Station

Botanisk
Have

St Mark's
Church

Den
gamle
By

Vesterbro

Vor Frue Kirke

Vesterbro-
Torv

Vestergade

Viking
Museum

Library

Cathedral

Art
Hall

Theatre

Goods
Station

Concert Hall

Europa-
plads

Town Hall

Catholic
Church

Bus
Station

Main
Station

FREDERIKS-
BJERG

LANGENÆS

St Paul's Church

Frederiksb.
Torv

Århus

500 m

© Baedeker

Skanderborg

Tivoli, Stadium, Marselisborg Castle
Aboretum, Wild-life Park

Museum Moesgård
Odder

developments in the 20th c., with displays covering everyday life, art and
handicrafts (open: Sept. 18th–May 31st Tue.–Sun. 10am–4pm, June 1st–
Sept. 17th daily 10am–5pm).

City Hall

On the south side of the busy Rådhus Plads, the hub of the city's traffic,
stands the City Hall, built in 1938–42 to plans by Arne Jacobsen and Erik
Møller and faced with Norwegian marble. From the 60m/200ft high tower
there is a fine view of the city and the bay (ascent of the tower from
mid-July to mid-September daily at noon and 2pm). In summer there are
guided tours which enable visitors to see the civic hall, the council chamber
and the marriage room.

Århus: altar-piece in the Vor Frue Kirke ▶

On the west side of the square is the attractive "Pig Fountain" (Grisebrønden) by M. Boggild, and at the foot of the City Hall tower is the fountain "Agnes and the Water Carrier".

Concert Hall

From here it is but a few steps to the concert hall, built in 1982, the headquarters of the Århus Symphony Orchestra and the Jutland Opera Company; many events of the Århus Festival Week are held in this building.

**Church of Our Lady

North-west of the cathedral in Vestergade stands the Church of Our Lady (Vor Frue Kirke), built in the 13th–15th c. Originally part of a Dominican priory it is now a purely Gothic building with frescoes and a magnificent altar-piece from the workshop of Claus Berg (1520).

In 1955, in the course of excavation work beneath the choir of the Church of Our Lady, a little church built of tufa stone was found. After careful restoration this old vaulted *krypta* is now a church within a church.

The chapter-house which served as an old people's hospital from the Reformation was also dedicated as a church, so there are now three churches in all. The chapter-house is adorned with medieval wall-paintings. Remains of the Gothic cloister of the former Dominican monastery have also been preserved.

Botanical Garden

West of the Church of Our Lady, Vesterbrogade borders the Botanical Garden (Botanisk Have), where in summer entertainment is provided for children and adults. Here also are hothouses in which subtropical plants from all over the world can be seen (open: Mon.–Sat. 1.30–3pm, Sun. 10.30am–3pm).

*Open-air Museum "Den Gamle By"

In the southern part of the Botanical Garden lies the open-air museum, The Old Town (Den Gamle By), a collection of some 75 houses from all parts of Denmark and one of the most popular places in Århus. The houses date from the 16th c. up to the early 20th c. and have been faithfully reconstructed in line with the originals.

The buildings include old town houses, shops, workshops with their equipment and windmills. The central feature is a burgomaster's house of 1597 which contains a collection of furniture. Visitors can also see a merchant's house from Ålborg, a house built on stilts, a two-storeyed stone house, a storehouse and a brewery. A toy museum, a textile museum and a historical musical collection are housed in a building from Næstved. In a house from Viborg there is a bicycle museum. In addition, visitors can admire an apothecary's shop complete with healing herbs, candlemakers', coopers' and shoemakers' workshops, a tobacco factory, a sailmaker's and a windmill housing the museum's office. The museum also holds special exhibitions of historical costumes and old silver objects. In addition, there is an open-air inn and a restaurant. In the high season there are guided tours with commentaries in English, German and Danish.

The North of the City

University

Århus University, founded in 1928, lies in a park in the northern part of the city. The main building was erected in 1946; the "Book Tower" being designed by Christian Frederik Møller.

In the College of Journalism to the north of the university site is the Danish Press Museum, which houses a large archive devoted to the history of the press (open: Mon.–Fri. 10am–4pm).

Natural History Museum

In the southern part of the park can be found the Natural History Museum (Naturhistorisk Museum). Exhibitions cover the topography of Denmark – heathland and forest, dunes, coast and sea, as well as zoology, anatomy and geology (open: Tue.–Sun. 10am–4 or 5pm).

*Århus Museum of Art

To the south of the Natural History Museum, in Vennelystpark, stands the Århus Museum of Art (Århus Kunstmuseum). It boasts one of the oldest

In the open-air museum "The Old Town" (Den Gamle By)

and most interesting collections of Danish art, including paintings, sculptures and drawings dating from 1750 to the present day. In recent years the museum has been able to build up a sizeable collection of modern Danish art, as well as works by foreign artists, especially from Germany and the United States. Special exhibitions are also held (open: Tue.–Sun. 10am–5pm).

The South of the City

In the south of the city, surrounded on three sides by the Marselisborg Woods, lies the amusement park known as "Tivoli Friheden" (Tivoli Freedom), which provides fun and games for young and old alike. Concerts and appearances by well-known artists are included in the entertainment programme. Nearby are a sports hall, a stadium, the Jutland Racecourse (horse-racing) and a cycle-track.

Tivoli Friheden

Further south still, in a park on the far side of Carl Nielsens Vej, stands Marselisborg Palace. It was built in 1902 and is the summer residence of the Danish Royal Family. When the queen and her family are in residence the changing of the guard takes place at noon every day. There is a rose garden in the palace park.
Between Marselisborg Palace and the coast to the east a memorial park (Marselisborg Mindepark) has been laid out in memory of the Danes from northern Schleswig who fell in the First World War. A monument is engraved with the names of 4144 Danish soldiers.

Marselisborg Palace

The Marselisborg Woods extend for several kilometres along the coast towards the south. Part of the woods has been fenced in and made into a wildlife enclosure (Dyrehaven), where visitors can observe sika deer from Japan, fallow deer and wild boar in a natural environment.

Wildlife Park

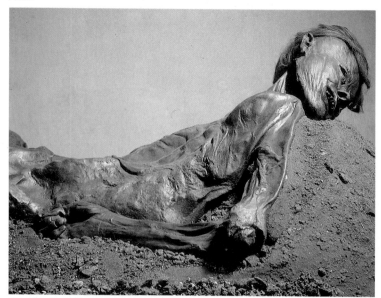

The "Grauballe Man", in the Moesgård Prehistoric Museum

Southern Surroundings

* Prehistoric
Museum

About 9km/6 miles south of the city (leaving along Strandvej) stands the Århus Prehistoric Museum (Forhistorisk Museum Moesgård), housed in the old Moesgård manor-house. Here the visitor can gain an interesting insight into Denmark's history from the Stone Age up to Viking times. A particular attraction is the Grauballe Man, a corpse dating back more than 2000 years and perfectly preserved in a bog. The museum also houses the Institute of Prehistoric Archaeology and Ethnography of the University of Århus (open: daily throughout year; closed Mon. in winter).

In the open-air section of the museum a Prehistoric Trail (Oldtidssti) has been laid out, leading through woods and fields and past reconstructions of prehistoric houses and burial mounds.

Every year since 1977, on the last weekend in July, an open-air Viking Event (Vikingetræf) has been held on Moesgård beach. It shows the local Vikings returning in their ships from their summer raids and trading expeditions. Above all else, however, this event is a fun festival, with plenty to eat and drink and the Olaf market to visit.

Skanderborg

Leaving the town centre in a south-westerly direction along Road No. 170 (with the E45 motorway running parallel a little way to the north-west) the visitor will pass through the villages of Hasselager, Hørning and Stilling (by the lake of the same name) and after travelling some 22km/14 miles will arive at the town of Skanderborg, on the north bank of Skanderborg Lake (Skanderborg Sø).
The town grew up around an old royal castle which medieval Danish kings often used as their residence. All that remains of the castle is a part of the south wing and the castle church (built *c.* 1570, now a parish church), and a

round tower from which there is a fine view. A small museum has a local history collection. In the castle park stands a bust of King Frederick VI by the Danish sculptor Bertel Thorvaldsen. From Skanderborg a detour to Himmelbjerg (see entry) is recommended.

Northern Surroundings

Leaving Århus in a northerly direction and following the wide arc of Kalø Bay, the A 15 road leads to the Djursland Peninsula.

Djursland Peninsula

Near Løgten a road branches off left to Rosenholm Castle just beyond Hornslet. This 16th c. Renaissance building has been owned for more than four centuries by the Rosencrantz family, an old Danish aristocratic line. The rooms are decorated with paintings and tapestries. In the park is a lake and a Renaissance pavilion which is open to the public. (Open: end Apr. to early Aug.)

*Rosenholm Castle

About 1km/1100yd from the village of Rønde on Kalø Bay a little road branches off on the left to Thorsager, the site of Jutland's only surviving round church, part of which dates from 1200. It is two-storeyed, with the vaulting of the lower storey being supported on four columns. The upper storey, reached by a winding staircase, was probably used as a gallery for the local nobility. Note the 1525 crucifix.

Thorsager
*Round church

The A 15 continues to Rønde and from there a road leads south-east to Ebeltoft. To the right on a spit of land projecting into Kalø Bay can be seen the ruins of Kalø Castle (Kalø Slot), built in 1314 by King Erik Menved. At one time it was joined to the mainland by a drawbridge. Gustav Vasa, later King of Sweden, was held prisoner here in 1518, but escaped. On the return journey the visitor will enjoy a view of the peninsula of Mols.

Kalø Castle

Ebeltoft, on the bay of the same name, is a charming little country town with a small Town Hall (now a museum), the Farvegård, an old dyer's

Ebeltoft

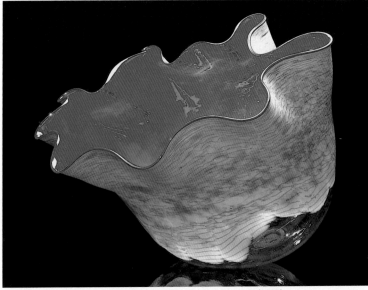

Ebeltoft Glass Museum – a phantastic creation by Dale Chihuly (1985)

workshop, and a Glass Museum. The 19th c. frigate "Jylland" is anchored in the harbour. Ebeltoft also boasts a remarkable plant for the production of energy. On a pier extending 800m/875yd out into the sea stand a large number of "wind turbines", with a larger energy-converter on the land. This "wind farm" produces enough current in a year to meet the needs of several hundred private houses.

Billund   B 3

Jutland
District: Ribe amt
Population: 8000

Situation and Importance

The little town of Billund lies in Central Jutland, some 30km/19 miles west of Vejle (see entry). It is the headquarters of "LEGO A/S", the factory which produces Lego plastic bricks for children. For some years now Billund has also possessed a further attraction in the shape of a Transport Museum Centre.

"Lego"

"Lego" in Latin means "I read" or "I put together". However, the inventor of the bricks, Ole Kirk Christiansen, did not know that; he composed the name from two Danish words "leg godt" (play well). Like many Danes, Ole Kirk Christiansen found himself unemployed in the 1930s. A cabinet-maker by trade, he had the idea of producing wooden toys which would arouse the imagination of children. The present factory was founded in 1932. It was in the mid-1950s that the firm went over to making plastic bricks which can be locked together to make houses, etc.

*Center Mobilium

The Center Mobilium on Ellehammers Allé in Billund is worth a visit. It consists of three museums – an Aviation Museum (Danmarks Flyve-

Legoland: the safari-jeep comes into contact with an elephant

museum), a Motor Museum (Danmarks Bilmuseum) and the Falck
Museum (Falck Museet).

In the Aviation Museum visitors can see jet-planes and models of space-
craft, as well as a DC3 and a Spitfire; some of the exhibits are under cover,
others in the open air. The Motor Museum illustrates the development of
the motor car from 1897 to the present day by means of carefully selected
specimen cars. In the Museum of the Falck Rescue Service there are fire-
engines, breakdown and rescue vehicles, etc. The Falck Rescue Service
was founded by Sophus Falck (open: daily June–Sept.; rest of year Sat. and
Sun.).

*Legoland

Designers of the firm had often made large coloured models from Lego
bricks for fairs and exhibitions, and these were greatly admired. This led to
the setting up of a park with miniature buildings made of Lego bricks. On
June 7th 1968 "Legoland" was opened near Billund. The extensive site,
originally a barren area of heathland, became a large leisure park of various
complexes. Every year over a million people visit the park.

*Park and
miniature
buildings*

The central feature is Miniland. Well-known buildings from all over the
world have been imitated in Lego bricks on a scale of 1:20, including
Amalienborg Palace and the Nyhavn (harbour) of Copenhagen, an airport
modelled on large Scandanivian airports, narrow gabled houses from
Holland, the Emperor Wilhelm Memorial Church (Berlin), the Statue of
Liberty (New York), the Wat-Phra-Keo Temple (Bangkok) and much more.
Danish fishing villages and well-known sights such as the Dybbøl Mill are
also to be seen.

Another attraction is Lego Safari, with elephants, lions, zebras and other
animals. There is also a revolving lift which provides a panoramic view of

The Monorail travels at three metres above the park

Billund and the surrounding countryside, a Legorail giving rides around the complex, miniboats for a "round-the-world cruise", a giant wheel and a traffic school for children. In the "Lego Technic Land" workshop the whole family can build models. Pirateland and the Red Indian Camp offer exciting experiences for the youngsters. (Open: end Apr.–mid-Sept. daily 10am–8 or 9pm).

Inside
exhibitions

On the south side of the park is an Exhibition Hall. Of particular interest is the collection of dolls and dolls-houses, one of the world's largest with 500 exhibits dating from the 16th to the 20th c., and a collection of toys.
Of special interest, too, is "Titania's Palace", an exquisite creation by the Englishman Sir Nevile Wilkinson for his little daughter, who believed she had seen elves in the garden. The palace was intended as a dwelling for the fairy queen Titania, her husband Oberon and their children. This palace, the rooms of which are furnished with valuable furniture, was auctioned by Christie's in London in 1978.

Note

In 1993 a new system of charging was introduced; after paying the entrance fee all activities are free, with the exception of the driving school for which an extra charge is made. There are picnic sites and bistros in the park.

Bornholm   G/H 3/4

District: Bornholms amt
Area: 588sq.km/227sq.miles
Population: 45,000

**Situation

The island of Bornholm lies in the Baltic 37km/23 miles off the Swedish coast and about 150km/95 miles from Copenhagen. There are ferries to Rønne on Bornholm from Copenhagen and from the German port of Sassnitz.

Topography

The island consists of a great mass of granite, much of it with only a thin layer of soil; on the north it is bounded by beautiful, steep cliffs and on the south-east and west by sand dunes; the region near Dueodde is particularly popular. The interior is partly wooded and partly heathland.

History

Until the 2nd c. B.C. Bornholm was inhabited by Burgundians (Burgundarholm). In the 12th c. the island fell to the Archbishopric of Lund (Hammershus Episcopal Castle). The Romanesque round churches, such as those at Østerlars and Olsker, were used as fortresses in the war against the piratical Wends. In 1525–75 the island belonged to Lübeck and from 1658–60 to Sweden. Bornholm has been Danish since 1660.

Economy

In the Middle Ages Bornholm was an important trading-post. Today the population lives mainly by fishing and fish-processing (smoked herrings) and farming, although the ceramic industry is also important, and several ceramic factories in Rønne offer guided tours.

Holiday centre

The mild climate, pleasant atmosphere and sandy beaches, together with the many opportunities for walks and cycle rides, have led to the development of a lively holiday and tourist trade.

Tour of the Island

Rønne

The capital and administrative centre of Bornholm is Rønne, which also has the island's airfield and its principal harbour. The harbour is separated into ferry, fishing and yachting basins. There is also a yacht harbour for pleasure-boats farther north at the beginning of the northern coastal road (Nordre Kystvej).

Bornholm

15° ö. L.

Tat
Græsholm
Frederiksø
Christiansø
(Ertholmene)

Hammeren Sandvig
Våde Ovn 1 2 Allinge
Hammershus
Vang   ▲124 m   Tejn
    Jons
    Kapel   Olsker
Teglkås
            Stenby   Rø   Gudhjem
Rutsker   125 m   Rebro   Melsted
        ▲   Lensgård
Hasle   Saltune
    Tøfte   Klemensker
Muleby   Østerlarsker   Bølshavn
        Arsballe   Østermarie   Listed   Svaneke
Nyker   99 m   Travbane   Runesten   Louisen-
    ▲   Almindingen   lund
Rønne   Lilleborg   104 m   Årsdale
    Westermarie   162 m ▲ Gamleborg   127 m   Rokkestenen
    Knudsker   Gamleborg
    Grisby   Lobbæk   Gryet
    Lufthavn   Nylarsker   Neksø
    Arnager   Åkirkeby   Myregare   Bodilsker
                Egeby   Balke
            Saksebro   Agårds   Snogebæk
                Mølle
            Pedersker   Povlsker
                    Kirke   ▲18 m
            Slusegårdens Mølle
                        Dueodde

1 Tommelhuset
2 Madsebakke
3 Windmill
4 Rytterknægten
    (observation tower)
5 Svanemølle
6 Brændgårdshavn

5km

© Baedeker

SaßnitzSaßnitz, Travemünde, Copenhagen, Ystad

55°10' n.Br.

55°10' n.Br.

15° ö. L.

On a hill above the harbour in the oldest part of the town stands St Nicholas' Church, originally 14th c. but largely rebuilt in 1918. Note the font from the island of Gotland.

Many old houses survive in the streets around the church, including the half-timbered Erichsens Gård (1807) in Lakesgade and the main police station (1745) in Søndergade. The interesting Bornholm Museum at Skt.-Mortens-Gade 29 possesses a collection covering seafaring history and the natural history (granite, limestone, coal and kaolin specimens) of Rønne and Bornholm; there is also a history of art department with works by Bornholm painters as well as drawings and examples of the decorative arts.

In the south of Rønne stands the castle, built about 1650, with its massive round tower. It has been converted into a defence museum where weapons, maps and models of fortifications are on display.

Ruins of Hammershus Castle

Ny Kirke

8km/5 miles north-east of Rønne stands the round church of Nyker (1287), which has two storeys and is the smallest on the island. It has a round barrel-vaulted roof resting on a massive central pillar. The inner walls have frescoes depicting scenes from Our Lord's Passion, Entombment and Resurrection, using mainly shades of yellow, green and light brown. Also to be seen are two fragments of a runic stone.

*Brogårdsten

9km/5½ miles along the road to Hasle north of Rønne can be found the Brogårdsten, the most important runic stone on Bornholm. It was discovered in 1868 as a coping-stone on a bridge over the Bagå and set up at this spot. Dating from about 1100, the stone bears the following inscription: "Svenger had this stone erected for his father Toste and for his brother Alvlak and for his mother and sisters".

Hasle

2km/1¼ miles further along the coast lies Hasle, a little port with a sturdy 14th c. stone church with a half-timbered tower; the beautifully carved and painted winged altar is the work of a Lübeck artist and dates from around 1450. In July the Herring Festival is celebrated in Hasle.

South of the town a sandy beach lies beyond some pine woods, and 7km/4½ miles to the north stretches a steep granite coast with a crag known as Jons Kapel (John's Chapel), which is 40m/130ft high.

Allinge-Sandvig

Following the road further north the visitor will come to the twin resorts of Allinge-Sandvig, one of the most attractive holiday places on the island ("Sandvig" means "sandy bay"). Tømmehuset, at Vestergade 3 in Sandvig, houses a little local museum.

In Allinge there are a number of attractive half-timbered houses, an interesting old Town Hall and a church, the oldest parts of which are Gothic. Outside the cemetery in Allinge stands an obelisk in memory of Russian soldiers who fell in the Second World War.

There is a rewarding walk northwards from Allinge-Sandvig to the Hamme-ren Lighthouse, passing the Stejleberg (84m/276ft), the highest cliff on the island. Strategically placed on a rocky plateau to the south-west of the lighthouse lie the ruins of Hammershus Castle; these medieval castle ruins are the largest in Northern Europe. The former castle, built about 1250 as a protection against the Danish kings, was fought over violently on several occasions and then used as a quarry for building stone until placed under a preservation order in 1822.

*Ruins of Hammershus Castle

There is a magnificent view from the 74m/240ft high cliff, and interesting boat trips can be made from Hammershus, for example to the Våde Ovn, a cave 55m/180ft long. The walk along the footpath to the Slotslyngen wood-land is considered one of the most beautiful in Denmark.

Built in the 12th c. and restored in 1950–52, the round church of Ols (Ols Kirke) is situated 4km/2½ miles south of Allinge. Dedicated to St Olaf, the church is 30m/100ft high and is the tallest on Bornholm. Because of the small diameter of the circular nave the church possesses something of the character of a fortress tower. When it was restored a ceramic relief by the sculptor Gunnar Hansen ("The Women at the Tomb") was set on the new altar-table. In the porch are several 16th c. tombstones.

*Round church of Ols

To the south of Allinge the sea is fringed with cliffs along which winds a rocky path. Important places include Sandkås, Tejn, Stammershalle, the Helligdom Cliffs and the cliffs at Stevelen. 17km/10 miles south of Allinge lies the fishing village of Gudhjem, with a harbour blasted out of the rock and numerous winding lanes and steep streets. The Municipal Museum is housed in the former station building. 3km/2 miles to the south of the village the open-air Melstedgård Agricultural Museum at Melstedvej 25 is recommended; the museum is housed in a half-timbered farmhouse typical of those on Bornholm. The employees are dressed in period clothes and work the land with implements in use 200 years ago.

Gudhjem

The round church in Ols

Bornholm

*Bornholm's Art Museum

A new Art Museum was opened to the north of Gudhjem in 1993. On display is a magnificent collection of paintings and decorative arts produced by the island's inhabitants. It concentrates on the Bornholm School, with works by such artists as Edvard Weie, Karl Isakson, Olaf Rude, Kræsten Iversen, Niels Lergaard and Oluf Høst providing fine examples of modern Danish painting. There are also sculptures and earlier paintings, together with Denmark's largest collection of arts and crafts outside Copenhagen (open: Apr. 1st–Oct. 31st daily 10am–5pm, Nov. 1st–Mar. 31st Tue. and Thur.–Sun. 1–5pm).

*Round church of Østerlars

In the south in Østerlars, a village inland from Gudhjem, stands the largest round church on the island; it was built in the 11th c. and dedicated to St Laurence. The central pillar is hollow with internal ribbed vaulting. The space inside, known as the "oven", is joined to the rest of the nave by six arcades. On the exterior of the "oven" can be seen wall-paintings of about 1350 portraying scenes from the life of Jesus and the Last Judgment. When the church was restored in 1955 the "oven" was converted into a baptistry with a granite font.

Almindigen

South of Østerlars stretches the State Forest of Almindingen, with a number of small lakes and the highest hill on the island, the Rytterknægten (162m/530ft, viewing tower). Further north are the ruins of Lilleborg, which ranked with Hammershus as one of the two most important fortresses in Bornholm.

Svaneke

On the coast 7km/4½ miles south-east of Gudhjem are the Randkløveskår Cliffs, and 8km/5 miles further the picturesque little fishing town of Svaneke, with old houses and a post-mill of 1634. 3km/2 miles south-west lies the Brændegårdshaven amusement park.

Neksø

The road to the south leads past the beautiful wooded Paradisbakkerne (Paradise Hills) to the port of Neksø, the largest fishing port on the island. Whereas the north of Bornholm is mainly granite, the subsoil near Neksø is predominantly sandstone. Many roads are, therefore, paved with sandstone and garden walls made of red sandstone. The old Town Hall now houses a museum mainly devoted to fishing.

Memorial to Martin Andersen Nexø

A memorial to the writer Martin Andersen Nexø (see Famous People) has been installed in his parental home. The collection comprises a selection of books in various languages by or about Nexø, photographs and some of his personal belongings (open; in summer on weekdays 10am–4pm; on Sun. by prior arrangement).

Dueodde Lighthouse

3km/2 miles south of the town lies Balke with a beach of fine sand. 7km/4½ miles beyond this the southern tip of the island is reached; here are the Dueodde Lighthouse, rolling sand-dunes and a beach.

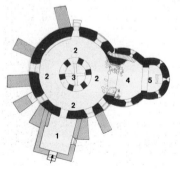

Round Church of St Laurence

in Østerlars on Bornholm

1 Porch
2 Parish room
3 Central pillar
4 Choir
5 Apse

⊢ 10 m ⊣

© Baedeker

The only town on Bornholm away from the coast is Åkirkeby, 15km/10 miles inland. It boasts a handsome 12th c. stone church, the largest medieval church on the island, with a Romanesque font embellished with reliefs and runic inscriptions, as well as a Renaissance altar and pulpit carved by a Swedish artist from Lund.

Åkirkeby

The Church of the Rosary (Rosanskranskirke; 1932; R.C.) is one of the most attractive modern churches in Denmark. Its adornments include frescoes by the Finnish artist Birgitta Reckelsen and an oak altar-table.

The road to Rønne (16km/10 miles) passes through Nylars, where the latest and best preserved of Bornholm's round churches stands. In this church can be seen wall-paintings depicting the Creation and the Fall of Man. In the porch hangs a huge cross dating from the Renaissance.

Round church at Nylars

Pea islands

In the Baltic Sea north-east of Bornholm lies the group of islands called Ertholmene (Pea Islands); they can be reached by boat from Allinge, Gudhjem and Svaneke. On the main island of Christiansø can be seen extensive fortifications installed by Christian V in 1684. When Christiansø lost its importance as a naval base in the 19th c. a number of poets and artists settled here.

Christiansø

The neighbouring island of Frederiksø was once notorious as a place of exile; its most interesting building is the Lille Tårn (Little Tower), now a museum with a 17th c. model of the castle on Christiansø, rifles and cannon, old furniture and utensils. On Græsholm, which is closed to the public, there is a bird sanctuary.

Copenhagen (København)   E 3

Zealand
District: Københavns amt
Population: 620,000 (with suburbs 1,700,000)

The description of Copenhagen in this Guide has deliberately been kept comparatively brief, as there is a separate Guide for the city available in the "Baedeker" series.

Note

Copenhagen, the capital of the Kingdom of Denmark, lies on the east side of the island of Zealand and on the island of Amager in the Øresund. The conurbation of Copenhagen (Store København) is a municipal agglomeration which came into being through the incorporation of a number of places including Frederiksberg. With a total area of 570sq.km/220sq.miles and a population of some 1,700,000, Copenhagen is by far the largest city in Denmark. The seat of government, the Parliament (Folketing) and the residence of the Royal Family are all in the city.

Situation and Importance

Copenhagen is first mentioned as "Havn" in 1043. In 1167 Valdemar I made a present of the fishing and trading settlement to Bishop Absalon, who had the fortress of Slotsholmen built as a protection against Wendish pirates (remains can still be seen beneath Christiansborg). Around the fortress, the area known as "Købmandenes Havn" (merchants' port) soon developed into a thriving trade centre and in 1254 received its municipal charter. In 1416 control of Copenhagen passed to King Erik of Pomerania who made it his capital, and the town formed the centre of the three kingdoms of Denmark, Norway and Sweden, which had been united since 1397.

History

The Reformation came to Denmark in 1536 and the Lutheran doctrine was declared the State religion. From this time onward Copenhagen became the royal seat. The heavily fortified town was provided with some fine buildings during the time of the popular King Christian IV (1588–1648) and

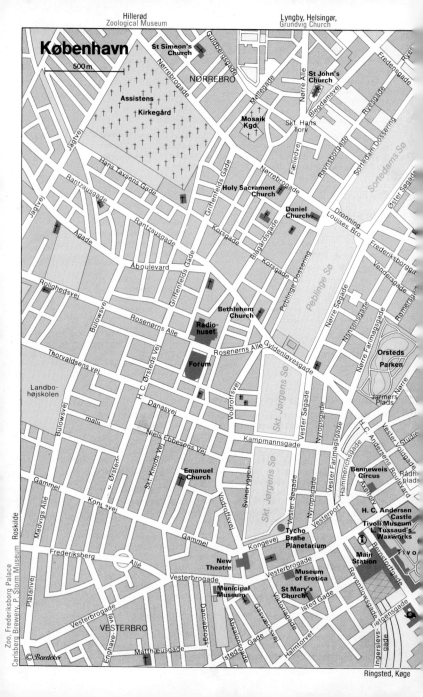

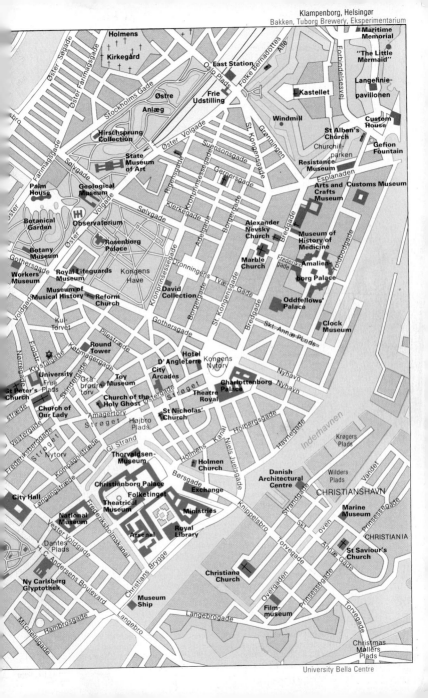

successfully resisted attacks by the Swedes in 1658 and 1659 and by the combined English, Dutch and Swedish fleets in 1700. The old town of Copenhagen was largely destroyed by fire in 1728 and again in 1795, and in 1807 suffered considerable damage from bombardment by the British navy.

Under Christian VIII (1839–48) the city was granted a comprehensive statute of self-government. After the absolute monarchy had been changed into a constitutional government Copenhagen became, in 1848, the seat of the new government and the function of the city as the political hub of the country was strengthened. Copenhagen then reached out beyond its defensive walls. In 1867 the fortifications were demolished and several parks were laid out where the ramparts had been. The opening of a free port in 1894 and of Kastrup Airport in 1924 gave a decisive boost to Copenhagen's economy and transport system.

During the First World War many refugees came to Copenhagen, especially after the Russian Revolution in 1917. At the beginning of the Second World War Denmark declared itself neutral, but was occupied by German troops in 1940. Resistance organisations were formed which were especially concerned with helping Danish Jews, living principally in Copenhagen, to escape to Sweden. On the evening of May 4th 1945 the German surrender was announced. The early post-war years were difficult for the city because of the heavy destruction it had suffered, but in 1948 the Marshall Plan brought relief. At the end of the 1950s there was a boom. In 1962 "Stroget", a pedestrian zone measuring 1·8km/2000yd in length, became one of the first traffic-free streets in Europe. In 1987 Kastrup Airport was declared "airport of the year" because of its newly-opened elegant shopping precinct.

Economy

Copenhagen is Denmark's largest commercial and industrial city. There are shipyards, motor works, textile and clothing factories, chemicals, foodstuffs and breweries (Carlsberg and Tuborg). The porcelain industry (Royal Porcelain Factory and Bing og Grøndahl) grew from the discovery of large china-clay deposits on the island of Bornholm in 1755.
Copenhagen owes its importance as a transhipment port to its position at the entrance to the Baltic. The quays have a length of 44km/26 miles. A bridge over the port (Knippelsbro) leads to the island of Amager.

Cultural life

Copenhagen is also the cultural centre of Denmark. Of the many theatres the Royal Theatre is the most versatile and mounts theatrical, operatic and ballet productions. Although most of the Theatrical performances are in Danish, the Mermaid Theatre at Ny Vestergade 7 puts on all its plays in English.
Every week concerts are performed in the hall of Danish Radio at Julius Thomsens Gade; these are given either by the Radio Symphony Orchestra, the Radio Concert Orchestra or the Radio Big Band. The Zealand Symphony Orchestra gives concerts in the concert hall in Tivoli. In Copenhagen there are also many jazz clubs and bars with music; Danish and foreign jazz musicians take part in an annual jazz festival.
There is ample provision in Copenhagen for those interested in art. Besides the four main museums – the Ny Carlsberg Glyptothek, the National Museum, the Thorvaldsen Museum and the State Museum of Art – there are a number of private galleries. In the "Latin Quarter" around the university and in Nyhavn there are many antique shops.

Sightseeing in Copenhagen

The busy pedestrian zone of Strøget forms the city centre. To the south of this area lie Tivoli and "Castle Island" (an island surrounded by canals). On the far side of the harbour is the Christianshavn district. The northern part

Copenhagen: street musicians in the pedestrian zone

of the inner city extends as far as Langelinie at the entrance to the port. On the far side of the lakes which border the inner city on the west lie the districts of Frederiksberg, Nørrebro and Bispebjerg. From April to mid-September there is a 50-minute canal tour every ½ hour. In July and August a water bus operates stopping at all major sights.

Pedestrian Zone and Old Town

The 1·8km/1 mile long pedestrian zone, known as "Strøget" (meaning straight line or stretch), traverses the inner city. It is Copenhagen's most popular shopping street. Strøget consists of several roads criss-crossing one another, beginning at Town Hall Square (Rådhuspladsen) and ending at Kongens Nytorv. Some adjoining streets on the north have also been pedestrianised. The streets are lined by many shops, boutiques and cafés. The busy Town Hall Square (Rådhuspladsen) is dominated by the Town Hall, which was built between 1892 and 1905 and is based partly on the Italian Renaissance and partly on medieval Danish architecture. The tower is 106m/350ft high and the building is richly adorned with sculpture and painting. Above the main entrance can be seen a figure of Bishop Absalon in gilded copper and in the Great Hall are busts of Martin Nyrop, the architect who designed the building (d. 1921), the sculptor Bertel Thorvaldsen (1770–1840), Hans Christian Andersen (1805–76) and the physicist Niels Bohr (1885–1962). The World Clock at the main entrance which was designed and constructed by Jens Olsen in 1955 shows not only the time and date but also various astronomical constellations (open: Mon.–Fri. 10am–3pm, also guided tours).

In Town Hall Square stands Dragon Fountain (sculpture "Contest of the Bull with the Lindworm" by Joachim Skovgaard, 1923), a memorial to Hans Christian Andersen and – in front of the Palace Hotel on a stone column 12m/40ft high – two lur-players in bronze by Siegfried Wagner (1914).

**"Strøget"

**Town Hall

87

Gammeltorv/ Nytorv	To the north-east of Town Hall Square Strøget widens out to form Gammeltorv and Nytorv Squares, with old patrician houses of around 1800, lawns and beautiful fountains.
*Church of the Holy Ghost	Continuing along Strøget the visitor will come to the Church of the Holy Ghost (Helligåndskirke) and the Helligåndshus, which formerly belonged to a monastery and is Copenhagen's only medieval edifice. Amagertov 6 is believed to be the oldest private house in the city; it was built in 1616 by Burgomaster Hansen in the Dutch Baroque style and has a beautiful sandstone doorway. It now houses the showroom of the Royal Porcelain Factory. No. 10 is the well-known Illums Bollinghus store, which sells Danish handicrafts and designer goods.
*Kongens Nytorv	Past the Stork Fountain lies the busy Kongens Nytorv (King's New Market), a large square laid out at the end of the 17th c. In the centre stands an equestrian statue of King Christian V. This is an important traffic junction and Copenhagen's largest square with a dozen or so streets radiating from it.
Theatre Royal	On the south side of the square stands the Theatre Royal, erected in the Late Renaissance style in 1872–74. In front of the main entrance stand bronze memorials to the Danish comic dramatist Ludwig Holberg (1684–1754) and the tragic dramatist Adam Oehlenschläger (1779–1850).
Church of Our Lady	A good starting-point for a walk round the Old Town is Nytorv. In the square are the former Law Courts which are considered to be the finest example of Danish Classicism. Proceeding north from here by way of Gammeltorv and Nørregade the visitor will come to the Church of Our Lady (Vor Frue Kirke), Copenhagen's "cathedral". The present church is the sixth to be built on the same site. After the fifth church was burned down during the bombardment of the town in 1807 the architect Christian Friedrich Hansen created

Decoration on the doorway of the Church of the Holy Ghost

the present Classical building in 1811–29. In the vaulted two-storeyed interior can be seen numerous works by Thorvaldsen – behind the altar his well-known figure of Christ and along the walls the Twelve Apostles (on plinths). The font has a figure of a kneeling angel. The characteristic square tower with a flat roof is topped by a gleaming cross.

To the north of the church, behind Bispetorv, lies the main building of the University, founded by Christian I in 1479. The present building, influenced in style by that of English university buildings, was erected by Peter Malling between 1831 and 1836. The assembly hall, with historic paintings, and the entrance hall with frescoes by Constantin Hansen portraying mythological themes and dating from about 1850, are of interest. On the bordering square stands a row of busts of important graduates of the college, including one of the physicist and Nobel Prizewinner Niels Bohr (see Famous People).

*University

On the other side of Nørregade stands one of Copenhagen's oldest churches, St Peter's, originally late Gothic and restored in 1816. It has a 78m/255ft high tower. Inside the church and in the herb garden are a number of tombs.

St Peter's Church

From Nørregade narrow lanes lead into Fiolstræde, a parallel street with many bookshops and antique-dealers. In Krystalgade can be seen the Synagogue, built in 1833 in yellow brick. Passing this the visitor will come to Købmagergade, a shopping street, with the Round Tower (Rundetårn), 36m/120ft high and 15m/50ft in diameter, which was built as an observatory in 1642 and now houses a small collection of material connected with the Danish astronomer Tycho Brahe. The platform, from the top of which there is a magnificent panoramic view of Copenhagen, is reached by a wide spiral ramp. The tower is the one referred to in Hans Christian Andersen's story "The Tinder Box": "eyes as big as the Round Tower . . .".

**Round Tower

The tour continues by way of Skindergade and Kejsergade to Gråbrødre-torv, one of Copenhagen's most charming squares with its brightly coloured old houses. From here it is a short distance back to Nytorv by way of Strøget.

Southern Inner City

Starting from Town Hall Square and crossing H. C. Andersens Boulevard brings us to the famous Tivoli amusement park and pleasure gardens (main entrance in Vesterbrogade), with more than twenty attractions including a roller coaster, roundabouts, halls of mirrors and halls of horror, pantomime theatres, puppet theatres, open-air theatres, etc., restaurants and cafés, a flower garden and a concert hall (open: May 1st to mid-Sept. daily 10am–midnight).
The best time to visit the park is in the evening in order to enjoy the full effect of the illuminations. There are firework displays at 11.45pm on Wed., Fri. and Sat.

**Tivoli

In addition to the entrance on Vesterbrogade there are three others, including one for parties on H. C. Andersens Boulevard. In the entrance building here can be found Louis Tussaud's Waxworks, with figures of Danish and foreign personalities, including King Christian IV, H. C. Andersen, Karen Blixen, Albert Einstein, Pablo Picasso, Gandhi, ex-President Bush, etc. (open: Sept. 17th–Apr. 23rd daily 10am–4.30pm, Apr. 24th–Sept. 15th daily 10am–11pm).

*Louis Tussaud's Waxworks

On three floors in Hans Christian Andersen Castle will be found the newly-opened Tivoli Museum. It portrays in a graphic and amusing manner the 150 years and more of the history of the world-famous leisure park (open:

Tivoli Museum

Copenhagen (København)

Tivoli Amusement Park

© Baedeker

N

AMUSEMENTS

1 Flying Carpet
2 "Ladybird"
3 Children's Giant Wheel
4 "Wild Swans"
5 The Viking Ship
6 Boating pool
7 "Mini Go-go"

8 Glass House
9 "Circus Roundabout"
10 Comet
11 Vintage cars
12 Flying Shell
13 Tramline 8
14 Driving school
15 Dodgems
16 Blue Cars

17 "Little Flyers"
18 Animal Roundabout
19 Odin Expressway
20 Merry-go-round
21 Galleys
22 Tub-track
23 Balloon Swing
24 Slide
25 "Devil's Fire"

Sept. 21st–Apr. 26th Tue.–Sun. 10am–5pm, Apr. 27th–Sept. 15th daily 10am–10pm).

Municipal Museum

At Vesterbrogade 59 is Copenhagen City Museum (Københavns Bymuseum), where the visitor can obtain a general idea of the history of the city. Room 14 contains the Søren-Kierkegaard Collection, which was inaugurated in 1960 (open: May 1st–Sept. 30th Tue.–Sun. 10am–4pm, Oct. 1st–Apr. 30th Tue.–Sun. 1–4pm). In summer a model of the city of Copenhagen is displayed in front of the building.

Tycho Brahe Planetarium

From the main entrance to Tivoli it is worth making a small detour westwards via Axeltorv to one of Copenhagen's latest attractions, the Tycho Brahe Planetarium at Gammel Kongevej 10. It is the largest of its kind in Europe. The highly technical laser and film shows in the domed cinema with its 23m/75ft screen have proved very popular. The cylindrical building was designed by the Danish architect Knud Munk (open: Tue.–Sun. 10.30am–9pm; Mon. as well between June 20th and Sept. 9th).

Ny Carlsberg Glyptothek

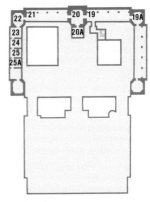

© Baedeker

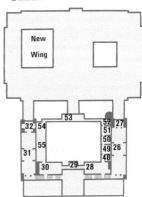

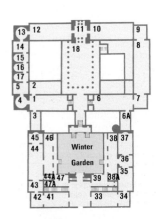

The museum has two major features:
sculptures of the last 3500 years and works
by modern, especially French, painters.
These two departments of the museum are
linked by a winter-garden.

Rooms 19–22: Etruscan Collection
Most of the items are associated with
burials, including urns for ashes,
sarcophagi, as well as cube-shaped
tombstones, bronzes and vases. Etruscan
graves contained vases, and even bronzes.

Room 23: Magna Graecia from Sicily

Room 25A: Cypriot Collection

Room 27: Richard Winther Collection

Rooms 28–30: French Impressionism
Bronzes by Degas, works by Cézanne,
Sisley, Pissarro, Monet and Renoir; later
artists (Maillol) are also represented.

Rooms 48–53: The "Golden Age"
Paintings by the Danish artists Juel,
Eckersberg, Lundbye, Bissen and Købke.

Rooms 26, 31, 32: From David to Gauguin
Works by David, Corot, Courbet, Manet,
van Gogh and Gauguin.

New Wing
The Glyptothek is being extended by a large
new wing which is to house the collection
of French impressionist paintings (opening
in 1996). The pictures by Danish artists will
then be accommodated in other rooms.

Rooms 1–4: Egyptian Art
Funerary art: gods, animals, humans

Room 5: Ancient Oriental Art
Assyrian, Persian, etc. sculpture.

Rooms 6–9: Greek Art
Geometrical vases; grave and votive reliefs;
copies of Greek works.

Rooms 10–17: Portraits
Examples of Graeco-Roman portraiture
(sculptures and coins).

Rooms 33–47: Modern Sculpture
Works by Rodin and the 19th c. Danish
sculptors H. W. Bissen and J. A. Jerichau;
also Gerhard Henning and Kai Nielsen.

Room 38 A: Icons

Room 18: Large Hall

Copenhagen (København)

*Ny Carlsberg Glyptothek

From Tivoli H. C. Andersens Boulevard leads south-east to Dante Square (Dante Plads). Here can be found the Ny Carlsberg Glyptothek, in front of which stands the Dante Column, a gift from the city of Rome. The museum contains the collections of Carl and Ottilia Jacobsen (Carlsberg Brewery), who presented them for public exhibition in 1888. The building was erected in two phases, the first part in 1892–97 with three wings and a richly decorated façade facing Dante Square, the second in 1901–06. The central feature, known as the Winter Garden, is a pillared marble hall in the style of an ancient temple court. The front building contains the modern collection. There are rooms with works by Danish sculptors, particularly by two pupils of Thorvaldsen – H. V. Bissen (1798–1868) and J. A. Jerichau (1816–83) – as well as rooms devoted to French sculpture with an extensive collection of Rodin's work (1840–1917). The upper floors contain further sculpture, including bronzes by Edgar Degas, and a collection of pictures by French and Danish masters of the 19th and 20th c., including some by the French Impressionists Cézanne, Sisley, Pissarro, Monet and Renoir. In the Winter Garden can be seen the decorative fountain group "The Water Mother and her Children", by Kai Nielsen (1882–1924).

The Collection of Antiquities in the rear building was assembled with the help of the German archaeologists W. Helbig and P. Arndt and is regarded as one of the finest of its kind north of the Alps. It contains many Roman portraits and busts, and the Egyptian and Etruscan collections are also very fine. Every period of Egyptian sculpture is represented, and the Greek sculpture includes outstanding original examples of 6th and 5th c. B.C. Archaic art and some of the best work from the time of Phidias, Polycletus, Praxiteles and Lysipp (open: May–Aug. Tue.–Sun. 10am–4pm; Sept.–Apr. Tue.–Sat. noon–3pm, Sun. 10am–4pm).

Note

A further wing is currently being added to the Ny Carlsberg Glyptothek; it is hoped to complete it in 1996, when it will house the collection of French paintings. Therefore references in the text to the placing of the paintings and sculptures as well as the plan of the museum in this Guide will be accurate for a limited time only.

**National Museum

Along Vestergade, opposite the Glyptothek, lies the National Museum (Nationalmuseet), bordered by Ny Vestergade and the Frederiksholm Kanal.

Between 1989 and 1992 the museum was completely modernised and considerably extended. The spacious vestibule is generously proportioned and its domed glass roof gives it a friendly ambience. Spiral staircases lead to the upper floors. The main building is linked to other sections by a covered glass walkway; some impressive runic stones are displayed in a pavilion. In one room the visitor can obtain information about the museum's various departments and exhibits with the assistance of modern aids such as videos and a computer.

The museum has a notable collection illustrating Danish history, including a "sun chariot" (cult object in the form of a cart) more than 2000 years old, Romanesque and Gothic church fittings as well as Danish porcelain and silver and collections of antiquities and coins. In the collection of Danish Peasant Culture of the 18th and 19th c. costumes, household furnishings and equipment, etc., are exhibited. (Note: closed at present because of building work.)

The important ethnographical collection, including items from Greenland, gives an excellent impression of life among the Eskimos; other areas covered include Asia, Africa and Oceania as well as the culture of the Indians (open: all the year round, Tue.–Sun. 10am–5pm).

Incorporated in the National Museum is the Prince's Palace (1744), a Rococo building influenced by the French style of the period.

**Christiansborg Palace

From the National Museum cross the Frederiksholm Kanal to the island of Slotsholm on which stands Christiansborg Palace, seat of the Danish Government and Parliament (Folketing). This building also houses the

Christiansborg Palace

Foreign Ministry, the Supreme Court and the Queen's Audience Chambers. Parliament and the Royal Rooms can be visited on guided tours.
The palace occupies the site on which Bishop Absalon built the earliest fortifications of the city in 1167. Ruins of the bishop's castle, which was destroyed in the 14th c., as well as of the medieval fortress which passed to the crown under Erik of Pomerania, were discovered when the present palace was being built and can now be seen by visitors.

The foundation-stone of the first palace to be erected on the site of the original castle was laid by Christian VI in 1733, but the building was not completely finished and was subsequently destroyed by fire in 1794. Of that huge palace of four wings, only the Riding School survives. A new palace was built in the first 20 years of the 19th c. to designs by the Classical master architect C. F. Hansen, but was used only rarely as a royal residence. In 1849 it became the home of the new Parliament. In 1884 this palace, too, was burned down. Among the sections which survived was the palace church, the dome of which was decorated with angels by Bertel Thorvaldsen. The "third" Palace of Christiansborg was erected between 1907 and 1928 to the design of Thorvald Jørgensen. The façade of the four-winged palace is of dressed Bornholm granite and its tower is 90m/295ft high.

On the square in front of the palace stands an equestrian statue of Frederik VII by H. V. Bissen. In 1927 an equestrian statue of Christian IX by Carl Nielsen was erected on the former riding arena.

Equestrian statues

Within the Riding School complex, where the royal horses are exercised every morning, stands the old Court Theatre, built in 1767 and now the Theatre Museum. The museum illustrates the history of Danish theatre from the time of Ludvig Holberg up to the present day. On display are photographs, prints, theatrical costumes, programmes, etc. (open: Wed. 2–4pm, Sun. noon–4pm).

Theatre History Museum

Copenhagen (København)

Royal Arsenal (Museum)	On the other side of Tøjhusgade can be found the Arsenal (Tøjhus), which now houses the Military Museum (Tøjhusmuseet), with its collection of weapons, armour and uniforms (open: Tue.–Sun. 10am–4pm).
Royal Library	By attractive gardens near the Arsenal stands the Royal Library (Det Kongelige Bibliotek), with 1,700,000 volumes and 52,000 manuscripts. It is the National Library and also functions as a Danish book museum. Note the old reading-room.
**Thorvaldsen Museum	North-west of Christiansborg Palace stands the Thorvaldsen Museum, with works by Bertel Thorvaldsen (1770–1844), the greatest of all Danish sculptors. The building, in Neo-classical style, was constructed in 1839–48 to designs by Gottlieb Bindesbøll. On the exterior facing the canal are frescoes depicting Thorvaldsen's return from Rome in 1838. In addition to Thorvaldsen's works, the museum contains his own private art collection (open: Tue.–Sun. 10am–5pm).
*Fishwife	In Gammel Strand, on the opposite side of the canal, can be seen the statue of an old fishwife (Fiskerkone) as a reminder of the time when the daily fishmarket was held here.
**The Stock Exchange	South-east of Christiansborg, facing the harbour, is the Stock Exchange (Børsen), built in 1619–20 in the Dutch Renaissance style. Its tower is 54m/177ft high, with a spire formed by the intertwined tails of four dragons. This and the green patina of the copper roof are characteristic of the building, which is one of Copenhagen's emblems. The business of the Stock Exchange is now carried on at Nikolaj Plads 8, while the old building houses the offices of the Copenhagen Chamber of Trade.
*Holmens Church	The 17th c. Holmens Church (Holmens Kirke), on the opposite side of the canal, was intended as a church for seamen. The "Royal Doorway" was brought here from Roskilde Cathedral in the 19th c. Fine features of the interior are a Baroque altar of unpainted oak and a carved pulpit by Abel Schrøder the Younger, both dating from around 1660. In a side chapel can be seen various tombs including that of the naval hero Niels Juel (d. 1697).

Christianshavn

From Børs Gade a bascule bridge, the Knippelsbro, with a span of 29m/95ft, leads into the district of Christianshavn on the island of Amager. The older quarter, transversed by a number of canals, has something of the atmosphere of Amsterdam. Pretty houses front the waterside by which stands Christians Kirke, flanked by two pavilions; in the church note the font of Norwegian marble, a christening shawl with an inscription in German and the crypt with its burial chapel.

**Church of Our Saviour	The Church of Our Saviour in Skt. Annæ Gade (Vor Frelsers Kirke), has a splendid Baroque altar decorated with figures and cherubs, a beautiful font and a richly carved organ case. The characteristic spire, with an external spiral staircase of 400 steps and a gilded figure of Christ standing on a globe, offers extensive views from the top.
Christiana	Since it was at Christianshavn originally that the Royal Fleet was to be protected, military establishments were set up there. In 1971 the old barracks on Bådsmandsstraede were vacated. Drop-outs, members of the "alternative society" and hippies moved into the building and proclaimed it the "Free State of Christiana". After protests by the Danish public this establishment was recognised as a "social experiment" between 1973 and 1975. Christiana still exists today and is visited by many tourists.
Royal Naval Museum	The Royal Naval Museum (Orlogsmuseet) at Overgaden oven Vandet 58A in Søkvasthuset, the former naval hospital, is worth a visit. On display are

Pop-art greets the visitor to Christiana

model and full-size ships, nautical instruments and naval uniforms; special exhibitions are also held (open: Tue.–Sun. noon–4pm).

Northern Inner City

Charlottenburg Palace, on the east side of Kongens Nytorv, has been the home of the Royal Academy of Art since 1754. To the rear of the palace lies Nyhavn (New Harbour), which is flanked by a street of the same name. At the end of the harbour can be seen an anchor, placed there as a memorial to Danish sailors who lost their lives in the Second World War. Nyhavn was once a disreputable quarter of the city but now, with its brightly painted little gabled houses many of which contain restaurants or cafés, it is a very charming part of Copenhagen. Idyllic museum ships lie at anchor, including a lightship (Fyrskib) dating from 1885.
From Nyhavn there are hydrofoil and catamaran services to Sweden, as well as sightseeing trips round the harbour and along the canal. **Nyhavn

Bredgade leads northwards from the upper end of Nyhavn to the Marble Church, the building of which began in 1749 but was not completed until 1894. It is also known as Frederik's Church, because it was intended to be the main church in the Frederiksstad district. Features of the interior include an ivory Crucifix, an oak carving of the Descent from the Cross and Grundtvig's seven-branched golden candelabrum. The church has a dome 84m/275ft high and the façade is decorated with statues of great figures in ecclesiastical history, including St Ansgar, the Apostle of the North, and the religious reformer Grundtvig. *Marble Church

Frederiksgade leads from the church to Amalienborg Palace, the residence of the Queen. It was built by Niels Eigtev about 1750, during the reign of King Frederik V. The spacious octagonal Palace Square is surrounded by **Amalienborg Palace

95

Façades and boats at the Nyhavn

four palaces; in the middle of the square stands an equestrian statue of Frederik V (1771). The palace originally provided residences for noble families, including Counts Christian Frederik Levetzau and Adam Gottlob Moltke, Baron Joakim Brockdorff and Counsellor Severin Løvenskold. When Christiansborg Palace was burned down in 1794 the King took over Amalienborg as his residence, and Danish kings continued to use the palace from time to time. Queen Margarethe II and her family today occupy the upper storey of Christian IX Palace (formerly Løvenskjold). The Moltke Palace is used for official purposes; the palaces are not open to the public. The soldiers of the Royal Guard with their bearskins and blue (on festive occasions red, white and blue) uniforms are a symbol of the city. When the Queen is in residence the Changing of the Guard takes place at noon.

By following Bredgade from the Marble Church in a northerly direction the visitor will come to the Russian Alexander Nevski Church, with its three gilded domes, and to St Ansgar's Church, the oldest Roman Catholic church in Copenhagen. On the exterior, note the beautiful sculpture of St Ansgar and those of saints above the main door.

*Museum of Applied Art

A Rococo building near St Ansgar's Church, built in the 18th c. by Niels Eigtved and Lauritz de Thurah, houses the Museum of Applied Art (Kunstindustrimuseet). The museum was founded in 1890 by the Ny Carlsberg Foundation and has been here since 1926. The collections comprise European applied art from the Middel Ages to the present day, together with objects from China and Japan. The emphasis is on domestic furnishings and household items – carpets, porcelain, ceramics, Danish silver, glass, textiles and jewellery; modern Danish design is also represented (open: Tue.–Sun. 1–4pm).

The house also has a garden which is open to visitors and has some notable sculptures, including "The Sea-horse" by Niels Skovgaard.

Gefion Fountain

The "Little Mermaid"

Bredgade leads into the esplanade to the north; on the left is the sailors' home, the Nyboder, built in the 17th and 18th c.

In Churchill Park near the Esplanade is the Resistance Museum (Frihedsmuseet), designed by the architect Hans Hansen. It contains documents relating to the Danish resistance against the Nazis from 1940 to 1945, including photographs, newspaper articles, letters, etc. Close by stands St Alban's Church, the Anglican church of the British colony in Copenhagen. Next to the church is a large fountain, the Gefion Springvandet, erected in 1908; according to legend the goddess Gefion with her oxen ploughed the island of Zealand out of Swedish soil.

Resistance Museum

Langelinie, the landing-place for a promenade along the shore, starts at the Gefion Fountain. From here the visitor will arrive at the Kastellet, the former Citadel of Frederikshavn, the oldest parts of which date from 1625. When, in 1658, Denmark lost her possessions on the eastern side of the Øresund, Copenhagen found itself a frontier town and so its defences were strengthened accordingly. The buildings within the Citadel are well maintained and include two gates, the Zealand Gate and the Norwegian Gate.

*Kastellet

From the Citadel it is a short distance to the "Little Mermaid" ("Den lille Havfrue") on the Langelinie; it is the official emblem of Copenhagen. The bronze sculpture was created by Edward Eriksen in 1913, based on a theme from one of Hans Christian Andersen's fairy-tales. The story says that the little mermaid once came up out of the depths of the sea because she had fallen in love with a prince but, as the prince did not return her love, she was forced to leave the world of humans and return whence she had come. When, in April 1964, her head was sawn off by some unknown perpetrator the whole of Copenhagen was outraged. Fortunately the moulds used in 1913 had been preserved, so it was possible to give the mermaid a new head.

**The Little Mermaid

*Hirschsprung Collection	Going west from the Citadel and passing Østerport Station the visitor will come to Østre Anlæg Park. On its north side, at Stockholmsgade 20, is the Hirschsprung Collection (Hirschsprungske Samling), an art collection bequeathed to the city by Heinrich Hirschsprung. Its principal items are Danish painting and sculpture of the 19th c., including some by the "Skagenmaler", who represented the modern "breakthrough" (c. 1880). The collection has now grown to 600 paintings, 200 sculptures and over 1000 water-colours (open: Wed.–Sat. 1–4pm, Sun. 11am–4pm).
*State Museum of Art	In the southern part of Østre Anlæg stands the State Museum of Art (Statens Museum for Kunst), built in 1891–96. It consists of a main building with rooms for paintings and sculpture and an engraving department, as well as an annexe for special exhibitions. In the painting collection can be seen works representative of European art from the 13th to the 18th c. In the Italian department are some important works by Titian, Tintoretto and others; the Dutch and Flemish schools are represented by Rubens and Rembrandt. The German collection includes work by Lucas Cranach the Elder and his successors. The museum also owns a collection of Danish Biedermeier painting as well as numerous works from the early part of the 20th c. Eighteenth century Danish artists include Nicolai A. Abildgaard and Jens Juel, while the Golden Age of the early 19th c. is represented by C. W. Eckersberg and his pupils. Also worthy of note is a private collection of works by French painters, including Braque and Picasso, which has been donated to the museum. The Engraving Collection, which has been removed from the Royal Library, contains some 100,000 items (open: Tue.–Sun. 10am–4.30pm, Wed. 10am–9pm).
Botanic Garden	Adjoining the Østre Anlæg on the south lies the Botanic Garden (Botanisk Have) which, like other parks, was laid out on the remains of former fortifications. The principal features are the Palm House, the Botanic and Geological Museums, an artificially arranged biotope devoted to the wild plants of Denmark, and an Alpine Garden (open: daily 8.30am–4pm or 6pm; Palm House daily 10am–3pm).
**Rosenborg Palace	In a park to the east of the Botanic Garden stands Rosenborg Palace (Rosenborg Slot), built by Christian IV between 1608 and 1634 as a summer palace and used by the Danish Royal Family from the middle of the 18th c. as a spring and autumn residence. In 1833 the palace was opened to the public as a museum. It houses the private collections of the Danish kings, including furniture, paintings, sculptures, etc. In the treasure chamber in the cellar vaults the royal insignia, including the Crown Jewels, are on display. Of particular interest are the Marble Room, a Baroque reception room, and the Knights' Hall with the Coronation Throne which was used from 1871 to 1940. Porcelain is also exhibited, including the famous "Flora Danica" service. Open: Jan. 2nd–Mar. 30th and Oct. 24th–Dec. 18th: Palace Tue., Fri., Sun. 11am–2pm, Treasure Chamber Tue.–Sun. 11am–3pm; Mar. 31st–Oct. 23rd: Palace and Treasure Chamber Mon.–Sun. 11am–3 or 4 pm; Dec. 19th–Dec. 25th: Palace and Treasure Chamber closed; Dec. 26th–Dec. 30th: Palace and Treasure Chamber Tue.–Sun. 11am–3pm.
Kongens Have	The adjoining park, Kongens Have (or Rosenborg Have), was laid out in 1606 in the reign of Christian IV, and is the oldest park in Copenhagen. Here can be seen many statues, including one of Hans Christian Andersen (see Famous People), surrounded by listening children. Here, too, are the barracks of the Royal Guards, from where the new guard leaves shortly before 11.30am every day for the Changing of the Guard ceremony at Amalienborg Palace.

Frederiksberg

Vesterbrogade leads from the inner city to the district of Frederiksberg in the west. In the south of the extensive Frederiksberg Have park stands Frederiksberg Palace, built in the Italian style with an ochre-yellow façade.

Statens Museum for Kunst

State Museum of Art

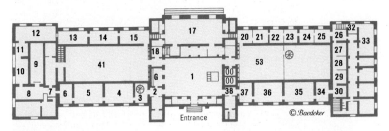

GROUND FLOOR

1 Entrance hall; 20th c. Danish art
2 Information kiosk
3 Cafeteria
4–18 Danish art (1900–60)
   (including Jerichau, Nielsen, Giersing,
   Weie, Isakson, Lundstrøm, Carstensen,
   Jorn, Raadal, Bille, Pedersen, Jacobsen,
   Mortensen, Søndergard, Henning)

20–30 Exhibition rooms; print room
30 Entrance to Museum Library
33 Study room for prints
34–41 20th c. foreign art (Rump Collection)
53 Danish and international art after 1960
   (including Brøger, Polke, Mertx, Brøgger,
   Warhol, Richter, Judd, Beuys, Nørgaard,
   Penck, Kirkeby, Baselitz, Frandsen)

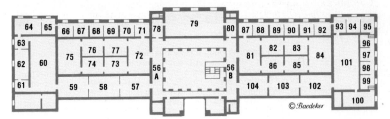

FIRST FLOOR

57–71 Flemish, Dutch and German art of the
   15th–18th c. (including P. Brueghel,
   Valchenborch, Rembrandt, Frans Hals,
   Rubens, Gijsbrechts, de Momper, Pieter
   de Hooch, de Vries, van de Velde, Both,
   Memling, Lukas Cranach the Elder)
56 A, 14th–18th c. Italian art
72–75 (Rosa, Mantegna, Titian, Tintoretto, Lippi,
   Bernini, Tiepolo, Guardi)
76–77 17th and 18th c. French art (including
   Poussin, Boucher, Robart, Claude)

78–80 Nolde, Munch, Strindberg, Willumsen
56 B, Danish and Scandinavian art of the
81–104 18th and 19th c. (including Juel,
   Lundbye, Eckersberg, Jensen,
   Dahl, Christiansen, Skovgaard,
   Dalsgaard, Krøyer, Anna and
   Michael Ancher, Marstrand,
   Købke, Abildgaard, Gottschalk,
   Hammershøi, Henningsen, Nielsen,
   Larsen Stevns, Philipsen, Hansen,
   Zahrtmann)

To the west of the palace lies the Zoological Garden (Zoologisk Have), one of the largest zoos in Europe. The enclosures are laid out so as to imitate the animals' natural surroundings as closely as possible. Visitors can watch polar bears, seals, lions and other animals being fed. At the entrance there is an observation tower. The zoo can boast a reptile house, a bird lake with storks and pelicans, a lion's den, a giraffe house, a monkey house, etc. (open: daily 9am–4, 5 or 6pm).

**Zoological Garden

In the adjoining suburb of Valby stands the large Carlsberg Brewery building. The entrance in Ny Carlsberg Vej is known as Elephant Tower, actually a cooling tower resting on four massive granite elephants. Guided tours

*Carlsberg Brewery

Rosenborg Palace and its park

take the visitor through the various parts of the brewery including the fermenting cellar and the brewery museum. Every visitor is given the opportunity of tasting the product (guided tours: Mon.–Fri. 11am–2pm). As the Carlsberg Brewery has for many years donated part of its profits to Danish cultural life it has written on its delivery vans "Skål for Kunsten" ("Here's to the Arts!"). The founder of the brewery, J. C. Jacobsen, set up the charity foundation in 1886, and his son has perpetuated his interest in the arts.

Nørrebro

*Assistens
Kirkegård

In Nørrebro, a district north of Frederiksberg, lies the "Assistens Kirkegard", Copenhagen's large and certainly most interesting cemetery. Here several celebrated Danish figures lie buried, including Hans Christian Andersen, Søren Kierkegaard and Martin Andersen Nexø, the working-class novelist.

Workers'
Museum

On May 1st 1984 a Workers' Museum was opened at Romersgade 22, in the district of Nørrebro. The museum is devoted to the cultural history of the workers' movement in Denmark from 1850. There are permanent exhibitions on various themes. The exhibition named "The Sørensens – a working class family 1885–1990", for example, describes the experiences of three generations who spent their lives in a Copenhagen house which now belongs to the Workers' Museum and has not been altered since 1915 (open: Tue.–Fri. 10am–3pm, Sat. and Sun. 11am–4pm; July 1st–Oct. 31st Mon. in addition 10am–3pm).

**Zoological
Museum

Following Jagtvej in a northerly direction from Nørrebro we come to the Zoological Museum (Zoologisk Museet) on the university campus. The museum is divided into two sections, the "Fauna of Denmark" and "From

Tombstones of Martin-Andersen Nexø . . .   . . . and Søren Kierkegaard

Pole to Pole'' (animals of the world). Animals can be seen in their natural habitat (open: Tue.–Sun. 11am–5pm).

Bispebjerg

Half-way between Nørrebro and the Zoological Museum Tagensvej leads north-west from Jagtvej to the district of Bispebjerg. Here stands Grundt-vig Church (Grundtvigs Kirke), built between 1921 and 1940 by Peter Wil-helm Jensen Klint and named after the founder of the Adult Education movement.

**Grundtvig Church

Inspired by the style of the typical country churches of Denmark, the architect designed a tall and massive church building of yellow brick and clinker. The west front of the triple-aisled church resembles a gigantic organ. Indeed, as the church houses one of the largest organs in Scan-dinavia concerts are often held here. Below the choir and part of the nave lies a large crypt.

Southern Surroundings

Tårnby, the southernmost part of Copenhagen, lies on the island of Amager, which is joined to the inner city by a large lift bridge (Langebro); when a ship passes this can be raised or lowered in a very short time. On Amager is situated the ''Bella Center'' exhibition and congress centre and Copenhagen Airport south of Kastrup.

Amager Island (Copenhagen Airport)

On the east coast of the island lies the little town of Dragor, a popular holiday resort which has retained the character of a rural fishing commu-nity – more than 50 houses are listed buildings. A visit is recommended to the Local Maritime History Museum at Havnepladsen (open: May–Sept. Tue.–Fri. 2–5pm, Sat. and Sun. noon–6pm).

**Dragor

ıleby

Store Magleby, in the south of the island, was once known as "Dutch Town", as its first inhabitants were 16th c. Dutch settlers who drained and cultivated the land. A half-timbered 18th c. building houses the Amager Museum, which exhibits, for example, costumes worn by those early Dutch immigrants.

Saltholm

Off the island of Amager to the east is the island of Saltholm, a bird sanctuary, linked to Kastrup by ferry.

Planned bridge
across the
Øresund

In 1991 an agreement was signed by Denmark and Sweden to build a bridge across the Øresund, from Malmö to Copenhagen. The plan is for a suspension bridge with supporting pillars which will lead from the Swedish coast to two artificial islands south of Saltholm. There the road will enter a tunnel which will come to the surface near Copenhagen Airport (Kastrup). A start was made on the work at the Copenhagen end in 1993, but has since been stopped because the Swedish prime minister Bildt came up against problems; his coalition partners, the Centre Party, disapproved of the plan and threatened to undermine the coalition. It is hoped that a solution will be found by the autumn of 1994.

Part of the Øresund project includes plans for an improved road and rail link from Kastrup (Copenhagen Airport) southwards towards Rødby, as well as from the Main Station to Kastrup.

Northern Surroundings

Lyngby
Sorgenfri Palace

The Lyngbyvej motorway leads to Lyngby. There, in a park, stands Sorgenfri Palace, built in the 18th c. and since 1789 the property of the Royal Family (entrance to the southern part of the park).

*Open-Air
Museum

Near Lyngby is also the extremely interesting Open-Air Museum (Frilandsmuseet), which belongs to the Danish National Museum. Within its area of 35ha/86 acres are farmhouses, dwellings and mills from all parts of Denmark and some from the Faroes, each building furnished with old fittings and utensils. There are also old houses from Schleswig-Holstein and Sweden, as well as picnic-sites (open: Apr. 3rd–Sept. 30th Tue.–Sun. 10am–5pm; Oct. 1st–Oct. 15th Tue.–Sun. 10am–3pm; Oct 16th–Oct. 24th daily 10am–4pm; closed Oct. 25th–Mar. 25th).

Bredemuseet

Beautifully situated in Brede, not far from Lyngby, is an Ethnological Museum, with a restaurant, cafetaria and cinema attached. Exhibitions are held on such subjects as "Fashion and Clothes" and "Industrialisation and Society in the Mølleåen Region" (open: Apr. 3rd–Sept. 30th Tue.–Sun. 10am–5pm; Oct. 1st–Oct. 15th Tue.–Sun. 10am–3pm; Oct. 16th–Oct. 24th daily 10am–4pm; during the winter Tue.–Sun. 10am–3pm, noon–5pm at weekends).

*Tuborg Brewery

Leaving Copenhagen by Østerbrogade and Strandvej we come to Hellerup, north of the port installations. Here are the headquarters of the Tuborg Brewery, which is now merged with the Carlsberg Brewery. On the brewery site stands the largest "beer bottle" in the world (26m/80ft high), originally made for the Nordic Industrial Exhibition in 1888, with a lift to take visitors to the top. Guided tours for groups of 10 or more by appointment only.

Experimentarium

The old brewery bottling plant now houses an "Experimentarium", a centre for new technology. Visitors are invited to carry out their own research experiments on such subjects as aerodynamics and astronomy and natural science in general (open: Mon., Wed., Fri. 9am–6pm, Tue. and Thur. 9am–9pm, Sat. and Sun. 11am–6pm).

*Aquarium

A short distance to the north in Charlottenburg will be found Denmark's Aquarium (Akvarium), with about 3000 brightly coloured fish and other

Frilandsmuseet

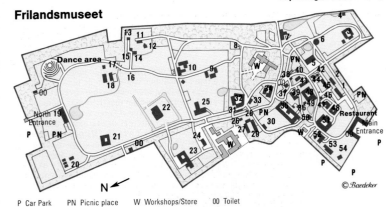

P Car Park   PN Picnic place   W Workshops/Store   00 Toilet

(DK)=Denmark   (D)=Germany   (S)=Sweden

1 Fisherman's house, Agger, North Jutland (DK)
2 Seaman's house from Sønderho, Fanø (North Sea island) (DK)
3 Farmhouse (early 19th c.), Øster Larsker, Bornholm (DK)
4 Watermill, Pedersker, Bornholm (DK)
5 Farmhouse (late 16th c.), Ostenfeld, South Schleswig (D)
6 Tower windmill, erected on the present site in 1832, in use until 1906 (no access)
7 Watermill (pre 1800), Ellested, Funen (DK)
8 Boundary stone of hunting territory (1743), Løve, Central Jutland (DK)
9 Farmhouse (c. 1850), Kølvrå, Karup Heath, Central Jutland (DK)
10 Farmhouse (from 1736), Læsø Island (Kattegat; DK)
11 Peasant's house (1866), Múla, Borðoy (Faroes; DK)
12 Store hut, Viðarejðí, Vidoy (Faroes; DK)
13 Watermill for domestic use, Sandur, Sandoy (Faroes; DK)
14 Buckwheat drying kiln, Múla, Borðoy (Faroes; DK)
15 Stone used in weight-lifting contests, Múla, Borðoy (Faroes; DK)
16 Milestone (2nd half of 17th c.), Holstebro district, West Jutland (DK)
17 Quarry (2nd half of 18th c.), Smedevad, near Holstebro, West Jutland (DK)
18 Farmhouse (from 1770), Vemb, West Jutland (DK)

19 Barn (originally c. 1600), from a farm at Fjellerup/Djursland, East Jutland (DK)
20 Fishermen's houses, Nymindegab, West Jutland (DK)
21 Farmhouse (1803), Lønnestak, West Jutland (DK)
22 Peasant's house (1653, partly older), Eiderstadt, south-west Schleswig (D)
23 Farmhouse (originally 17th c.) Sønder Sejerslev, North Schleswig (DK)
24 Pillow-lace making school (19th c.), Nørre Sejerslev, North Schleswig (DK)
25 House from Toftum (whaler-captain's house; 18th c.), Rømø Island (DK)
26 Fuel shed, Sode, North-east Schleswig (DK)
27 Barn (17th c.), Øsby, North-east Schleswig (DK)
28 Barn (1605), Grønninghoved, North-east Schleswig (DK)
29 Peasant's house (1766) Barsø, North-east Schleswig (DK)
30 Cottage from Dyndved (2nd half of 18th c.); Alsen, North Schleswig (DK)
31 Peasant's house with shoemaker's workshop, Ødis Bramdrup, near Kolding, East Jutland (DK)
32 Farmhouse (17th/18th c.), True, near Århus, East Jutland (DK)
33 Potter's workshop (1844), Sorring, East Jutland (DK)
34 Farmhouse (originally 2nd half of 17th c.), Halland (S)

35 Double farm (18th c.), Göinge, Schonen (S)
36 Bath House, Småland (S)
37 Two-storey storehouse, South-east Småland (S)
38 Small watermill, West Småland (S)
39 Smallholder's steading (18th/19th c.), Dörröd, Schonen (S)
40 Weaver's house, Tystrup, Zealand (DK)
41 Rural craftsman's house, Kalvehave, Zealand (DK)
42 Farmworker's house, Engelrup, Zealand (DK)
43 Farmhouse (before 1800), Greve, Zealand (DK)
44 Almshouse (1710), Greve, Zealand (DK)
45 Boundary stone (1757), Virum, Zealand (DK)
46 Fire-station (c. 1850), Kirke-Såby, Zealand (DK)
47 Small farm (1760), Årup, Funen (DK)
48 Wooden shoemaker's house (19th c.), Kirke-Søby, Funen (DK)
49 Village green, with place of assembly, Funen (DK)
50 Village smithy (c. 1845), Ørbæk, Funen (DK)
51 Farmhouse (1747), Lundanger, Funen (DK)
52 Small farmhouse, Dannemare, Lolland
53 Cottage (small farmhouse; pre 1800), Tågense, Lolland (DK)
54 Post-mill (c. 1662), Karlstrup, Zealand (no access)

Karen Blixen: bourgeois or aristocrat?

Whenever the name of Karen Blixen was mentioned a murmur went through the classroom, followed by a rapt silence; this would then be broken by a continuous string of questions – who was this lady, what inspired her? Even at that early stage, in a small Danish provincial town, it was clear that there was more to

TANIA BLIXEN

AFRIKA
DUNKEL LOCKENDE WELT

*Aus dem Englischen übertragen
von Rudolf von Scholtz*

MANESSE BIBLIOTHEK DER WELTLITERATUR

the riddle of Karen Blixen than just an interest in literature. Sometimes it was as if Baroness Blixen herself tried to help people towards a deeper understanding of what made her tick. "Live as I have lived" she would say in her uniquely deep voice, as if speaking from beyond the grave.

Her life, which she lived to the full, begins on April 17th 1885 on the Rungstedlund estate near the gates of Copenhagen. Although Karen and her four sisters lack nothing in a material sense the contrasts within the family circle are very marked. The mother, Ingeborg Westenholz, daughter of a wealthy businessman, the grandmother and Karen's aunt are all very strict but charitable and self-sacrificing, with little interest in self-indulgence or material matters.

In stark contrast are the Dinesens, the male branch of the family, freedom-loving army officers and landowners related to the most powerful aristocratic families in the country and passionately radical in their views. At an early stage in her life William Dinesen recognises the special talent and rebellious potential present in his second-oldest daughter and makes her his ally. Long walks, sometimes together, sometimes alone, provide them with an escape from the maternal and domestic strait-jacket.

In 1895 the ten year-old Karen suffers a dreadful personal tragedy such as she had never imagined. Her father, a political outsider who appears to be climbing up the Danish parliamentary ladder, commits suicide. Now, more than ever, Karen feels the need to escape the shackles that are suffocating her. She makes her first attempts at writing, joins courses at the Academy of Fine Arts in Copenhagen and tries once more to base her life on those freedom-loving ideals in which she had temporarily lost faith following the death of her father and which, she now fervently believes, are to be found only among the aristocracy. Her endeavours take her across the Øresund to Sweden.

Her engagement to her Swedish cousin, Baron Bror Blixen-Finecke, is met with blank amazement in the Westenholz household. However, it proves to be much more than just a *mariage de convenance*; as well as genuine mutual attraction they also share a common desire for a fresh beginning far away from restrictive family influences, and elect to go to Africa.

They are married in 1913 on the day of their arrival in Mombasa in the later Crown Colony of Kenya.''. . . I suddenly found myself in the very heart of Africa, in a *vita nuova*, which for me was what life truly should be like'', she writes some years later.

The first impressions the newly-wed Baroness gains of her new home are almost overwhelming. She sinks happily into the "quicksand paradise" of East Africa, enjoys the wide open spaces and the simplicity of nature, and experiences at last the bringing together of her two worlds into one. However, this newly-won freedom soon shows its more fickle and unhappy side. The coffee-farm in Ngong Hills, on which they had both pinned their hopes, produces only minimal profits, while back in Copenhagen the Westerholz's – who have invested considerable capital in the venture – are pressing for quick returns. Even though she is now abroad Karen realises she has not shaken off the family shackles and with a heavy heart she feels obliged to leave her husband Bror after five years of marriage, in the first of which he infected her with syphilis.

It is owing to her determination and faith in her Odyssey that, in spite of her illness, she refuses to give up hope of finding her Shangri-la here in Africa. Her beloved Kenya gives her the strength to carry on, but increasing problems on the farm finally convince her that she must face reality.

The final act in the African saga of Karen (Tania) Blixen revolves around Denys Finch-Hatton, a British aristocrat and airman, who shares her passion for Africa like no other. Long conversations through the night on art and literature, when Denys shows himself to be an excellent listener, help Karen to realise her true purpose in life. He is the first person to whom she relates her psychologically enigmatic tales which are later to make her world-famous. During their flights together over the vast expanses of Kenya she feels happier than she has ever felt before; when close to Denys, her great love, she awakes from her inner dreams and experiences new dimensions in her existence.

The curtain falls when, in 1931, Denys is killed in a tragic flying accident. In that same year Karen makes the most difficult decision of her life – to return to Rungstedlund.

At the age of 46 she finds herself once again threatened with the chains of a bourgeois existence but now knows how to avoid them. The true identity she has been seeking for so long now materialises in her writing. In reaction to her failure to succeed as an aristocrat she takes as her main themes those which she now realises are the ones that really matter – a return to basics, universal tolerance, spontaneity, freedom. Africa, her lost paradise, remains a source of inspiration to her to the very end.

In addition to her autobiograpical novel "Out of Africa", which was made into an the award-winning film in 1985, she also published psychological tales of mystery such as "Seven Gothic Tales".

denizens of the deep, which is very popular with visitors. The fish include fluorescent fish, sharks, electric eels and exotic species such as the notorious piranhas (open: Mar. 1st–Oct. 31st daily 10am–6pm, Nov. 1st–Feb. 28th Mon.–Fri. 10am–4pm and Sat., Sun. 10am–5pm).

*Dyrehave
(*Bakken)

Finally the visitor will come to Dyrehave, a large park with a game reserve where deer can be seen grazing. In the magnificent beech-wood lies the Eremitage, a royal hunting-lodge built in 1736 in Rococo style which is still used today. From here there is a fine view of Øresund and Sweden beyond. On the southern edge of the park lies the Bakken leisure centre, a folksy version of the Tivoli, with restaurants. Nearby is Klampenborg, with villas and good bathing.

Sommers
Oldtimer Museum

On the E 47 north-west of Dyrehave lies the little village of Nærum, with the interesting Sommers Oldtimer Museum. The collection consists of more than 20 vintage cars (1923 Bugatti, 1925 Bentley, 1937 Jaguar, etc.) and numerous oldish model cars (open: Mon.–Fri. 9am–5pm, Sat. 9am–1pm, Sun. 11am–3pm).

*Karen Blixen
Museum

Further north, a Karen Blixen Museum (Karen Blixen Museet) was set up in 1991 in the Rungstedlund mansion at Strandvej 111 in Rungsted. The Danish authoress (also known by the name of Tania Blixen and other noms-de-plume) was born in this house and after her return from Africa lived here until her death in 1962. (See Baedeker Special pp. 104–105.)
On display are books and pictures, including portraits of members of the Kikuyu tribe, which she painted (open: May–Sept. daily 10am–5pm, Oct.–Apr. Wed.–Fri. 1–4pm, Sat. and Sun. 11am–4pm).

Esbjerg   A 3

Jutland
District: Ribe amt
Population: 82,000

Situation and
Importance

Esbjerg, the fifth largest town in Denmark, lies on the west coast of Jutland facing the northern tip of the island of Fanø. It is the country's most important North Sea harbour and largest fishing port; in addition it is the base for Denmark's oil and gas exploration in the North Sea. A lightship lies in the harbour.

History

After the Treaty of Vienna of 1864, under the terms of which Denmark had to cede the Duchies of Schleswig-Holstein and Lauenburg to Germany, the ports on the west coast of Schleswig were available to the Danes only on payment of customs duties. Therefore it was decided in 1868 to build a port on the site where Esbjerg now stands, especially with a view to trading with Britain. The port was completed in 1878 but later modernised and extended on several occasions. Esbjerg received its town charter in 1898.

Economy

Exports and imports and the processing of fish form the major branches of the town's economy. The principal exports are the products of agriculture and fishing. There are fur farms outside the town. Passenger traffic is also of significance; there are ferry services from Esbjerg to Great Britain (Newcastle and Harwich) and to the Faroes (Tórshavn).

Sights

Within the town there are wooded areas and parks with lakes and sports facilities, including Strandskoven, Vognsbøl Park and Nørreskoven.

Water Tower
Art Gallery

In the municipal park near the extensive harbour stands the Water Tower (1897), the town's landmark. At Hanvegade 20 can be found the Art Gallery,

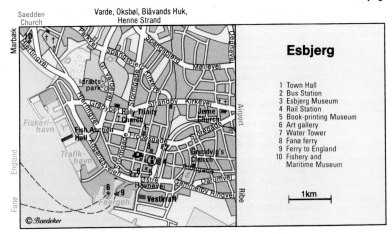

Esbjerg

1 Town Hall
2 Bus Station
3 Esbjerg Museum
4 Rail Station
5 Book-printing Museum
6 Art gallery
7 Water Tower
8 Fanø ferry
9 Ferry to England
10 Fishery and
   Maritime Museum

1km

housing a comprehensive collection of 20th c. Danish paintings and sculpture. Among the exhibits are works by Harald Giersing, Wilhelm Lundstrøm, Richard Mortensen, the Jørgen brothers and Arne Haugen Sørensen. Special exhibitions and concerts of international repute are held in the Art Gallery (open: daily 10am–4pm). In the entrance stands the ironwork sculpture "Esbjerg", by Robert Jacobsen (1962).

Amber in the Esbjerg Museum

Esbjerg

*Esbjerg Museum/ West Jutland Amber Museum

The Esbjerg Museum at Nørregade 25 is well worth a visit. The museum has a collection of several hundred pieces of natural amber in many colours as well as processed amber. More amber is found here on the west coast of Jutland than anywhere else in Denmark. The exhibition explains how amber was formed many millions of years ago. The museum also displays objects illustrating life during the Viking era, as well as dioramas of towns with market-places and shops, etc. (open: daily 10am–4pm; closed Sept. 1st–May 31st).

Museum of the Printing Press

South of the town centre, at Borgergade 6, this museum is set out like a Danish printing-works, with apparatus and demonstrations of traditional methods of printing books by hand. It is a working museum, and visitors may, on request, obtain finished examples of the craft (open: daily 10am–4pm; closed Sept. 1st–May 31st).

Kongensgade

Running parallel to Borgergade is Kongensgade, a busy pedestrian zone and shopping street with a number of Art Nouveau houses and 19th c. buildings; to the east is the railway station.

Fishing harbour

On the quay of the fishing harbour stands the Fish Auction Hall, covering an area of 8000sq.m/9570sq.yd; the first auction is at 7am every weekday. A little way north can be seen a memorial to fishermen lost at sea. This is in the form of a granite rotunda engraved with the names of Esbjerg fishermen who have lost their lives at sea since 1900. Motorboat tours depart from Fanø ferry berth.

*Fisheries and Maritime Museum

In Tarphagevej, to the north-west of the memorial, will be found the very interesting Fisheries and Maritime Museum (Fiskeri og Søfastsmuseet). It houses a comprehensive collection of fishing-boats and equipment, with photographs and diagrams.

There is also a fresh-water aquarium containing fish found in the seas around the Danish coasts, and a large seal basin with a viewing window.

A fishing harbour on the North Sea coast

The seals are fed daily at 11am and 2.30pm and give birth to their pups in July (open: daily 10am–4pm; mid-May–Sept. to 6pm; July and Aug. to 8pm).

Esbjerg can boast a number of interesting churches. To the north of the town centre, in Grådbyet, stands Holy Trinity Church (Treenighedskirken), built in 1961 to designs by Erik Flagsted Rasmussen and Knud Thomsen. The building has four triangular gables; three have glass mosaic windows by Jens Urup Jensen, while the organ fills the fourth. Adjoining the church on the north is Vognsbøl Park.

Holy Trinity
Church

In Fyrvej, in the Sædden district of the town, stands Sædden Church, which forms part of a shopping centre. It is an impressive building, designed by the architects I. and J. Exner and dedicated in 1978. The gallery and steps are of wood, the altar and font stand in the middle of the church, and the organ has 33 stops.

Sædden Church

There are two other notable churches to the east of the town centre; Grundvigs Church in Ribegade, built in 1969 by Ole Nielsen with a V-shaped roof, and the Romanesque Jerne Church, which was mentioned in the records as early as 1306. The latter is built of granite and was later provided with a brick tower; inside can be seen an altar of 1634 and a granite font. The organ, installed in 1989, has 20 stops.

Grundvigs Church
Jerne Church

Suroundings

By way of Hjerting, an attractive coastal suburb with a view of Ho Bay, the road leads to Marbæk Nature Park, some 12km/7 miles north-west of the town. Large areas of heather and scrub are a feature of the landscape. Two Iron Age settlements have been excavated here. The steep coasts at Ho Bay are impressively picturesque, as are the lakes inhabitated by flocks of birds. The Marbækgård, with an agricultural exhibition and a restaurant, is situated in the centre. 18km/10 miles of signposted trails offer walkers the opportunity to explore the area.

Marbæk Nature
Park

20km/12 miles north of Esbjerg lies the busy little township of Varde, with some interesting old houses and the 12th–13th c. St Jacob's Church on Torvet. The Town Hall is embellished by two sculptures – "Laksedrengen" (Boy with Salmon) and "Brøndpigen" (Maiden of the Fountain), by Anker Hoffmann. On display in Varde Provincial Museum are silver, furniture, Jutland stoneware and paintings, especially works by the Danish artist Christian Lyngbo. A model of old Varde as it was in 1866, scale 1:10, can be seen north-west of the town centre in the Arnberg complex. Tambours Garden makes a pleasant outing and boat trips can be made on the river between the harbour and Sommerland.

Varde

Varde Sommerland, a large leisure park for young and old, includes among its attractions a tour on the Colorado Express, excitement of the Colorado River and a traffic school (open: mid-May–early Sept. 10am–6pm).

Varde
Sommerland

14km/9 miles west of Varde lies the town of Oksbøl. In the Romanesque Ål Church are some beautiful 13th c. wall-paintings, including scenes from the legend of St Nicholas and a frieze of a cavalry battle, and a Romanesque font. In the Local Museum in Oksbøl are displayed objects from a refugee camp which was situated there during the Second World War. Farther south, at Blåvands Huk, the most westerly point in Denmark, stands a lighthouse. The nature reserve on nearby Skalligen Peninsula will be of interest to ornithologists.

Oksbøl

Driving west from Varde the visitor will come to the seaside resort of Henne Strand. In this region will be found the most beautiful dunes on the coast of Jutland. From the 64m/210ft high shifting dune known as Blåbjerg there is a superb view. A little north stretches Blåbjerg Plantation, a wooded area.

Henne Strand

Fåborg

Fåborg

Funen Island
District: Fyns amt
Population: 18,000

*Situation

Fåborg, an attractive little town, lies in the south of Funen on the Fåborg Fjord. To the west stretches the peninsula of Horneland with the ferry port of Bøjden, from where boats ply to Fynshav on the island of Als. Today the harbour is popular with amateur yachtsmen and anglers.

History

In the Middle Ages Fåborg belonged at different times to the Kingdom of Denmark and the Duchy of Schleswig. It was fortified and had a castle which is mentioned in records of 1377. During the "Counts' Wars" (1534–36) the fortifications were destroyed apart from the West Tower at Vesterport (see below).
In the 19th c. the town merchants were engaged in the cereal trade. By the mid-19th c. Fåborg had a regular boat service to Copenhagen and in 1880 the railway arrived.

Sights

Vesterport

There are some well-preserved old streets, many of which are cobbled, including Nygade and Holkegade ("Schmedehusene", or "blacksmiths' houses"). The West Gate in Vestergade, a medieval town gate with a passage for vehicles, is very impressive. It was built in the 15th c. and together with the wall and ditch formed the boundary between the town and the surrounding countryside. It was not until the 19th c. that the town began to expand beyond these limits.

Market-place

In the Market-place (Torvet), formerly the commercial centre, and now traffic centre, busy with traffic, is the "Ymer Fountain", a copy of the original by the sculptor Kai Nielsen. In 1913 it was donated to the town by Mads Rasmussen. At house No. 9 in the market-place is a pottery dating from 1850, named "Pottemageri".

Bell-tower

In Lille Tårnstræde stands a Bell-tower (Klokketårnet) which was originally built for a church. On the east wall of the tower can be seen remains of the oldest building in Fåborg – parts of the wall which linked the tower with the church which once stood here. From the tower there is a superb view over the town and the little islands off the coast of Funen.

Egeskov Castle, near Fåborg, is built on piles in a lake ▶

Fåborg

*Fåborg Museum

The Fåborg Museum at Grønnegade 75 is especially worth seeing, as it houses a comprehensive collection of works by Funen painters from about 1900 and thereabouts. In 1910 Mads Rasmussen, a prosperous merchant, took the initiative founding the museum, which was constructed according to plans by the architect Carl Petersen. Exhibits include works by the painters Peter Hansen, Fritz Syberg, Johannes Larsen, Jens Birkholm and Harald Giersing. In 1985 N. F. Truelsen designed an extension to the building to house the work of the Danish sculptor Kai Nielsen (1882–1924), who created a statue of Mads Rasmussen which can be seen in the museum (open: daily 10am–4 or 5pm).

"Den Gamle Gård" Museum

The house named "Den Gamle Gård" (The Old Farm) at Holkegade 1 was built in 1725 and made into a museum in 1932. Early life in Fåborg is documented in one section, with a luxurious Rococo Room containing a fine collection of glass, porcelain and china. In an adjoining house there is an exhibition of articles associated with seafaring, formerly an important facet of the town's economy. The third department displays objects from the island of Lyø, to the south of Funen, including textiles and embroidery (open: May – Oct.).

Surroundings

Kaleko Mølle

2km/1¼ miles east of the town stands the water-mill known as Kaleko Mølle, the oldest part of which dates from 1600. In the early 1900s the mill was opened up as a museum and then renovated in 1968 and made a listed building. The rooms contain old furniture and household utensils, so that the visitor will gain an impression of how a miller's family would have lived more than 100 years ago.

Horne

To the west of Fåborg lies the peninsula of Hornerland and the little village of Horne. On a hill stands a round 12th c. church built of stone. Note the embrasures for use in defending the church against attack. The altar-painting is by C. W. Eckersberg (1812).

Brahetrolleborg Castle

From Fåborg the A 8 road leads east to what are known as the Funen Alps; on the left rises the Lerbjerg (126m/413ft). 9km/5 miles further on stands the 15th c. Brahetrolleborg Castle, rebuilt several times, with a large park. At the entrance is the "Humlehaven" restaurant in which exhibitions of art and antiques are mounted (park is open daily 9am–5pm).

*Egeskov Manor-house

Continuing along the A 8 the visitor will come to the Renaissance manor-house, one of the best-preserved moated houses in Europe. Constructed on oak piles between 1524 and 1554, it has two round towers at east end and a square tower with staircase at west end. The fine rooms are furnished with antiques, hunting trophies and family portraits (open: daily June, July, Aug. 9am–6pm, May and Sept. 10am–5pm).

The house is situated in a large park with beech hedges and gravel paths leading to several gardens: English, fuchsia, Renaissance garden, as well as a large bamboo maze (open: as Manor-house above).

Museums

In the grounds are two museums: the Veteranmuseum, which houses a gleaming collection of vintage and veteran cars, motor-cycles and aircraft, and the Hestevogns og Landsbrugsmuseum (Horse and Carriage and Agricultural Museum) where old wagons and agricultural implements are displayed (open: as Manor-house above).

Færøerne

See Faroe Islands

Falster   D/E 4

District: Storstrøms amt
Area: 514sq.km/198sq.miles. Population: 45,000

The island of Falster lies between the two larger islands of Lolland (west) and Zealand (north), to which it is joined by bridges. Together with the southern part of Zealand, Lolland, Møn and a few smaller islands Falster forms the administrative district of Storstrøm, so named after the Sound between Zealand and Falster. Gedser Odde, the southern tip of the island, is the most southerly point in Denmark. On the east coast there are some beautiful sandy beaches.

Sights

From Lolland the Frederik IX Bridge crosses Guldborg Sound to the island's largest town, Nykøbing. At the end of the 12th c. fortifications were constructed on a peninsula on Guldborg Sound for protection against the Wends, and these were later converted into Nykøbing Castle. The town grew up around the fortifications. After the Reformation the castle became the residence of widowed Danish queens. Several of whom were of German descent thus attracting many other Germans to the town.

In 1767 the castle was sold and later pulled down. Since there was no longer any income from the court, the inhabitants began to concentrate more on trade and industry. Today there are tobacco, margarine and cement factories in Nykøbing Falster.

A few beautiful half-timbered houses of the medieval old town still remain, such as the Ritmestersgård (a Renaissance building) in Store Kirkestræde, the old corn store in Slotsgade and buildings in Langgade, where the two-storeyed house at No. 18 is the oldest in the town, dating from 1580.

A notable building is the Abbey Church (Klosterkirken), built about 1500 as part of a Franciscan monastery; after the Reformation it became the town church. Note the grave monuments inside, one of which contains a picture

Holidaymakers on the beach at Marielyst

113

(1450) by Lucas Cranach the Elder. The "Mecklenburg Family Tree" (*c.* 1630) by Antonius Clement, is composed of more than 30 portraits. In the herb garden near the church, originally laid out by Franciscan monks, herbs have once again been cultivated since the 1970s.

The Falster Museum at Langgade 2 is housed in Czarens Hus (Czar's House), built in 1700 and so named following a visit by Peter the Great of Russia. In addition to documents, costumes and other material relating to the island of Falster and its people, ceramics and copper and pewter articles are displayed. There is also a goldsmith's workshop.

Væggerløse

In Væggerløse, south of Nykøbing, there is an old village church; in the ceiling of the tower can be seen interesting paintings dating from the Late Middle Ages. One scene shows Jesus dining with two young men following His Resurrection. Note also the crucifix and the pulpit. Nearby stands an old post-mill.

Corselitze Castle

12km/7 miles east of Nykøbing stands Corselitze Castle, the main wing of which dates from 1777. The castle is surrounded by a park laid out in the English style, with lakes and streams. The park is open daily Apr.– Oct. From the castle a main road leads to the coast near Tromnæs. North of Tromnæs stretches the longest strip of coastal woodland in eastern Denmark.

Marielyst

On the east coast lies the bathing resort of Marielyst, with beautiful beaches and a number of holiday homes. Nature walks are arranged during the season.

Further south, near Bøtø, is the Sommerland Falster activity park, a large area with many facilities for sport and amusement including a water-chute, a model boat pond and a track for go-carts (open: late May–Aug).

Gedser

In the extreme south of the island lies Gedser (pronounced "yehser"), Denmark's southermost town. There are ferry services from here to Travemünde (3½ hours) and Warnemünde (2 hours) both in Germany. In autumn large flocks of birds can be seen flying over this part of Falster on their way south. The town has a lighthouse, Railway Museum (Gedser Remise) and a Geological Collection (Skolegade 2B).

Nørre Alslev

From Nykøbing the A 2 leads north-west through fertile fields and meadows to Nørre Alslev. The Gothic church has a three-sided apse and a Late Medieval west tower. Note the wall-paintings inside, including a frieze with heraldic figures and a *danse macabre.*

Stubbekøbing

In Nørre Alslev a road branches off east to Stubbekøbing, an ancient little town beautifully situated on the Grøn Sound. It has the oldest church on the island, with a Renaissance altar and a carved pulpit; there is a panoramic view from the tower. On the Town Hall can be seen an original inscription reading "Lad dem styre som forstaae det" (Let those who understand, govern). A Motor Cycle Museum displays vintage vehicles. From Stubbekøbing it is just 12 minutes by ferry to the island of Bogø, from where a bridge crosses to the island of Møn (see entry).

Storstrøms Bridge

To the north of Nørre Alslev the Storstrøms Bridge (Storstrømsbro, 3200m/3520yd long), crosses the Strostrøm to the little island of Masnedø and from there the road continues over a bascule bridge to Vordingborg (see entry) on the island of Zealand.

Farø Bridge

The E 47 from Lolland leads north-east from Nørre Alslev across the Farø Bridge (Farøbro, 3322m/3644yd long) which is in two sections. The first section leads to the island of Farø and from there the second section continues to Zealand. These motorway bridges, opened in 1985, form a relief route for the Storstrøm Bridge.

Fanø

District: Ribe amt
Area: 55sq.km/21sq.miles
Population: 3200

The North Sea island of Fanø, developed from a sandbank in the sea, lies off the coast of South Jutland opposite the port of Esbjerg (see entry). With its miles of sandy beaches it has become a popular holiday resort. During the holiday season there are ferries every half an hour from Esbjerg; the crossing takes about 20 minutes.

Places of interest on Fanø

The chief place on the island is the fishing village of Nordby on the east coast, with its thatched fishermen's cottages. In the Fanø Museum can be seen a typical Fanø house, with replicas of Danish trading ships, ceramics and curiosities brought home by local sailors from their trips abroad. Before Esbjerg became the major port on the south-west coast of Jutland Fanø was an important marine trading centre with a large merchant fleet. This history is documented in the Skipperhus in Hovedgade, which also houses a large costume collection. There are many models of ships hanging from the ceiling of the 18th c. church, which has a hipped roof with glass tiles. There are numerous camping sites near the town of Rindby.

Nordby

About 3km/2 miles south-west of Nordby lies the resort of Fanø Vesterhavsbad, with an attractive beach extending south along the west coast of the island. The state forest, which practically covers the interior of the island, has been cultivated since the turn of the century and contains pine, oak and beech trees.

Fanø
Vesterhavsbad

In the dunes on the North-sea island of Fanø

Sønderho   Sønderho, on the southern tip of the island, is a 15km/9 mile drive from Nordby. The village has some pretty thatched fishermen's houses. Hannes Hus (*c.* 1770) houses a local museum, with furniture and antique wall-tiles. The local inn is one of the oldest buildings on Fanø. Many model ships, including a warship and a lifeboat, hang from the roof of the little church. The pulpit has a canopy, and there is an interesting sculpture "Fanøkone med barn" (Fanø woman with child), by Elof Nielsen (1949).

Farøe Islands/Færøerne/Føroyar

Autonomous Island Group
Total area: 1400sq.km/540sq.miles
Population: 48,000

Situation   The Farøe Island (Danish "Færøerne", Farøese "Forøyar"), meaning "Sheep Islands", is a group of 18 islands and several skerries which together form an autonomous part of Greater Denmark. They lie some 600km/373 miles west of the Norwegian coast, in latitude 62° north.

The islands can be reached by air all the year round from Copenhagen, the airport being on the island of Vågar. In the summer months (June to August) there are ferries from Esbjerg and other Danish ports to Tórshavn on the island of Streymoy.

Topography and climate   The islands, of volcanic origin, are of basalt with a thin layer of tufa. They have steep rocky coasts and fjords which bite deep inland. The landscape consists chiefly of meadows, fen and heathland. Trees and bushes are found in only a few places. The animal life of the islands comprises birds (including puffins), fish, seals and whales. Many of the birds live on the rocky coasts.

As the islands lie within the sphere of the Gulf Stream precipitation is considerable; rain falls on 280 days a year and the annual rainfall totals 1200–1700mm/47–66in. The oceanic climate means that summers are cool (11°C/52°F) and winters relatively mild (3°C/47°F). The influence of the Gulf Stream ensures that the sea temperature in summer and winter varies little and the sea remains free of ice.

History   The Farøes were settled from the 7th c. by Irish monks but were conquered around 800 by Norwegian Vikings and from 1035 onwards they belonged

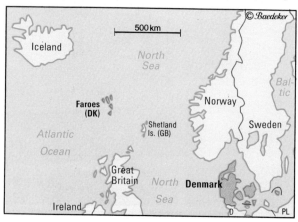

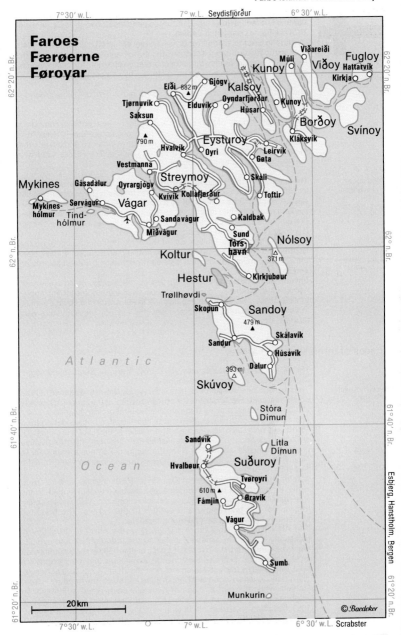

Faroes
Færøerne
Føroyar

7°30' w.L.   7° w.L. Seydisfjörður   6°30' w.L.

62°20' n.Br.

Viðareiði
Múli   Viðoy   Fugloy
Kunoy   Hattarvík
Kirkja
Gjógv   Kalsoy
Eiði   882 m   Oyndarfjørður   Kunoy
Tjørnuvík   Elduvík   Húsar
Saksun   Borðoy   Svínoy
790 m   Hvalvík   Eysturoy   Klaksvík
Oyri
Vestmanna   Leirvík
Streymoy   Gøta
Mykines   Gásadalur   Oyrargjógv   Skáli
Mykines-   Sørvágur   Kvívík   Kollafjørður
hólmur   Tind-   Vágar   Toftir
hólmur   Sandavágur   Kaldbak
Miðvágur   Sund   Nólsoy
Tórs-
havn   371 m
Koltur
62° n.Br.
Hestur   Kirkjubøur
Trøllhøvdi
Skopun   Sandoy
479 m
Sandur   Skálavík
Húsavík
393 m   Dalur
Skúvoy
Stóra
Dímun
61°40' n.Br.
Sandvík   Lítla
Dímun
Ocean   Hvalbøur   Suðuroy
Tvøroyri
610 m   Øravík
Fámjin
Vágur
61°20' n.Br.
Sumb
20km   Munkurin
© Baedeker

Atlantic

7°30' w.L.   7° w.L.   6°30' w.L. Scrabster

Esbjerg, Hansholm, Bergen

to Norway. In 1380 both Norway and the Farøes came into the possesion of Denmark. After the break-up of the union between Norway and Denmark in 1814 the Farøes remained Danish.

During the Second World War British troops occupied the islands. In 1848 they acquired autonomous status with internal self-government under the Danish Crown; the Danish parliament is responsible only for their interests in the fields of foreign policy and defence. They do not belong to the EU.

The Farøes have their own coat-of-arms – a ram argent on a blue ground – and, since March 23rd 1948, their own flag.

The legislative body of the country is the parliament (Løgting), consisting of 32 elected representatives; parliamentary elections are held every four years. Executive power is in the hands of the government (Landsstyret), the members of which are appointed by the Løgting. The Farøes send two members to the Danish parliament.

Population and economy

The language of the Farøes is one of the Germanic family of languages. Like Icelandic, to which it is closely related, it was originally derived from the old Nordic tongue, to be succeeded by a number of dialects. Modern Farøese spelling rules were laid down by V. U. Hammershaimb in 1846, and this has brought in its wake a unique and original form of Farøese literature. Danish is a compulsory second language in schools.

Until 1992 there were limitations on the consumption of alcohol on the islands, and spirits, wine and beer were not sold on the open market. Now they can be purchased in certain state-controlled shops; hotels can provide details.

Sheep-rearing has long been important on the islands, which are indeed named after the sheep. Today the principal source of income for the inhabitants is fishing. Some of the people work in shipyards and spinning-mills. Pullovers in beautiful colours and designs are popular souvenirs with tourists.

Places of interest in the Farøes

The largest islands are Streymoy, Eysturoy, Suduroy, Sandoy and Vágar. Most are separated by narrow sounds.

Streymoy with *Tórshavn

The largest island in the archipelago is Streymoy (Danish "Strømø"). On its south-east coast lies Tórshavn, the port and capital of the Farøes. It has only 15,000 inhabitants, making it the smallest capital in Scandinavia.

The oldest part of the town, with pretty little wooden houses dating from 18th c., lies on a spit of land in the harbour area. At the tip of this peninsula, at Cape Tinganes, the Vikings established their first *thingstead* (legislative council), probably about 930. Near the peninsula stands a memorial to Niels Ryberg Finsen (1860–1904), who was born in Tórshavn and won the Nobel Prize for Medicine in 1903.

Also of interest is the fortress of Skansin (*c.* 1580) near the harbour, from which in years gone by the entrance into the town was defended. In the National Museum, with its ethnological collections, etc., visitors can obtain information on the history and culture of the Farøes. The Maritime Museum is housed in a neighbouring building.

The Art Gallery (Listaskálin Art Gallery) in the north of Tórshavn is pleasantly situated in parkland, including Vidarlundin Park and exhibits works by Faroese artists. "Nordic House", built in 1983 in the Scandinavian style, is a cultural centre where concerts, exhibitions and other events are held. Designed by the Norwegian architect Ola Steen, it was built of Norwegian stone, Swedish wood and Danish glass and steel. The furniture is from Finland, while the roof is made of materials contributed by Iceland. To celebrate its ten years of existence a big cultural event was arranged in 1993, including an art exhibition with works by the Farøese artist Ingálvur av Reyni, who has also made a name for himself abroad.

To the south-west of Tórshavn lies Kirkjubøur, a place inhabited by Irish monks as early as the 8th c. Here stand the ruins of the 13th c. St Magnus' Cathedral, an unfinished building with tall basalt walls and Gothic pointed windows, and St Olaf's Church which has been restored. The medieval timber-framed house known as "Stokkastovan" is now a museum.
North of Tórshavn it is worth visiting Kvívík, where a house dating from the Viking Age has been excavated.

In a deep valley about 10km/6 miles from Tórshavn, on the north-west coast of Streymoy, lies Saksun, now a museum depicting life in the Middle Ages, with good fishing nearby. The Dúvugarður, a farmhouse built of boulders and peat, is furnished much as it was in the Middle Ages.

A runic stone can be seen near Sandavágur, on the island of Vágar to the west of Streymoy. The Bøsdalafossur Waterfall is scenically most impressive. The unique rock formation known as the "Trøllkonfingur" (Witch's Finger), on the extreme east coast, stands 350m/1150ft high; King Frederik VII, who visited the island in 1844, was most impressed by it. There is a Folklore Museum in Miðvágur, a small island south of Vágar.

Vágar

From Sørvágur on the west coast of the island there is a boat service in summer to the little island of Mykines, where the rocks inhabited by birds are easily accessible and extremely attractive. Seagulls, guillemots and puffins abound; the inhabitants catch birds for food. Birthplace of artist Mikines (1906–79).

Mykines

Eysturoy is the second largest of the Faroe Islands, and linked to Streymoy by a bridge. Two picturesque villages in the north are Gjógy and Eiði and between them tower the highest cliffs in the Farøes, reaching heights up to 882m/2895ft above sea-level. They can be climbed in clear weather and from the top there is an extensive view over the sea and the islands.

Eysturoy

In the Faroes: a picturesque village by the water

On Streymoy Island

At the northern tip of Eysturoy the Rison and Kellingin rocks tower up out of the water.

Borðoy

To the north and north-east of Eysturoy lie many sizeable and smallish islands. Klaksvik, on Borðoy, has a population of 5000, making it the second largest town in the Farøes. The town began to grow when fishing became more important than agriculture, for Klaksvik has a good natural harbour surrounded by hills.

Note the History Museum and St Christians Church, from the roof of which hangs a boat which was the only one of four to return safely to land on a stormy winter's night in 1923.

Viðoy

Viðareiði, in the middle of a hilly area on the island of Viðoy, is the northernmost point in the Farøes. From Cape Enniberg (750m/2460ft) there is a fine view of several islands. The cliffs to the north of Viðareiði are home to immense colonies of sea-birds.

Sandoy

To the south of Streymoy lie Sandoy and Suðuroy, between which flows the Suðuroyar Fjord. Sandoy ("Sand Island"), named after the sandy beaches near Sandur and Húsavik, is the flattest of the islands. The land is used for agriculture and there is excellent fishing. In the pretty village of Húsavik can be seen an old house with an open fireplace and chimney; until a few years ago this house was inhabited.

Suðuroy

Sumba on Suðuroy is the most southerly of the Farøe Islands. The road to it passes the impressive Beinisvorð Cliffs on the west coast, a nesting-place for numerous sea-birds. This island has bays and harbours on the east coast but a very steep west coast. Note also the votive church which was a gift from a Norwegian lady.

Føroyar

See Farøes

Fredericia   B 3

Jutland
District: Vejle amt
Population: 47,000

The town of Fredericia lies on the east coast of Jutland, on the Little Belt,   Situation
north of the place where a road bridge (E 20) leads east from Jutland to the
island of Funen. The bay is a nature reserve.

In the mid-17th c. Frederik III (1648–70) had a fortress built here to protect   History
northern Jutland against enemy attacks and to enable the crossing from
Jutland to the island to be made in safety. Within a semi-circular rampart
across the island the fortress-builder Gottfried Hoffmann laid out streets in
a rectangular pattern. The name "Fredericia" dates from 1664. Fredericia
was one of the few towns in Denmark where people could live who were
not adherents of the Evangelical-Lutheran faith. Therefore Jews could be
found here from 1679 and, since the 18th c., members of the Reformed
Church, many of whom were engaged in growing tobacco.

In 1864, during the Second German-Danish War, Fredericia was besieged
and after severe bombardment the inhabitants fled to Funen. Not until
1909, when the fortifications were demolished, did Fredericia expand.

Fredericia: "The Valiant Soldier" monument

Sights

Memorial	In the course of the First German-Danish War (1848–50) the Danes succeeded in capturing Fredericia on July 6th 1849. This victory over the forces of Schleswig-Holstein is commemorated by the bronze statue "The Valiant Soldier" in front of the main police station; it was sculpted by H. V. Bissen (1796–1868), a pupil of Thorvaldsen.
Fredericia Museum	The Fredericia Museum, housed in several buildings in Jernbanegade, boasts a notable collection of lamps, paintings, furniture, and tiled stoves, as well as documents on the history of the religious denominations which found sanctuary in the town in days gone by (open: daily mid-June–mid-Aug.; at other times of the year Tue.–Sat. afternoons).
Ramparts	There is an enjoyable walk to be had along the ramparts (Voldene) of the demolished fortifications which are among the largest in Denmark; there is a panoramic view from the top. The walls guard the approach to the Bersodde peninsula, on which Fredericia lies. Of the original town gates only Prince Gate (Prinsenport), built about 1750, has survived. A castle on the tip of the peninsula and a gun-tower also form part of the old fortifications.

Surroundings

Hvidberg	North of the town on Trelde Næs stretches an area of dunes, and to the west, on the coast, lies the resort of Hvidberg, with its broad sandy beach and white dunes up to 27m/90ft high.

Frederikshavn   C 1

Jutland
District: Nordjyllands amt
Population: 35,000

Situation and Importance	Frederikshavn, the largest town north of the Limfjord, lies on the east coast of northern Jutland. From the fortified natural harbour, ferries sail to Gothenburg in Sweden, Larvik, Moss and Oslo in Norway and to the Danish island of Læsø. There are also yacht basins.
History	Where the present town now stands was in medieval times the site of the fishing settlement of "Fladstrand". When, during the Thirty Years' War, a defence entrenchment was built here the place gained in military importance. A fortifications expert erected a powder-tower surrounded by a wall. In 1818 Fladstrand received its municipal charter and was named Frederikshavn, after Frederik VI. In the 19th c. the citadel, apart from a few buildings, was pulled down. The town is proud of its pedestrian area.
Economy	Fishing (flounders, oysters) and fish-processing are important branches of the town's economy, together with such industries as shipbuilding, engineering and iron-foundries.

Sights

Gun-Tower (Museum)	At Havnepladsen, near the harbour, stands the town's emblem – the Krudttårnet, the former gun powder magazine, built of stone in 1688 as part of the fortifications designed by the architect Anthon Coucheron; at one time there were also several cannons here. Today the tower houses a Museum of Military History, exhibiting weapons dating from 1600 to 1900 (open: Apr.–Oct.). Events of recent history are shown in the Bunker Museum (Batteri Nord), which comprises a Second World War German bunker.

Frederikshavn: the Powder Tower now serves as a museum

The oldest part of the town, Fiskerklyngen, lies to the north of the fishing harbour and here can be seen a number of well-preserved 17th c. houses. Note also the North Entrenchments (Nordre Skanse), which were built by Wallenstein's troops during the Thirty Years' War.

Fiskerklyngen

Fladstrand Church (Fladstrand Kirke), dating from 1690, has been renovated several times. In the cemetery will be found the graves of German and British soldiers killed in the Second World War.

Fladstrand Church

Sognefogedgården, on the western edge of town, is worth a visit; in the "Schulzenhof" (18th c.) the kitchen, dairy, alcoves, stable and workshop have been retained in their original form.

Sognefoged-gården

4km/2½ miles to the south-west of the town, at an altitude of 165m/540ft above sea-level, stands a 58m/190ft high observation tower, Cloos Tower (Cloostårnet), from which there are extensive views of the Vendsyssel countryside and the sea. Close by, in Gærumvej, are Iron Age Cellars (Jernalderkældrene), with Early Iron Age material found in the locality.

Cloos Tower

Surroundings

3km/2 miles south-west of Frederikshavn along Møllehus Allé, set in 50ha/124 acres of woodland, lies Bangsbo Manor (1750), a three-winged half-timbered building which is now a museum. In the maritime section can be seen a collection of galleon figureheads and models and paintings of ships. Most impressive is the "Ellingåschiff", a former trading ship similar to Viking ships.
In addition, this museum is the largest Resistance Museum outside Copenhagen, with exhibits covering the period of German occupation 1940–45 (open: daily 10am–5pm; closed on Mon. Nov.–Mar.).

Bangsbo (Museum)

A model ship in Bangsbo Museum

Near the museum are a deer park and Boolsen's Stone Garden, a collection of more than 1000 stones with carvings or inscriptions (millstones, baptismal fonts and boundary stones), the oldest dating from prehistoric times. From the Pikkerbakken, a range of low hills to the south of Bangsbo Manor, there are magnificent views of Frederikshavn, the countryside beyond and the sea.

*Sæby

12km/7½ miles south of Frederikshavn on the E 45 and A 10 lies the fishing port and seaside resort of Sæby. Near the beach stands the whitewashed St Mary' Church, which originally belonged to a monastery (*c.* 1460) which no longer exists. The church, with its four groin vaults, is famous for its rich 16th c. frescoes showing scenes from the life of Jesus, the "Adoration of the Magi", the "Entry into Jerusalem" and the "Last Judgment", as well as coats-of-arms of noble families. The Dutch altar-table dates from 1520. On the walls are numerous epitaphs from different centuries. Nearby is Voergaard Castle (open: daily end-June–Aug.).

Frederikssund   E 3

Zealand
District: Frederiksborg amt
Population: 17,000

Situation
and Importance

The port of Frederikssund is situated in the north of Zealand on the east shore of Roskilde Fjord.
4km/2½ miles to the south the remains of five Viking ships (now in the Viking Ship Museum in Roskilde; see entry) were recovered from the fjord in 1962; they had probably formed part of an underwater barrier.
Frederikssund is also known for its Viking plays, which are held there every summer.

As the Roskilde Fjord at Frederikssund is at its narrowest, it is here that the easiest crossing from North Zealand to the Hornsherred peninsula can be made. Therefore there was already a ferry here in the Middle Ages, and in the course of time a trading-station grew up which in 1573 received the right to levy customs duties. At the end of the 16th c. a bridge of ships was built, to be followed by a more permanent bridge across the sound in the 19th c.

History

Sights

The interesting J. F. Willumsen Museum, built 1955–57, contains works by the artist of that name, who left them to the state on condition that a museum would be built to house them. Jens Ferdinad Willumsen (1864–1958), born in Copenhagen, lived for many years in France and worked both as a painter and sculptor and also as an architect. Although his work was criticised as well as respected he played an important role in Danish art for some 70 years.

J. F. Willumsen Museum

One hundred and twenty-five works by this artist are on display in the museum, which was the first modern museum to be built in Denmark after the Second World War. There is also an interesting collection of works by Gauguin.

Surroundings

On the Hornsherred spit of land 6·5km/4 miles west of the town Jæerspris Castle stands in a magnificent wood. The three-winged building, which has been extended several times, was once a hunting-lodge and the summer residence of King Frederik VII. In the castle park stand memorials by J. Wiedeveldt to famous Danes, Norwegians and Holsteiners. The King's consort, Countess Danner, owned a fashion house before her marriage; she is buried in the park, and there are commemorative rooms in the south wing. North of the castle lie the beautiful Nordskoven, or Northern Woods.

Jægerspris Castle

Selsø Castle, further to the south on Roskilde Fjord, is also worth a visit. The castle was built in the Renaissance style and later converted to the Baroque; note the Knights' Hall with its stuccoed ceiling, the paintings of battles and the two large mirrors.

Selsø Castle

Driving north from Frederikssund along ths shores of Roskilde Fjord the visitor will come to the port and industrial town of Frederiksværk, with its iron and steel works. On the site of the former powder and cannon factory stands the Krudtværk Museum ("krudt" is Danish for powder), with implements dating from the period when the factory was built. In the market-place stands the sculpture "Woman Foundry-worker", by Axel Poulsen (1956).

Frederiksværk

On the shore to the north of Frederiksværk lie the popular resorts of Liseleje and Tisvildeleje and betweem them stretches the "Tisvilde Hegn", a woodland area which was originally planted in order to stabilise the shifting sand of the dunes.

Liseleje Tisvildeleje

To the west of Frederiksværk, on a spit of land at the confluence of the Isefjord and the Kattegat, will be found the fishing village of Hundested, once the home of the polar explorer Knud Rasmussen (1879–1933). At the Spodsbjerg Lighthouse (view) there is a Knud Rasmussen Museum with souvenirs of the explorer and his expeditions.

Hundested

Nykøbing Sjælland, on Nykøbing Bay on the far side of the Isefjord, is one of the oldest trading-posts in Denmark. The Anneberg Collection on Egebergvej is considered to be one of the most important collections of

Nykøbing Sjælland

antique glass in northern Europe. The Oddsherred Local Museum has interiors representing peasants' and fishermens' houses; adjoining is a bakery museum. Sommerland Sjælland is an amusement park and aquascape, with over 60 activities (open: mid-May–end Aug.).

Funen/Fyn   B/C 3/4

District: Fyns amt
Area: 3482sq.km/1344sq.miles
Population: 398,000

Situation and Topography

Funen, Fyn in Danish, the second largest island of Denmark, lies between Jutland and Zealand. Its west coast is washed by the Little Belt, the east coast by the Great Belt. The area is generally flat; only in the south-west is there a wooded morain ridge known as the "Funen Alps". The fertile marl soil yields an abundance of agricultural produce, which has resulted in the island being called the "Garden of Denmark".

Funen can be reached from Jutland by one of the two bridges spanning the Little Belt. The older of the two (1935), to the south, is a reinforced concrete structure 1178m/1300yd long with a clear height above the water of 33m/108ft. The newer bridge (1970), to the north within sight of the older one, is Denmark's first suspension bridge; it is 1080m/1200yd long, with a span of 600m/650yd and a clear height of 42m/138ft.

Towns to visit

The cultural centre of Funen is Odense (see entry), the birthplace of Hans Christian Andersen. The coastal towns of Middelfart, Nyborg, Fåborg and Svendborg (see entries) are also worth seeing.

Greenland/Grønland/Kalaallit Nunaat

Autonomous Region
Area: 2,175,600sq.km/839,782sq.miles
Population: 55,000

Situation and Topography

Greenland (Danish Grønland, Greenlandic Kalaallit Nunaat), the largest island in the world, is situated north-east of the North American continent; it lies between latitude 59°46' and 83°39' north and longitude 11°39' and 73°8' west. In the west the island is separated from the Canadian Archipelago by Davis Strait, Baffin Bay and Smith Sound, in the east from Spitzbergen by the Greenland Sea and from Iceland by the Denmark Strait.

By its nature the island forms part of the Arctic; 85% of the surface is covered by a gigantic sheet of ice averaging some 1500m/4900ft in thickness. The ice-free area, 341,700sq.km/132,000sq.miles in extent or 15% of the whole, lies principally on the coast; this is a region of fjords and skerries, the land resembling the Alps (although in the north and north-west there are also plateaux), reaching heights of 1200–1500m/3950–

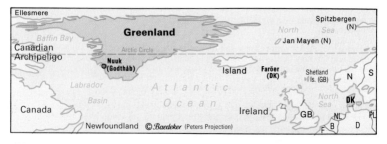

4930ft. The highest point is the Gunnbjørn Field (3733m/12,252ft) in the east of Greenland. Disko Island lies off the west coast.
There is an air service between Denmark and Greenland throughout the year.

In the parts of the country close to the edges of the ice the vegetation consists mostly of birch and alder trees with junipers and rhodendrons. Further north the vegetation is characterised by polar pasture, grasses, mosses and lichens.
Animals, found mainly on the coasts, include reindeer, foxes and hares; in the north and east there are also musk-oxen, Arctic wolves, polar bears and lemmings. In the coastal waters seals, whales and walruses abound as well as about 100 kinds of fish. More than 200 species of birds get their food from the sea. Eagles, falcons and snowy owls are protected species.

Flora and fauna

As is usual in countries with ice and tundra there are considerable differences in climate. In the interior and in the north of Greenland conditions of extreme polar temperatures hold sway, whereas in the south the weather is milder but there is more precipitation. Generally speaking, the best and most stable weather conditions are to be found in the innermost fjord regions and in Disko Bay.
On the east coast the cold East Greenland current keeps the temperatures low. As the air over Greenland is mainly dry temperatures are viewed in a somewhat different light, 15°C/59°F is regarded as very warm indeed!.

Climate

The earliest inhabitants of Greenland were Eskimos (Inuit). In 982 Eric the Red, a Norwegian Viking, landed on the island and named it Greenland, although it had already been discovered in 875 by the Norman Gunnbjorn. From 1261 the island was subject to the Norwegian Crown. Most of the European settlers succumbed to the wretched living conditions in the Middle Ages, and not until the missionary Hans Egede landed in 1721 on

History

Drift ice on the Bredefjord near Narsaq

Greenland
Grønland

Kalaallit
Nunaat

250 km

© Baedeker

Girls in tradtional Greenland costume

the west coast in the region of present-day Nuuk did Greenland again become settled by Europeans.

When Norway and Denmark separated in 1814 Greenland remained Danish. A dispute about the island in 1933 was settled by the International Court of Justice in the Hague in favour of Denmark. During the Second World War the United States established air bases on Greenland. In 1963 it became part of the Kingdom of Denmark with equal rights, and since 1985 it has enjoyed internal autonomy; Denmark represents the interests of the country in the fields of foreign policy and defence.

The legislative body is the Parliament (Landsråd) which is composed of elected representatives; general elections are held every four years. Executive power lies in the hands of the Government (Landsstyre), chosen by Parliament. The electorate also sends two members to the Danish parliament (the Folketing).

Greenland has its own flag, in red and white. The round disc symbolises the midnight sun setting in the sea. The flag, the result of a worldwide competition to decide on the design, was first raised on June 21st 1985, the Day of the Midnight Sun. The island's coat-of-arms – a polar bear argent on a white ground – symbolises the "Land of the Polar Bears".

Population

The people known as "Greenlanders" have developed from a mixture of Eskimos and Europeans. In addition there are a few pure-blooded Eskimos and Europeans. In Greenland both the local language and Danish are spoken. Greenlandic is derived from the language of the Eskimos and the written language is several hundred years old. Many of the younger people also speak English.

Economy

The principal branches of the economy are fishing and fish-processing, together with seal-hunting and sheep-rearing. Lead, zinc and silver are mined in Marmorilik. Many people work at home, producing objects in

129

stone, wood, bone, skin and pearls. In recent years a modest tourist industry has developed but it is not yet by any means a centre of mass tourism.
The Royal Greenland Trading Company which, from 1774, supplied Greenland with imported goods and which was supported until the end of 1985
by the Danish State, has been named "Kalaallit Niuerfiat (Greenland Trade)
since January 1st 1986, when its headquarters were transferred from
Copenhagen to Nuuk (Danish Godthåb).

Holiday Areas

Most vacation areas are on the west coast, which has the mildest climate.
Prominent features of coastal towns are fishing vessels and small, gaily
painted wooden houses. Icebergs move into the sea from the coastal
waters.

Southern
Greenland

Narsarsuaq in southern Greenland is a base for walking tours; information
about these can be obtained from tourist offices and hotels. Excursions to
sights in the vicinity include those to ruins of the period 985–1500, including the Hvalsey Viking Church, to the inland ice and to fishing settlements. There is also a South Greenland Programme which includes a stay
in Narsaq, Qaqortoq/Julienehåb and Nanortalik. Nanortalik is a busy place,
especially in early summer when seals swim along the coast. A visit to the
museum in the Old Town is recommended, and popular excursions include
those to the mountains near Nanortalik and the islands off the coast with
their colonies of birds.

Nuuk/Godthåb

Nuuk/Godthåb, population 13,000 and the capital and administrative centre of Greenland, is also a popular place with visitors. The town has a
number of schools, specialist shops and cafés.
The Local Museum is of interest; it contains a collection of hunting-equip-
ment, kayaks, carvings and Viking finds, and also mounts exhibitions of
geology, applied arts and folk-art. Visitors will also be interested in the
mummies of women and children which were found in 1978 in the grave of
Qilakitsoq near Uummannaq; they are so well preserved that some of the
facial tattoos and the various colours of the material of the 15th c. clothes
are still recognisable. Note Hans Egede's house in the Old Harbour (see
History).

Nuuk is the starting-point for tours of the Godthåb Fjord, one of Greenland's most beautiful regions. Here there is a mild climate, with grass and
flowers growing on the cliffs; fishing is possible.

Sisimiut/
Holsteinsborg

On the west coast north of Nuuk lies Sisimiut, a fishing port with a wharf.
East from here at the end of the fjord lies Kangerlussuaq/Strømfjord, with
Greenland's major airport. Between Nuuk and Sondre Strømfjord walking
tours (including a visit to the inland ice) are organised and in winter there
are safaris on skis. To the south, near Manitsoq, there is a ski centre.

Disko Island

Disko Island lies off the west coast of Greenland, and Disko Bay is to the
south of the island. Qeqertarsuag/Godhavn, the largest place on Disko
Island, was once a base for whalers. Nearby the University of Copenhagen
has set up a research station with the aim of studying biological and
ecological conditions in the Arctic.

Ilulissat/
Jacobshavn

On Disko Bay lies Ilulissat/Jacobshavn, a section of coast where huge
glaciers "calve", meaning that icebergs break off from them and float out
into the coastal waters. Holidaymakers can watch this natural spectacle.
The Danish explorer Knud Johan Victor Rasmussen (1879–1933), the son of
a pastor, was born in Jacobshavn; the family's wooden house is now a
museum.

Tasiilaq/
Ammassalik

For a long time few visitors came to the eastern side of Greenland because
of the severe climate. Today, however, Tasiilaq/Ammassalik is the destination of short trips from Iceland. In addition to the impressive landscape
visitors will find some beautiful traditional handicrafts.

Nuuk/Godthåb, the chief place on Greenland

There are only two towns on the east coast of Greenland. Near the second of these, Ittoqqortoormiit/Scoresbysund, stretches the world's largest National Park, covering an area of 972,000sq.km/375,000sq.miles, or more than Great Britain and France combined. Examples of almost all Greenland's fauna are to be found here – polar bears, musk-oxen, walruses, sea-lions, foxes and numerous birds.

National Park

In 1910 Knud Rasmussen and Peter Freuchen founded a trading-post in north-west Greenland and named it after the legendary island of Thule, which is said to have existed north of the British Isles. The US air base of Dundas, which was set up on the site of the old trading-post during the Second World War, has since been extended. The village of Thule (Greenlandic Oaanaaq) was moved north in 1953 to Murchison Sound, 200km/120 miles to the north, because the noise of aircraft disturbed the seals and birds on which the Eskimos depend for their living. Present-day Greenlanders are in the main descendents of the Thule Eskimos.

North-west Greenland

From Thule Rasmussen undertook seven expeditions into the Arctic where he investigated the various Eskimo tribes and researched their myths and legends especially those relating to their mutual interests. In 1921–24 he crossed the American Arctic as far as the Bering Strait. "Knud Rasmussen Land", in northern Greenland, is named after him; he died in Copenhagen in 1933.

Grenå

C 2

Jutland
District: Århus amt
Population: 19,000

Grenå

The resort of Grenå, the centre of a popular holiday region, lies on the Kattegat on the coast of the Djursland peninsula, part of Jutland. From the town, which is important as a ferry and fishing port, car ferries leave for Varberg and Halmstad in Sweden. There are excursion ships to the island of Anholt (see entry). Two districts of Grenå are of importance – the town centre and the harbour area.

Sights

Danish Museum of Fisheries/ Djursland Museum

This attractive place boasts many old half-timbered houses, in one of which (Torvet, dating from 1750) at Søndergade 1 in the market-place, can be found the Danish Museum of Fisheries (Dansk Fiskerimuseum) and the Djursland Museum. The Fisheries Museum provides an insight into the history of the Danish fishing industry and also has a collection of model ships. There is a separate department devoted to eel-fishing. The Djursland Museum displays coins and beautiful Danish pottery from the 17th to 20th c., together with an exhibition documenting archaeological digs which have been carried out in recent years (open: mid-June–end of Aug. Tue.–Fri, 10am–4pm, Sat. 10am–1pm, Sun. 1–4pm; rest of the year Tue.–Fri. and Sun. 1–4pm).

Old Smithy

Near the Town Hall is an old smithy (Den Gamle Smedje), which was set up in 1849 and now forms part of the Djursland Museum. From June–Sept. visitors can watch the blacksmith at work every Wed. 1–3.30pm.

*Kattegatcentret

One of Grenå's special attractions is the new Kattegatcentret near the harbour, an impressive modern building with several aquaria where fish of every kind including tropical sharks, and other marine creatures can be observed. In a "Science Center" adults and children can perform experiments and another section provides information about underwater life.

A holiday complex "Djurs Sommerland" near Grenå

Surroundings

A few miles north-east of the town lies Fornæs, the most easterly point in Jutland, where a lighthouse was built in 1892. From here an excursion can be made to Sostrup Slot near Gjerrild in northern Djursland. This castle, built about 1600, was taken over by Cistercian nuns in 1960 and extensively renovated. It is surrounded by a park containing holiday homes which visitors can rent.

Sostrup Castle

25km/15 miles inland from Grenå at Nimtofte is Djurs Sommerland, a theme park near the beautiful Løvenholm Woods (Løvenholm Skov). The attractions for young and old include gold-panning in "cowboy country" and an aquapark (open: mid-May–end of Aug.).

Djurs Sommerland

Haderslev   B 3

Jutland
District: Sønderjyllands amt
Population: 40,000

Haderslev, an industrial and commercial town, lies in the south of Jutland on the narrow Haderslev Fjord which penetrates inland from the east and is fed by several small rivers.

Situation

Haderslev was founded, probably in the middle of the 12th c., at a fork in the road where there was also a ford and developed into an important town and ecclesiastical centre. Because of its position, the town was involved on several occasions in the wars for the Duchies of Schleswig and Holstein. Between 1864 and 1920 Haderslev belonged to the Prussian province of Schleswig-Holstein. When the Duchy of Schleswig was divided up in 1920, Haderslev became Danish.

History

Sights

The Cathedral (Church of Our Lady; Vor Frue Kirke/Domkirke), dating from the 13th–15th c. and built of brick, stands high on a hill. The interior is notable for its light choir, a bronze font (1485) by Peter Hansen, the altar with a Romanesque crucifix (c. 1300), statues of Mary and John and alabaster figures of the Apostles.
In nearby Slotsgade are some old half-timbered houses from the 16th c.; No. 20 contains a collection of beautiful pottery and ceramics, as well as domestic items and 16th c. wall-paintings.

Cathedral

Ehler's
Collection
(ceramics)

The Haderslev Museum in Dalgade consists of an open-air section with half-timbered farmhouses from East Schleswig and a windmill, as well as an indoor section which covers the prehistoric period of South Jutland. This comprises weapons and flint tools, Bronze Age gold dishes and cult objects, as well as a copy of the dress worn by the "Skrydstrup Maiden" found in an oak coffin in 1935 can be seen here.

*Haderslev
Museum

Surroundings

On the A10 north of the town lies Christiansfeld, a town founded by the Moravian Brethren with the consent of King Christian VII in 1773. The town is impressive in its simplicity and has many mementoes of the Brotherhood from Saxony – the Brødremenighedens Kirke (church) of 1776, plain and undecorated, the interior whitewashed; the cemetery subdivided into large

Christiansfeld

View of the Cathedral of Haderslev

plots and the Brotherhood Museum with ethnographical collections of their missionary work. In the cellar is housed the South Jutland Fire Brigade Museum.

Helsingør

E 2/3

Zealand
District: Frederiksborg amt
Population: 57,000

Situation

The old Danish port and trading town of Helsingør (more familiar in English as Hamlet's Elsinore) lies in the north-east of the island of Zealand, only 4·5km/3 miles from the Swedish town of Helsingborg on the other side of the Øresund; a bridge is planned.

History

The origins of the town can be traced back to the first half of the 13th c. After the Norwegians had burned down the settlement in 1288 King Erik of Pomerania began, in 1420, to build a new castle on the outermost spit of land; this castle was called "Krogen" or "Ørekrog". In 1426 the town was granted its charter. Erik introduced tolls for vessels passing through the Øresund; both banks of the channel then belonged to Denmark and every ship which sailed through the Sound had to pay a toll; this lasted until 1857. The King made the town an ecclesiastical centre and three monasteries were founded. When, in 1658, the easterly provinces of the country (Schonen, etc.) fell to Sweden, Helsingør lost much of its former importance. During the 17th c. several epidemics led to a decline in population. At the end of the 18th c. English and Scottish merchants settled in Helsingør; the town obtained a land link with Copenhagen. Since the end of the 19th century many holiday villas have sprung up

Copenhagen, Fredensborg, Humlebæk

between Helsingør and Copenhagen and tourism has benefited the town considerably.

Helsingør possesses a shipyard as well as engineering, brewing and textile industries. A rail ferry plies across the Øresund to Helsingborg.

Economy

The town is divided into an inner district, a north-western and a north-eastern area where, on a peninsula, stands Kronborg Castle .

The town

Inner Town

The railway station, post office and tourist information office lie opposite the terminal of the Danish Railways ferry. North of the railway station lies Harbour Square with the Swedish Pillar (Danish "Sveasøjlen"); 11·75m/ 39ft high, it was erected in 1947 as an expression of gratitude to Sweden for taking in Danish refugees in the Second World War. Many of these refugees were able to flee across the Øresund.

To the north-east lies Stengade, the main street of Helsingør and the main artery of a pedestrian zone. The street is lined with fine old houses. The

Town Hall

135

Town Hall (1855) has glass mosaics in the Council Chamber with motifs depicting the town's history; they date from 1936–39 and are by Poul and Fanny Sæbye. On Strandgade, which marks the eastern edge of the pedestrian zone, more beautiful houses are to be seen, including the Old Pharmacy (1577 and 1642) at Nos. 77–79 and the Court Building (1520) at Nos. 72–74.

St Olaf's Church
St Olaf's Church, a Late Gothic brick edifice, was completed 1480–1559. Note the remains of its Romanesque predecessor, the Baptistery with paintings by Joakim Skovgaard, the Chapel of the Holy Trinity and numerous epitaphs. The church has been a cathedral since 1961.

St Mary's Church
Well worth seeing is St Mary's Church, about 150m/165yd further north in Skt. Anna Gade. Built in the Late Middle Ages, the church boasts a fine interior and a magnificent organ. The composer Dietrich Buxtehude (1637–1707) was organist here between 1660 and 1668 and lived at Skt. Anna Gade 6. St Mary's Church forms the south wing of a Carmelite monastery, built about 1430 and later restored. The courtyard, enclosed on all sides by open arcades, the church and the chapter-house are the venues for concerts and lectures.

Municipal Museum
The Helsingør Municipal Museum (Bymuseum), housed in the former poorhouse near the monastery portrays history of the town from the Middle Ages by means of historical documents, a model of the town as it was in 1801, and a doll collection.

Axeltorv
Axeltorv, to the west of Skt. Anna Gade, is the town's main square where the fountain by Einar Utzon-Frank (1926) was erected in memory of King Erik of Pomerania who gave Helsingør its charter. A market is held in Axeltorv on Wednesdays and Sundays, and from May to October there is also an antique market each Friday.

North-western District

Veteran Railway
On Sundays between June and September steam trains ply between Grønnehavevej on the North Harbour (Nordhavnen) and Gilleje, a distance of 24km/15 miles.

Øresund Aquarium
On Strandpromenaden lies the Øresund Aquarium, with ten types of marine animals found in the Sound. Their biosphere includes sand-flats, a rocky reef, the wreck of a sunken galleon and mud from the deepest part of the Sound (open: daily noon–4pm).

Mansion of Marienlyst
From Axeltorv we proceed in a north-westerly direction through Nygade and Marienlyst Allé to the Mansion of Marienlyst. Originally built in 1587 and conceived as an observation pavilion overlooking the Sound, it was reconstructed after 1760 by Nicolas Henri Jardin for Queen Juliane Marie, the widow of Frederik V. Today the mansion, surrounded by a park, serves as a museum with Louis XVI furniture. In the park is a commemorative grave for the Danish Prince Hamlet, a granite sarcophagus by the sculptor Einar Utzon-Frank and erected here in 1926.

Technical Museum
On Nordre Strandvej stands the Danish Museum of Technology (Danmarks Tekniske Museum), adjoining which is a Transport Museum. The museums portray the development of natural science and technology as well as transport from its origins to the present day. On display are models of aircraft, trains of the Danish State Railway, trams and buses including the Danish "Hammelvognen" (1886) and Ellehammers aeroplane (1906). There is also a collection devoted to the astronomer Ole Rømer. The museum also mounts special exhibitions (open: daily 10am–5pm).

North-eastern District

**Kronborg Castle
In the north-east of the town, on a peninsula in the Øresund, towers Kronborg Castle, a landmark visible from afar. Originally a fortress built

Kronborg Castle

about 1420 by Erik of Pomerania stood here. The new castle – a four-winged edifice with an enclosed inner courtyard – was built between 1574 and 1584 under Frederik II, by the Dutch architects Hans van Paescheng and Anthonis van Opbergen. After a catastrophic fire in 1629 King Christian IV had the castle rebuilt between 1635 and 1640, finance being provided by raising the tolls on ships passing through the Øresund. For over a hundred years the castle served as a garrison; in 1924 it was renovated. In the south wing is the Castle Chapel, which survived the fire of 1629; it has a

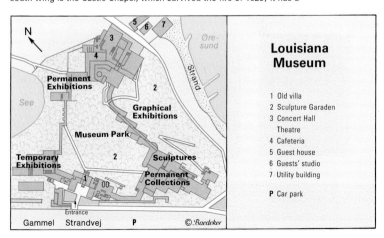

Louisiana Museum

1 Old villa
2 Sculpture Garaden
3 Concert Hall
   Theatre
4 Cafeteria
5 Guest house
6 Guests' studio
7 Utility building

P Car park

N

Øre-sund

Strand

Permanent Exhibitions

See

Graphical Exhibitions

Museum Park

Temporary Exhibitions

Sculptures

Permanent Collections

Entrance

Gammel   Strandvej   P   © *Baedeker*

magnificent Renaissance interior, with German woodcarvings. The North Wing contains the great Ballroom or Knights' Hall. Tapestries are on display in the West Wing.

Maritime Museum

The Danish Commercial and Maritime Museum which is also housed in the castle, celebrated its 75th anniversary in 1990. The collection illustrates the history of Danish maritime trade during the Colonial period and the development of ship-building. Separated rooms are devoted to trade with India and China, for example, or navigational instruments, etc. (open: 10.30 or 11am–4 or 5pm).

Ramparts

In the casemates (fortified walls) below the inner ramparts is a seated statue by H. P. Pedersen-Dan of the sleeping "Holger Danske", the national hero who, according to legend, will awaken only in the country's hour of need. A walk along the outer bastions can be recommended. The "platform before the castle" is that on which, in Shakespeare's "Hamlet", the ghost of the Danish king appears striding past the guard.

Southern Surroundings

Humlebæk:
** Louisiana Museum

10km/6 miles south of Helsingør, on the coast road, lies the village of Humlebæk. Here, in a park overlooking the Øresund, stands the Louisiana Museum of Art, founded in 1958 by the merchant and art-lover Knud W. Jensen, who instructed the architects Jørgen Bo and Vilhelm Wohlert to build a museum complex here which has since been extended on several occasions, the last time being when an underground Graphic Arts Wing was added. The ground floor of the museum complex is a former noble-man's house, built in 1860 and numbering among its previous occupants three gentlemen, each with a wife named Louise; as a result the house was called "Louisiana".

Yves Klein: Single colour panels in Louisiana Museum

Sculptures by Henry Moore in the park of the Lousiana Museum

The museum has a collection of Danish and international modern paintings, including works by Josef Albers, Georg Baselitz, Mark Rothko, Asger Jorn, Per Kirkeby, Max Bill, Sam Francis, Mark Tobey, Andy Warhol, Pablo Picasso and many others.

In the beautiful old park stand some exceptionally fine sculptures, including works by Hans Arp, Alexander Calder, Max Ernst, Alberto Giacometti, Henry Moore and Jean Tinguely. Every year – mainly in winter – there are special exhibitions of modern art. Concerts are frequently held here; bookshop and cafeteria. The museum is open daily 10am–5pm. Wed. to 10pm.

15km/9 miles along the A 6 to the south-west of Helsingør is the town of Fredensborg on the Esrumsø, with Fredensborg Castle (Fredensborg Slot). Built in 1719–22 in the Italian Baroque style, it is the spring and autumn residence of the Royal Family. King Frederik IV named the castle "Fredensborg" as a memorial to the peace which ended the Second Nordic War (1700–20). The castle in its present form, with its Classical façade, is the work of the architect Caspar Frederik Harsdorff. When the Queen is in residence the ceremony of the Changing of the Guard takes place every day at noon. The castle is open to visitors during June only (daily 1–5pm). ****Fredensborg Castle**

The park, extending north-west to Lake Esrum, was laid out by King Frederik IV. There are 69 statues of workers, farmers and fishermen and these, together with its fine avenues of birches, make this one of the most impressive parks in Denmark; it is open all the year round. ***Castle park**

From Helsingør to Gilleleje

The road leads past many seaside resorts to the northern tip of Zealand. Leave Helsingør on the Strandvej, passing the Mansion of Marielyst, and **Hornbæk**

Fredensborg Castle

after 4km/2½ miles Julabæk will come into view, with its old water-mill, the "Hammermøllen". This mill, built for Frederik II at the same time as Kronborg Castle, served for a time as an arms factory and was restored in the 1980s. From Hellebæk a stretch of coast road leads to the popular resort of Hornbæk.

Dronningmølle (Tegner Museum)

From Hornbæk the road continues through Villingbæk to Dronningmølle. 2km/1¼ miles south, in a nature reserve, is a museum containing paintings and sculptures by Rudolph Tegner (1873–1950). The artist, who lived and worked in Denmark and France, adopted a monumental style, using such materials as plaster, clay, bronze and marble. The museum – a pleasing blend of architecture, sculpture and nature – was designed by the artist himself. In the park stand statues, some on plinths, embodying mythological forms (such as "King Oedipus") or people of his time ("My wife Elna"). Open: during the holiday season Tue.–Sun. 9.30am–5pm.

Gilleleje

Shortly before Gilleleje, on a high cliff to the right of the road, can be seen Nakkehoved Lighthouse (54m/177ft; extensive views). From here it is 4km/2½ miles to Gilleleje, an old fishing village and popular holiday resort. From the breakwater there are good views over the Kattegat to the Swedish coast. Items of local interest, such as fishing equipment, costumes, etc., are displayed in the Gilleleje Museum at Rostgaardsvej 2 (open: June 15th–Sept. 15th Tue.–Sun. 2–5pm). About 1km/½ mile west lies Gilbjerg Hoved, the most northerly point on Zealand.

Herning

A/B 2

Jutland
District: Ringkøbing amt
Population: 57,000

The town of Herning lies on Jutland Heath between Ringkøbing and Silkeborg, and is the centre of the Danish textile industry. At the end of the 17th c. there were just a few farms here, but in the 19th c. Herning developed quickly to become an important centre of communications and industrial enterprises were established. Large numbers of fairs and exhibitions are now held in the town.

Situation

Sights

Sculptures placed along the streets and in the squares help to add colour and atmosphere to the town. They include works by famous sculptors such as Henry Moore ("A Woman Seated", near the Congress Centre), Carl Visser, Erik Heide, Ole Christensen, Jørgen Haugen Sørensen, Helge Holm Skov and Yonghin Han.

Sculptures

In the Municipal Museum at Museumsgade 32 the life of the once-poor people of the heathland is presented by means of reconstructed farmhouse interiors and wax figures dressed in period costumes. The Knitting Room gives an impression of the way the textile industry has developed; piecework knitting at home was at one time essential for the peasant's survival. A visit is also recommended to the exhibition called "A Year on Jens Nielsen's Farm", mounted by the lady artist Inge Faurtoft. Nearly 70 scenes using tiny figures in peepshow cases create a three-dimensional picture, helping to convey an idea of family life from ploughing in spring, through to Christmas. Outside stand an old farmhouse, smithy and cottage, typical of the region (open: Tue.–Fri. 10am–5pm and Sun. noon–5pm).

Municipal Museum

At Museumsgade 28 lies Denmark's Photographic Museum. Here visitors can see a panoramic photograph of Copenhagen measuring 100 by 1170cm/3ft 4in. by 39ft 6in., as well as a collection of holographs (open: Tue.–Sun. 1–5pm; Mon. also during July).

Photographic Museum

The Herningsholm Mansion, a major historical building in central Jutland, also merits a visit. After careful restoration it was equipped as a museum in 1980 to commemorate the author Steen Steensen Blicher (1782–1848), the writer of popular novels on life in the region and known affectionately as the "Poet of the Heathland". The exhibits include illustrations by Danish artists for inclusion in his books, first editions and original manuscripts (open: May 1st–Oct. 31st Tue.–Sun. 11am–4pm).

Blicher Museum (Herningsholm)

3km/2 miles east of the town centre at Birk, lies the Angligården, the building of a former textile factory. Built to plans by Carl Theodor Sørensen and Christian Frederik Møller the house had a circular layout; in the inside courtyard is an interesting 200m/650ft ceramic frieze "Phantasy Playing round the Wheel of Life", by Carl Henning Pedersen. The art collection has works by Danish masters, including Asger Jorn, Robert Jacobsen, Svend Dalsgaard, Paul Gadegaard and Richard Mortensen, as well as pictures by foreign artists such as Piero Manzoni and Victor Vasarely (open: Tue.–Sun. noon–5pm; June and July also open Mon.).

*Herning Art Museum

In the adjoining circular Sculpture Park can be seen a number of sculptures dating from the 1950s, by both Danish and foreign sculptors. Near the park are the Geometric Gardens, laid out by the Danish landscape architect C. Sørensen who was also responsible for the Sculpture Park.

Sculpture Park

Close to this complex stands a museum which was opened in 1976 and displays works by the Danish artists Carl-Henning Pedersen and Else Alfelt; both were members of the international body of artists known as COBRA. Here, too, the external wall is decorated with a ceramic frieze by Pedersen which is reflected in a moat surrounding the building.

Pedersen Alfelt Museum

Pedersen-Alfelt Museum, with its ceramic frieze

Surroundings

Rind Kirke

A few miles south of the town along the A 18 on the edge of a wood can be found a Romanesque church, Rind Kirke, which is about 800 years old.

Jutland's Minizoo

12km/7½ miles west of Herning, near Havnstrup, is Jutland's Minizoo (Jyllands Mini-Zoo; open: Apr.–Sept.).

Hillerød   E 3

Zealand
District: Frederiksborg amt
Population: 34,000

Situation

The town of Hillerød, a railway junction, lies in the north of the island of Zealand, not far from Helsingør and Copenhagen (see entries).

History

Hillerød became a settlement in the early Middle Ages. Some years later a nobleman built a mansion on an island in what is now the castle lake; this house was acquired by Frederik II (1559–88) who wanted to use the area for hunting. In 1562 the king built a castle and called it "Frederiksborg". However, the king's son, Christian IV (1588–1648) had it pulled down and a new one built between 1602 and 1620 in the Renaissance style, to designs by Hans van Steenwinkel the Elder and his son. During the period of Absolutism all Danish kings were anointed in the castle church, the last being Christian VIII in 1840. The town of Hillerød also came into being in the time of Christian IV.

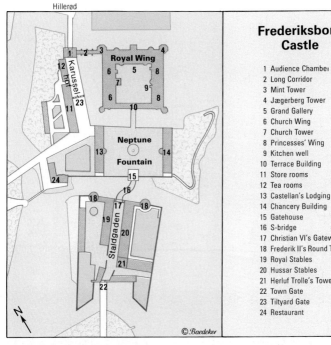

Frederiksborg Castle

1 Audience Chamber
2 Long Corridor
3 Mint Tower
4 Jægerberg Tower
5 Grand Gallery
6 Church Wing
7 Church Tower
8 Princesses' Wing
9 Kitchen well
10 Terrace Building
11 Store rooms
12 Tea rooms
13 Castellan's Lodging
14 Chancery Building
15 Gatehouse
16 S-bridge
17 Christian VI's Gateway
18 Frederik II's Round Towers
19 Royal Stables
20 Hussar Stables
21 Herluf Trolle's Tower
22 Town Gate
23 Tiltyard Gate
24 Restaurant

© Baedeker

In 1658, during the war with Sweden, King Frederik III and Karl X of Sweden met at Frederiksborg. On their departure in 1658, the Swedes sacked the castle and, among other things, took away the Fountain of Neptune by Adrian de Vries (1623). Later the castle was used only as a summer residence. When the Royal Family gave preference to Fredensborg (see Helsingør) the heyday of Frederiksborg was finally past.

There has been a stud in Hillerød since 1720 and the Frederiksborg horse has always been important in Danish breeding.

**Frederiksborg Castle

Frederiksborg Castle lies on three islands in the little Frederiksborg Lake. The castle, restored in its original style after a fire in 1859, is considered to be the epitome of Danish Renaissance architecture. Since 1888 the main courtyard has been adorned with a copy of the fountain by Adrian de Vries. After the completion of Fredensborg Castle, Frederiksborg gradually acquired the character of a museum in the course of the 18th and 19th c. and the Knights' Hall was turned into a picture gallery. (Open: daily 10 or 11am–3, 4 or 5pm).

The actual castle is situated on the third island. It has three wings – the north Royal Wing, the west Chapel Wing and the east Princesses' Wing. A low Terrace Wing joins it to the central island. Since 1877 it has been furnished as a Museum of National History, with financial assistance

Main building
(Museum)

143

bestowed in accordance with the scientific and artistic aims of the Carlsberg Fund. The museum provides the visitor with an overall view of Danish history and culture by means of pictures, portraits, valuable furniture and *objets d'art*.

The castle church in the West Wing escaped damage in the fire of 1859. The nave with its Gothic stellar vaulting is supported on columns of gilded sandstone. The magnificent interior includes marble inlay and alabaster figures, pews with marquetry inlay, an ebony pulpit, a silver font and an organ with a fine tone; organ concerts are given in the church.

Castle church

Interesting rooms in the castle include the Knights' Chamber – with groined vaulting, carved chests and cabinets – and the Knights' Hall (originally the Ballroom) above the castle church; the latter is decorated with superb ornaments and silver figures, while the ceiling is adorned with expensive wood-carvings. Unfortunately, tapestries portraying the Coronation of 1596 fell victim to a fire. The chandeliers were designed around 1900 by the architect Carl Brummer. Portraits of Christian IX and other Danish kings also hang in the Hall.

Knights' Hall

The early 19th c. saw a blossoming of Danish literature, art and science. Portraits of well-known personalities of the period can be seen in Room 55, including those of the sculptor Bertel Thorvaldsen, the poet Adam Oehlenschläger, the physicist H. C. Ørsted and Nicolai Frederik Grundtvig, founder of the Adult Education Movement. Also of interest is the painting of the inaugural meeting of the Imperial Assembly in Room 61 on October 23rd 1848 when Denmark's new constitution was formulated.

Portraits of famous people

North of the castle, beyond the lake, lies the park, with terraces and avenues bordered by lime trees. It is considered one of the most outstanding Baroque designs in the north of the country.

Castle park

Surroundings

In the direction of Frederiksværk, 6km/4 miles west of the town, is the unusual Æbelholt Monastic Museum, housed in the ruins of a monastery. Human skeletons dating from the Middle Ages give clues to diseases which were then common and to the healing methods used. There is a garden with medicinal herbs.

Æbelholt Monastic Museum

To the north of Hillerød stretches the Gribskov, a wood with oak, beech and birch trees. A monument stands in memory of the philosopher Søren Kierkegaard, who loved to walk through these woods.

Gribskov

Himmelbjerg   E 2

Jutland
Altitude: 147m/482ft

The Himmelbjerg (Heaven Mountain), which has long been considered the highest hill in Denmark, overlooks Lake Julsø in Central Jutland.
From the 25m/82ft high observation tower, erected in 1874 in honour of Frederik VII, there is a splendid view of the surrounding forests and lakes which stretch as far as Skanderborg in the east. Various other viewpoints are linked with one another by paths through the forest. Many political and religious meetings took place here during the 19th c. and these are commemorated by a number of monuments. One such monument is in memory of the poet Steen Steensen Blicher (see Herning).
During the summer months the paddle-steamer "Hjejlen" sails on Lake

Situation and
*scenery

◀ *Frederiksborg Castle*

The paddle-steamer "Hjejlen" on Lake Julsø

Julsø as far as Silkeborg, passing through two smaller lakes, Borresø and Brassø, on the way.

Gammel Rye

An enjoyable excursion can be made to Gammel Rye, a distance of 15km/9½ miles along the southern slopes of the Himmelbjerg. During the Middle Ages there was a miracle-working spring here to which pilgrims flocked and also a church dedicated to St George. In the summer of 1534 secular and ecclesiastical dignitaries assembled in Gammel Rye to elect Christian III as king. Near the town is the Gudenå Museum, housing a private collection which will give the visitor an idea of life in the region bordering the Gudenå river.

Hjørring   B/C 1

Jutland
District: Nordjyllands amt
Population: 35,000

Situation

The old town of Hjørring, the capital of the Vendsyssel district north of the Limfjord, is an industrial centre.

History

The hill, which still forms the central point of the town, was a place of assembly during the whole of the Middle Ages; it was here that the "Thing" (Council) of Vendsyssel was held. The oldest known privileges of the town date from 1243. When assemblies of the "Thing" ceased at the beginning of the 16th c. a period of decline set in.

In the 19th c. the fortunes of Hjørring improved; the economy thrived and industries came to the town, including dyeworks, iron-foundries, etc. In the middle of the 19th c. the roads to Hjørring were improved and in 1871 the town was linked to the regional rail network.

Sights

Some 18th c. half-timbered houses are to be found in the older quarters of the town. These include the Provestgården (Presbytery), the Købmand Riis' Gård, a listed building, and a magnificent merchant's dwelling, J. P. Jacobsens Gård. The Plejestiftelsen in Overgade is a finely proportioned building erected in 1858 as a poor-house.

Half-timbered houses

In the Old Town three churches stand close together. St Catharine's Church (c. 1250), basically a Romanesque edifice, is situated on Kirkestræde. The original gable was replaced in the 18th c. by curved North Jutland Baroque gables. Of interest inside, are the 13th c. Gothic crucifix and the carved altar-panel in Baroque scrollwork dating from 1650.

St Catharine's Church

The Historical Museum of Vendsyssel (Vendyssels Historiske Museum) at Museumsgade 3 is housed in several old buildings, including a presbytery; it is surrounded by a garden with prehistoric tombstones and herbal plants. On view are items from the prehistoric epoch together with ecclesiastical art, agricultural items and decorative crafts (open: daily July and Aug. 10am–5pm; May and June 11am–4pm; rest of year 1–4pm).

Historical Museum

Hjørring also has a Museum of Art (Kunstmuseum) at Brinck Seidelingsgade 10, with paintings, lithographs and a few sculptures. The emphasis is on contemporary Danish art, with particular reference to North Jutland. The visitor will find works by Poul Winther, Agnete Bjerre, Poul Ekelund, Svend Engelund, Arne L. Hansen and many others. Note particularly the collection of work by the embroideress Berit Hjelholt, the ceramic artist Tove Anderberg and the goldsmith Bent Exner (open: Tue.–Sun. 10 or 11am–4 or 5pm).

Museum of Art

Surroundings

North of the town on the Skagerrak lies the port of Hirtshals. From the harbour, which was constructed between 1919 and 1930 and extended in 1966, there is a ferry service to Kristiansand in Norway. The fish-processing industry is of considerable importance. In Hirtshals is the North Sea Museum (Nordsømuseet) devoted to fishing and marine biology. As well as archives the museum has salt-water pools for seals and dolphins (open: daily 10am–4pm). Sand-dunes lie to the east of Hirtshals.

Hirtshals

Driving west from Hjørring we reach the coast the fishing village of Lønstrup. In nearby Mårup Church can be seen the anchor of a stranded English frigate, a memento of the many shipwrecks in Jammer Bay. The shifting sands in this area have also caused much damage. The Sandflugtsmuseum (Shifting Sands Museum) in a former lighthouse at Rubjerg Knude, a steeply sloping bank, gives details of the movement of the sands. The lighthouse has been out of commission since 1968, as the movement of the sand resulted in new dunes being formed between the North Sea and the lighthouse.

Lønstrup; Rubjerg Knude

To the south on Jammer Bay lies the popular resort of Løkken, with a fine wide beach along which it is possible to drive (subject to a strict speed limit) to the resort of Blokhus, about 16km/10 miles away.

Løkken Blokhus

Near Saltum, between Løkken and Blokhus, the Fårum Sommerland theme park is the largest in Denmark. It offers a huge range of attractions on land and water, from jungle trails to speedboats, water chutes, a traffic school and a trip on the "Colorado River" (open: daily, mid-May to August, 10am–6, 7 or 8pm).

Fårup Aquapark and Sommerland

It is worth while visiting the Premonstratensian Monastery of Børglum, some 6km/4 miles to the east of Løkken. This dates from the 12th c. and until well into that century it was a Royal Court. Part of the building was converted about 1150 into a diocesan centre. In the mid-18th c. the entire

Børglum Monastery

In Hirtshals Harbour

complex was restored by the Danish architect Laurids de Thura and converted to a Baroque mansion. Visitors can see the courtyard and the monastic church which was left unaltered and is a good example of Early Gothic. The church has some remarkable Rococo furnishings.

Hobro B 2

Jutland
District: Nordjyllands amt
Population: 14,000

The old town of Hobro lies at the western end of Mariager Fjord, surrounded by heath and farmland. Its woods and meadows, lakes, coastal inlets and yacht basin make it an attractive holiday region, especially for amateur sailors.

History

Hobro came into being where a bridge crossed the fjord; this can be seen in the town arms of 1584. In the 18th c. the town became important for maritime trade and from 1859 there were regular shipping links with Copenhagen. After the harbour was made deeper in 1910–13 Hobro developed into an industrial town (foodstuffs, engineering).

Sights

Church

The church was built in 1851–52 in red and yellow brick in the Neo-gothic style, to plans by Gottlieb Bindesbøll who also designed the Thorvaldsen Museum in Copenhagen. Note the mosaic of Christ by Joakim Skovgaard on the altar-wall.

The Hobro Museum at Vestergade 21 displays finds from the town's history, including a collection of silver and porcelain as well as archeological finds from the nearby Viking site at Fyrkat (see below). Open: Apr. 1st–Oct. 31st daily 11am–5pm.

The Ibsen Art Collection (Ibsen Samling af Nyere Kunst) at Sdr. Kajgade 18a is worth a visit. It contains over 700 works including paintings by Sven Dalsgaard, Hans Henrik Lerfeldt and Poul Pedersen.

Surroundings

3km/2 miles south-west of the town (follow the sign "Vikingeborgen Fyrkat") are the remains of a circular stronghold dating from 980. The Danish National Museum has reconstructed the 1000-year-old circular rampart (Fyrkatborgen) and a Viking house. The circular rampart, broken through in four places, shows that the site was strongly fortified and probably served the Viking army as a training camp and winter quarters. However, archaeological digs indicate that women and children also lived within its walls and that craftsmen worked there. Before the Danish National Museum started digging in the 1950s there was nothing here but fields (open: Mar.–Oct. daily 9am–7pm).

In the 1980s a replica of a Viking house was constructed near the stronghold. All the walls of the house were supported on planks placed at an angle. The roof is covered with about 25,000 oak shingles and the beams over the doors leading into the hall are decorated with carvings in the Nordic style. It is planned to build a complete Viking village about 500m/550yd from the Fyrkat stronghold; it will consist of eight or nine houses, both large and small.

Fyrkat: reconstruction of a Viking house

Snæbum

Under a hill near Snæbum, a few miles west of Hobro, are three "passage graves" from about 3000 B.C.; they are among the best preserved of such graves to be found anywhere in Denmark.

Mariager

To the east of Hobro, on the south bank of the Mariager Fjord, lies the little township of Mariager ("Mary's Field"), which grew up around the Convent of St Bridget (founded 1430). The picturesque township is characterised by numerous old half-timbered houses and an abundance of roses, which is why Mariager is also known as the "town of roses".

In the cruciform Gothic church, which once belonged to the Convent, can be seen some beautiful wall-paintings and the "Coffin of Christ", a carved chest containing a wooden sculpture. The ancient tombs include those of Bishop Stygge Krumpen and his brother.

The Mariager Museum is housed in an old merchant's dwelling and contains archaeological collections and furniture of the 18th and 19th c.

Every Sunday in June, July and August a "museum" train runs to Handest (17km/10½ miles) drawn by steam or diesel engines. The locomotives and carriages date from the first half of the 20th c.

South of the town lies the Hohøj burial barrow.

Holstebro   A 2

Jutland
District: Ringkøbing amt
Population: 39,000

Situation
and importance

Holstebro is an old commercial and industrial town on the River Storå in north-west Jutland. It is the centre of a rural catchment area, with a technical college, museums and theatre. A laser sculpture is particularly worthy of note.

Holstebro: sculpture in the inner courtyard of the New Town Hall

The town, first mentioned in 1274, grew up at the place where there was a crossing over the Storå River at a confluence of a number of roads. The oldest recorded municipal privileges date from 1552, and in the 16th c. merchants from Holstebro traded with the Netherlands. The 17th c. saw an economic decline, but in the 19th c. came a resurgence of industrial activity, aided by the extension of the port in Struer, a new road system and rail link as well as the setting up of various industries.

Sights

Around the Store Torv (Market Place), set in the town centre, the roads form a pedestrian precinct with shopping streets and specialist shops. The fountains and works of contemporary art are impressive; these include the sculptures "Woman on a Cart", by Alberto Giacometti, erected in 1966 in front of the Old Town Hall and, further northwards in Nørregade, "Water Art" ("Vandkusten") by Helge Bertram (1975), a high stone wall surrounded by water-basins. South of the Market Place, by the River Storå, lies Red Square (Røde Plads) with a fountain which was unveiled in 1977.

In 1992 a museum was opened at Herningvej 1, which now houses the Holstebro Museum of Art – with its adjoining Sculpture Park – and the Holstebro Museum. The Museum of Art exhibits Danish painting and sculpture, including works by Henry Heerup, Laurits Hartz and Ejler Bille, as well as international prints of the 20th c. and collections of non-European art, including pre-Columbian ceramics from Peru, porcelain from Thailand and Cambodia as well as African art (open: Tue.–Sun. noon–4pm).

*Holstebro
Museum of Art

The Holstebro Museum boasts a variety of historical collections; these include Viking and medieval finds as well as silver cutlery, pipes and cigars, dolls and pewter figures.

Holstebro
Museum

Allied to the Holstebro Museum is the Dragoon and Freedom Museum. It exhibits historical documents about the local regiment of Dragoons, uniforms, etc., as well as exhibits relating to the Danish Resistance Movement during the Second World War.

Dragoon and
Freedom Museum

Weapons from 30 countries and dating from the 18th and 19th c. are contained in the Historic Weapons Collection at Sønderlandsgade 8; this collection also includes literature, weapons, etc. from the period of German occupation and Danish Resistance (1940–45; visits by prior arrangement).

Historic Weapon
Collection

On Døesvej, north of the town centre, stands Nørreland Church (consecrated in 1969), a building designed by the architects Inger and Johannes Exner. The church is circular in form so that the congregation and minister can gather round the altar and font. Near the main building is a steel mast supporting the belfry. There are 44 bronze bells which can be operated both manually and electronically.

Nørreland
Church

Near the church, at Nørrebrogade 1, can be found the Jens Nielsen and Olivia Holm-Møller Museum (Jens Nielsen og Olivia Holm-Møller Museet), which was also designed by Inger and Johannes Exner. As well as works by Nielsen and Holm-Møller the museum contains paintings by Kirsten Lundsgaardvig and sculptures by Niels Helledie. Jens Nielsen's studio can also be seen. Open: Mon.–Sat. noon–4pm, Sun. 11am–5pm.

Nielsen and
Holm-Møller
Museum of Art

Surroundings

Some 18km/11 miles west of Holstebro lies the village of Vemb, and not far south from there the Mansion of Nørre Vosborg. At one time it was ringed with walls for protection both from attack and from floods. The main building is of four wings, with the oldest part dating back to 1552.

Nørre Vosborg

About 1780 the property came into the possession of the merchant Peder Tang, a former servant who had come into money; he built the Classical gatehouse and a courtyard with a bell-tower, based on the Dutch model. In 1859 Hans Christian Andersen (see Famous People) was a guest here.

Horsens   B 3

Jutland
District: Vejle amt. Population: 55,000

Situation

The important industrial town of Horsens lies on the east coast of Jutland at the head of Horsens Fjord, to the north of Vejle and to the south of Århus (see entries).

History

As far as is known, the oldest privileges granted to the town go back to the year 1442. Many churches and monasteries were established but were used for other purposes after the Reformation. In the 16th c. landed gentry from the surrounding areas moved into the town and built houses there. After suffering from the effects of war in the 17th c., in the following century Horsen enjoyed a trade revival, especially with Norway. A new port was constructed in 1850 and Horsens developed into an industrial town.
The explorer Vitus Bering (1680–1741), who gave his name to the Bering Strait between Alaska and Cape Dezhneva in Asia, was born in Horsen, where Vitus Bering Park is named after him. A commemorative plaque is flanked by two cannons, recovered from Aleutian Islands, where he died.

Sights

Market-place

In the market-place (Torvet) stands the Town Hall, a new building inaugurated in 1986 and known for its magnificently colourful interior. The Church of the Redeemer (Vor Frelsers Kirke), built at the end of the 12th c. and restored in 1935–36 stands nearby. Inside, note the beautifully carved pulpit and the brick triforium. Above the altar hangs a 1950 figure of Christ by Einar Utzon-Frank.

Friary Church

The Friary Church (Klosterkirken) in Borgergade is the only surviving feature of a 13th c. Franciscan foundation. It was restored in 1892 when efforts were made to re-introduce the Late Gothic form of the building. The carved altar dates from around 1500, as do the choir-stalls and the triumphal cross. The pulpit has cartouche and scrollwork (c. 1650). Note the tombstones which include those of an important merchant and the Russian princes and princesses who once lived in the Lichtenbergs Palæ (see below). There are also 18th c. tombstones in the churchyard.

*"Lichtenbergs Palæ"

In Søndergade, where influential merchants once operated, there are still some buildings of note, including No. 17, Lichtenbergs Palæ (palace), an old half-timbered house which was rebuilt in the Baroque style in 1744. The German architect N. H. Riemann gave it a magnificent stone façade, similar to others which can be seen in Schleswig. An open staircase leads up to the doorway; inside are stucco ceilings. From 1810 to 1829 Queen Charlotte Frederike, mother of Frederik VII, resided here. Today it is a hotel (Jorgensens Hotel).

Lunden Art Museum; Horsens Museum

"Horsens Kunstmuseum Lunden" and the Horsens Museum are both situated in Caroline Amalie Park. As well as a collection of contemporary art, a sculpture park exhibits "The Red Dog", by Bjørn Nørgaard. In the Horsens Museum is a local history collection which includes finds from the Grønhøj "passage grave" and from the settlement and cemetery near Hedegård; note also the Jutland stoneware and silverware (open: Tue.–Sun. 10 or 11am–4pm).
Also part of Horsens Museum are the "Flensburgs Enkebolig" in Nørregade; these are widows' cottages, a gift made by the mayor Andreas Flensburg in 1786 for the benefit of poor widows of the town.

By the harbour stand a number of 19th c. houses, which, together with the former municipal electricity power station (1906) have been converted into a Museum. Visitors can watch working machinery such as printing presses and visit flats furnished to show living conditions in the 19th c.

Museum of Workers and Industrial Craftsmen

To the west of the town is a modern church, Sønderbro Kirke. Completed in 1971, it was designed by the architect Paul Niepoort, who lived for a long time in Finland and France. Asymmetric in form, its outer walls are white-washed. The tower is free-standing.

Sønderbro Church

In a beautiful park on the western edge of town lies Bygholm Castle, which was built in the early 14th c., converted to a manor house in 1775 and later renovated. It is now the Scandic Hotel.

Bygholm Castle

Surroundings

South-east of Horsens, on a spit of land which divides Horsens Fjord on the north from Vejle Fjord on the south, the little resort of Juelsminde lies in the midst of meadows and dunes. The resort has a beautiful beach and a ferry service operates to Kalundborg on Zealand.

Juelsminde

Jutland/Jylland

A–C 1–4

District: Sønderjyllands amt, Vejle amt, Viborg amt, Nordjyllands amt

Jutland (Danish Jylland), a peninsula in northern Europe, is the largest part of Denmark. The Jutland Peninsula, also known as the "Danish Continent", is bounded to the north of Flensburg by the German-Danish frontier sep-

Situation and Topography

In the Himmerland at eventide

arating Danish territory from the German province of Schleswig-Holstein. Danish Jutland extends north, surrounded by the North Sea, the Skagerrak and the Kattegat. The distance from Cap Skagen in the north to the German-Danish frontier in the south is some 310km/193 miles, and that from the west to Fornæs near Grenå in the east is 172km/107 miles. The southern part of the peninsula, which was ceded to Denmark by Germany in 1920, is called Sønderjylland in Danish. Heath and moors, fields and woodland are characteristic of the landscape, as are long beaches on the coast. Formerly devoted exclusively to farming and fishing, Jutland now has some well-developed industries, although agriculture still plays a very important role in its economy. Industrial concerns are found principally in the coastal towns. Jutland has a low population density.

Places of interest

There are many places of interest on the east coast, including the port of Frederikshavn, Grenå and Århus (see entries), the latter being the second largest city in Denmark with an interesting open-air museum. Viking burial sites can be found in the countryside around Ålborg (see entry). The young town of Esbjerg (see entry), on the southern part of the west coast, is the country's major North Sea port. Also of interest to visitors are the cathedral in Ribe (see entry), Legoland leisure park near Billund (see entry) and the runic stones at Jelling. Towns inland, such as Silkeborg and Viborg (see entries), are also worth a visit. An area of outstanding natural beauty is the Limfjord (see entry) in the north of Jutland, a holiday paradise for anglers, surfers and sailors.

Kalaallit Nunaat

See Greenland

Kalundborg   D 3

Zealand
District: Vestsjællands amt. Population: 19,000

Situation

Kalundborg, an important industrial town, lies on the fjord of the same name on the west coast of Zealand. From the harbour there are ferry services to Jutland (Juelsminde, Århus) and to the island of Samsø.

History

Near the place originally named "Hærvig" (Army Bay) where the fleet used to assemble before embarking on punitive expeditions, the fortified town of Kalundborg burgeoned in the 12th c., It was surrounded on all sides by walls and had a strongly defended castle, the towers of which included the "Folen", Denmark's largest medieval tower (see below). In 1285 the fortress was sacked by pirates.
In the 13th c. Kalundborg carried on extensive maritime trade. The oldest town privileges date from 1485. After Valdemar Atterdag had taken Kalundborg about 1340 he razed the old castle to the ground and replaced it with a larger one in the east of the town. It was here that the "Danehof" (later the parliament) met between the 14th and 17th c., and the king often stayed in Kalundborg. By the end of the Middle Ages the town's halcyon days were over. From 1658 to 1660 Swedish troops occupied the town, and the castle was taken by them and blown up.
Since 1684 ships have been sailing twice a week between Kalundborg and Århus; after 1874 a rail link was formed with Copenhagen and trade was established with Norway and England. At the end of the 19th c. various industries were set up in Kalundborg.

Sights

*Church of
Our Lady

The town's landmark is the five-towered Church of Our Lady (Vor Frue Kirke) on the castle mound in Adelgade, which was built about 1170. The

The five-towered church is the symbol of Kalundborg

walls stand on a granite base and the plan of the church is in the form of a Greek cross with four arms of equal length. It has five towers – an octagonal one on each arm of the cross and a massive square one (41m/135ft high) in the centre. The towers are surmounted by pointed spires and four of them have names – St Gertrude, St Catherine, St Anne and St Magdalene.

Inside, the pilasters and sunken semi-circular columns together with the lines of the window-arches on the outside suggest the work of a master builder from Lombardy. Note the altar-piece (1650) in the traditional Baroque style by the carver Lorents Jørgensen, and the granite font with palm motifs which dates from the time the church was built. Traces of wall-paintings can be detected.

The old half-timbered mansion in Lindegård, to the west of the church, houses the Kalundborg and District Museum (Kalundborg og Omegns Museum). The Knights' Hall in the north wing has some beautiful stucco work on the walls and ceiling. The museum displays traditional costumes of many kinds, implements for craftwork and peasants' rooms. In addition, temporary exhibitions are mounted and carnival festivities and cultural events are held here.

Municipal
Museum

In Skolegade stands the Folen, a tower which survived when the Swedes sacked Kalundborg castle in 1659.

Folen

Near the Town Hall stands the house in which the Norwegian authoress Sigrid Undset was born in 1882. Having fled from the Nazis and gone to the USA, she returned to Europe in 1945 and died in Lillehammer in 1949. She received the Nobel Prize in 1928.

Birthplace of
Sigrid Undset

Surroundings

On the Gisseløre Peninsula 1km/½ mile west of Kalundborg towers the Kalundborg radio transmitter, the mast of which is 143m/470ft high.

Gisseløre

Kalundborg

Ulstrup Mølle	Further north, on the spit of land called Rosnæs, can be seen a restored mill, the Ulstrup Mølle. It is a Dutch "gallery mill", which means that the cap of the windmill can, if necessary, be turned manually from the gallery which surrounds it so that the sails face the wind. The mill was in use until the 1950s and is the symbol of the village of Ulstrup.
*Lerchenborg Palace	5km/3 miles south of the town on the peninsula of Asnæs stands Lerchenborg Palace (Lerchenborg Slot), built in the Baroque style in 1745 for General Lerchen, a rich Danish landowner. The three-winged edifice, the lower ancillary buildings, offices, stables, riding arena and park are grouped around a central axis. The stuccoed Knights' Hall is the venue for concerts in summer (Lerchenborg Music Week). Two memorial rooms in one wing of the palace are dedicated to Hans Christian Andersen who was often a guest here. The park, laid out partly in the French style and partly in the English, has a beautiful rose-garden.

København

See Copenhagen

Køge   E 3

Zealand
District: Roskilde amt. Population: 38,000

Situation	Køge, an old port with some important industries, is situated south of Copenhagen on Køge Bay, on the east coast of Zealand.
History	The town was probably founded as a result of the profitable catches of herring in the Øresund and the associated fishing trade; it received its first privileges in 1288. Although until the end of the 16th c. trade was principally with towns in North Germany, the Dutch now came more to the fore; in addition, Køge became the home of wood-carvers, goldsmiths and shoemakers and Køge beer became famous. The town suffered severely in the wars of the 17th c. The Danish maritime hero Niels Juel inflicted considerable damage on the Swedish fleet in Køge Bay in 1677. The town enjoyed a fresh upswing in the 19th c.

Sights

	The central part of the town is old, with many pretty 16th and 17th c. timber-framed houses; the oldest, dating from 1527, is in Store Kirkestræde. In the very centre of town lies the market-place (Torvet), where the stocks once stood; witches' trials and the executions of those found guilty were carried out in Køge. A market is held on Wednesdays and Saturdays.
Municipal Museum	In Nørregade is the Municipal Museum, around a courtyard, where local collections of traditional costumes, embroideries, agricultural implements and silver coins are on view. Two living rooms show life in 1800 and 1900 and there are displays of peasant furniture and articles from Iron Age graves.
St Nicholas' Church	Also of interest is St Nicholas' Church, a Gothic building dating from 1450–1500. From the tower of this church King Christian V followed the Battle of Køge Bay in 1677, in the course of which the hero Niels Juel sank many Swedish ships. Inside the church, note the altar-piece by Lorents Jørgensen, the pulpit, choir-gallery and pews and several tombs of merchants from Køge.
Oluf Jensens Gård	Oluf Jensens Gård, a former merchant's residence at Brogade 7, has storehouses in the interior courtyard and various other buildings, all of which

combine to give a good idea of the design of such merchants' mansions in times gone by. The storehouse to the north houses the Køge Gallery, in which temporary exhibitions are held.

The monument "Battle in Køge Bay", which will be found near the harbour, is of considerable interest. This 9m/30ft high granite obelisk bears the name of the maritime heroes Niels Juel and Ivar Huitfeldt. Juel (as already mentioned) led the Danes to a decisive victory over the Swedes in 1677 and Huitfeldt commanded the ship "Danebrog" which caught fire when bombarded in 1710; he continued to fight on until the ship finally exploded.

Monument at the harbour

Surroundings

About 7km/4 miles south of the town stands Vallø Castle, a distinguished Renaissance building of 1586 which was completely rebuilt after a fire in 1893. It has two impressive towers, one round and the other square; it is surrounded by a park. Originally a royal palace, it was converted in 1738 into a home for gentlewomen.

Vallø Castle

Travelling south-east from Køge the visitor will arrive at the Stevens Peninsula and in another 22km/14 miles reach the little country town of Store Heddinge, with its interesting octagonal church, built about 1200 and later altered.

Store Heddinge

6km/4 miles to the east Stevns Klint, a chalk escarpment, extends along the shore and from it there is a magnificent view over the sea.
The white crag, 41m/135ft high, near Højerup is particularly beautiful, and here stands a little church of 1357 in the choir of which can be seen an even older chapel. According to legend this was built by a fisherman who had been rescued at sea. Since the sea has constantly eroded the chalk cliffs, the church – so the legend continues – moves inland a fraction on each New Year's night so as not to fall into the sea! In 1928 the choir collapsed and the rest of the church has now been made safe.

*Stevns Klint

Kolding

B 3

Jutland
District: Vejle amt
Population: 58,000

The lively port of Kolding, nestles among hills on the fjord of the same name on the east coast of Jutland. This region is an angler's paradise.

Situation

The oldest privileges enjoyed by the town date from 1321. Where the little Kolding Au flows into the fjord was the junction of several roads from the interior in the Middle Ages. In 1248 the Danish King had Koldinghus Castle erected here and this was later rebuilt on several occasions. In the 16th and early 17th c. the cattle trade in Kolding was very profitable. The customs boundary with the Duchy of Schleswig lay immediately south of the town. During the 17th c. Kolding suffered severe war damage. In the 19th c. the castle was burned down, and in both the wars against Schleswig-Holstein Kolding was occupied by German troops. After the Treaty of Vienna in 1864 a new customs boundary was drawn between Denmark and Germany.In the second half of the 19th c. the harbour was extended and industry came to the town.

History

Kolding is Denmark's largest export market for cattle. As well as abattoirs the town has textile, engineering and iron industries.

Economy

Sights

By a lake, the Slotsøen, in the centre of town stands Koldinghus Castle, built in 1248. For centuries Koldinghus Slot, a four-winged edifice, was the

Koldinghus (Museum)

Koldinghus Castle

In the Trapholt Museum

favourite residence of the kings of Denmark. In 1808, when Denmark had allied itself with Napoleon and Spanish soldiers were billeted in the castle, it was destroyed by fire. A start was made on rebuilding it in 1890, but it was to be another hundred years before it was finished.

In the restored ground floor of the north wing is an Historical and Cultural Museum, with exhibits covering the history of the town and the surrounding area, Romanesque and Gothic sculptures and handcrafted articles including porcelain, stoneware and silver.

There is a special exhibition devoted to the wars against Prussia in 1848–50 and 1864 (open: Apr.–Sept. daily 10am–5pm, Oct.–Mar. Mon.–Fri. noon–3pm. Sat. and Sun, 10am–3pm).

Concerts and other cultural events are also held in the castle.

Town Hall

The Neo-Romanesque Town Hall (1873–75) stands in the market-place; in the stairwell can be seen a mural by Otto Bache, "Attack by the Hussars on the German trenches 23.4.1849". Opposite the Town Hall lies Borchs Gård, a beautiful timbered house (1595), with carved beams, formerly a pharmacy.

Geographical Garden

Also worth a visit is the Geographical Garden (Geografisk Have og Rose-have) on the southern edge of town, which adjoins a rose-garden. This garden was laid out by Axel Olsen, owner of a tree nursery, and now has some 2000 species of trees and shrubs from all over the world, including North and South America, China and Burma. The garden is designed on geographical lines, and includes a herb garden and the longest bamboo grove in northern Europe.

*Trapholt Museum

For some years now Kolding has had a new attraction – Trapholt Art Museum, situated to the north of the town at Æblehaven 23, near Kolding Fjord. An interesting modern building situated in a park, it is home to a large collection of contemporary Danish paintings and applied art, including ceramics, textiles and design. The picture department is divided into two sections of landscape and figure forms and abstract art, and includes works by Richard Mortensen and Egill Jacobsen (open: May–Sept. daily 10am–5pm, Oct.–Apr. Mon.–Fri. noon–4pm, Sat. and Sun. 10am–4pm).

Surroundings

"Skamlingsbanken", to the south of Kolding, is 113m/370ft high, making it the highest point in the south of Jutland and offering a fine view. About 1850 the Danish Language and Culture Society used to meet here.

Skamlingsbanken

To the west of the town lies the town of Vejen, visited mainly for its Art Gallery, which houses sculptures by Niels Hansen-Jacobsen (1861–1941) and drawings by Jens Lund. In front of the museum stands the sculpture "Trold, der vejrer Kristenkød" (Troll, who scents human flesh), by Hansen-Jacobsen; in the municipal park is the bronze sculpture "Militarismen".

Vejen

Near Vejen is situated the Askov People's College, the model for other such institutions in Denmark and other Scandinavian countries. After the first Danish adult college in Rodding had closed down as a result of the German-Danish War, instruction continued in Askov in 1865. At first an old farmhouse was used, then new buildings were erected earlier this century.

Askov

Korsør   D 3

Zealand
District: Vestsjællands amt
Population: 20,000

The port of Korsør lies on the west coast of Zealand overlooking the Great Belt. To the east stretches the Korsør Nor, a coastal lake. Korsør is a passenger traffic port with ferry services to Funen, Langeland and Kiel, and a fishing port; it also has shipyards.

When the bridge over the Great Belt from Halsskov in Zealand to Nyborg in Funen is completed it will be of great advantage to the port of Korsør.

Situation and Importance

A castle has stood here as early as the 12th c., built as a defence against attack by the Wends. A new fortress was built near the Nor in the early 14th c., which consisted of a tower surrounded by a wall. Protected by this castle, Korsør soon developed and was granted its first town privileges in 1425. In 1661 Korsør, together with Copenhagen, became an official trading centre. The railway between Korsør and Copenhagen was completed in 1856. Ships from Kiel, which until then had called at Copenhagen, now sailed to Korsør. In the second half of the 19th c. industry, including glass-manufacture, became established in the town.

History

Sights

Of the old fortress (Søbatteri) by the harbour only the 23m/75ft high 14th c. tower and a 17th c. arms store have survived. From the tower there is a fine view over the town and the Belt; inside can be seen a large collection of model ships. There are also panoramas showing the breaking-up of the ice on the Great Belt.

Fortress tower

In Adelgade stands a row of old houses which were once blacksmiths' or shops. The King's House (Kongegården), built in 1761, was where the royal

King's House

Korsør

The marina of Korsør

personages used to stay when they passed through the town in years gone by. The façade is decorated with sandstone figures representing the Four Seasons. Exhibitions are mounted on the ground floor.

Monument   Also of interest is a monument on Havnepladsen near the harbour which is dedicated to the Danish writer Jens Baggesen (1764–1826), who was born in Korsør. In his hand he is holding a pansy as a symbol of how he was treated in Denmark.

Surroundings

Halsskov   The town of Halsskov, north of Korsør, will be the exit from the East Bridge over the Great Belt. The Great Belt Exhibition Centre (Storebælts Udstillingscenter) is worth a visit; its aims are explained in a large hall near the building site, from where visitors can gain access to a viewing platform (open: May–Sept. Tue.–Sun. 10am–8pm, Oct.–Apr. Tue.–Sun. 10am–5pm).

Skælskør   On Skælskør Fjord, to the south-east of the town, lies the harbour town of Skælskør, with its old timber-framed houses and St Nicholas' Church, dating from the 13th c. The church is unusual in that the nave and choir are the same width. Note the altar, pulpit and triumphal cross (1500). In one corner of the churchyard can be seen the former church barn, a brick building with stepped gables.

Borreby Manor   2km/1¼ miles south of Skælskør lies Borreby Manor (16th c.), one of the best-preserved Renaissance country houses; it is surrounded by a rampart and a moat. Situated in a park, the manor was built about 1550 for Johann Friis, Christian III's chancellor. It has a stepped tower on the south side and three towers on the north side. In the upper mezzanine floor there was a battlement walk with embrasures. The porter's lodge and parts of the administrative buildings date from the 17th c. The interior was restored in 1884.

From Borreby manor the road leads east to Ørslev, which has an interesting church with a frieze portraying a medieval round dance. From there the road continues to the 17th c. Holsteinborg Castle, a Renaissance building of four wings, situated in a beautiful park with a long avenue of limes by the waterside (Holsteinborg Nor). Since 1707 the castle has been owned by the Holstein ducal family. Hans Christian Andersen stayed here on several occasions.

*Ørslev;
Holsteinborg
Castle*

Læsø   C/D 1

District: Nordjyllands amt
Area: 116sq.km/45sq.miles
Population: 2500

The island of Læsø lies in the northern Kattegat. It first surfaced when the sea-level sank about 5000 years ago; parts in the south are often flooded. There is a car ferry between Vesterø Havn on Læsø and Frederikshavn on the coast of Jutland; the crossing takes about 1½ hours. There is also an air-taxi to Copenhagen.

Situation

Two thirds of the island consists of uncultivated land, principally of fen and heath. In the north lies the Højsande area of dunes which reaches a height of 30m/100ft; this – like some other parts of the island – has been designated a nature reserve. The south of the island has low-lying meadows along the shore, and many waders and sea-birds rest here during May to

Topography

A house thatched with seaweed on Læsø Island

July. The eastern point, with Danzigmand Dune, is an attractive area and is under a protection order; the dunes are named after a ship, the "Danzig" which was once stranded there. Flat beaches of fine sand attract bathers. The Knotten Peninsula, reached via a narrow sound, is particularly popular.

Byrum

Farmhouses with their roofs covered in seaweed are a feature of the island's capital, Byrum. When the islanders found they could no longer obtain sufficient reeds with which to thatch their houses they simply used seaweed, of which there was a plentiful supply. The Local Museum (Museumsgården) is housed in a half-timbered homestead of four wings with a seaweed-covered roof; here silver and costumes are on display. A windmill stands in front of the museum. The 13th c, church boasts a limewash painting of St George and the Dragon and an altar of 1450.

Langeland

C 3/4

District: Fyns amt
Area: 185sq.km/71sq.miles
Population: 17,000

Situation

The island of Langeland, some 50km/31 miles long from Hov at its northern tip to Dovns klint in the south and 3–9km/2–6 miles wide, is situated to the south-east of Funen in the Great Belt. The island can be reached by car or by ship. From Svendborg on Funen a huge bridge, built in 1967, leads to the island of Tåsinge and from the southern side of this island a causeway and a bridge (1962) via the little island of Siø form a link with Langeland. As well as the ferry services to other Danish islands, there is one between Kiel and Bagenkop in the south.

Tranekær Castle

Langeland is a long and narrow island popular with holiday-makers, with many beautiful beaches, magnificent beech woods and several steep cliffs, especially in the south, including Gulstav Klint and Dovns klint, south-east of Bagenkop.

Sights and Places of Interest

On the west coast lies the capital Rudkøbing, a picturesque place with narrow winding streets and stately merchants' mansions. Most of the old houses are in Brogade, Østergade and Gåsetorv.
The Old Pharmacy (det gamle Apotek) at Brogade 15, now a museum with old pharmaceutical equipment, is the birthplace of Hans Christian Ørsted (1777–1851). He was one of the great 19th c. physicists who established the theory of electromagnetism, and his statue, by the sculptor H. Vilhelm Bissen, stands in Gåsetorv.

Rudkøbing

The church is interesting; the oldest part of the nave is Late Romanesque, (c. 1100) and the tower dates from 1621.

The Langeland Museum at Jens Winthersvej 12 and at Østergade 25, contains items from prehistoric times to the early part of this century, much of it discovered locally by archaeologists. The exhibits include swords and armour from the Viking period, old boats and fishing tackle, and silver.

In the southern part of the island near road No. 26 lies Hennetved, and not far to the south is Skovsgård Mansion. The mansion's former corn-mill was restored in the 1980s and a new wing added to house an electric generator. The estate is run on ecological lines, with a collection of horse-drawn wagons, etc. (Open: mid-May–end Sept. Mon.–Fri. 10am–5pm, Sun 1–5pm; July Mon.–Fri. 7–9pm.)

Skovsgård

Langeland has many examples of prehistoric finds. A particularly interesting site, at Humble in the south of the island, is "Kong Humbles Grav" (King Humble's Grave), an impressive Megalithic "corridor grave". Another such grave, Hulbjergjættestuen, lies near Søgard to the south-west of Bagenkop.

Kong Humbles Grav

12km/7½ miles north of Rudkøbing, Tranekær Castle, the oldest and largest castle in Langeland, stands on a hill. The angular building, which was reconstructed in 1863 (tower in 1859) embraces the remains of a medieval royal castle. From the car park by the road to the south of the castle, a path leads round the castle lake. In the castle mill a Mill Museum has been set up, because there are many mills on Langeland – old windmills and others which generate electrical power. Some picturesque houses have been preserved in the nearby village of Tranekær By.

Tranekær Castle (not open to the public)

In Lohals, a resort in the north of the island, Tom Knudsen's Safari Museum is worth a visit. On display are hunting trophies and ethnographic collections from Africa (open in summer).

Lohals

Limfjord

Jutland
Districts: Viborg amt and Nordjyllands amt

The Limfjord, a stretch of water 180km/112 miles long, between the North Sea and the Kattegat, divides Nørrejyske Ø, the island of north Jutland, from the rest of the peninsula. This region extends from Thyborøn in the west to Hals in the east; in the west it has an almost lagoon and lake-like appearance. Shallows make the passage of ships somewhat difficult.

Fjord region

With its beautiful scenery and calm waters, Limfjord offers ideal conditions for sailing and water sports of all kinds. A vacation on the water is made

Water sports

particularly attractive by the presence of many little towns with harbours and mooring-places.

Tip

Car-drivers should note that the Limfjord can be crossed only at certain places; there are bridges over the Oddesund, Vilsund and Sallingsund (south of Nykøbing Mors) and over the Aggersund further south as well as a bridge and tunnel at Ålborg (see entry).
In addition, several ferries cross the fjord in a few minutes, including one at the west end and one at the east end.

Towns and islands in the fjord region

Thyborøn Canal

The western entrance to the Limfjord from the North Sea is the Thyborøn Canal (ferry), which flows from the North Sea into the lagoon known as Nissum Bredning. On the north side of the canal lies the popular holiday area around Agger and Vestervig.

Vestervig

In the 11th c. Vestervig was the seat of the Bishop of Vendsyssel, the most northerly part of Jutland. Today it is a small village with less than 1000 inhabitants. The church, Denmark's largest village church, reminds us of its proud past even though the once-majestic basilica suffered over the centuries as the result of unsympathetic rebuilding and restoration. Careful renovation in the 1920s brought the church back to something like its original condition. It contains a number of Romanesque tombstones, including the oldest ones in Denmark (1210).
Vestervig lost its importance when the harbour silted up, and the same is true of many other places along this stretch of coast. The silting alternated with storm tides which did further damage to the soil and much fertile land and several towns disappeared. The tiny Church and Lodbjerg Lighthouse bear witness to this destruction.

Agger Tange

Today the Agger Tange promontory is protected by dykes and breakwaters similar to those in the Netherlands.

Lemwig

On the south shore of the Nissum Bredning, a lagoon at the south end of the Limfjord, lies Lemvig, a pretty town in a hilly area. The church, with an onion tower of 1936, has a Rococo interior decorated by Bodil Kaalund. The Lemvig Museum (Vesterhus) contains items associated with the history of life-saving at sea and also pictures of stranded ships, a weaving-room and a goldsmith's workshop. Particularly interesting is the study used by the writer Thøger Larsen (1875–1928), complete with many of his books; in the garden there is a bust of the author by Thorvald Vestergaard (1958).
With expanses of woodland, moor and heath as well as sand-dunes on the west coast, the suroundings of Lemvig are a veritable paradise for nature-lovers and many rare waterfowl can be observed. 12km/7 miles west of the town a steep cliff, the 43m/141ft high Bovbjerg Klint, borders the sea.

Struer

The industrial town of Struer on Venø Bay, in the south of the fjord, is the home of the Bang and Olufsen electronics company. In the local museum, housed in a converted rectory, visitors can see an interesting collection of model ships and other exhibits. Struer also boasts some beautiful sculptures – "Young Girl from Sarpsborg" (1948) near the harbour and "Young Girl from Struer" (1927) in the park on Vestergade.
To the north-west of Struer, near Kilen, will be found some strange moraine landscape – a nature reserve – with U-shaped glaciated valleys.

Mors Island

In the Limfjord itself there are numerous islands both large and small, the most important of which, Mors (Morsø), is reached by bridges over the Sallingsund to the south-east and the Vilsund to the north-west, or by ferries across the Nees Sund and Feggesund. The charm of Mors lies mainly in its magnificent scenery. Especially impressive is the Hanklit in the north, a 65m/200ft high crag which falls almost vertically down to the sea and contains animal and plant fossils of the Tertiary period. Ice Age glaciers have worn the rock into fantastic shapes. At the northern tip of Mors lies Feggeklit, the place where – according to legend – Hamlet is said to have killed his stepfather King Fegge. The Moler Museum exhibits fossils and diatomites (open: daily May–Oct. 10am–4pm; July until 7pm).

The chief town on Mors is Nykøbing Mors, a smallish town on the Salling-sund, known for the culture of oysters and for herring fishing. In a restored wing of the former Dueholm Abbey, founded about 1370, is now housed the Historical Museum (Morslands Historiske Museum). On display are collections from the Stone Age up to 1900 documenting life on Mors, together with *objets d'art* from churches on the island, porcelain and traditional costumes. The writer Aksel Sandemose was born in Nykøbing Mors in 1899 and later emigrated to Norway. In Færkenstræde there is a memorial plaque to him, designed by Erik Heide in 1969.

Nykøbing Mors

A visit is recommended to the Jesperhus Flower Park (Blomsterpark) south of Nykøbing Mors. This is a large area with half a million plants and an aquarium containing tropical fish and coral (open: mid-May–Sept. daily 9am–6 or 9pm).

Jesperhus
Flower Park

East of Mors lies the little island of Fur, with moler deposits and sandstone in the north. About 1120 a sandstone church (Sct. Mortens Kirke) was built in Nederby in the Romanesque style. In the Fur Museum can be seen fossils and geological finds. A panoramic view of the island's beautiful natural scenery can be enjoyed from the Stendalshøj.

Island of Fur

Going east from Struer the visitor will come to Skive, on the fjord of the same name, a southern arm of the Limfjord into which the Skive Å flows at this point. There is an old 12th c. Romanesque church, Den Gamle Kirke, which was extended in the Late Middle Ages. The wall-paintings of 1522 show the Holy Family and the Apostles.
The historical and cultural exhibits in the Skive Museum include items from Greenland, an impressive amber collection and paintings.
In a wood behind the harbour stands Krabbesholm Manor, dating from the 16th c., which since 1907 has been a College of Adult Education. The central wing in brick was built by Iver Krabbe. In the Knights' Hall, richly furnished in the Jutland Rococo style, the wall and ceiling paintings are worthy of attention.

Skive

In the west of the Salling Peninsula, north of Skive, stands Spøttrup Castle, one of the best examples of medieval fortress architecture in Denmark. It was built in the 15th c. for the Bishops of Viborg and is surrounded by a double moat with a dividing rampart. For a long time it was considered impregnable. After threatening to collapse in the 18th c. it was purchased by the state in 1840 and restored. Note in particular the Gothic vaulting in the east wing, the Knights' Hall in the south wing and the battlement walk. To the east of the castle lies a garden with medicinal plants and spices (viewing: in Apr. Sun. 11am–5pm, May–Oct. daily 10 or 11am–6pm).

*Spøttrup Castle

South-west of Skive, and accessible via Vinderup, by Lake Flynder lies Herjl Hede Nature Park, 1000ha/2500 acres in area. It is named after H. P. Hjerl-Jansen, who acquired the site in 1900. The chief attraction is the Open-air Museum (Frilandsmuseum), known as "Den gamle Landsby" (The Old Village), with a forge, inn, fire-station, mills, shops and a church, together with one of the oldest Danish farm settlements, the Vinkelgård from near Viborg (see entry). A former forest ranger's lodge now houses the Jutland Forest Museum; outside a Stone Age settlement has been constructed as well as a Bronze and an Iron Age house. (Open: daily Apr.–Oct.)

Hjerl Hede;
*Open-air
Museum

The road from Skive continues eastwards and northwards along the Lim-fjord, sometimes at a distance from the shore. By taking a side turning near

Ålestrup

Spøttrup Castle on the Salling Peninsula

Gedsted the visitor will reach Ålestrup in the western Himmerland home of the Danish Bicycle Museum (Danmarks Cykelmuseet). It contains a collection of more than 100 bicycles from 1860 to 1970 which shows how they developed over that period.

Vitskøl Abbey

It is well worth making a detour north of Gedsted to take in Vitskøl Abbey, a Cistercian monastery founded by Valdemar the Great. Of the church, only ruins remain. The abbey was dissolved in the 16th c. and thereafter known as "Bjørnsholm" after its owner Bjørn Andersen. The three-winged manor, much extended, now houses a Botanical and Forestry Research Establishment. Medicinal plants and herbs grow in the old abbey garden.

Løgstør

The town of Løgstør lies on the Aggersund. a narrow part of the Limfjord further north, across which there has been a bridge since 1942. The Limfjord Museum is in the former residence of the Canal Supervisor and displays a collection of fishing gear and items connected with shipping and ferries.

Aggersborg

Across the bridge lies Aggersborg, on the north bank of the fjord. Nearby stood the Viking Castle of Aggersborg, built about 1000 at the behest of the king. A circular wall 240m/790ft in diameter has survived; in each quarter of the circle there once stood twelve long-houses. For a time the castle was a royal court, but was destroyed by fire during a peasants' uprising in the 15th c. About 1860 Aggersborggård Mansion, a half-timbered building, was erected here.

Thisted

Thisted is an industrial town on Thisted Bay (Thisted Bredning). In the old cemetery is the grave of the writer Jens Peter Jacobsen (1847–85), who was born here and whose psychological novel "Niels Lyhne" (1880) is well known both in Denmark and abroad. On the east side of the cemetery in Jernbanegade stands the Local Museum, with a collection of Stone and

Boats at Nørre Harbour

Bronze Age finds, items showing the development of Thisted, and rooms furnished in 18th and 19th c. styles with mementoes of Christen Kold and J. P. Jacobsen.
Thisted possesses an imposing Town Hall, designed in 1853 by M. G. Bindesbøll. A bust on the Lilletorv is in memory of the priest Hans Christian Sonne, who in the 19th c. founded Denmark's first consumers' co-operative society in an attempt to improve the lot of the workers.

The fishing and ferry port of Hanstholm lies 20km/12½ miles north of Thisted; there are ferries to the Faroes and other places. The 30m/100ft high lighthouse was built in 1843 and is visible from a considerable distance. In the Second World War German troops occupied Hanstholm and the local people were evacuated.
From the town a road along the dunes leads to the resort of Klitmøller (12km/7 miles).

Hanstholm

Continuing south along the coast, we come to the fishing village of Nørre Vorupør, where the North Sea Aquarium has a fine collection of fish and marine animals caught by local fishermen.

North Sea Aquarium

In Fjerritslev, a town between the Limfjord and Jammer Bay, is a Museum of Brewing and Local History, both housed in an old brewery on Gamle Bryggergård.
On Jammer Bay to the north, between Skarreklit and Slettterstrand there is a beautiful stretch of coast with sand dunes and camp sites.

Fjerritslev
Brewery Museum

To the east of Fjerritslev the A 11 leads to Åbybro and then continues south-east to Ålborg (see entry), the largest town in the region. From there to Hals, in the east, the Limfjord is known as the Langerak.

In Hals, an attractive resort on Ålborg Bay, remains of the old fortifications can be seen. A ferry connects Hals with the south shore of the Limfjord.

Hals

Lolland
C/D 4

District: Storstrøms amt
Area: 1241sq.km/479sq.miles. Population: 85,000

Situation

The island of Lolland lies to the west of Falster, facing the German Baltic coast. Not counting Greenland, Lolland is the third largest Danish island after Zealand and Funen. The islands of Lolland, Falster and Møn, together with the nearby smaller islands, are known by the Danes as the "South Sea Islands".

Economy

Lolland is still an area with little industry. The largest undertakings are concentrated around Nakskov. The most important branch of the economy is the growing of sugar-beet, with sugar refineries at Nakskov and Sakskøbing; fishing has declined in importance. A network of ferries has opened up Lolland for tourism.

Communications

The E 47, the shortest route between Germany and Copenhagen, passes through Lolland; its southern section is known as the "as the crow flies" stretch, and a bridge is planned over the Femer Belt. A ferry plies between Puttgarden in Germany and Rødbyhavn in the south of Lolland. A second ferry service from Tårs, near Nakskov, to Spodsbjerg on Langeland, links Lolland, Langeland and Funen. Two bridges over the Guldborg Sound lead from Lolland to Falster.

Tour of Lolland

Rødbyhavn

From Rødbyhavn the E 47, now mainly a motorway, leads towards Copenhagen. Although it is possible to cross Lolland in about half an hour the following tour is intended for those who wish to travel more leisurely.

Rødby

Following the E 47 from Rødbyhavn and then taking a side turning the visitor will come to Rødby, now 5km/3 miles from the sea, which was a port before the new harbour in Rødbyhavn was opened in 1912. In Østergade is a reminder that ships were once moored here. The town was often flooded and a comprehensive system of dykes cut Rødby off from the sea. A Flood Column in Nørregade shows the high-water mark of the great flood of 1872, when large areas of Lolland and Falster were completely under water.

*Tirsted Church

6km/4 miles north-west of Rødby lies Tirsted Church, a 13th c. Romanesque brick building. The upper and lower sections of the tower open up into two arches above the nave. Note the 15th c. frescoes in the choir portraying the Creation and other Bible scenes. In a niche stand two wooden figures of Mary and John the Baptist, from the workshop of Claus Berg.

Ostofte Church

From Rødby the E 47 continues and after about 10km/6 miles comes to Maribo; in the south of the town the A 9 goes off to the left to Nakskov. On this road the visitor will first come to Ostofte Church, a Romanesque brick building with a Gothic tower and porch, 15th c. vaulting in the nave and a transept of 1656. In the choir frescoes from about 1400 depict scenes from the Old Testament, including the story of the Creation and the Expulsion from Paradise, as well as various dragons. Stokkemarke has a pleasing church with a massive tower.

In Halsted there is a 12th c. monastery which was later almost completely destroyed and was converted into a mansion in the 19th c. The park is open to the public.

Nakskov

Nakskov, in a sheltered position on Nakskov Fjord, is an industrial town with a shipyard and Scandinavia's largest sugar factory. The town enjoyed its heyday in the 16th c. but has succeeded in retaining its medieval ambience to this day – narrow lanes and old houses between the harbour and Axeltorv, the market-place in which stands an old pharmacy. St Nicholas' Church is Gothic and dedicated to the patron saint of sailors; it has an impressively carved altar and a fine Baroque pulpit. A Swedish cannon ball from 1659 is still embedded in the chancel arch. Jews have lived in Nakskov since the 17th c., and so a synagogue was built here which is now used as business premises.

Along the south coast of Lolland stretch the finest beaches on the island, from Maglehøj Strand. They are primarily sandy beaches with shingle along the water-line.

Beaches on
the south coast

The Romanesque Løjtofte Church north of Nakskov is worth a visit; note the magnificent font and a sandstone sculpture (1100) by the Gotland artist known as the "Master of the Christ in Majesty". The road continues to Kong Svends Høj, a Neolithic "corridor grave".

Løjtofte Church

South of here near Pederstrup the Reventlow Museum (founded 1938–40) is housed in a mansion, built in 1820 for Count Christian Ditlev Reventlow, which is set in a park. In the elegantly furnished rooms hang portraits of important people who took part in the great Land Reform of 1788, when Count Reventlow aimed to improve the lot of the peasants.

Reventlow
Museum

From Kong Svends Høj continue north along the coast to Kragenæs, from where ferries serve the islands of Fejø and Femø. There is good sailing to be had in these coastal waters.

Kragenæs

Instead of turning off to Kragenæs the visitor can continue on the main road past Ravnsborg Castle, an old ruin with an attractive view of Smålandsfarvand. 13km/8 miles further on lies Bandholm, the port of Maribo, with a car ferry to Askø. On summer week-ends a small steam-train with old-fashioned carriages runs between Maribo and Bandholm.

Ravnsborg:
Bandholm

South of Bandholm lies Knuthenborg Safari Park, Scandinavia's largest manor-house park (600ha/1500 acres). It was laid out in the 19th c. in the English style on the Knuthenborg estate and converted to its present use in 1970. The park, which is surrounded by a wall 8km/5 miles long with only four gates, contains several hundred species of deciduous and coniferous trees, as well as Denmark's largest collection of animals – antelope, giraffes, zebras, camels, rhinoceroses and elephants. A motor road passes through the park and through an enclosure containing Siberian tigers. There is also a children's zoo with pony-rides (open: May 1st–Sept. 15th daily 9am–6pm).

*Knuthenborg
Safari Park

Shortly after leaving Knuthenborg the road re-joins the A 9 which leads back to Maribo. Maribo enjoys a beautiful setting by Sønder Lake in the heart of Lolland. The town grew in the 15th c. around Maribo Abbey, which was endowed by Queen Margarethe in 1408. All that remains of the abbey are some ruins in a garden to the north of the church, from where there is a beautiful view of the lake.

Maribo

Maribo Cathedral was erected between 1413 and 1470 as the church of an abbey of the Order of St Bridget. Built of brick, it is almost 60m/200ft long and the central nave has stellar vaulting. Originally the church had two choirs, one for monks and one for nuns. The plan of the church is roughly similar to that of the church designed by St Bridget for the principal abbey of her order at Vadstena in Sweden; Maribo was the first daughter house of Vadstena Abbey. It contains a 15th c. triumphal crucifix, a Renaissance painted pulpit, a Baroque altar carved by Henrik Werner about 1640, a painting on leather and an exhibition of ecclestiacal relics including the sponge which – according to legend – was handed to Christ on the Cross. Leonora Christina Ulfeldt, daughter of Christian IV and wife of Corfitz Ulfeldt, later governor of Copenhagen, was imprisoned for a long time and spent the last years of her life here in Maribo. She is buried in the cathedral.

Lolland

Maribo Cathedral

Watertower in Sakskøbing

Maribo also boasts an interesting Museum with an historical section (runic stones from Sædinge and Skovlænge) and an art collection, with paintings by Kristian Zahrtman, including pictures portraying scenes from the life of Leonora Christina (see above). There are also documents relating to Polish girls who worked in Lolland's sugar-beet fields in the early 20th c.
On the outskirts of Maribo is an Open-air Museum (Frilandsmuseum) reflecting the old peasant culture of Lolland and Falster. Visitors will find houses, farmsteads, a school, a church and various workshops.

Engestofte

There are opportunities for pleasant walks around the Maribo Lakes; on the north side lies the Classical Engestofte Manor House and to the south Søholt with a garden laid out in the French style. Particularly beautiful is Røgbølle Lake with old oak trees along its shores.

Sakskøbing
Berritsgård

From Maribo the E 47 continues east to Sakskøbing; in the market-place stands a sculpture ("Sugar-beet Girl") erected in 1940 by Gottfried Eickhoff in memory of the Polish girls who helped with the sugar-beet harvests. 4km/2½ miles north-east of the town stands the Renaissance manor-house of Berritsgård, which has an octagonal tower with a copper spire. The house was built in 1586 for Lisbet Friis, the widow of Jacob Huitfeldt; their coat-of-arms is above the door.
In a beautiful setting on Sakskøbing Fjord lies Orebygård; this 16th c. manor-house was later remodelled in the Late Renaissance style.
Near Sakskøbing the A 9 branches off to the right and leads south-east towards Nykøbing Falster.

Krenkerup

Just beyond the turn-off on the right stands the Neolithic Dolmen of Radsted, and behind it the fine Krenkerup Manor House, first referred to in the time of Queen Margarethe I. The tower was built in the early 17th c. by the state official Palle Rosenkrantz.
Just before Nykøbing a road leads off to the right and after 17km/11 miles

south-west it reaches Nysted, passing Frejlev Forest on the way (Bronze Age remains).

Nysted is one of the smallest towns in Denmark. Note the Gothic church, built about 1300, the tower of which has a high spire made of copper; inside can be seen a burial chapel for Count Otto Ludvig Raben, a Gothic crucifix dating from 1400 and a 17th c. bronze font. The Egholm Ulvecenter (Wolf Centre) near Nysted is an exciting new venture, comprising a wolf park and museum.

Nysted

This attractive town on the Baltic grew up around Ålholm Castle, which was built in the 12th c.; the west wall is 14th c. About 1330 King Christopher II mortgaged the castle to a count from Holstein; later he was to be a prisoner in his own castle. In the late 19th c. it was converted to a knight's castle. It has some interesting portraits as well as paintings by the Danish artist Jens Juel and beautifully furnished rooms (open: daily June–Aug. 11am–7pm).

Ålholm

Near the castle, is the Automobile Museum, with Denmark's largest collection of veteran and vintage cars, numbering some 200 and dating from 1896 to 1936. There is also a model railway layout set in mountain scenery. A train pulled by a steam-engine resembling an 1850 model, runs to the beach through the castle grounds.

Ålholm
Automobile
Museum

From Nysted a road to the west brings the visitor back to the motorway which leads to Rødbyhavn. On the way, it passes through Holeby, one of the smallest townships in Denmark, but so widely dispersed that it has an exceptionally long main street.

Holeby

Middelfart

B 3

Funen
District: Fyns amt
Population: 18,000

Middelfart, an important seaport and seaside resort, is situated in the extreme north-west of the island of Funen on the Little Belt. From Jutland the town can be reached by means of one of two bridges – one a rail bridge, the other a road bridge – leading from Jutland to Funen.

Situation

Middelfart was already populated in prehistoric times. The Royal Castle of Hindsgavl (Hindsgavl Slot) which stood here was first mentioned in 1295, when the Danish King Menved and the Norwegian king concluded an armistice there; in the 14th c. the castle passed to King Valdemar IV. Hindsgavl was destroyed in a storm in 1694. In 1784 a mansion was built on the site. The people of Middelfart operated ferries across the Little Belt. About the year 1500, dolphins were hunted here.

History

Sights

St Nicholas' Church by the harbour was built in Romanesque style in the 12th c. and later extended; the work was financed in part by selling "letters of pardon" to heretics and other criminals. It boasts a beautiful pulpit (1596), a font by Hermann Wilhelm Bissen and a Baroque altar (1650) with a painting of about 1840 by C. W. Eckersberg.

St Nicholas'
Church

Middelfart Museum is located in Henner Friisers Hus, a gabled half-timbered house. It displays articles concerned with dolphin-hunting about 1500, and items of local history and a collection of ladies' hats. Mands Samling Cultural History Museum at Damgade 26, displays local glass, china and furniture, as well as workshops (open: daily end June and July 2–6pm).

Museums

Middelfart: carved figures on a door

Hindsgavl Castle

This castle stands on a peninsula west of the town centre. It was built in Neo-classical style in 1784, with two floors and two wings, and stands in a beautiful park. For some years now it has been a conference centre, with a hotel. Nearby foundations and walls have been excavated which formed part of the original Hindsgavl Castle. The barn in the grounds displays prehistoric items and a section on the castle's history. The evolution of the landscape is also illustrated.

Northern surroundings

Bogense

About 20km/12 miles north of the road from Middelfart to Odense (see entry) the pretty little town of Bogense lies on the north coast of Funen. In the Middle Ages this was where ferries left for Jutland; since 1976 their mooring-place has been a marina for small yachts and boats. In Bogense many old houses have survived – Landbohjemmet (17th c.) in Østergade and in Adelgade the Bryggergården with an old monastic cellar. Furniture, costumes and coins are exhibited in Nordfyns Museum.

Glavendrup

Glavendrup, 18km/11 miles to the south-east of Bogense, is also worth a visit to see the restored Viking ship-building rig. On a runic stone is a detailed inscription ending with a threat to damage the stone.

Southern surroundings

Assens

The old township of Assens on the Little Belt about 40km/25 miles south of Middelfart has a number of timbered houses dating from the 16th and 17th c. Of especial interest is Willemoes House (1675) at Østergade 36, which contains mementoes of the famous seafarer Peter Willemoes, who was born in this house. His statue stands in front of the Kogehus near the harbour. (Open: all year 10.30am–noon and 2–5pm; closed Mon. Jun.–Aug. and weekdays in May.)

The Seven Gardens (De 7 Haver) are situated at Ebberup, south-east of Assens, the warmest spot in Denmark, and cover 30,000sq.m. On display are rare plants, rockeries and many varieties of rhododendrons and roses, as well as special features from seven European countries.

Ebberup

There are ferries from Assens to the two islands lying to the north-west in the Little Belt, Bågø (30 minutes) and Brandsø (1 hour 15 minutes).

Bågø
Brandsø

Driving east from Assens on Road 168 the visitor can see on the left after 8km/5 miles the Øksnebjerg (85m/279ft), with a memorial tablet to Count Johann von Rantzau, who in 1535 defeated a force from Lübeck and a peasant army; there is also a fine windmill dating from 1859.

Øksnebjerg

Krengerup Castle, to the east of Assens, is one of the most beautiful Classical mansions in Denmark. It was built in the 18th c. for F. S. Rantzau. On the roof cornice can be seen coats-of-arms, vases and a cornucopia. Admission to grounds only.

Krengerup

Taking route 161 south-east of Middelfart visitors with children might like to visit a family park at Årup and a reptile park and aquarium at Vissenbjerg. Fyns Sommerland occupies 200,000sq.m. and includes a range of activities including pony rides, aerial ropeways, archery, roller skating, rowing boats and rally cars. Also on site is an aquascape, comprising three pools and ten water chutes. (Open: mid-May to early Sept.)

Årup and
Vissenbjerg

Scandinavia's largest collection of reptiles and amphibians is at Vissenbjerg. (Open: daily all year; 9am to 6pm Apr.–Aug.; to 4pm rest of year.) Also in Vissenbjerg is Funen Aquarium (Fyns Akvarium). (Open: daily, 10am–7pm, Apr.–Oct.; 10am–6pm rest of year.)

Møn   E 3/4

District: Storstrøms amt
Area: 217sq.km/85sq.miles. Population: 12,000

The island of Møn lies at the east end of the Størstrommen, the channel which divides the islands of Zealand and Falster. It is connected with Zealand by a bridge from Kalvehave and can be reached from Falster by crossing the Farø bridge (branch to the island of Bogø) or by taking the ferry from Stubbekøbbing to the island of Bogø and crossing the causeway from there to Møn. The white chalk cliffs on the east of the island are one of Denmark's most beautiful natural features and a great tourist attraction. In addition, Møn, flat and fertile in the west, is interesting on account of its varied landscape – heathland, fields, meadows and marshes, as well as some fine bathing beaches. Many prehistoric remains have been found on Møn, including a "number of particularly interesting Neolithic chambered tombs known as "giants' graves". Popular legend associated these tombs with two giants – Grønjæger, the Green Huntsman, who ruled over western Møn, and Upsal, king of the cliffs, who held sway in the east end of the island. Upsal was long regarded as the island's protector, since it was he who caused enemy ships to be shattered on its rocky coast.

Situation and access

Topography

Cultural history

Tour of Møn

The bridge from Zealand crosses the Ulvsund to Møn. Only one road crosses the island lengthwise; 2km/1¼ miles from the bridge a side road goes off on the right and meanders south through beautiful scenery – there is a fine view of the Sound from Borre – to the Neolithic tombs known as Kong Askers Høj, a burial chamber about 10m/33ft long, and Klekkende Høj, a passage grave 9m/29½ft long and 1·25m/4ft high. 11km/7 miles along the main road from Zealand lies the capital of the island, Stege. It grew around a castle built by Valdemar I about 1175 as a defence against enemy forces. In the 15th c. it had a wall and a moat; only one of the three town gates, Mølleporten (Mill Gate), has been preserved; apart from the one at Fåborg it is the only surviving medieval gate in Denmark.

Kong Askers Høj:
Klekkende Høj

Stege

St Hans' Church, built about 1250 in Romanesque style, was enlarged by the addition of a three-aisled choir in the 15th c.; it has rich fresco decoration in the choir and nave.

In Møn Museum can be seen geological and archaeological finds, photos. costumes, silverware and seamen's chests.

Ulvshale

From Stege a minor road leads north into the Ulvshale (Wolf's Tail) Peninsula, a nature reserve with rare birds and gnarled old trees. Birds such as water-rails, razorbills and snipe live on the mud-flats. From Ulvshale a bridge leads to the nearby island of Nyord, where birds can be observed from elevated seats.

*Keldby Church

This seldom-visited part of Møn boasts some of the island's finest beaches. The main road to the east from Stege passes through Keldby and past Keldby Church, built of brick between 1200 and 1250 and with some rich frescoes; those in the choir, arranged in two rows, date from the 13th c. On the walls are vividly imagined Bible scenes from the Old and New Testaments, including the Last Judgment and the Shepherds with their flocks. The vaulting has paintings by the Master of Elemunde, whose work is frequently found in many Møn churches. His primitive paintings, full of humour, contain many details reminiscent of everyday life, such as Joseph making gruel for the infant Jesus.

Hans Hansens Gård

South of the church, by way of Keldbylille, the road leads to Hans Hansens Gård, a thatched square building dating from about 1800 and arranged around an inner courtyard. The rooms are furnished with 19th c. furniture and objects and are now open to visitors as a museum.

Elmelunde

The road continues to Elmelunde. The church, a prominent landmark for sailors, is in the style typical of rural churches in eastern Denmark and contains frescoes by the Master of Elmelunde; these include "Entry into Jerusalem", "Flagellation of Christ", "Last Judgment", "St Peter with the Key to Heaven", "St Paul with a Sword", as well as ploughing and harvest scenes. Beautiful patterns of flowers, climbing plants, birds and stars fill

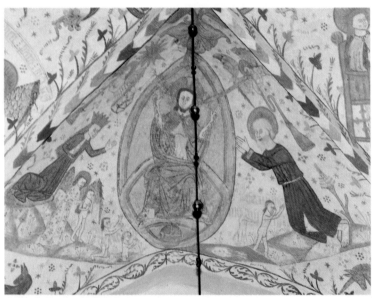

Fresco in Elmelunde Church

the spaces between the many Bible scenes. The altar and pulpit were gifts from Corfitz Ulfeldt – who lived on Møn for a time as a feudal lord – and his consort, Leonora Christina (see Maribo).

10km/6 miles further on the road reaches the main attraction of the tour, the chalk cliff known as Møns Klint, the highest point of which is 128m/420ft above the sea. The brilliant white of the chalk standing out against the deep blue of the sea is particularly striking when the sun is shining. There are footpaths around the cliffs, with walks lasting about an hour, and two steep flights of steps lead from Storeklint and Jydeleje down to the sea. Fossils of marine animals and plants can be found on the shore. An expanse of beech forest along the cliff-top contains rare species of plants hidden in the undergrowth. A superb view can be enjoyed from Sommerspiret, a peak 102m/335ft high; at Taleren remarkable echoes can be heard. There is an archaeological and geological museum near the car park.

**Møns Klint

From Møns the visitor is recommended to make a short detour to see the Romantic small summer residence of Liselund, built about 1795 by the Governor of the island, the French immigrant Antoine Bosc de la Calmette, for his wife and named after her. In the course of his travels he had acquired a taste for French architecture and was influenced by the "Back to Nature" movement; the house was, therefore, designed in the style of a simple peasant house and the roof thatched with dark reeds.

Liselund Manor

The house is surrounded by beautiful gardens with many Romantic features, including artificial lakes and canals, a "Swiss cottage" and a "Chinese tea pavilion". Hans Christian Andersen wrote his story "The Tinder Box" while staying in the Swiss cottage. Other buildings in the park were destroyed by a rockfall in 1905.

The return journey is on the same road back to Stege. By turning off to the south at Magleby we come to Klintholm, a mansion built in 1875 in the

Klintholm Mansion

Møns Klint

175

Møn

Neo-Renaissance style. Through the northern part of the park – with its lakes and avenues of lime trees – there is a marked footpath which leads into the forest and on to the cliffs on the coast.

Klintholm Havn
Further to the south on Hjelm Bay lies the fishing port and sailing harbour of Klintholm Havn.

Grønjægers Høj
From Stege a detour of 7km/4 miles south can be made to Æbelnæs, where there is another Stone Age "passage grave". At the south of the island lies Grønjægers Høj, the "Hill of the Green Huntsman", also known as "Grønsalen", a megolithic tomb of three chambers surrounded by some 140 massive stones and one of the largest of its kind anywhere.

*Fanefjord Church
Near the tomb stands the brilliant white church of Fanefjord, decorated with a rich series of paintings (c. 1500) by the Master of Elmelunde. The paintings form a kind of "Biblia Pauperum" (Bible of the Poor) but do not adhere rigorously to the biblical accounts. The themes are taken from the Old and New Testaments and from Christian legends, including "The Anunciation", "Birth of Jesus", "Adoration of the Magi", "Baptism of Jesus", "Slaughter of the Innocents" and "St George and the Dragon". Note also the frescoes of the High Gothic period (c. 1350) on the choir arch showing St Christopher, St Martin and medallions with emblems of the Apostles.

Island of Bogø
From the southern tip of Møn a causeway crosses to the island of Bogø, which was once known as the "Island of Mills". Today there is but one survivor – Bogø Mølle, a windmill of Dutch origin. From Bogø we can travel north to Zealand (see entry) by the Farø Bridge or south to Falster (see entry) via the Farø Bridge or by ferry from Nyby to Stubbekønig.

Næstved   D 3

Zealand
District: Storstrøms amt. Population: 45,000

Situation
Næstved, an industrial town and port, lies on the south-west coast of Zealand where the River Suså flows into Karrebæk Fjord, providing a link between the town and the Bay of Karrebæksminde.

History
Næstved developed around a medieval monastery, and trade and fishing were the main occupations of the inhabitants. Until the wars with Sweden in the 17th c. the town had commercial links with North Germany, Scotland and Norway. The extension of the port, enabling it to be used by large ships, the improvement of communications with Copenhagen and the south of the island, as well as the arrival of various industries all brought a renewed upsurge in the town's fortunes in the 19th c. Important branches of industry now include engineering, ceramics, wood and paper. A squadron of brightly dressed cavalry rides through the town every Wednesday morning.

Sights

St Peter's Church
The oldest part of the town is that near St Peter's Church (Skt. Peders Kirke), the largest Gothic church in Denmark. Most of the building dates from the 13th c.; it was comprehensively restored between 1883 and 1885. During this restoration wall-paintings of about 1375 were found in the choir, including a representation of King Valdemar IV and his Consort, Hedwig, kneeling at a penitent's stool. Also to be seen are a choir screen by Abel Schrøder the Elder (c. 1600), a 13th c. Crucifix, a copper font and a pulpit of 1671.

"Boderne" (museum)
In Church Square stands the old Town Hall and medieval brick houses with arched windows bedded in mortar. These 15th c. stone booths (Stenbo-

derne) are the only remaining medieval terraced houses in Denmark; they were once occupied by craftsmen. Today they house a museum of local crafts, glassware and silver.

The very beautiful House of the Holy Ghost (Heiligåndshuset) at Ring-stedgade 4, was built in the 15th c. and formerly used as a hospital. It now houses the Municipal Museum (Næstved Museum), exhibiting medieval and more modern wood carvings.

House of the Holy Ghost (museum)

Among the many half-timbered houses the Apostelhuset (Apostle House) in Riddergade is of particular interest. It has carved figures of the Apostles on the beams of the facade (c. 1500); each Apostle is carrying an object symbolising his martyrdom.

Apostelhuset

Nearby stands an old pharmacy (Løveapoteket), a recently-restored half-timbered building of 1853 in the Dutch Renaissance style. Medicinal herbs and spices are grown in the garden.

Pharmacy

About 2·5km/1½ miles north of the town centre stands a former Benedictine Mønastery (Skovkloster, c. 1200), which houses the Herlufsholm boarding-school. The late medieval monastery church is one of the oldest brick churches in Denmark. It has an unusually wide nave and is notable for some magnificent tombs, which include those of Admiral Herluf Trolle, who endowed the monastery as a school, and of his wife Birgitte Goye. Note the impressive Gothic ivory crucifix (c. 1230) and the Baroque pulpit of about 1620 by Ejler Abelsen.

Herlufsholm

A visit can also be recommended to the glassworks at Holmegård, a few miles outside Næstved. Artistic and everyday articles in blown glass are produced here, together with bottles, preserving jars and medicine bottles. Visitors can watch the glass-blowers at work. (Open: Mon.–Thurs. 9.30am–1.30pm, Fri. 9.30am–noon, Sat. and Sun. 11am–3pm.)

Holmegård Glassworks

Surroundings

There are a number of interesting stately homes in the countryside around Næstved. On the island of Gavnø south-west of Næstved stands Gavnø Manor. The estate, a former nunnery, became privately owned in 1584 and in 1755 the house was converted into a Rococo mansion by Otto Thott (1703–85). It possesses one of Denmark's largest picture collections and a magnificent library, which at the time of Thott's death contained some 138,000 volumes. Note also the church in the south wing, with an altar and pulpit carved by Abel Schrøder.
In the park, tulips bloom in the spring followed by summer flowers, orna-mental shrubs and roses (open: May–Aug. daily 10am–4 or 5pm).

*Gavnø Manor

See Korsør, Surroundings

Holsteinborg

Another stately home, Sparresholm (1609) lies 14km/9 miles west of the town. It was built in Renaissance style for Jens Sparre and has a beautiful flight of steps leading to the courtyard. In a former cowshed is a collection of horse-drawn vehicles of all kinds, both carriages and carts. Nearby is a wheelwright's shop, a stable and a running track of Olympic proportions (open: summer, Sat. and Sun. 10am–5pm).

Sparresholm

25km/16 miles east of Næstved is the little town of Fakse by a limestone hill 76m/250ft high with a quarry which has been used since the Middle Ages. In the Geological Museum are displays of minerals and fossils found in the coral reef of the Cretaceous period. Now only limestone and chalk for industrial purposes is quarried here. Surrounded by woods on Fakse Bay, to the south-east of Fakse, is the resort of Fakse Ladeplads. From this harbour, local limestone has been shipped since the Middle Ages.

Fakse

The Mansion of Gisselfeld

Vemmetofte Abbey	About 8km/5 miles east of Fakse, Vemmetofte Abbey, which has been rebuilt several times, is situated in a park; since 1909 it has been a Baroque mansion. In 1735 the estate became a home for ladies of the nobility; since then the deeds have been amended to allow married couples to reside here. The old abbey has attractive gardens.
*Mansion of Gisselfeld	The Mansion of Gisselfeld (1554), an impressive Renaissance building which has been altered several times, lies to the north-west of Fakse and is surrounded by a moat. The house is situated in a very beautifully maintained park laid out in the English style and containing a lake, a grotto with a waterfall, a fountain, a rose-island and 400 different species of trees and bushes, including a bamboo grove. (House not open to the public.)
Bregentved Manor	Bregentved Manor, the largest estate in Zealand, is situated 4km/2½ miles to the north-east. Since 1746 it has been owned by the ducal family of Moltke. The manor-house, the buildings of which date partly from about 1700 and partly from the 19th c., is surrounded by a large park. Some parts of the gardens are maintained in the Baroque style (entrance to the park: Wed. and Sun. 9am–8pm).
Præstø	25km/16 miles south-east of Næstved the little town of Præstø is charmingly situated on Fakse Bay and has a pretty 15th c. church. On the northern edge of the town stands Nysø Mansion, the main buildings of which are 17th c.; in the garden is a studio built by Baroness Stampfe for the sculptor Bertel Thorvaldsen; a side wing of the manor houses a collection of the artist's works.

Nyborg

C 3

Funen
District: Fyns amt. Population: 18,000

The important port of Nyborg is situated on the east coast of the island of Funen, on the Great Belt.

The castle, built in the 11th c. in order to control the Great Belt, led to the development of the town. Nyborg obtained its charter in 1271 and in 1282 King Erik Klipping signed Denmark's first constitution in Nyborg castle. From 1354 until the early 15th c. the meetings of the "Danehof", the annual assembly of important personages of the kingdom in audience with the king, were held in Nyborg. From 1560 until 1857 a patrol ship in the Great Belt collected tolls from all ships using this waterway. The war against Sweden (1658–59) led to a long impoverishment of the town. In 1869 the fortifications were pulled down but the west wing (King's Wing) was restored between 1917 and 1923. Today Nyborg is an important centre of communications. A bridge and tunnel across the Great Belt between Funen and Zealand is under construction; the West Bridge, between Funen and the little island of Sprogø (a road and rail bridge 6·6km/4 miles long) has already been completed. The Great Belt Exhibition Centre explains what is happening. (Open: May–Sept. daily 10am–8pm, Oct.–Apr. 10am–5pm; closed Sun.) Nyborg also has a marina.

Sights

The present Castle (Nyborg slot), situated near the market-place, consists of only the "King's Wing", where the Danish kings held their court between 1250 and 1413. After restoration the medieval character of the castle – fortifications, Knights' Hall and Imperial Council Chambers – can again be appreciated. The castle now houses a collection of weapons. (Open: Jun.–Aug. daily 10am–5pm, Mar.–May and Sept.–Oct. Tues.–Sun. 10am–3pm; guided tours).

A beautiful timbered house (1601) in Slotsgade, Mads Lerches Gård, now houses the Nyborg Museum (Nyborg og Omegns Museum). Its exhibits

Mads Lerches Gård in Nyborg

illustrate the history of the town; an annexe contains some interesting sculptures by Carl Aarsleff (open: as castle above).

Landporten

On Torvet, north of the castle and market, is "Landporten" gatehouse, a 40m/130ft long building with an entrance gate. It was built in 1660 by Frederik III who, following the war with Sweden, strengthened the fortifications and extended the ramparts. At that time the Landporten was the only entrance to the town from the land side. Some of the ramparts still exist. Bells are rung at 9.45pm each evening as a reminder of the time when the gate was closed at 10pm.

Church of Our Lady

A visit should be made to the three-aisled Church of Our Lady (Vor Frue Kirke) in Adelgade; the interior was restored in 1973. Inside are some 17th c. epitaphs and a font with a carved lid. The tower, 67m/220ft high, is covered in copper.
Near the church stands the Korsbrødregård, a stone building with a Renaissance gable of 1614 and cellars with Gothic vaulting.

Surroundings

Knudshoved

About 4·5km/3 miles south-east of the town lies the promontory of Kundshoved from where ferries cross the Great Belt, which is only 26km/16 miles wide at this point, to Halsskov (see Korsør, Surroundings) on Zealand. A bridge and tunnel project, providing a link from Knudshoved via the little island of Sprogø to Zealand, is complete.

Holckenhavn Palace

2km/1¼ miles south of Nyborg stands Holckenhavn Palace, a Renaissance building (1590–1631) considered one of the most magnificent mansions in Denmark. It is surrounded by a large park with well-tended lawns, flowerbeds and trees (entrance to the park Tue. and Sat. 2–6pm).

Kerteminde

Some 40km/25 miles north of Nyborg on Kerteminde Bay lies the pretty fishing town of Kerteminde, where many of the old houses have been preserved. The Johannes Larsen Museum (in Møllebakken) is the artist's former house containing a selection of his work (closed Mon. in summer; open Wed., Sat., Sun. rest of year). In St Lawrence's Church, built probably about 1200 and later remodelled, visitors can see models of ships.

Ladby

A short distance south-west of Kerteminde is the village of Ladby. 1·5km/1 mile to the north (signposted!) lies "Ladbyskibet", where a Viking ship, 22m/72ft long and originally constructed as a burial site, was found in 1935. A roof has been built over the ship and a museum building constructed around it; the museum exhibits replicas of burial objects found here, including horses' bridles. (Open: Tue.–Sun. all year, 10am–6pm, summer; 10am–3pm rest of year.)

Hindsholm

North of Kerteminde stretches the peninsula of Hindsholm which, compared with Funen, has a rough climate. At first the land is hilly and then becomes flat towards the northern point of Fyns Hoved. The road ends near the village of Nordskov. The peninsula has numerous bays and some beautiful beaches.

Odense   C 3

Funen
District: Fyns amt
Population: 180,000

Situation

Odense, after Copenhagen and Århus the third largest town in Denmark, lies on the island of Funen on the important E 20 main road from Jutland to

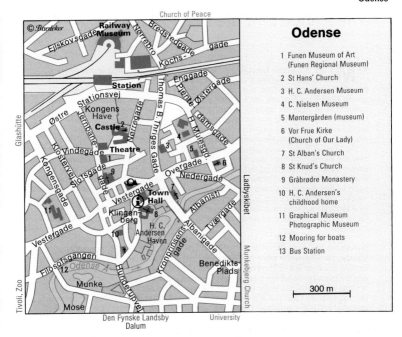

Odense

1 Funen Museum of Art
   (Funen Regional Museum)

2 St Hans' Church

3 H. C. Andersen Museum

4 C. Nielsen Museum

5 Møntergården (museum)

6 Vor Frue Kirke
   (Church of Our Lady)

7 St Alban's Church

8 St Knud's Church

9 Gråbrødre Monastery

10 H. C. Andersen's
   childhood home

11 Graphical Museum
    Photographic Museum

12 Mooring for boats

13 Bus Station

300 m

Copenhagen; the town is located on the little Odense Å river which flows into Odense Fjord a short distance north of the town.

The name of Odense first appears in the records in 988, when the Bishop of the town was granted a letter of safe conduct by the German Emperor Otto. No doubt it was originally a cult site devoted to the worship of Odin (Wotan); hence its name. In 1086 the Danish king Knud (Canute) was murdered in St Alban's Church here. Fifteen years later he was canonised by the Pope. An ecclesiastical centre and place of pilgrimage in the Middle Ages, Odense survived secularisation after the Reformation and remained an important commercial town. At the beginning of the 19th c. Kerteminde, 15km/10 miles away, became the port of Odense. The Old Town was gradually occupied by shops and businesses, so that although it has preserved its original layout, few old buildings remain. (See Travel Discounts.)

History

Odense's most celebrated son is the fairy-tale writer Hans Christian Andersen (the initials H. C. are pronounced ho-tsay in Danish; the "d" in Andersen is silent). He was born here on April 2nd 1805, but moved to Copenhagen – where he became famous – because he felt unappreciated in his native town, a resentment which can be "read between the lines" in his tale "The Ugly Duckling". Andersen died in Copenhagen on August 4th 1875 (see Famous People and Baedeker Special "The Prince and the Pea", pages 182–183).

Odense has developed into a major industrial town; the harbour is linked by a canal to the Odense Fjord on the Great Belt. It has a wharf and iron and steel, electro-technical and textile industries as well as timber-processing.

Economy

181

The Prince and the Pea

"**M**y life is a pretty fairytale . . . rich and happy" are the first words of Hans Christian Andersen's autobiography "The Fairy Story of My Life". That sounds happy and carefree, but in truth things were quite different; in front of the young man from Odense lay a winding path through life, a difficult climb from conditions of extreme squalor, a "truly thorny road to fame and honour". His happiness lay in the fact that he could himself experience this "pretty fairytale", be welcomed at the finest courts in Europe and see his work become a part of the world's great literature. He changed his life from that of the "Ugly Duckling" to that of the "Proud Swan", enjoyed the patronage of the King of Denmark himself and saw his stories find their way into the homes of countless readers. However, his early life had been anything but easy. At the age of fourteen Andersen ran away to Copenhagen to seek his fortune in the theatre, but met with little success and was soon in dire financial straits. In Jonas Collin he found a well-to-do patron who made it possible for him to study; but what he really wanted to do was to write. As well as other writings he published travel notes – such as "A Walk from Holmen's Canal to the East Point of Amager" (1829) – on which his later fairytales were modelled.

During his life Hans Christian Andersen made thirty extensive journeys through Europe. He frequently went to Germany, where he had many friends and benefactors. On June 3rd 1831 he noted ". . . in the Royal Court Theatre of Saxony. Tieck was there and greeted me most kindly. We went home by boat down the Elbe. The bridges were reflected in the water and the domes and towers of Dresden could be seen against the clear sky. We went over the Brühl Terrace and enjoyed the scent of jasmine. From the windows there was a beautiful view over the Elbe and of the vineyards on its banks."

He met Adalbert von Chamisso in Berlin; he "was the first man who translated my works and introduced them into Germany". Of Andersen himself Chamisso wrote at that time "Gifted with wit, a lively mind, humour and folksy *naïveté*, Andersen possesses the ability to awaken deep responses in his readers."

Time and again Andersen travelled to Weimar, Jena, Leipzig, Dresden and Hamburg; the latter he regarded as "more poetical than Berlin". He became acquainted with many of the great names of his era: Schelling, the Brothers Grimm, Mendelssohn-Bartholdy, Clara and Robert Schumann, Franz Liszt, Richard Wagner, Heinrich Heine, Alexander von Humboldt, Franz Grillparzer and Johann Strauss. He was a guest at the royal courts of Dresden and Munich, dined in Potsdam and was decorated by the King of Prussia in 1845. He was very friendly with the Grand Duke of Sachsen-Weimar.

"Travelling is living! Travelling has provided me with the best form of schooling. For me it is like a refreshing bath for the mind, like Medea's potion of eternal youth. My teachers are life itself and the world, I have the gift of being able to interpret and portray them; but I must have a place in which to work, which means I must travel the world". These are the words of a restless man seeking the good fortune which eluded him in his private life.

Thus Andersen became one of the greatest itinerants of his time, eagerly absorbing all the people whom he met, all the towns and landscapes he saw, and portraying them in his stories. On his journeys he felt the "galoshes of good luck" on his feet, which seemed also to endow his mind with "seven-league boots"; to quote his own words, "To travel along the Rhine is like a living fairytale. The knights' castles hang on the slopes of the green vineyards like . . . the grapes of one's memory. The Rhine provides a nostalgic and wistful picture of days of yore". Thus inspired, he wrote "A Poet's Bazaar" (1842) and "In Sweden" (1851), using a free form of expression which enables him to cast off the restrictive strait-jacket of the novel. "Here his skill as a writer of tales blossoms with witty associations and poetic digressions. With both he enters new territory in literature. His book "In Sweden" heralds a new epoch; until then not even the Swedes themselves had appreciated the unspoilt natural beauty of their land which he unveils in his books. In his travel books pictures of romantic nature alternate with flashes of everyday life, historical sketches with visions of the future."

In his books on Spain and Portugal Andersen lights a sparkling firework display of brilliant and fantastic pictures which won praise even from the critics: "A veritable Orpheus, this poet, whose prose sings so beautifully that not only do the very animals, plants and stones listen and understand but toys become alive, goblins and elves actually exist – a true magician", wrote Strindberg.

His first fairytales were written during his journeys through France and Italy in 1833 and 1834. Without his "Eventyr" Andersen would probably now long since have been forgotten. "The Emperor's New Clothes", "The Princess and the Pea", "The Swineherd", "The Brave Tin Soldier", "The Ugly Duckling", "The Little Mermaid" – in all these his seemingly naïve style transports his readers to another world in which the horrors and injustices of the real world are taken and dealt with in a fanciful way. With ironic bite, sarconic sharpness and witty humour he uses the most minor and everyday events as material for his tales.

His novels are little known, his major works – the travel diaries – even less so. The latter reveal the true magnitude of the man, his gifts of observation, the art of describing people, places and scenery. However, it was abroad that Andersen, who as a fourteen year-old had gone to Copenhagen "to seek fame and fortune", was first discovered

Salvador Dali: "The Little Mermaid"

in all his many talents, before at the age of 62 he was eventually made a freeman of his native Odense. When he celebrated his 70th birthday on April 2nd 1875 half of Denmark joined in the celebrations and organised street-parties. He lived for a further four months, finally departing this life on August 4th. The town and the royal court honoured him with a state funeral, the first ever accorded to a commoner.

His work has for many years filled an important role in world literature – today the tales of this magician of fantasy and sorcerer of language, the "Prince of Denmark", are read by children all over the world in more than 80 different languages.

The South of the Town

Town Hall

The town centre around the Cathedral and Town Hall is a pedestrian zone. In Flakhaven, a square bordering the long street known as Vestergade, stands the Town Hall, the oldest part of which was built in red brick in the late 19th c., modelled on the Italian style. Further building took place between 1936 and 1955 in reinforced concrete faced with red tiles. It contains many works of art, including a sculpture "Spring in Funen". On St Knud's Square in front of the Town Hall can be seen a statue of St Knud by Utzon Franck. The Town Hall is open Mon.–Wed. 9am–3.30pm, Thur. 9am–5.30pm, Fri. 9am–noon.

*St Knud's Church

To the south of the Town Hall stands St Knud's Church (Skt. Knuds Kirke), the cathedral of Odense. It is named after the Danish saint, Knud IV, who had himself begun the building which was dedicated to his name about 1100. This church was burned down in the 12th c. After a further great fire Bishop Giscio made a start on a three-aisled replacement in the 13th c., but this in fact took almost 200 years to complete. The present brick church has a square tower with a spire above the west end of the main nave.

A feature of the interior of this Gothic edifice is the crypt below the choir, with the tombs of King Knud and his brother Benedict as well as sundry other kings and their consorts. Behind the High Altar stands a huge reredos with magnificent carvings, the work of Claus Berg between 1515 and 1534 on instructions from Queen Christina. In the centre of the main panel Christ is portrayed on the Cross, while scenes from Our Lord's Passion appear on the side-panels. Paintings of the royal family adorn the predella. Note also the epitaphs, bronze font of 1620 and pulpit of 1750. The carillon in the tower is played several times a day.

To the east of the Cathedral a park named after H. C. Andersen (H. C. Andersen Haven) stretches along the waterfront; in it stands a statue of the writer.

St Alban's Church

On Albani Torv nearby is St Alban's Roman Catholic Church.

H. C. Andersen's Childhood Home

To the south-west of the Cathedral, in Munkemøllestræde (Nos. 3–5) stands the house of Hans Christian Andersen's parents (H. C. Andersens Barndomshjem), a half-timbered house with a memorial plaque on the gable. Andersen lived from 1807 to 1819 with his parents in one of the little apartments in this house. In 1930 the building was furnished as a museum and is now a branch of the main Andersen Museum (see below). (Open: Apr.–Sept. daily 10am–5pm, Oct.–Mar. noon–3pm).

The East of the Town

**Hans Christian Andersen Museum

At Hans Jensens Stræde 37–45 stands a single-storey, half-timbered house which is believed to have been the birthplace of Hans Christian Andersen (1805) and is now the heart of the Hans Christian Andersen Museum, which contains furniture, pictures, manuscripts and books belonging to the writer. Since its foundation in 1905 the museum has been extended on two occasions. On view is a large library with Danish and foreign editions of Andersen's works as well as a collection of illustrations to these stories. The domed hall of the museum, which was set up as a memorial hall in 1930, is decorated with scenes from the autobiographical book "Story of My Life"; the frescoes are by Niels Larsn Stevns (open: Jan.–May daily 10am–4pm, June–Aug. daily 9am–6pm, Sept.–Dec. daily 10am–4pm).

Carl Nielsen Museum

In 1988 a museum was opened at Claus Bergs Gade 11 in memory of the town's second famous son, the composer Carl Nielsen. It is a modern

H. C. Andersen Museum   *Portrait of H. C. Andersen*

glass-fronted building with a well-lit interior. Visitors can see the room in which Nielsen composed, and all his works can be heard through an excellent stereo system, linked to a videoshow. The life and work of his wife, the sculptress Marie Carl-Nielsen, is also documented (open: daily 10am–4pm).

Going south from the Carl Nielsen Museum the visitor will come to the Møntergården at Overgade 48–50. This is the Old Mint, which now serves as a Museum of Local and Cultural History (open: daily 10am–4pm). The complex includes other typical houses of old Odense from the 16th and 17th c., as well as a Baroque warehouse. The buildings are furnished with interiors of various periods, as well as collections of costumes, ceramics, ecclesiastical art, toys, silver, clocks and coins. Particularly interesting is the exhibition "Odense in the Middle Ages".   Møntergården

To the south-east of the Mint stands the Church of Our Lady (Vor Frue Kirke), a Late Romanesque single-aisled brick and granite-block building with a partly preserved group of Late Romanesque round-arch windows on the east wall. The tower is late medieval. Note the carved pulpit (1639) and font.   Church of Our Lady

The North of the Town

At Jernbanegade 13 is the Museum of Art (Fyns Kunstmuseum), which dates from 1883–84 (open: daily 10am–4pm, Wed. also 7–10pm). Early Danish painting is represented by Jens Juel, Dankvart Dreyer and the Funen painters Peter Hansen, Fritz Syberg, Johannes Larsen and Jens Birkholm. More recent works include those by Asger Jorn, Richard Mortensen, Robert Jacobsen and Carl-Henning Pedersen. A special exhibition of Danish Concrete and Constructive Art forms a considerable part of the collection.   Fyns Kunstmuseum

Odense

St Hans' Church	Further north near Kongens Have Park stands St Hans' Church (Skt. Hans Kirke), the oldest parts of which are 13th c., the choir being 15th c. The church was once part of a monastery of the Order of St John of Jerusalem. On the north wall can be seen a large 15th c. Crucifix, while the font is Late Romanesque. Outside the south-west wall is a pulpit which can be reached from inside the church; this is Denmark's only external pulpit.
Mansion	The old monastery buildings were converted in the time of Frederik IV into a mansion, which lies behind St Hans' Church in Kongens Have. Frederik VII had it redesigned in 1841 in the Classical style. Today it houses council offices.
*DSB Railway Museum	In the northern part of Odense the visitor will find the DSB Railway Museum in a semi-circular building at Dannebrogsgade 24. The museum was modernised and extended in 1988. As well as locomotives and railway carriages dating from 1847 to the present day there is a ferry-ship exhibition and a large model railway (open: May–Sept. daly 10am–4pm, Oct.– Apr. 10am or 1pm–4pm).
Peace Church	Outside the town on the north on Skibhusvej stands the Peace Church (Fredenskirke), built 1916–20 to plans by the architect Jensen Klint; the design was originally intended for the Church of St Paul in Århus but this was never built. The Peace Church, an adaptation of Gothic brick churches and a preliminary study for Jensen Klint's famous Grundtvig Church in Copenhagen, is in yellow brick with a red-tiled roof and has five bays. Unusually, the choir is at the west end and the entrance at the east end. The front of the tower is divided into two gables ("tveje") with high vertical screens arranged like organ-pipes.

The West of the Town

**Brandts Klædefabrik	In the west of Odense, at Brandts Passage 37–43, lies "Brændts Klæde-fabrik", a former textile factory which is now an Arts Centre, with museums, shops, restaurants and cafés. Visitors are particularly attracted by the Funen Academy of Fine Arts on the top floor, an exhibition hall covering an area of 1600sq.m/17,200sq.ft. In rooms which once housed spinning-jennies and weaving-looms can now be seen paintings, sculptures and works from the fields of architecture, design and handicrafts. In addition, video demonstrations, concerts and lectures are given (open: Jan.–Dec. Tue.–Sun. 10am–5pm).
Museum of Photographic Art	The former textile factory is also home to an interesting Photographic Museum on the second floor. Its collections are currently being built up and are the subject of temporary exhibitions (open: as per Art Hall above).
Danish Museum of Printing	This museum (Danmarks Grafiske Museum/Dansk Pressemuseum) on the 3rd floor illustrates the history of graphics and printing during the last three hundred years. There are workshops for paper manufacture, book-printing and bookbinding, where old machines and tools are used (open: as per Art Hall above).
Moorings	To the south of Brandts Klædefabrik on the Odense Å, is a mooring jetty (Filosofgangen) from where river trips can be made.

Surroundings

Munkebjerg Church	There is an interesting modern church to be seen in Munkebjerg, to the south-east of the town. Munkebjerg Church in Østerbæksvej was the result of an architectural competition in 1942. The winning design was for an unusual polygon structure, but local resistance prevented construction of the church until 1962, when another team of architects took over and produced a building similar to the original plan, the unconventional style

Brandts Klædefabrik: exhibition in the art gallery

having in the meantime become generally accepted. The church is hexagonal, with the air of a huge tent, and has a free-standing tower.

Attractions to the south-west of Odense include the Tivoli Amusement Park (open: Apr.–Aug. daily 2–10pm) and the Zoological Garden (open: daily 9am–4, 5 or 6pm), both situated on Sdr. Boulevard.

Tivoli
and Zoo

4km/2½ miles south of the town centre lies the Open-Air Museum in Hunderup Skov. This is "Den Fynske Landsby" (The Funen Village), with reconstructed farms and houses, many with thatched roofs, from the island of Funen, together with a water-mill, a brick-works, a school, a smithy and other workshops. Agriculture is practised using old methods. The oldest building in the village is a barn of 1666 next to the entrance; nearby can be found a "Kro" (Krug=jug, or inn). During the summer there are often opportunities, on request, to practise weaving or make pottery, etc. Andersen's fairy-tales are performed in the open-air theatre (open: Apr., May, Sept., Oct, daily 9am–4pm, June–Aug. daily 9am–6.30pm, Nov.–Mar. Sun. 10am–4pm).

Open-Air
Museum
(Den Fynske
Landsby)

The town of Dalum, to the west of the Funen Village, is also worth seeing. Its church was once part of a Benedictine monastery which was moved here from Odense about 1600; note the interesting frescoes.

Dalum

From Dalum Volderslevvej leads south to Carl Nielsens Barndomshejm (Childhood Home), now a museum. It was here that the Danish composer Carl Nielsen (1865–1931) spent a part of his childhood and youth (open: May–Aug. 11am–3pm). Nielsen, who from 1908 to 1914 held the post of director of music at the court in Copenhagen, composed several operas, including "Saul and David" (1902) and "Masquerade" (1905), as well as symphonies, string quartets and works for piano and organ.

Carl Nielsen's
Childhood Home

Odense

*Hollufgård Museum and Art Centre

A visit to the Hollufgård, a museum and Cultural Centre on the south-eastern edge of Odense will be found rewarding. The centre of the complex is a stately home of 1577 which has been restored. There are sculptors' workshops (where visitors can try their hand), a Museum of Funen Pre-History ("Fyns Oldtid") with reconstructed houses from the Bronze and Viking Ages, and lecture rooms of the Odense Municipal Museums. Members of the research centre devote themselves to the theme "Man and Nature". There are also sporting facilities available, and the Odense Golf Club has its club-rooms here (open: Jan. 1st–Apr. 30th Sun. 11am–4pm, May 1st–Oct. 31st Tue.–Sun. 10am–5pm, Nov. 1st–Dec. 31st Tue.–Sun. 11am–3pm).

European Automobile Museum

For those interested in cars a visit to the European Automobile Museum 7km/4½ miles east of Odense is strongly recommended. There are some 70 cars on show which provide a picture of driving in the 1950s, together with a wide range of tools, manuals and brochures connected with the purchase or technical development of motor cars (open: July 1st–Aug. 31st daily 10am–5pm; Apr., May, June and Sept. Sat. and Sun. 10am–5pm).

Fraugdegård

Further east lies the town of Fraugde, with a half-timbered 16th c. manor-house, Fraugdegård. In the late 17th c. it belonged to Denmark's most celebrated ecclesiastical poet, Thomas Kingo, who later became a bishop. Inside can be seen a crucifix by Claus Berg.

Randers   C 2

Jutland
District: Århus amt. Population: 62,000

Situation

The town of Randers lies on the Gudenå, Denmark's longest river, near where it flows into Randers Fjord on the east coast of Central Jutland.

History

Since Randers was easily accessible from the interior of Jutland the town developed at an early date into an important trading centre. There was a Royal Mint here in 1080. During the Middle Ages several churches and monasteries were founded. In the middle of the 14th c. Valdemar IV built a castle near the town. The Franciscan monastery was dissolved in 1530 and converted into a royal palace.
Between 1627 and 1629 Imperial troops under Wallenstein occupied the town, which suffered in the years that followed from the effects of the war, from a large conflagration in 1672 and from the plague. During the 19th c. the disputes regarding Schleswig-Holstein had an adverse effect on Randers, and in the Second World War it was occupied by German troops.

Economy

There have long been craftsmen of various kinds in Randers – bell-foundry workers, silversmiths, woodcarvers and shoemakers – but the town became particularly well known for its salmon; at the last salmon-farm in operation in 1820 well over 1000 salmon were caught. Foodstuffs, metal-working, shoe production and vehicle manufacture are the major branches of industry today.

Sights

Church of St Martin

In Kirkegade, in the Old Town, stands the Church of St Martin, a 15th c. Gothic brick building. The choir, with three sides facing east, is lower than the three-aisled nave. The interior fittings date from the 17th and 18th c. and include a Baroque pulpit, font, altar and organ-case (1750). It was intended to build a monastery near the church, but this never materialised.

House of the Holy Ghost

Of the old houses near the church special mention should be made of the Helligåndshus (House of the Holy Ghost), dating from about 1435. The building, the remains of a dissolved monastery, was restored between 1894 and 1897 by Hack Kampmann. Note the 15th c, wall-paintings on the ground floor and the 16th c. ones on the first floor.

Passing along Torvegade the visitor will come to the old Town Hall, built in 1778 to the designs of Christian Mørup. The hipped roof is topped by a belfry. On a plinth in front of the Town Hall is the seated figure of Niels Ebbesen, who in 1340 killed a Duke of Holstein when he attempted to gain control of Denmark.
Immediately opposite the Town Hall, at Rådhustorvet 7, stands a Gothic brick building which is the oldest stone house in the town and now a café; it has gable steps leading to the neighbouring house. | Town Hall

At Stemannsgade 2 can be found the Culture House (Kulturhuset), consisting of an old and a new building; the latter was erected in 1964–69 by the architect Fleming Lassen and has two interior courtyards. On the first floor is the Historical and Cultural Museum, including three interesting burghers' rooms decorated with paintings by Rembrandt and Ostade. The Art Museum on the second floor houses works by 20th c. Danish painters, including Ejler Bille and Asger Jorn. In the inner courtyard is an abstract sculpture. | Culture House

North of the Culture House, in Østergade, stands the Amtmannshof (1928), a house typical of the Biedermeier period. | Amtmannshof

Surroundings

Near Ammelhede a commemorative stone marks the spot where – according to legend – Hamlet is buried. | Ammelhede

On the Djursland Peninsula, 25km/16 miles east of Randers, lies the little township of Auning. It has an interesting Romanesque church with wall-paintings of 1562 showing Christ sitting in judgment. In a chapel can be seen the tomb of Jørgen Skeel, owner of Gammel Estrup (see below). | Auning

3km/2 miles west of Auning stands Gammel Estrup, a stately home surrounded by a moat, built about 1500 and rebuilt in the Renaissance style. The owners of Gammel Estrup, members of the noble families of Brok and Skeel, were for many years linked with the Danish royal family in the rôles of advisors and confidants. In the early 20th c. the building was fitted out as the Jutland Manor House Museum (Jyllands Herregårdsmuseum). The architects were Matthias Bygmester and Jørgen Skeel. The south wing and staircase tower have been newly built. | *Gammel Estrup Manor-house

The building now houses two museums; in the house itself is the Jutland Manor House Museum, while in the old administrative part will be found the Danish Agricultural Museum. In the Manor House museum furniture and fittings from various eras help to convey the right atmosphere to the rooms – the Knights' Hall, Renaissance Room, Chapel and Watchman's Lodge. (Open: Apr.–Sept. daily 10am–5pm, Oct.–Mar. Tue.–Sun. 10am–3pm).
The Agricultural Museum (Dansk Landbrugsmuseum) is over 100 years old and consists of several buildings. Permanent exhibition on 200 years of Danish farming life and 25,000 agricultural implements. Between April 1st and October 31st members of the Gammel Estrup Blacksmiths' Guild give demonstrations of the way artefacts are produced by hand in an old smithy. (Open: daily 10am–5pm.) | Museums

Clausholm Manor, 13km/8 miles south-east of Randers, is occasionally used for concerts. The five-winged Baroque building was erected between 1699 and 1723 for Grand Chancellor Conrad Reventlow (bust above the main entrance). Later it came into the possession of Frederik IV, who had a love affair with Anna Sophie, the daughter of the Reventlow family, and | *Clausholm Manor

Gammel Estrup Manor

Clausholm Manor, a Baroque building

later married her even though his first wife was still alive. Note the Dining Salon with stucco-work, the so-called "Royal Suite" and the Chapel which has the oldest organ in the country (open: in summer daily 10am–noon and 2–5.30pm; park daily 9am–6pm).

About 20km/12½ miles south-west of Randers lies the village of Ulstrup, where there is a three-winged mansion dating from the 16th/17th c., which was built for Christen Skeel and extended for his son; notable is the sandstone doorway.

Ulstrup

Around Randers can be seen a number of fine country churches. One of these is at Råsted (8km/5miles north-west of Randers). Its large-scale frescoes make it an interesting example of Romanesque church decoration; the paintings portray scenes from the Old Testament (the Fall of Man, etc.) as well as the Nativity and Childhood of Jesus.

Råsted

Ribe

A 3

Jutland
District: Ribe amt
Population: 18,000

Ribe, one of the oldest towns in the country, lies on the Ribe Å, not far from the place where the river enters the North Sea in the Bay of Fanø.

Situation

Ribe developed on an estuary which formed one of the few harbours on the west coast of Jutland. Excavations in the 1970s have established that at one time Ribe lay north of the present river, as shown by the discovery of a Viking settlement of about A.D. 700 near Skt. Nicolaj Gade. In the year 860 Ansgar, Archbishop of Hamburg and Bremen, obtained permission to build a church here; and in 948 Ribe became the episcopal see. From the early 12th c. the town was surrounded by a rampart and outside its gates a castle was built. The kings resided here around 1200.

In the Middle Ages the town traded with England and Germany, exporting cattle and fish. However, the Reformation led to a decline in the population, and it was not until after the re-unification of South Jutland (North Schleswig) with Denmark in 1920 that Ribe began to thrive once more.

History

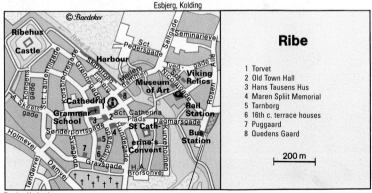

Esbjerg, Kolding

Ribe

1 Torvet
2 Old Town Hall
3 Hans Tausens Hus
4 Maren Spliit Memorial
5 Tarnborg
6 16th c. terrace houses
7 Puggaard
8 Quedens Gaard

200 m

Tønder, Haderslev

Sights

The twisting lanes and streets with their many 16th and 17th c. half-timbered houses (storks' nests) bestow a particular charm. From May 1st to September 15th every year a watchman makes his evening tour of the town, singing his song and telling the story of old Ribe; the one-hour tour begins on Torvet at 10pm (also at 8pm during the high season).

*Cathedral

In the centre on the Torvet stands the Romanesque Cathedral (Vor Frue Kirke), building started about 1150 and it was later rebuilt on several occasions. Today it is the only five-aisled church in Denmark. There is a panoramic view from the 50m/164ft high tower, which has a bell, formerly rung to warn the citizens of floods or fires. The relief above the door shows Jesus being taken down from the Cross. In the light and airy interior can be seen tombs and epitaphs including one erected by Valdemar the Victorious for his son who died in 1231. Note also the beautiful wood-carving of St George and the Dragon, the pulpit of 1579, a bronze font and the choir-stalls. On Cathedral Square stand statues of Hans Adolph Brorson, who was Bishop of Ribe in the 18th c., and of the reformer Hans Tausen (see below).

Hans Tausens Hus (museum)

Opposite the Cathedral stands Hans Tausens Hus, an old timbered building. The house is a relic of Denmark's oldest existing episcopal see (16th c.). Here Hans Tausen (1494–1561), a disciple of Luther and the first Danish Reformer, spent the last ten years of his life. Today the house is an archaeological museum, displaying Viking finds including handcrafted objects and merchants' goods (open: Tue.–Sun. 10 or 11am–3 or 5pm; also Mon. June 1st–Aug. 31st).

Old Town Hall

The Old Town Hall (1496), to the south-east of the Cathedral, was originally a private residence. Anders Bording (1619–77), who published the first

Ribe Cathedral: painting and mosaics by Carl-Henning Petersen

Danish newspaper, was born here. The building served as the Town Hall from 1709 until the administration was moved in 1966, although there are still collections of council items to be seen in the former Council Chamber. The former debtors' prison is now a museum of weapons, etc.

Further east lies St Catherine's Church (Skt. Catharinæ Kirke), part of a Dominican abbey. The present church dates from the 15th c. but incorporates remains of the original building of 1228. Passing through the church the visitor will come to the medieval monastery court which is surrounded by two cloisters lying one above the other; in the lower cloister note particularly the arcades with pointed arches and vaulting.

St Catherine's Church and Abbey

After the Reformation the abbey served as a hospital until 1864, then as a home for the elderly (not open to the public). Outside the church stands a fountain with a statue of St Catherine, patron saint of Dominicans. The fountain was the work of Anders Bundgaard (c. 1930).

From Torvet the street called Overdammen leads to Quedens Gård (c. 1580), a half-timbered merchant's house with four wings. The Classical dwelling was built 200 years later. Today Quedens Gård is a museum, with interiors of 1580, a 19th c. citizen's home as well as documents on commerce, handicrafts and industry. The museum also mounts a special exhibition on Ribe in the Middle Ages (open: Tue.–Sun. 10 or 11am–3 or 5pm: also Mon. June 1st–Aug. 31st).

Quedens Gård (museum)

The Museum of Art is situated in Skt. Nicolaj Gade. It contains sculptures and paintings by Danish artists of the "Golden Age" (first half of the 19th c.) as well as later works.

Museum of Art

An old street in Ribe

Michael Ancher's picture "Baptism of a Child" is representative of the Skagen school; there are also works by Funen artists and a selection of paintings of Ribe scenes (open: Tue.–Sun. 11am or 1pm–4pm).

Skibbroen (harbour)

Skibbroen, along the river, is Ribe's harbour, which today is used only for leisure purposes and as a mooring for the "Riberhus" excursion boat, which, between May and September, takes passengers through the marshlands to the Kammer sluice.

Nearby lies the "Johanne Dan", a barge designed to sail through the shallows. Every Wednesday in summer a market is held at Skibbroen.

Flood Column

The flat marshland has been subject to flooding by storms for many years. On the harbour a Flood Column (Stormflodssøjle) shows the height reached by the water in the floods of 1634, when it rose more than 6m/20ft above the norm; countless houses were destroyed and several thousand people lost their lives. In 1976 the dike was strengthened.

Riberhus Castle

On a hill to the north-west of the town can be seen the excavated remains of Riberhus Castle (Riberhus Slotsbanke); built in the 12th c, it was for several centuries a residence of the Danish kings. All that remains are the ruins of a fortress, the moat and a statue of Queen Dagmar, the consort of Valdemar the Victorious (1170–1241).

Surroundings

Vester Vedsted

To the south-west of the town, near the coast, lies Vester Vedsted. The mud-flats which stretch from Blåvands Huk in Denmark to Den Helder in Holland are the main resting-place and winter home in Europe for a plethora of water-fowl. In just one square metre of mud-flats live several thousand microscopically small animals and plants on which the birds feed. A chain of islands separates the mud-flats, most of which are a conservation area, from the North Sea.

Island of Mandø

Offshore lies the little island of Mandø (area 7.5sq.m), comprising salt meadows and sand dunes. It can be reached only at low tide from Vester Vedsted in a bus drawn by a tractor. On Mandø there is a museum and an Ornithological Collection, as well as a Visitors' Centre where nature conservancy exhibitions are mounted. On the island terns, sandpipers, waders and ducks, including eiders breed. In order not to disturb the birds, visitors are asked to observe them only from the marked roads and pathways.

From Mandø trips are arranged to Koresand, a sandbank in the mud-flats west of the island; the trips last some three hours and include a visit to the seal-reserve.

Ringkøbing

Jutland
District: Ringkøbing amt
Population: 17,000

Situation

The little town of Ringkøbing lies on the northern bank of Ringkøbing Fjord on the west coast of Jutland. The lagoon-like fjord, bordered in the south by Holmsland Klit, is connected to the sea by a narrow channel. In the 17th c. the entrance to the fjord began to shift southwards and to silt up, making it more difficult for ships to enter from the North Sea. It was 1931 before the problem was finally solved by the opening of the lock in Hvide Sande.

History

The oldest known privileges enjoyed by the town date from 1443. Agriculture, fishing, oyster-catching and shipping formed the principal sources of income for the inhabitants, followed later by trade in cattle. The 17th c. brought a period of decline, caused by the wars with Sweden and the silting up of the channel to the North Sea. In 1793 the district administration was moved to Ringkøbing.

In 1869 Ringkøbing was the first small town in Denmark to provide free universal education. In 1904–5 the town received a new harbour. Today the citizens are very enthusiastic about environmental protection; they help to keep the beaches clean and, as far as possible, use environmentally-friendly sources of energy.

Sights

Beautiful old houses, such as the Customs Building in Østergade, are a feature of the townscape. On the market-place stands the old Mayor's Palace (1807), built in the Empire style. A fountain was erected in the market-place to commemorate the town's 500th anniversary in 1943. From the market-place (Torvet), the busy street of Vester Strandgade with houses dating from 1800, as well as shops and inns, leads down to the harbour.

Townscape

The museum on Kongevejen displays local history items, a coin collection, ecclesiastical artefacts, ships' figureheads and pictures of stranded ships. Also of interest is the collection of items relating to the writer and Polar explorer Ludwig Mylius-Erichsen (1872–1907), who led an expedition to Greenland in 1906 but died on the return journey. His statue stands nearby. A museum (Smedenes Hus), devoted to the development of forging and wrought metalwork through the ages has recently been opened at Lem, south east of Ringkøbing.

Museums

Surroundings

14km/8 miles north-east of the town lies Ølstrup, worth a visit to see the church with a painted reredos by Emil Nolde (1867–1956) showing Christ in Emmaus (1904).

Ølstrup

In Hee, 7km/4 miles north of Ringkøbing stands a 12th c. Romanesque church of granite slabs, which was restored about 1880. The north and south sides of the tower have a false roof in which were kept documents of the "Thing" (local assembly) which met in Hee during the Middle Ages. On the door of one of the cupboards in which ecclesiastical artefacts are stored is a representation of "The Man of Sorrows" framed by the arms of some famous families. Note also the granite font and a Triumphal Cross dating from about 1450.

Hee

The Sommerland West leisure park at Hee includes four lakes and a small zoo. Activities include speedboat racing, terrain cars, pony rides, and a traffic school. (Open: end-May–Aug. 10am–5 or 6pm.)

Sommerland West

To the west of Ringkøbing, on the North Sea coast, the tourist centre of Søndervig nestles amid the dunes. To the south stretches the promontory of Holmsland Klit with the Nørre Lyngvig Lighthouse, 53m/174ft high. Near Hvide Sande is the narrow channel through which ships from Ringkøbing Fjord reach the North Sea. In Hvide Sande, one of Denmark's major fishing ports, visitors can see ships of all kinds – trawlers, fishing smacks, etc. The fish are transported to the processing factories in large refrigerated lorries. In the fjord there are shipyards where the vessels are overhauled and repaired. Rides on horseback across the heath and through the dunes down to the beach or night-time rides are favourite leisure pursuits.

Coastal region

Svend Lodberg, a child prodigy and now a famous landscape painter, was born in Hvide Sande in 1945. His pictures show the countryside close to the sea and the fjord, emphasising the effect of light and the kaleidoscope of colours in the sky; there is a permanent exhibition of his work in Ringkøbing.

Ringsted

Zealand
District: Vestsjællands amt. Population: 29,000

Situation	The town of Ringsted, situated in Central Zealand, is an important traffic hub; road 14 from Næstved to Roskilde intersects the east-west highway E 20 from Koge to Korsør.
History	Until well into the 4th c. Ringsted was the location of the "Thing" (local assembly), just as Odense was for Funen and Viborg for Jutland. On the occasion of religious festivals people from all over the island assembled here; justice was also dispensed at the "Thing" site.

In the Middle Ages Ringsted was one of the most important towns in the country. The first church was built about 1080; the body of Duke Knud Lavard, who was slain by Magnus the Strong, a son of King Niets (1104–34), was buried here. In 1169 Knud Lavard, who was revered by the people, was canonised. After 1160, King Valdemar I had a new and larger church built, and until 1341 the kings of Denmark were buried here. The town grew up around the church and the Benedictine Monastery, which had been founded several decades earlier, was destroyed by fire in 1800. Industries became established in the town in the 19th c. and the railway arrived.

Sights

"Thing Stones"	Two towers remain of the town wall which formed part of the medieval fortifications. In the market square three stones, the "Tingstener" still stand, recalling the earliest days of Ringsted.
St Benedict's Church	Also in the market square stands St Benedict's Church (Skt. Bendts Kirke), dating from the 12th c. and one of Denmark's oldest brick churches. Later, following a fire, it was given an Early Gothic vaulted roof and a Gothic tower above the crossing. The church contains the tombs of many Danish kings of the 12th and 13th c. A brass plate in the choir marks the resting-place of King Eric Menved (d. 1319) and his queen. Frederik VII had the royal tombs opened in 1885; in a chapel can be seen the grave goods found, including a lead tablet from the tomb of Valdemar the Great and silken materials from that of Valdemar the Victorious. On the canopy of the choir-stalls are scenes from the Old Testament (north side) and the New Testament (south side). There are also some notable chalk-paintings, including those in the choir and on the cross-vaulting.
Town Hall	In 1920 the land belonging to the former monastery passed into the possession of the town, and on the south and west of St Benedict's Church a park was laid out. Later the east side of the church was also opened up. In 1936–37 the Town Hall was built on the north side of the open space; designed by Steen Eiler, it is a two-storeyed brick building with a copper roof. Nearby stands a statue of Valdemar the Great.
Fantasy World	Mechanical fairytale figures, north-west of Ringsted. (Open: daily 10am–5pm end Feb; end March–mid Sept.; early Oct.–end Dec. Closed Mon. mid Apr.–mid May.)

Surroundings

Fjenneslev	Fjenneslev, 8km/5 miles west of the town, is a village with a twin-towered church which was originally built of flint and limestone. Note the Crucifix by Claus Berg on the altar and the 12th c. frescoes portraying the "Adoration of the Magi" and the "Flight into Egypt".
Gyldenløves Høj	In a wooded region 15km/9 miles north of Ringsted rises Gyldenløves Høj, at 126m/414ft above sea-level the highest point in Zealand, with a fine view.

The E 20 from Ringsted leads in a westerly direction to Sorø. Just before reaching Slaglille a country road branches off to the village of Bjernede. Here there is an interesting two-storey round church, the only one in Zealand, dating from 1150–75. The interior vaulting is borne on four pillars. The roof and small octagonal tower were added in the course of restoration in 1890–92. Note the granite font and Triumphal Cross.

Bjernede

In Sorø, on the lake of the same name, stands a notable 12th c. church, the largest monastic church in Denmark; it is dedicated to the Virgin Mary. In 1199 Bishop Absalon gave the church to the Cistercian Monastery of Sorø, which he had founded. Within the church are a large number of tombs, including those of Bishop Absalon (d. 1201), King Christoph II (d. 1332) and his wife, Valdemar IV (d. 1375), and King Oluf (d. 1387). The playwright Ludvig Holberg (1684–1754) is buried in a side chapel. Note also the very impressive Triumphal Cross hanging above the transept, the work of Claus Berg (*c.* 1530).

*Sorø
Church

In 1586 Frederik II had set up a school in the monastery building and this became an academy for the sons of noblemen. Holberg left his property and his library to the academy, but most of this was destroyed in a fire in the 19th c. Today it is a boarding school. In the academy gardens, which are laid out in the English style and extend to the shores of Lake Sorø (Sorø Sø), there is an open-air theatre and a statue of Holberg.

Rømø

A 3

District: Sønderjyllands amt
Area: 99sq.km/38sq.miles
Population: 1000

Rømø, off the west coast of Jutland, one of the North Friesian Islands, is the largest Danish island in the North Sea. Many birds nest here. A stone causeway 10km/6 miles in length through the mud-flats links the island with the mainland. Rømø is separated from the German island of Sylt by the Lister Deep (Listerdyb). There is a car ferry to List.

Situation

The west coast of this popular island has a broad sandy beach. The island is divided into Nørreland and Sønderland, with a road running diagonally through it to the seaside resort of Lakolk, near the west coast. The landscape of the eastern part is characterised by woodland, heath and marsh. On the east side of Rømø lie the small towns of Juvre, Toftum, Nørre Tvismark, Kongsmark, Rømø Kirkeby, Østerby and Havneby; Mølby and Sønderby are further inland.

Topography

Sights

In the Kommandørgården at Toftum, the home of an 18th c. "Kommandør", or whaling captain, the ceilings and doors are painted with Biblical subjects, while the exterior walls are clad with Dutch tiles. The house is now a Local Museum, where examples of the architecture and domestic life of the island of Rømø can be seen.

*Toftum:
Local Museum*

Kirkeby church is dedicated to St Clement, the patron saint of seamen. It dates from the 16th c. and has a ceiling with wooden beams from which hang beautiful models of ships. Concerts are held here in the summer.
In the churchyard, note the gravestones of ships' captains, with epitaphs and pictures telling their life stories.

*Kirkeby:
St Clement's
Church*

From the fishing village of Havneby a ferry serves the island of Sylt. In years gone by daring seafarers embarked from here on voyages to Greenland, generally on St Peter's Day (February 22nd).

Havneby

The Kommandørgård on Rømø Island

Rømø Ny Sommerland	Rømø Ny Sommerland, a leisure centre in the south of the island, has a village of typical, old, half-size farmhouses. Many activities include pony-rides, water cycles, water chute and trampolines (open: daily May–end Oct., 10.30am–6pm).

Roskilde   E 3

Zealand
District: Roskilde amt
Population: 51,000

Situation	Roskilde, which in the Middle Ages was at times a royal seat and a diocesan town, is situated in the east of Zealand on Roskilde Fjord, which bites deep into the island. Within the town there are several natural springs, the largest being the "Maglekilde", which delivers 15,000 litres/3,300 gallons of water every 24 hours. Roskilde can be reached from Copenhagen by train or car in about half an hour.
History	Roskilde is one of the oldest towns in Denmark. As early as 960 a wooden church stood on the northern edge of the terrace from which the land slopes down to the fjord. Harald Bluetooth, the ruler who converted Denmark to Christianity, is believed to have founded this church; this, at least, is the tradition, although there is no real evidence to support it. Nevertheless it is a fact that in 1030 a start was made on rebuilding the church in stone. In the 11th c. Roskilde became a royal and episcopal residence and in the following centuries it enjoyed its period of greatest prosperity. It was principally the centre of an ecclesiastical area, possessing great power and wealth, particularly after King Valdemar arranged the appoint-

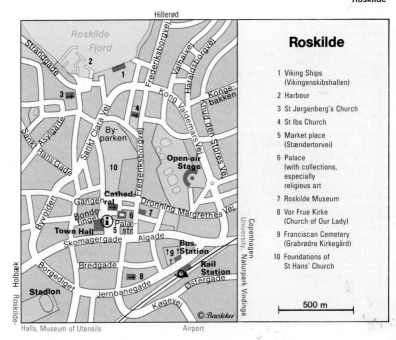

Hillerød

Roskilde

1 Viking Ships
  (Vikingenskibshallen)

2 Harbour

3 St Jørgenberg's Church

4 St Ibs Church

5 Market place
  (Stændertorvei)

6 Palace
  (with collections,
  especially
  religious art)

7 Roskilde Museum

8 Vor Frue Kirke
  (Church of Our Lady)

9 Franciscan Cemetery
  (Grabrødre Kirkegård)

10 Foundations of
   St Hans' Church

500 m

© Baedeker

Halls, Museum of Utensils   Airport

ment of a young Paris-educated priest as bishop. This was the great Bishop
Absalon of the Hvide lineage (1128–1201). In 1168 Valdemar presented to
his favourite the town and castle of Havn; thus Absalon became the virtual
founder of Copenhagen, then a fishing village of little consequence. Thereafter the focus of power lay in Roskilde. The situation changed, however,
with the Reformation, when eleven parish churches and all the town's
religious houses were closed, and the economic and intellectual life of
Roskilde declined. The town later recovered some of its importance, and in
1658 the peace treaty between Denmark and Sweden was signed in Roskilde Cathedral. By this treaty Denmark lost all its possessions beyond the
Kattegat and the Øresund. Much of the old town was destroyed in a series
of fires during the 18th c.

The economic revival of Roskilde did not begin until the mid-19th c., after
the construction of a railway link with Copenhagen. Roskilde is now one of
the major industrial, educational and scientific areas of Denmark, with the
Roskilde University Centre (RUC), concentrating on the social sciences, and
an atomic research centre at Risø, to the north of the town.

The Cathedral, one of Denmark's great national monuments, is the central
feature of the town, which extends northwards to Roskilde Fjord and
southwards to the motorway (21 or 23).

Townscape

The Town Centre

The imposing Cathedral of St Luke stands on slightly raised ground on the
site of three earlier churches, including the wooden church believed to
have been built by King Harald Bluetooth. The building of Bishop Absalon's
cathedral began about 1170 to the plan of a Romanesque basilica with

**Cathedral of
St Luke

199

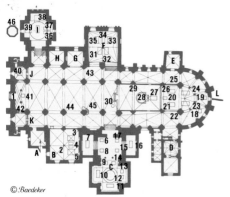

© Baedeker

Roskilde Cathedral

A Entrance
B Christian I's Chapel
  (Chapel of the
  Three Kings)
C Frederik V's Chapel
D Chapter House
E Oluf Mortensen's Porch
F Christian IV's Chapel
G St Andrew's Chapel
H St Birgitte's Chapel
I Christian IX's Chapel
J North Tower Chapel
K South Tower Chapel
L Absolon's Arch

1 Main entrance
2 Royal Column
3 Monument of Christian III
  and Queen Dorothea
4 Tomb of Christian III
  and Queen Dorothea
5 Monument of Frederik II
  and Queen Dorothea
6 Coffin of Caroline Amalie
7 Sarcophagus of Sophie
  Magdalene
8 Coffin of Christian VIII
9 Coffin of Marie Sophie
  Frederike
10 Sarcophagus of Queen
   Louise
11 Sarcophagus of Frederik V
12 Coffin of Juliane Marie
13 Coffin of Christian VII
14 Coffin of Frederik VI
15 Coffin of Louise Charlotte

16 Sarcophagus of Christian VI
17 Coffin of Frederik VII
18 Helestens Sten
19 Tombstone of Bishop
   Peter Jensen Lodehat
20 Monument of
   Duke Christopher
21 Sarcophagus of Frederik IV
22 Pillar, with remains
   of Svend Estridsen
23 Sarcophagus of Christian V
24 Sarcophagus of Charlotte
   Amalie
25 Pillar, with remains of Estrid,
   sister of Knud the Great
26 Sarcophagus of Queen Louise
27 Sarcophagus of Queen
   Margrethe
28 High Altar
29 Choir-stalls of 1420
30 Font

31 Sarcophagus of Frederik III
32 Sarcophagus of Sophie Amalie
33 Coffin of Anne Cathrine
34 Coffin of Christian IV
35 Coffin of Prince Christian
36 Sarcophagus of Queen
   Alexandrine
37 Sarcophagus of Christian 10th
38 Double Sarcophagus of
   Christian IX and Queen Louise
39 Double Sarcophagus of
   Frederik VIII and Queen Louise
40 Sarcophagus of Anne
   Sophie Reventlow
41 Kirsten Kimer, Per Daver
   and St Jørgen
42 Armour of Vincentz Hahn
43 Royal Gallery
44 Orgen (1554–1654)
45 Pulpit (17th c.)
46 Tomb of Frederik IX

transepts, but this plan was modified around 1200 under the influence of French Gothic. The church, in red brick, thus displays a mixture of Romanesque and Gothic architecture, and the exterior is further altered by the addition over the years of several funerary chapels. For more than 500 years the Cathedral has been the burial-place of the kings and queens of Denmark. The two west towers were added in the 14th c., and their slender spires, sheathed in copper, are dated 1635–36. The "Royal Door" between the towers is opened only for royal funerals; visitors must enter by the south door.

Interior

The interior, with lateral aisles flanking the nave, is divided mainly into the central aisle, choir and upper choir. The central nave is bordered by the North Tower Chapel, originally known as St Siegfried's Chapel, and by the South Tower Chapel, endowed by Queen Margarethe I as the Bethlehem Chapel. Both served as burial-chapels for Danes of noble birth.

*Choir-stalls

The choir is particularly notable for the magnificent mid-15th c. carved choir-stalls; they were so constructed as to make it easier for the choirboys to stand during services. Above the stalls are reliefs with scenes from the Old Testament (south side) and New Testament (north side). An interesting feature of the New Testament series is the representation of the Ascension; the footprints left by Christ can be seen on the ground, while his feet are still visible at the top of the scene.

Roskilde Cathedral: the exterior . . .   *. . . and a view of the interior*

The large gilded winged altar in the choir, made in Antwerp in the 16th c., was originally intended for the Chapel of Frederiksborg Castle, but was presented to Roskilde by Christian IV. The pictures on the wings of the altar portray scenes from the Life of Christ – from the Nativity to his Crucifixion. The altar has been excellently restored following a fire in 1968; as part of the restoration the renowned needlewoman Anna Thommesen made a new altar-cloth. Behind the altar lies the tomb, artistically worked in alabaster, of Queen Margarethe I.

*Winged altar

Note also the bronze font (1602) and – in the central aisle – the pulpit of sandstone, marble and black limestone.

The ambulatory used by the members of the choir leads around the chancel. Note the "Hehlestens sten", a stone with no inscription which is said to mark the tomb of a "hehlest", a headless horse which heralds the approach of death; in fact it is probably the grave of a beheaded man.

Ambulatory

In the funerary chapels, built on to the cathedral and entered from the aisles, are the tombs of more than 30 Danish monarchs, commencing with that of Margarethe I (d. 1412), who reigned over three Nordic countries – Denmark, Norway and Sweden. Frederik IX, who died in 1972, was also initially buried in a chapel, but in 1985 his coffin was transferred to a tomb specially built outside the cathedral. It is octagonal in shape and clad with hand-painted tiles, to the designs of the architects Inger and Johannes Exner and Vilhelm Wohlert.

Tomb of
Frederik IX

The Chapel of Christian IV, on the north side of the cathedral, has massive ogival vaulting. On the walls can be seen paintings by William Marstrand, showing scenes from the king's life, while at the entrance is a bronze statue of Christian IV by Bertel Thorvaldsen. The chapel, containing several coffins, is separated from the church by an imaginatively designed grille.

Funerary
chapels

Also on the north side are the chapels of Christian IX, St Brigitte (frescoes of 1511) and St Andrew.

From the Chapel of Christian IV the visitor should proceed to the middle of the church where, on the north wall, can be seen the Royal Gallery and the Renaissance Throne of Christian IV, richly carved and gilded. Opposite the gallery is the organ, which was restored in 1988–91.

The Chapel of Christian I, known as the Chapel of the Three Kings, on the south side, has a roof of ribbed vaulting supported on a granite column. The column is marked with the heights of various kings: the tallest – that of Christian I and marked by the king himself – is 2·1m/6ft 9in, although in fact his skeleton measures only 1·88m/6ft 2in. It can be seen that Peter the Great of Russia, who stayed in Denmark in 1716, stood head and shoulders above most of the others. The walls are decorated with chalk drawings, mainly of Biblical subjects; also of interest are two coats-of-arms on the east wall. Christian I and his consort as well as other rulers and their wives are buried in this chapel. Originally Christian I intended that this chapel should be the assembly-room for an Order of Knights he had founded; this led to the story of the Order of the Elephant.

Also on the south side of the cathedral is Frederik V's Neo-classical chapel, modelled on the Pantheon in Rome, with a dome and high windows which let plenty of light into the chapel. On the roof can be seen the slender Margarethe Spire which – according to tradition – Erik of Pomerania had built.

Palace	The cathedral is linked to the Palace to the east by Absalon's Arch, a covered bridge built of limestone in the year 1200 or so. The Palace originally served as the Bishop's seat and later as accommodation for royalty who were passing through or were attending a funeral in the cathedral. In the 18th c. the present palace was built to the designs of the Danish architect Laurids Thura; the building has a handsome courtyard and staircase.
Historical Collection	Five rooms of the Palace now house a collection (Palæsamlingerne) which originated from a gift to Roskilde by the Kornerup family, who were important merchants of the 18th and 19th c. The exhibits include furniture, paintings – including portraits of Peter Kornerup and his wife – and works by the architectural artist Joseph Kornerup. Also on view are some 19th c. champion rifle-shooting targets.
Art exhibitions	One room in the palace is used by the Roskilde Art Club for their exhibitions. In summer sculptures are displayed in the palace garden.
Town Hall	In the market-place (Stændertorvet), south of the palace, stands the Town Hall, built about 1880. The tower, some 500 years old, once belonged to St Laurence's Church which stood on the site. Some of the remains of this church have been found and can be seen in a basement of the Town Hall.
Roskilde Museum	The Roskilde Museum is situated in a town house of 1804 at Skt. Ols Gade 18. The exhibits include prehistoric finds from the region (Gerdrup Grave) as well as medieval relics. The museum also has a collection of local embroidery and costumes. A merchant's house (Brødrene Lützhøfts Efterfølger) at Ringstedgade 6, captures the atmosphere of the period 1910–20.
Church of Our Lady	In Fruegade, in the south of the town, stands the Church of Our Lady (Vor Frue Kirke), the structure of which incorporates remains of the walls of an 11th c. church which, according to the Danish historian Saxo (d. 1220), was built by Bishop Sven Normand around 1080. Restoration at various dates has severely altered the character of the church. Note the altar of 1620 with 19th c. paintings by C. Hansen and F. C. Lund, and also the pulpit.
Museum of Old Tools	At Ringstedgade 68, a short distance south of the town centre, is the Tool Museum (Håndværkmuseet), a private collection of old woodworking tools as used by cabinet-makers, carpenters and factory workers.

The North of the Town

In the north of the town lies the Town Park, with a fine view over Roskilde Fjord. Nearby stands St Ibs' Church, a limestone building of about 1100. Over the years parts of the church have been demolished, so that today only the nave remains.

Not far away, on a hill near the fjord in a part of the town which was once a fishing village, will be found the Church of Skt. Jørgensbjerg, with a choir and nave dating from about 1100. The walled-up north doorway is even older and formed part of a previous building which has been dated at 1040. From the hill there is a magnificent view over the sea.

Roskilde's second main attraction, the Viking Ship Museum on the bank of the fjord, was opened to the public in 1969 (open: Apr.–Oct. incl. daily 9am–5pm, Nov.–Mar. incl. 10am–4pm). The fishermen of Roskilde had known for a long time that there was an underwater stone ridge in the fjord; according to local tradition the accumulation of stones covered a ship which had been sunk by Queen Margarethe (d. 1412). It was only when the Danish National Museum carried out underwater excavations in 1957 that the barrier at a narrow part of the fjord was found to date from the Viking Age and to consist of more than one ship. These had been sunk and covered with stones at some time between 1000 and 1050 in order to block the fjord and to protect the trading town of Roskilde from hostile attack – probably from Norwegian Vikings, who were then harassing the Danish coasts.

In 1962 the barrier area was drained and the ships brought to the surface. Although they had broken into thousands of pieces they were found to comprise an ocean-going freighter for trading with England, Iceland and Greenland, about 16·5m/54ft long; a trading vessel 13·3m/44ft long, used in the Baltic, the North Sea and on rivers – this was crewed by a maximum of six men and carried cargo stowed amidships; a warship some 18m/59ft

Roskilde: in the Viking Ship Museum

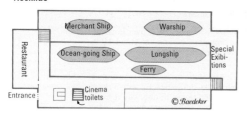

Viking Ship Museum Roskilde

These ships, found in Roskilde Fjord in 1957 and raised in 1962 have been thoroughly restored and preserved

long, for sails or 24 oarsmen; a ferry-boat, about 12m/38ft long, which was also used for fishing; and finally a longship so long – some 28m/92ft – that at first it was believed to be two vessels. The last was the dreaded Viking man-of-war, seaworthy and yet easily beached, fast and manoeuverable in battle. Then began the task of piecing together and restoring the ships. Although the Viking ships of Roskilde are of little significance to specialist archaeologists they are of great interest from a purely historical and artistic point of view.

There is a cinema in the museum where films are shown daily about the recovery of the ships (commentary also in English). A permanent exhibition provides the visitor with information about the Vikings, the construction of the ships and sub-aqua archaeology. The facilities include a cafeteria and a shop.

Surroundings

Tours

There is a lot to see and do in the surroundings of Roskilde. There are trips through Roskilde Fjord on board the "Sagafjord", which departs from the harbour and has a restaurant on board. The ship sails past Boserup Skov, a forest with beautiful flora, and the nature reserve on Bognæs Peninsula, where many species of birds are to be seen.

Vindinge;
Museum Railway

To the south-east of the town, near Vindinge, lies Roskilde Sommerland, a park with extensive open-air enclosures for animals and a games area. Nearby a narrow-gauge railway (the Hedelands Veteranjernbane), runs on Sundays from May to September. Since it was opened in 1977 it has been extended several times and there are now 4km/2½ miles of track; the buildings and stops along the line are named after local places. The trains depart from Hedehusgård Station in Hedehusene. The terminus is the Flintebjerg, 81m/266ft high, from where there are excellent views on fine days.

Ole Rømer
Museum

Still further east in the Vestskoven Forest the observatory of the celebrated astronomer Ole Rømer (1644–1710) was discovered in 1978. The place is now signposted, and in the nearby Vridsløsemagle Museum information can be obtained about Rømer's work as an astronomer.

Ledreborg
Castle

A few miles west of Roskilde, near Lejre, lies Ledreborg, one of Denmark's finest Baroque buildings dating from the 17th and 18th c. The main building was converted in the 18th c. for Count J. L. Holstein, under the guidance of the Rococo architect Niels Eigtved. The original furnishings and paintings have remained unspoiled. Note particularly the domed Salon and the magnificent Chapel in an adjoining building. The park is attractively laid out in the English and French styles, with terraces and walkways (open: daily, Jun.–Aug: park 10.30am–5pm; castle 11am–4.30pm).

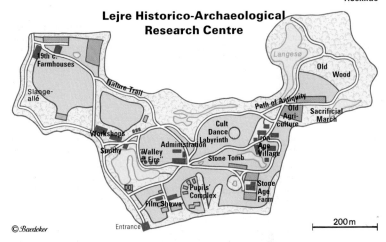

Lejre Historico-Archaeological Research Centre

In the Historico-Archaeological Research Centre 4km/2½ miles north-west of Lejre the past is brought to life! In September 1964 a research area of 25ha/62½ acres was opened up here. which seeks to secure the social and material culture of former times, which is in danger of being forgotten in our present technological age. The principal attraction is the "Iron Age Village", a reconstructed 2000 year-old Danish village with houses, fields and domestic animals. In their leisure time or on holiday "Iron Age families" attempt to exist in prehistoric conditions and to do without any modern aids; for example, they plough with a wooden plough drawn by oxen. In addition there are old workshops (pottery, weaving, smithy). In the "Valley of Fire" demonstrations are given on such themes as "Fire and Boat" or "Iron and Horse".

Archaeological analyses are also carried out. At one spot in the open "Sacrificial Marsh", visitors can see how the Iron Age people worshipped their gods. The centre's symbol, the Ask Yggdrasil Tree of Life. is taken from Norse mythology (open: May 1st–end of Sept.).

*Historico-Archaeological Research Centre of Lejre

The old village of Gammel Lejre, near Lejre, has in its small Kongsgården Museum (royal estate) the remains of a Viking ship burial and, near Øm, a passage grave of the Late Stone Age (c. 3000 B.C.), one of the best-preserved burial-mounds in Denmark. This consists of fifteen upright stones and four covering stones. The stone chamber measures 7m/23ft long and 1·8m/6ft wide. Visitors are recommended to carry a torch. In the course of archaeological digs stone objects have been found, including chisels, daggers and arrowheads, as well as pottery and human bones.

Ship burial; Passage grave

South-west of Lejre, in the wooded region of Skjoldenæsholm, near Gyldenloves Hoj, 126m/414ft high and the highest point on Zealand, is a Tramway Museum (Sporvejsmuseet) with a changing exhibition of trams, trolley-buses and buses. Trams of the period 1863 to 1949 are on display and a museum tramway operates. In 1952 the trams were replaced by diesel buses. Texts and pictures tell the story of public transport in Denmark.

Tramway Museum

The old town of Holbæk lies on Holbæk Fjord, an arm of the large Ise Fjord, 30km/19 miles north-west of Roskilde. The interesting Local Museum, exhibiting 17th c. furniture and tools, is at Klosterstræde 16; near the museum a half-timbered house of 1660 has been re-erected. Sailing and motor boats can be hired at the marina.

Holbæk

4km/2½ miles south of the town the visitor will find Tveje-Merløse Church, dating from around 1120 and restored in 1892–94. It is one of the oldest churches in the country and was originally built by members of the Hvide family, to which Bishop Absalon also belonged. Of special interest are the pulpit of 1571 and the wall-paintings of about 1175. In the churchyard stands a modern 20th c. sculpture, "Pottemageren" (Jug Maker), by Jais Nielsen.

Interesting wall-paintings by the Master of Isjeford dating from about 1450 and showing mainly scenes from the Childhood of Jesus can also be seen in the Romanesque village church of Tuse, 7km/4½ miles west of Holbæk. The font is of granite.

Samsø   C 3

District: Århus amt
Area: 114sq.km/44sq.miles
Population: 5000

Situation

The long island of Samsø, popular as a holiday centre, lies in the Kattegat. The north and south divisions of the island are linked by an isthmus, near which is a nature reserve. A car ferry operates between Sælvig on the west coast and Hov on the east coast of Jutland, and another between Kolby Kås (also on the west coast) and Kalundborg on Zealand.

Sights

The island can boast some fine beaches, a varied landscape and several ancient archaeological sites.

A picturesque thatched house on the Island of Samsø

Tranebjerg, in the middle of the island, is the largest town on Samsø and was once a venue of the "Thing" (early Danish assembly). Of interest are the 14th c. fortified church on the western edge of the town and the Museumsgård on Museumsvej, where the Samsø Museum is housed. On the east coast, near Tranebjerg, lies the fishing village of Ballen, an attractive seaside resort with a yacht basin. Onsbjerg, north-west of Tranebjerg, is worth a visit if only in order to see the rare Romanesque gold crucifix (about 1200) in the church.

Tranebjerg

In a park in the south of Samsø stands Brattingsborg Manor; the main wing of this country house was built in the English style in 1871–98 (admission to the park June to August, Tues. and Fri. 10am–4pm). The main road passes the park and leads on through a wood to the coast. The "Vesborg Fyr" lighthouse to the south acts as a landmark.

Brattingsborg

Beautiful old thatched half-timbered buildings, surrounding a village pond, and a bell-tower are features of the picturesque little village of Nordby in the north of the island. To the north-west lie Ballebjerg (64m/210ft high) and the spit of land known as Issehoved, now a nature reserve.

Nordby

Silkeborg   B 2

Jutland
District: Århus amt. Population: 49,000

Silkeborg lies on the Langsø (Long Lake), in an area of Central Jutland characterised by forests and lakes; these are the "Danish Lake Uplands", through which flows the Gudenå. During the summer months visitors can enjoy colourful illuminated fountain-displays on the banks of the Langsø.

Situation

In the Middle Ages there was a castle by the Langsø, close to the site of the present Viborg Bridge, but little now remains. In 1840 King Christian VIII conceived the plan of founding a town in the vicinity of present-day Silkeborg, in order to open up the interior of Jutland. In 1845 Michael Drewsen set up a paper factory and other industries soon followed, many of which made use of the water-power from the Gudenå river. In 1883 the first spa was established here, and in 1900 Silkeborg was elevated to the status of a town. Today various industries are well established and tourism plays an important role in the local economy.

History

Sights

The town extends along both north and south banks of the Langsø, the centre being in the south. Hovedgården, a town residence dating from 1770 (extended), houses the Historico-Cultural Museum. The most notable exhibit is the Tollund Man, a corpse some 2200 years old, found in a nearby bog. It is generally held to be the best-preserved body of a prehistoric man so far discovered. Also exhibited are documents relating to the town's history and some Danish glass dating from the Renaissance to 1900 (open: mid-Apr.–end Oct. daily 10am–5pm, rest of year Wed., Sat. and Sun. noon–4pm).

Historico-
Cultural Museum

*Tollund Man

The Museum of Art, situated at Gudenåvej 9 in a large park by the Gudenå, is worth a visit. The building dates from 1982 and was designed by the architect Niels Frithiof Truelsen and his colleagues. Jean Dubuffet designed the ceramic cladding for the façade, which was carried out by Erik Nyholm. Visitors to the museum pass through four large studios; here and there are "resting-places", with furniture by the Finn Alvar Aalto.
The museum has works by modern artists, including paintings by members of the COBRA group, founded in 1948, to which the Dane Asger Jorn

*Museum of Art
(Asger Jorn)

Silkeborg: the Museum of Art, with ceramic decoration

belonged. Jorn grew up and spent his life as a painter in Silkeborg; when he died in 1973 at the age of 59 he left to the town some 5,500 works by internationally-esteemed artists as well as several thousand of his own. He was sixteen when he painted his first picture – a seascape with sailing-ships. In the Second World War he produced "The Seasons" cycle of paintings, which can now be admired in the entrance hall but which at the time served as black-out blinds in an apartment block in Copenhagen! Jorn painted abstract pictures with a powerful use of colour, some with figures from Nordic folk-art. He became an art-collector after the war, many items being obtained in exchange for his own pictures. In this way he acquired works by Odilon Redon, James Ensor, Emil Nolde, Max Ernst, Francis Picabia, Man Ray, Fernand Leger, Jean Dubuffet, Karel Appel, Pierre Alechinsky, Lucio Fontana, Echauren Matta, Enrico Baj and other well-known artists. In addition to the exhibition rooms there are others used for the instruction of art students and those taking courses, a cafeteria and a children's workshop (open: Apr.–Oct. Tue.–Sun. 10am–5pm, Nov.–Mar. Tue.–Fri. noon–4pm, Sat. and Sun. 10am–4pm).

Surroundings

Steamer trip

In summer the world's oldest paddle-steamer, the 130-year-old "Hjejlen", takes visitors from its mooring on the lake in the Museum Park – through one of the most beautiful parts of Denmark to the Himmelberg (147m/482ft; see entry). From the top of the hill there is a splendid view over the surrounding forests and lakes.

Grønbæk

A 13th c. Romanesque church in Grønbæk, 13km/8 miles north of Silkeborg, has some interesting wall-paintings in the choir which date from the time when the church was built. The frescoes portray Christ enthroned, with Mary and Peter on one side and John and Paul on the other. The south door is beautifully decorated with granite reliefs.

15km/9½ miles north-west of Silkeborg, beyond Voel, is the Jutland Car Museum, which will prove attractive to all who are interested in old cars. On display are about 100 vintage vehicles from the period 1900 to 1942 (open: May–mid-Sept. 10am–6pm; Apr. and mid-Sept.–Oct. Sat. and Sun. 10am–5pm).

Gjern
(Jutland Car
Museum)

Skagen   C 1

Jutland
District: Nordjyllands amt
Population: 14,000

Skagen, the northernmost town in Denmark, lies at the northern tip of Jutland. On the far side of this popular seaside resort the Grenen Promontory stretches far out into the sea. Some years ago the remains of a shipwreck was found here.

Situation

Archaeological finds have established that the site was populated in the Stone and Bronze Ages. In the Middle Ages Old Skagen (Gammel Skagen or Højen) had a settlement on the coast facing the Skagerrak, but it was not until later that the Kattegat coast was also populated. The houses were scattered among the dunes. In 1413 the town received its charter, when the principal occupation was fishing. From the 17th to the early 19th c. storms and flooding caused great damage in Skagen. In the second half of the 19th c. an artists' colony, with Danes predominating, settled in the town. In 1858 a new lighthouse, 46m/151ft high, was brought into use near Grenen. The railway came to the town in 1890.

History

Sights

Skagen is characterised by low, yellow-painted early 19th c. houses. A stroll round both Skagen and Gammel Skagen will be found most interesting. Every morning a fish auction is held in the auction hall at the harbour.

Townscape

Skagen Museum at Brøndumsvej 4, contains paintings, drawings and sculptures by Danish, Norwegian, Swedish, British and German artists who have had some connection with the town. Most of the work dates from 1870–1930. Local artists in particular are represented by some superbly colourful paintings, including works by P. S. Kroyer (1851–1909) and Michael (1849–1909) and Anna (1859–1935) Ancher. The house of Michael and Anna Ancher (Michael og Anna Anchers Hus) at Markvej 2 is also furnished as a museum. Both museums are open daily 10am–6pm).

*Skagen Museum

The Open-air Museum (Skagens Fortidsminder) at P. K. Nielsensvej 10 consists of eight old buildings, including the Fishing Museum, illustrating the history of fishing in Skagen, a Commemorative Hall recording the work of local rescue services and items from wrecks, a lifeboat station with an old lifeboat and a windmill, later used as a cornmill. A small group of old fisherman's houses, basically furnished, portrays their very hard living conditions (open: daily 10am–4 or 5pm).

Open-air
Museum

Near the Open-air Museum stands Drachmanns Hus, the timber-frame house where the Danish author Holger Drachmann (1846–1908), also a member of the artists' colony, spent his twilight years. Inside are his paintings and sketchbooks.

Drachmanns Hus

"Den Tilsandede Kirke", a tower near Skagen

The sand-buried church	3km/2 miles west of the town the visitor will come upon the Den Tilsandede Kirke, the tower of the 14th c. St Laurence's Church. In 1775 the church was enveloped by sand and the parishioners had great difficulty in getting to it; in 1795 it was closed by royal decree. In 1810 the nave was torn away, and only the tower remained standing.

Surroundings

Grenen	3km/2 miles north of Skagen stretches the flat Grenen Promontory, Denmark's most northerly point and a favourite holiday spot, where there is an interesting Art Museum (Grenen Museet). Among the dunes of Grenen lies the grave of the Danish poet and writer Holger Drachmann (see above), the "singer of the sea". Beyond Grenen Lighthouse the road ends at a car park, from where visitors can ride in a "sand-worm" (sandorm – a tractor drawing a passenger-carrying trailer), or walk (15 minutes) to the northern tip of Jutland, where the Skagerrak and Kattegat meet. Whereas the North Beach is becoming wider, the sea is constantly eroding land from the South Beach on the Kattegat coast.
Råbjerg Mile	To the south of Skagen lies a large area of dunes, heathland and plantations. The most impressive natural phenomenon in this region is the Råbjerg Mile, a 41m/135ft high shifting dune which moves annually a distance of 8–10m/26–33ft to the east, burying any vegetation in its wake; the dune is legally protected. There are two paths leading to the dune; one starts from the entrance to the Bunken camp-site, the other from a small picnic area near Råbjergvej.
Eagle Sanctuary	15km/9½ miles south-west of Skagen, on the road between Tversted and Ålbæk at Tver Birdslev, an Eagle Sanctuary has been established. In summer visitors can watch golden eagles being fed and sea eagles demonstrating their aerial skills.

Slagelse

Zealand
District: Vestsjællands amt
Population: 35,000

Slagelse, an important trading centre in the Middle Ages because of its situation, lies on the E 20 in the south-west of Zealand. Roads lead from here to Kalundborg in the north, Næstved in the south and Copenhagen (see entries). The engineering and furniture-making industries play an important role in the economy.

Situation

As early as the 11th c. Slagelse had a mint, and the first privileges of the town date from 1288. The inhabitants were engaged in agriculture and trade or worked as craftsmen. For several years Hans Christian Andersen attended the local Grammar School which had been founded after the Reformation, but which was closed in 1852. For centuries the town suffered from serious fires and the effects of war, but by the 19th c. the economy had recovered and breweries, distilleries, canning factories and engineering works were established here.

History

Sights

The central feature of the town is St Michael's Church (Skt. Mikkels Kirke), built about 1330 on the highest hill in Slagelse and restored in 1873–76. It has a memorial, designed by the sculptor Gunnar Slot in 1959, to the Danish resistance movement in the Second World War; next to it can be seen the sculpture "Woman", by Keld Moseholm Jørgensen.

St Michael's Church

Nearby stands the former monastery barn, which was a Grammar School from 1616 to 1809. A prominent pupil was Jens Baggesen (1764–1826), who published the first modern Danish prose.

Fisketorv – note the granite sculpture of 1977 – leads to Gammel Torv. For many years this was the town's commercial centre and main meeting-place. Queen Margarethe I is said to have crowned her six year-old son Oluf here.

Gammel Torv

The oldest building in Slagelse is the Romanesque St Peter's Church (Skt. Peders Kirke), which was later enlarged and altered, partly in the Gothic style. Medieval tombs can be seen in the arms store, and in a chapel is the tomb of St Anders (d. 1205) who had been a leading figure in the town's development.

St Peter's Church

In the 12th c. there was a monastery of the Order of St John of Jerusalem in the south-east of Slagelse, near the road to Næstved. It was founded by King Valdemar the Great in 1165 and was the chief seat of the Order of St John in the Nordic countries. Hans Tausen (see Ribe), who became a Lutheran in Wittenberg in Germany, went to school in Antvorskov as a twelve year-old and later became a monk. In 1525 he preached the sermon in Antvorskov which opened the way for the Reformation in Denmark.

Antvorskov

In 1580 the monastery became a royal residence and was subsequently made into a palace. Today only the ruins can be seen in Antvorskov woods. Some excavated finds are on display in a small museum; these include some limestone keystones from the vaulting and fragments of tomb-stones. The Danish flag, originally the banner of the Order is flown from the flagpole by the ruins every Sunday.

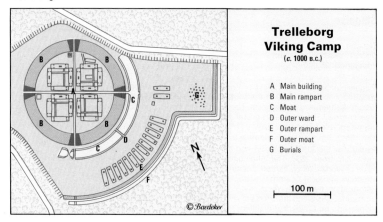

Trelleborg Viking Camp
(*c.* 1000 B.C.)

A Main building
B Main rampart
C Moat
D Outer ward
E Outer rampart
F Outer moat
G Burials

100 m

© *Baedeker*

Surroundings

*Trelleborg

7km/5 miles west of Slagelse lies the interesting reconstruction based on the finds from the excavated Viking settlement of Trelleborg, dating from the years 1000–1050. It consists of a circular rampart together with wooden stakes inserted into the ground, with four entrances. From there four streets, which divide the area into four quadrants, lead to the centre; within the ramparts were sixteen houses each 29·5m/97ft long with gently rounded walls, four houses being laid out in each quadrant. All the buildings were of wood with thick vertical wall-timbers which were sunk into the ground and supported the roof. There was also a row of houses arranged radially close to the ramparts, and a burial site to the east. The east side of the ramparts was protected by a moat, the other sides being flanked by marshy land and two small rivers. A Viking long house has been reconstructed outside the old settlement (open: mid-Apr.–mid-Sept. daily 10am–6pm, mid-Sept.–mid-Oct. week-ends 10am–6pm).

Svendborg   C 3

Funen
District: Fyns amt
Population: 39,000

Situation

The port of Svendborg lies in the south-east of the island of Funen, on the banks of Svendborg Sound. A ferry links the town with the island of Ærø to the south. Off the coast is a nature reserve.

History

The town's oldest charter dates from 1253. In the Middle Ages Svendborg had trade links with the Hanseatic towns and with the Duchies of Schleswig and Holstein. During the Counts' Wars (1534–36) Ørkid Castle in the east of the town was burned down. In the 17th c. Svendborg suffered great destruction as a result of the wars with Sweden. The 19th c. was a period of prosperity. In 1966 the bridge across Svendborg Sound was completed. The German poet and dramatist Bertolt Brecht and his wife Helene Weigel lived from 1933 until 1939 as emigrants in Svendborg. During this time Brecht wrote the "Svendborg Poems" and "Mother Courage".

Important industries include shipbuilding, engineering, tobacco, wood-working and food-processing.

Sights

A number of old houses are to be found in Svendborg. South of the market-place stands St Nicholas' Church (Skt. Nicolai Kirke), built of brick in 1220 in the Romanesque style and restored in 1892. Note particularly the granite font. In front of the church stands the sculpture "En lille pige" (A Little Girl) by Kai Nielsen.

St Nicholas' Church

Another brick building in the town centre which is worthy of note is the Church of Our Lady (Vor Frue Kirke). It was restored in Neo-Gothic style in the 19th c.. There is a carillon in the tower and the altar-piece ("Gethsemane") is by Christoffer Wilhelm Eckersberg.

Church of Our Lady

In 1993 a Toy Museum (Legetøjsmuseet) was opened at Skt. Nicolaigade 1B, with Danish and foreign toys from the last hundred years. The interesting collection includes dolls, tin-soldiers, wooden and lead toys; there is also a model railway, together with children's books and puzzles (open: June–Aug. daily 10am–5pm; rest of year: Wed.–Fri. noon–5pm, Sat. 10am–4pm, Sun. noon–4pm).

Toy Museum

This museum (Svendborg & Omegns Museum) exhibits in two buildings. At Fruestræde 3, is a half-timbered house (Anne Hvides Gård), dating from 1560 and renovated in 1976. Attractive interiors depict local life in 1700 and 1800. There are collections of silverware and glassware and changing social history exhibitions (open: daily, May–Oct. 10am–5pm; to 4pm May to mid-June). The second building, a former poor-house (Viebæltigard) at 13 Grubbemøllevej, displays prehistoric and later archaeological collections from Funen. Craftsmen, such as goldsmiths, demonstrate their skills. (Open all year: 10am–5pm, mid-Jun. to Oct.; to 4pm, May to mid-Jun.; rest of year 10am–4pm. Closed weekends Jan. and Feb.) Works by the sculptor and painter Kai Nielsen (1882–1924), a native of Svendborg, are on display in the museum and statues by him can be seen at various locations in the town, including near the library and at the swimming-pool.

Municipal Museum

In the former iron-foundry of L. Lang and Co. on Vestergade 45 there is a museum (L. Langs Ovnmuseum) exhibiting stoves manufactured between 1850 and 1984.

The Zoological Museum at Dronningemæn 30 is also worth a visit to see its collections of Danish mammals from prehistoric times as well as insects and birds. In the Whale House in the inner courtyard is the skeleton of a baleen whale 17m/56ft long which was stranded near Troense in 1955.

Zoological Museum

A few miles west of the town lies Hvidkilde Manor; the Baroque palace of 1742 was converted from a Renaissance building. About 300m/330yd west of the manor an avenue leads to a car-park from where visitors can walk in the woods along marked pathways.

Walks

Southern Surroundings

To the east of the bridge over Svendborg Sound a causeway leads to the little island of Thurø, which has a beautiful church and is a popular seaside resort. The sea south of Funen is ideal for a sailing holiday, because it is normally not far from the nearest harbour, with anchorage, a resturant or shopping facilities.

Thurø Island

From Svendborg a massive bridge 1200m/1300yd long and with a clear height of 33m/108ft crosses Svendborg Sound to the island of Tåsinge (area 70sq.km/27sq. miles). South-east of Vindby lies Troense, with a picturesque village street; the collections in the Maritime Museum (Søfartssamlingerne), housed in an old half-timbered building, reflect the history of seafaring in South Funen from the 17th c. until the present day (open: daily all year 9am–5pm, closed Sun. Oct.–Apr.).

Tåsinge Island

Less than a mile south of Troense stands Valdemarsslot (Valdemar's Castle), one of the most beautiful Late Baroque castles in Denmark.

* Valdemar's Castle

Valdemarsslot (Valdemar's Castle) near Troense on Tåsinge Island

Christian IV had it built in 1639 for his son Count Valdemar Christian. The estate later passed to the Naval hero Niels Juel; it is now a museum illustrating the history of manor houses in Funen.

The castle has some very tastefully furnished rooms; these include the Royal Room with portraits of Danish kings and princes, other rooms with priceless tapestries, the Library with several thousand volumes, the Knights' Hall and the Castle Church. Restaurants with plenty of atmosphere – "Den graa Dame" (The Grey Lady) and "Æblehaven" – and a tea-pavilion will entice the visitor to tarry awhile (open: daily May–Sept. 10am–5pm; rest of year, open only Sat. and Sun.).

Bregninge

From the tower of the village church in Bregninge (the porch dating from around 1500 and the north wing from around 1700), there are panoramic views of Funen and its archipelago. The local Folklore Museum (Tåsinge Skipperhjem og Folkmindersamling) contains a section devoted to the tragic love-affair of Count Sparre and Elvira Madigan, both of whom are buried in Landet cemetery as well as model ships and a 19th c. sailor's home (open: Mid-May–Aug.).

Bridge to Langeland

From the south-east side of Tåsinge a causeway and a bridge lead, by way of the little island of Siø, to the holiday island of Langeland (see entry).

Northern Surroundings

*Hesselagergård Castle

There are also some interesting places to be found north of Svendborg. 12km/7¼ miles along road No. 163 to Nyborg (see entry) a minor road branches off to the seaside resort of Lundeborg, and in another 2km/1¼ miles a road bears off to Hesselagergård Castle, 1·5km/1 mile away. The castle was built in 1538 by Johann Friis, the Chancellor of Christian III. The round gable, modelled in the Venetian style, was added in 1550. Some of the interior fittings have been preserved, and the chalk drawings of deer are especially worthy of note.

Further north in a meadow can be seen a boulder at least 12m/40ft high and 46m/150ft in diameter. it is the "Damestenen", which was deposited here from Norway during the Ice Age and is believed to be Denmark's largest erratic boulder. | Damestenen

A further 6km/4 miles along road No. 163, near the village of Langå, a side road to the left leads to Rygård Manor, built on piles in the 16th c. | Rygård

Near Rygård stands Glorup Manor, rebuilt in the Baroque style in 1743 and surrounded by a beautiful large park. In the park can be found several statues and a "Tuscan" Temple of Love (admission to the park: Thur., Sat. and Sun. 9am–6pm). | Glorup Manor

---

Tønder   A 4

Jutland
District: Sønderjyllands amt. Population: 13,000

The town of Tønder is situated in the fenland of South Jutland, north of the Danish–German border. | Situation

About 1130 the place is mentioned as being "a good harbour". At that time the town had access to the North Sea, thanks to a river (the Vidå) with a good depth of water. In 1243 Tønder was granted a charter by Lübeck, and in the centuries that followed it was alternately under Danish and German jurisdiction. Duke John the Elder had dykes built to protect the town from flooding, but these proved to be a disadvantage to shipping. | History

Tønder traded with the Netherlands and with North German ports, especially in cattle. In the early 17th c. the people of Tønder and its surroundings began to make lace. After 1813 lace-making declined in importance, but trading in cattle continued to play a role in the town's economy. When new frontiers were drawn in 1920 Tønder lost its extensive hinterland in the south.

Sights

The town boasts some fine old houses dating from the time when lace-making was at its height; these include Digegrevens Gård (Dike Administrator's House) in Vestergade and the old Pharmacy (Det gamle Apotek) in Østergade, with its Baroque sandstone doorway and 400-year-old thick-walled cellar, often used for exhibitions. Opposite stands the "Hop Barrow" inn, the name suggests its former popularity with hop-growers.

The Late Gothic Christ Church (Kristkirke) was built of brick in 1591. Note the tower with its octagonal spire, which had formed part of an earlier church. The richly decorated interior boasts an altar-table of 1696, a pulpit of 1586 and a font of Belgian marble, as well as 17th and 18th c. tombs of leading merchants of the town and their families. | Christ Church

In the 16th c. gatehouse of Tønderhus Castle, which was pulled down in 1750, and in a more recent building are housed the Tønder Museum and the South Jutland Art Museum. In the former, the municipal museum, can be seen 17th and 18th c. silverwork, lace and Dutch tiles and porcelain, as well as a "Kagmand", a wooden figure with a cane which once stood in the market-place; at one time anyone who had committed a crime was tied to a post (kag) and publicly whipped. | Museums

In the Art Museum are exhibited works by contemporary Danish painters and sculptors.

Surroundings

Møgeltønder, a few miles west of Tønder, is a very old town, with thatched brick houses and cobbled streets. The church has one of the oldest organs in the country. | Møgeltønder

Tønder

Schackenborg

Slotsgade leads to Schackenborg Manor; originally Baroque, the buildings in their present form date from the 19th c. In 1660 the house was bought by Marshal Hans Schack and since then has been privately owned.

Rudbøl

South-west of Møgeltønder lies the frontier village of Rudbøl; since 1920 the Danish–German border has run right through the middle of the village. In Sebüll, on the German side, is the Nolde Museum. Nolde, actually Emil Hansen, was born near Bylderup-Bov in Nolde in 1867; he died in 1956.

Højer

Højer, on the coast north-west of Møgeltønder, has an interesting Romanesque church. After Tønder had been cut off from the sea as the result of the construction of a dike, Højer developed into a cattle-exporting port. Near Højer stands a 30m/98ft high windmill of 1857, which now houses a museum and a restaurant. Also of interest is the Flood Column near the sluice, on which are marked the water-levels reached during all known floods which have occurred here; the last one was on January 3rd 1976, when the dike broke its banks and Tønder had to be evacuated.

Løgumkloster
**Løgum Abbey

The village of Løgumkloster, 18km/11 miles north of Tønder, grew up around Løgum Abbey. After Tønder, Løgumkloster was for a long time the second largest lace-making centre in the country. The former Cistercian abbey, founded in 1144 in an uninhabited and marshy plain, is now an ecclesiastical administrative centre.

Church

Of the old abbey buildings only a part of the east wing – including the chapter-house, sacristy, library and church – remains. The abbey church (1230–1330) is impressive, with spacious Early Gothic pointed windows and beautiful pillars. The original whitewashed walls were revealed only when restoration work was carried out early this century. Inside can be seen a winged altar (c. 1500), sumptuous choir-stalls, a reliquary with wings and a Gothic triumphal cross (c. 1300).

Opposite the main building, the "Refugium", stands a 25m/80ft high tower with a carillon named after King Frederick IX, which strikes at 8 and 11am, 3, 5, 6.30 and 9pm.

Art Museum

At Østergade 13 is an Art Museum dedicated to the artist and sculptress Olivia Holm-Møller (1875–1970).

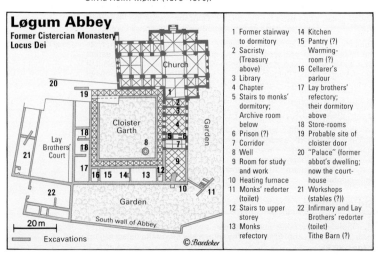

Løgum Abbey
Former Cistercian Monastery
Locus Dei

1 Former stairway to dormitory
2 Sacristy (Treasury above)
3 Library
4 Chapter
5 Stairs to monks' dormitory; Archive room below
6 Prison (?)
7 Corridor
8 Well
9 Room for study and work
10 Heating furnace
11 Monks' redorter (toilet)
12 Stairs to upper storey
13 Monks refectory
14 Kitchen
15 Pantry (?)
Warming-room (?)
16 Cellarer's parlour
17 Lay brothers' refectory; their dormitory above
18 Store-rooms
19 Probable site of cloister door
20 "Palace" (former abbot's dwelling; now the court-house
21 Workshops (stables (?))
22 Infirmary and Lay Brothers' redorter (toilet) Tithe Barn (?)

20 m
Excavations
© Baedeker

Vejle   B 3

Jutland
District: Vejle amt. Population: 52,000

Vejle, a busy industrial and commercial town, lies on the coast of Central   Situation
Jutland in a wooded area at the end of the Vejle Fjord.

Vejle grew up around a ford over the Vejle Å River and received its town   History
charter in 1327. In the 17th c. it suffered considerably from the effects of
wars. For a very long time it has had trading connections with other
countries, especially with the North German towns of Flensburg, Hamburg
and Lübeck, as well as with the Netherlands and Norway. From Lübeck
came iron and spices, while corn was exported to Norway. At the end of the
18th c. the district administration was removed to Vejle and between 1824
and 1827 a new harbour was constructed. From this time onwards the
production of akvavit (schnapps) played an important role in the town's
economy. During the Schleswig-Holstein Wars of the 19th c. Vejle was
occupied at times by German troops and until 1956 was a garrison town.

Sights

Town Hall Square (Rådhustorvet) forms the centre of the town. The Town   Town Hall
Hall was built in 1878 on the site of a medieval Dominican monastery. The
old monastery bell survives and marks the passing of the hours. In front of
the Town Hall stands a statue called "Trade, Industry and Agriculture".

The oldest building in the town is the 13th c. Gothic St Nicholas' Church on   St Nicholas'
Kirketorvet, which has been altered several times. Interesting features   Church
include a granite font, the Classical reredos (1791) by the sculptor Jens
Hiernoe, the 16th c. Renaissance pulpit and a processional crucifix.
In a side chapel can be seen a coffin containing the corpse of a queen; it had
been buried in a peat-bog and dates from around 450 B.C. Cavities in the
north wall contain skulls of criminals beheaded for theft.

In the west of the town, on Flegborg Street, there are two interesting   Museums
museums; at No. 16 is the Vejle Museum of Art and at No. 18 the Vejle
Museum. The former has pictures by 19th c. Danish artists as well as
Danish drawings and designs from the 19th c. to the present day; there are
also special exhibitions of Danish and European design. The Vejle Museum
exhibits finds from archaeological excavations and of local historic interest, such as "Man and Nature".

The 800-year-old history of the town, surviving wars and fires, is well told in   Den Smidtske
the half-timbered old merchant's house of 1799 (Den Smidstke Gård) at   Gård
Søndergade 14. The life of the ordinary citizen can be easily imagined from
displays of finds from Viking tombs, domestic utensils, and recreated
interiors and workplaces.

The Vejle Centret in Idrættens Hus, in the west of the town, is a municipal   Vejle Centre
sports centre with public baths and a concert hall. The Centre boasts a hotel
with conference and exhibition facilities.

The town's emblem is a windmill, the Vejle Mølle. built in 1847 and later   Vejle Mill
rebuilt following a fire. It is open to visitors in summer and an exhibition
documents its history.

Surroundings

A moving stairway takes visitors up to the Munkebjerg, a hill 93m (300ft)   Munkebjerg
above sea level, to the south-east of Vejle. From here there is a panoramic
view over the town.

12km/7 miles north-west of Vejle, and best reached by way of the beautiful   Jelling
road through the Grejsdal (wooded slopes, many viewpoints), lies Jelling,

The runic stones of Jelling

which was the political centre of the region about the year 1000. The two 21 and 24m/70 and 80ft high burial-mounds by the roadside are the oldest royal graves in Denmark, dating from about 935–50. After excavations in 1941–42 and 1978 it was established that the northernmost grave held the remains of King Gorm, who died about 940, and of his wife Thyra.

**Runic stones

The two runic stones on the site, with drawings and inscriptions, have provided considerable historical information. The smaller, which Gorm set up for his wife, bears the inscription, "Gorm the King set up this monument to Thyra his Queen, the pride of Denmark". Harald Bluetooth (940–985), the son of Gorm, embraced Christianity; he had the mound on the south erected over a pagan cult site and set up the larger runic stone. On the latter is written, "This stone was erected to the memory of Gorm, his father, and Thyra, his mother, by Harald Bluetooth, that Harald who won for himself Denmark and all Norway and who made the Danes Christian". Harald transferred his seat from Jelling to Zealand, probably to Roskilde.

Between the graves and the runic stones, a small church stands on the site where Harald Bluetooth had previously built a wooden church (11th c.), which was later altered on several occasions. In the present church can be seen copies of Romanesque wall-paintings by Magnus Petersen (1875); in the choir are modern paintings by J. T. Skovgaard.

Viking Games

Near Jelling lies the pretty Lake Fårup. There is an open-air theatre by the lake, and in summer plays with Viking themes are performed – with Gorm the Old, Harald Bluetooth, Sven Forkbeard and Knud (Canute) the Great, together with their wives.

Givskud
(safari park)

9km/5½ miles north-west of Jelling and 20km/12½ miles from Vejle we come to Givskud Løveparken, a lion park and a safari park with elephants, giraffe, etc. (Open: from May–mid-Oct.)

218

In the Lion Park of Givskud

Viborg   B 2

Jutland
District: Viborg amt
Population: 40,000

Viborg is attractively situated on two lakes, surrounded by forests and expanses of heathland. It is one of the oldest towns in Denmark, lying in the heart of the country, at the intersection of trade routes from north, south, east and west.

Situation

There are numerous opportunities for fishing and golf in the countryside around Viborg, and the town itself is a good starting point for excursions and walks, many of which follow in the footsteps of the local poet Steen Steensen Blicher. Borgvold, with the old castle mound, is now a lakeside park.

Archaeological finds have shown that there was a settlement in the area of the present town around 700. The town was originally known as Wibjerg (wi is an old word for sacred, hence Wibjerg meant "sacred hill") and is thought to have been a pagan cult site; this gave rise to trading activity and thus to the development of the town. After the coming of Christianity Viborg became a religious focal point and in 1065 the see of a bishop. At this time it was the capital of Jutland, and until 1340 Danish kings were elected in Viborg. For another 300 years it remained the place where the nobles paid homage to the newly elected king. Until 1650 it was the largest town in Jutland and until 1850 the seat of the "Landsting" (provincial assembly). Between 1525 and 1529 the preacher, Hans Tausen, made Viborg a centre of the Reformation. Most of the town's old buildings were destroyed by conflagrations in 1567 and 1727, and of its churches only the Cathedral (rebuilt in the 19th c.) and the Dominican church survived. Viborg is now primarily a commercial and industrial town.

History

Sights

The Cathedral on Sct. Mogensgade was built in the 12th c. and rebuilt between 1864 and 1876 as a copy of the original Romanesque building of granite ashlar. Only the three-aisled crypt of the original was preserved. The new church, built of brick and Swedish granite, was modelled on some of the German cathedrals and the churches of Lund and Ribe. Its most distinctive features are the twin towers with their pyramidal roofs, visible from afar. A few Romanesque sculptured stones have been incorporated into the external walls, including the two lions flanking a window in the apse.

*Cathedral

The interior is dominated by, and famous for, the Biblical wall-paintings which Joakim Skovgaard created between 1901 and 1906. In the side aisles are Old Testament scenes, in the transepts scenes from the life of Christ and in the choir the Resurrection and the Ascension. The ceiling paintings, in oil on mahogany, depict the Nativity, flanked by Moses and David and the Prophets. The altar is in gilt bronze. The three-aisled Romanesque crypt has twelve bays of vaulting borne on six columns and ten semi-columns with shafts of granite.

In nearby Sct. Mogensgade, the Latin Garden (Latinerhaven) has survived for over 200 years and the old brick summerhouse still stands.

On Gammeltorv, the square in front of the cathedral, stands the Old Town Hall, a Baroque building by Claus Stallknecht of Altona (Hamburg), who came to Viborg to supervise rebuilding after the fire of 1726; it now houses the Skovgaard Museum. On display are sketches, paintings and sculptures by Joakim Skovgaard (1856–1933), including his preliminary sketches for the frescoes in the cathedral, as well as works by some of his relations and friends. The latter include Constantin Hansen, Johan Thomas Lundbye, Niels Larsen Stevns and Thorvald Bindesbøll. Designs by 20th c. Danish artists can also be seen.

Skovgaard Museum

To the south of the cathedral stands the Søndre Sogns Kirke (Church of the Southern Parish), originally belonging to a Dominican monastery and dating from 1227; it was destroyed by fire in 1726 and then rebuilt. The choir and nave of the old church survive. The church has a magnificent carved and gilded Flemish Gothic altar of 1520, which originally stood in the church of Christiansborg Palace in Copenhagen but was presented to this church by Frederik IV.

Søndre Sogns Church

This museum (Viborg Stiftsmuseum) is found on Hjultorv (Wheel Market), in a building which was at one time the headquarters of the Heath Society, with statues of some of the society's pioneers. The museum tells the history of Viborg from the Ice Age to our times, with many exhibits from the Stone, Bronze and Viking Ages. One section is devoted to 16th and 17th c. commercial art. A weekly market is held on Hjultorv each Saturday.

Regional Museum

The Nytorv (New Market), a cemetery from 1040 to 1584, is surrounded by some beautiful patrician houses, including "Stillings Gård" and the Swan Pharmacy.

Nytorv

On the east side of town, beyond the bridge over the Nørresø and Søndersø, lie the remains of Asmild Church (c. 1100), of which only the walls survive. In the late 12th c. it was given to an Augustinian nunnery which was then situated to the south of the church but of which nothing now remains. Bishop Eskild of Viborg was murdered in front of the High Altar in 1132. The gallery, with portraits of Danish kings, the carved reredos and the pulpit of 1625 are all worthy of note, as is the runic stone in the vestibule.

Asmild Church

◀ *Viborg Cathedral*

Surroundings

Hald Hovedgård	On Hald Lake, 8km/5 miles south-west of the town, stands a manor-house, Hald Hovedgård; from the Middle Ages several castles were built on this site and later pulled down. The present main building, originally a porter's lodge and carriage-house, is now used as a cultural centre. Models of the old castles are displayed in a restored half-timbered barn.
Hald Lake	South of the manor-house a marked forest path on a peninsula jutting out into the lake, amid hills, woodland and heath, offers walkers an opportunity to experience the beautiful scenery.
Mønsted	Near Monsted, to the west of Viborg, lie limestone quarries (Kalkgruber) from where stone was dug nearly 1000 years ago, sometimes for 14 hours a day. It was used in building the cathedral at Ribe, but was closed down in 1953. Visitors can inspect the tunnels, which are some 35km/22 miles long and up to 20 metres (60ft) high. About 8,000 bats, Europe's biggest colony, spend the winter here. A Bat Museum and a Limestone Museum provide useful information. (Open: mid-May–end Oct.: daily, end Jun.–Aug. 10am–5pm; rest of time, 1–4pm, closed Mon.)
Dangberg	A little further west of Mønsted is another underground limeworks (Kalkgruber), first quarried in the 10th century. Above ground, a nature reserve has been created, to resemble forests in the Middle Ages. (Open: mid-Apr.–mid-Sept.: daily Jun.–mid-Aug.; rest of time, closed Mon.)
Hvolris	The Hvolris excavation site is to be found 17km/10½ miles north of Viborg. Here excavations have revealed Iron Age villages and burial-sites as well as Bronze Age mounds. Explanatory signs aid the visitor. Some of the finds are on display in a barn.

Vordingborg D 3/4

Zealand
District: Storstrøms amt
Population: 20,000

Situation	Vordingborg is delightfully situated on the south coast of Zealand, not far from the Storstrøm Bridge which links Falster and Zealand. There are ferries from Vordingborg to Germany (Warnemünde and Rostock) via Gedser.
History	In the 12th c. Valdemar the Great built a castle on the plateau which falls steeply away to the south. This castle formed part of the fortifications erected by the Danes on the coasts of the Baltic as protection against the Wends. In addition, Vordingborg was important because it was situated at the place where the ferry crossed to Falster. In the Middle Ages, Danish kings often resided in the castle and until the end of the 13th c. the Danish Court held its meetings in Vordingborg. The town later lost much of its importance and in 1658 the Swedish King Gustav took Vordingborg after his unopposed landing on Zealand. It is now a garrison town.

Sights

Castle ruins; *Goose Tower	Of the castle, one of the most important in the country, only the curtain-walls built by Valdemar IV (Atterdag) and the Goose Tower (Gåsetårn) near the harbour survive. The pointed copper roof of the 36m/118ft high tower, the town's landmark, is crowned by a golden goose – hence its name. The goose is a reminder of the remark made by Valdemar IV that the Hanseatic towns were like a flock of cackling geese. Vordingborg was Valdemar Atterdag's favourite castle.

The "Goose Tower", part of the ruined Vordingborg Castle

The Goose Tower is one of the best-preserved medieval towers in Western Europe. From the top there is a fine view of town and surrounding countryside (open: daily June–Aug.; closed Mon., Sept.–May).

Near the fortress ruins is the South Zealand Museum. Its exhibits include Stone Age finds as well as local and municipal history collections. Of special interest is an aquamanile, a medieval vessel from which water was poured over the priests' hands during Mass. Behind the museum lies a herb-garden, laid out in 1921, containing plants once used for medicinal purposes.

Museum

On Kirketorvet stands the Gothic Church of Our Lady (Vor Frue Kirke), built in brick and probably dating from about 1400. At that time the Pope allowed the parishioners to buy "letters of indulgence", thus granting them remission from temporal punishment for their sins; the income from this was used to finance extensions to the church.

Church of Our Lady

The choir is decorated with some notable frescoes (1450), portraying the Nativity and the Adoration of the Magi, etc. The interesting altar-piece is by Abel Schrøder the Younger; it shows Our Lord's Crucifixion, with Christian IV's monogram above.

Surroundings

North of the town lies Udby, where the Danish theologian and popular educationist Nikolai Frederik Severin Grundtvig was born in a rectory in

Udby

1783; he died in Copenhagen in 1872. A museum has been set up in his memory. A man of varied literary talents, he published sermons, hymns and translations, as well as writing a treatise on the history of the world. His main passion, however, was the education of the masses, and in 1844 he founded the first adult education college in Rødding (Jutland).

Sværdborg

From Udby it is worthwhile making a detour west to Sværdborg. In the medieval village church are Gothic frescoes with scenes from the life of Christ; note particularly the "Warning that the End of the World is Nigh", including "Stars Falling from the Heavens", "Life Comes to an End", etc.

Zealand/Sjælland   C–E 2–4

Districts: Københavns amt
         Frederiksborg amt
         Roskilde amt
         Vestjællands amt
         Storstrøms amt
Area: 7026sq.km/2712sq.miles
Population: 1,950,000

Situation and Topography

Zealand (Danish Sjælland) is the largest island of Denmark, bounded in the north by the Kattegat and in the south by the Baltic. Many fjords, spits and bays are features of the coasts. In the north-east of Zealand the Øresund, which separates the east coast of the island from the south-west coast of Sweden, is very narrow. A ferry links Helsingør (Denmark) with Helsingborg (Sweden); a bridge across the Øresund is planned. In the south, the Storstrøm and Farø bridges connect Zealand with the island of Falster. Fertile moraine deposits, with U-shaped glaciated valleys and "osers" (banks of sand or pebbles formed by meltwater during the Ice Age) characterise the landscape. While in the south agriculture plays a major role, the north of the island is extensively industrialised.

Sights

Copenhagen (see entry), in the east of the island, is particularly attractive and interesting, with its many palaces (Christiansborg, Amalienborg), museums and places of entertainment (Tivoli, etc.), beautiful squares, the "Strøget" pedestrian zone and the exciting atmosphere of Nyhavn, the harbour quarter. There are also interesting castles and palaces in the north of the island, in Hillerød (see entry; Frederiksborg Castle) and in Helsingør (see entry; Kronborg Castle). On the way there visitors can make a detour to the exciting Louisiana Arts Centre. Roskilde (see entry) also has much to offer – the Cathedral is famous as the last resting place of the Danish kings, while the Viking Ship Museum, where reconstructed ships are on display, illustrates how important ships and shipping were to the country in days of yore. The Vikings are also encountered in Trelleborg (see Slagelse). Kalundborg and Korsør (see entries) are important harbour towns for transport within Denmark.

Smoked herrings on Bornholm ▶

Practical Information

Air Transport

SAS

The main domestic airline serving Denmark and the other Scandinavian countries, Greenland and the Faroes included, is the Scandinavian Airlines System, (SAS).

Danair

The Danish airline Danair also has flights between Denmark's main cities as well as services to the Faroes.

Kastrup airport

Denmark's main airport is Kastrup International Airport. This is about 10km/6 miles to the south-east of Copenhagen on the island of Amager and half an hour from the city centre. See also Getting to Denmark.

Airlines

SAS has desks and ticket booking facilities at all Danish airports and in most of the major airports abroad. The other main international airlines also have their own offices in Copenhagen.

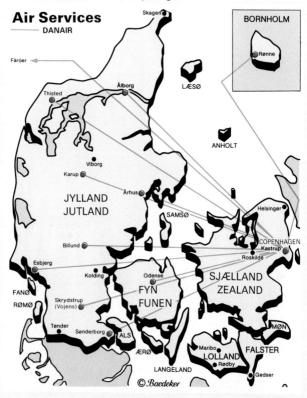

© Baedeker

Scandinavian Airlines System (SAS)
SAS Building, Hammerichsgade 1
DK-1611 Copenhagen V; tel. 32 32 68 48

British Airways
Rådhuspladsen 16
DK-1550 Copenhagen V; tel. 32 32 32 33

Flight reservations in Ireland and the UK:
Aer Lingus; tel. (0845) 737 747
British Airways; tel. 0181–897 4000
Business Air; tel. (01382) 66345
Maersk Air; tel. 0171–333 0066
New Air UK; tel. 0161–489 2800
Scandinavian Airlines; tel. 0171–734 4020

Bathing Beaches and Resorts

Denmark has over 7400km/5000 miles of coastline. The longest stretches of
bathing beaches, often in the shelter of dunes, extend almost without a

Bathing beaches

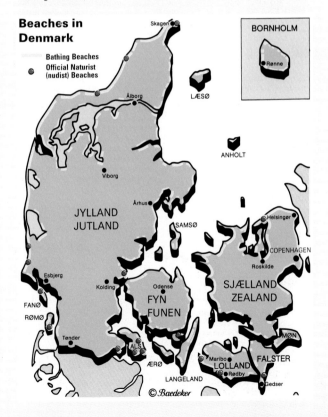

Beaches in Denmark

- Bathing Beaches
- Official Naturist (nudist) Beaches

BORNHOLM

Rønne

Skagen

Ålborg

LÆSØ

ANHOLT

Viborg

Århus

JYLLAND
JUTLAND

SAMSØ

Helsingør

COPENHAGEN

Roskilde

Esbjerg

Kolding

Odense

FYN
FUNEN

SJÆLLAND
ZEALAND

FANØ

RØMØ

Tønder

ALS

ÆRØ

Maribo

LOLLAND

Rødby

MØN

FALSTER

Gedser

LANGELAND

© Baedeker

227

break along the west coast of Jutland from the islands of Rømø and Fanø in the south to the country's northernmost tip at Skagen. Danish beaches have remained largely unspoilt, with few deckchairs or sun umbrellas to detract from the natural landscape.

Beach resorts

The best-known resorts are on the north coast of Zealand, the east coast of Falster and the southern tip of Bornholm. This is the only part of Denmark with any cliffs worth mentioning, although it has beaches of fine sand as well. Beaches on the Mol peninsula and east coast of Jutland often have tree belts down to the water's edge. Funen and its neighbouring islands also boast some excellent beaches.

Naturist beaches and resorts

Denmark has many freely accessible naturist beaches. In many places bathers with and without clothes swim and sunbath together. The only people who get into trouble with the police are those who provoke it.

Beach and water quality standards

A map published every year and available from bookshops and tourist offices (see Information) gives the beach and seawater conditions all round Denmark. Coastal areas considered unsuitable for swimming are also clearly marked and signed in several languages.

Holidaymakers in Denmark pay no special resort tax but this also means there are fewer beach facilities than in those countries which do levy a tax of this kind. Most beaches have parking nearby. This is usually free but is also unsupervised as a result.

Camping and Caravanning

Denmark has hundreds of official camp sites. These have to be approved by the Danish Camping Council (Campingrådet) who award one, two or three stars according to the amenities provided. Three-star sites have 24-hour supervision. They also have cabins and stationary caravans which can be rented in the high season. It is generally advisable to reserve a site in advance, enclosing return postage in the form of an international reply coupon. These are obtainable from most post offices.
Overnight camping in tents and campers is permitted on official sites only. This is strictly enforced, especially as regards dunes and beaches which are often nature conservation areas. Visitors from abroad also need the international camping permit. This can be obtained from any Danish camp site.

Danish tourist offices can supply a list of camp sites published by the national Camping Council. The address for further information is:

Campingrådet
Hesseløgade 16
DK-2100 Copenhagen Ø; tel. 39 27 88 44

Car Rental

In Denmark, as in most other countries, car rental has developed into a substantial service sector. Besides the usual international companies represented at train stations and international airports there are a number of Danish car hire firms and these are also listed in the local equivalent of the Yellow Pages.
Drivers must be over 25 and holders of a national driving licence plus in some cases an international driving licence, therefore it is advisable to have both. Price depends on the type of car, the time of year and the rental period.

Danish currency

Currency

The unit of currency is the Danish Krone (crown) with 100 øre to the krone (DKK). Banknotes are 50, 100, 500 and 1000 krone. Coins include some with holes and some without: 25 and 50 øre (copper, no hole), 1, 2 and 5 krone (silver, with hole) and 10 and 20 krone (brass, no hole). Travellers' cheques, Eurocheques and most of the international credit cards are accepted by banks, shops and the larger hotels.

Unit of currency

The Faroes have their own currency, with 1 Faroese crown equal to 1 Danish crown. They have their own banknotes but use Danish coins, and Danish money is accepted everywhere.
Danish coins and notes are also legal tender in Greenland.

Customs Regulations

Since the advent of the Single Market in 1993 no duty is payable on goods traded between the Member States of the European Union. There are, however, certain limits on items for personal use and up-to-date information about these can be obtained from the customs authorities.
Visitors both from Europe and overseas should also be sure to check with their travel agents on the duty-free allowances for re-entry into their own countries.

European Union internal market

Although items for personal use can be imported duty-free into Denmark from EU countries there are limits on the amount of alcoholic drinks and tobacco that may be brought in free of duty. Persons over 17 can import 1.5 litres of spirits above 22° or 20 litres fortified wine (maximum 22% alcohol content) and 90 litres table wine plus 300 cigarettes or 150 cigarillos or 75 cigars or 400 grams of tobacco.

Import into Denmark

The allowances for items bought in duty-free shops on board ship or at airports are less and are the same as for goods brought in from non-EU countries. In both cases items brought in free of duty may not exceed a value of 350 DKK.

The import of medication, fuel, arms and explosives is governed by special regulations and drugs may not be brought in under any cirumstances.

Faroes

The Faroes do not have EU status. For persons over 20 the duty-free allowances are 1 litre of spirits, 1 litre wine (maximum 22% by volume alcohol content), and 2 litres beer (bottled only), no drink in disposable containers is allowed in at all.

Persons over 18 may bring in 200 cigarettes or 100 cigarillos or 50 cigars or 250 grams of tobacco. There is a strict ban on taking in any pets.

Greenland

Although Greenland is politically part of Denmark it is classed as a foreign country so far as customs duties are concerned. Visitors over 17 can take in 1 litre of spirits or 2 litres sparkling wine, 1 litre table wine, 200 cigarettes or 100 cigarillos or 50 cigars or 250 g tobacco; other items may not exceed 350 DKK in value. Again, there is a ban on taking in pets.

Re-entry to EU countries

On re-entry to other EU countries such as Britain the guidelines for duty-free alchohol and tobacco items for personal use are 10 litres spirits and 90 litres table wine and 110 litres beer; and 800 cigarettes and 200 cigars and 1 kilo tobacco.

Re-entry to non-EU countries

For countries outside the European Union the allowances are as follows: Australia 250g tobacco products (eg 250 cigarettes), 1 litre spirits or 1 litre wine; Canada 200 cigarettes and 50 cigars and 400g tobacco, 1.14 litres spirits or wine; New Zealand 200 cigarettes or 50 cigars or 250g tobacco, 1.125 litres spirits and 4.5 litres wine (or 4.5 litres beer in 6×750ml bottles); South Africa 400 cigarettes and 50 cigars and 250g tobacco, 1 litre spirits and 2 litres wine; USA 200 cigarettes and 50 cigars and 2kg tobacco, 1 litre spirits or 1 litre wine. (NB. In the USA, state alcohol laws may be more restrictive than federal laws.)

See also Travel Documents

Cycling

Denmark's flat terrain makes it an ideal country for cyclists. Special cycle tracks exist in and between towns and there are also marked cycle routes. Local tourist offices provide information about renting a bike for a day, and they also offer cycling holidays. Cycling tour organisers include: Bike Denmark, Aboulevarden 1, 1635 Copenhagen V (tel. 35 36 41 00).

Diplomatic Representation

Australia
Embassy: Kristianiagade 21
2100 Copenhagen Ø; tel. 35 26 22 44

Canada
Embassy: Kr. Bernikowsgade 1
1105 Copenhagen K; tel. 33 12 22 99

Eire
Embassy: Østbanegade 21
2100 Copenhagen Ø; tel. 31 42 32 33

South Africa
Embassy: Gammel Vartovvej 8
2900 Hellerup; tel. 31 18 01 55

United Kingdom
Embassy and consulate: Kastelsvej 36–40
2100 Copenhagen Ø; tel. 35 26 46 00

USA
Embassy and consulate: Dag Hammarskjölds Allé 24
2100 Copenhagen Ø; tel. 31 42 31 44

Distances in Denmark

Kilometric Distances by road or time by ferry between selected towns in Denmark	Ålborg	Århus	Copenhagen	Esbjerg	Frederikshavn	Gedser	Grenå	Haustholm	Helsingør	Hillerød	Hirtshals	Kalundborg	Kolding	Odense	Ringkøbing	Roskilde	Rødby Færge	Skagen	Tønder	Vordingborg
Ålborg	•	111	382	234	62	399	132	95	415	394	64	330	196	244	174	349	405	103	275	347
Århus	111	•	283	157	173	303	62	192	314	292	174	3hrs	99	147	128	253	309	214	180	251
Copenhagen	382	283	•	276	445	147	345	404	46	36	448	100	206	136	320	32	152	486	383	92
Esbjerg	234	157	276	•	294	293	215	204	307	285	298	226	71	137	80	242	299	337	77	241
Frederikshavn	62	173	445	294	•	461	194	156	479	458	51	390	259	306	236	411	467	41	337	409
Gedser	399	303	147	293	461	•	365	426	180	172	461	161	228	155	339	134	68	502	308	55
Grenå	132	62	345	215	194	365	•	213	375	354	197	293	160	209	168	312	374	235	241	315
Haustholm	95	192	404	204	156	426	213	•	439	415	134	351	222	270	144	371	432	176	273	373
Helsingør	415	314	46	307	479	186	375	439	•	24	477	128	239	168	352	63	192	515	315	132
Hillerød	394	292	36	285	458	172	354	415	24	•	453	104	214	144	328	39	179	491	291	117
Hirtshals	64	174	448	298	51	464	197	134	477	453	•	392	260	308	238	414	470	38	338	412
Kalundborg	330	3hrs	100	226	390	161	293	351	128	104	392	•	156	78	262	67	159	425	225	101
Kolding	196	99	206	71	259	226	160	222	239	214	260	156	•	67	115	175	229	298	79	171
Odense	244	147	136	137	303	155	209	270	168	144	308	78	67	•	184	105	161	346	146	106
Ringkøbing	174	128	320	80	236	339	188	144	353	328	238	262	115	184	•	287	345	277	149	286
Roskilde	349	253	32	242	411	134	312	371	63	39	414	67	175	105	287	•	140	452	252	80
Rødby Færge	405	309	152	299	467	68	374	432	192	179	470	159	229	161	345	140	•	508	308	60
Skagen	103	217	486	337	41	502	235	176	515	491	38	425	298	346	277	452	508	•	377	450
Tønder	175	180	383	77	377	308	241	273	315	291	338	225	79	146	149	252	308	377	•	250
Vordingborg	347	251	92	241	409	55	315	373	132	117	412	101	171	106	286	80	60	450	250	•

Diving

Experienced divers wishing to hire equipment in Denmark should contact the tourist information centre in Middelfart (see Information).

Electricity

Electric current in Denmark is 220 volt AC (50 Hz). British and American visitors will need to bring a two-pin Continental adaptor.

Emergency Services

General emergency number: 112
Calls on this number are free.
Ask for police, fire or ambulance.

General emergency number

231

Emergency Services

Breakdown
services

Breakdown services are operated, for a charge, by the FALCK organisation and DAHU (Dansk Autohjælp). These have 170 breakdown stations on call round the clock.

The telephone numbers of the main ones are as follows:

FALCK		DAHU	
Ålborg	98 12 22 22	Ålborg	98 17 68 01
Århus	86 15 22 22	Århus	86 26 20 44
Copenhagen	33 14 22 22	Copenhagen	31 31 21 44
Odense	66 11 22 22	Odense	66 17 79 08

The numbers of the other stations can be found in the local telephone directory. The offices of FDM, the Danish Automobile Club (see Motoring), can also be of assistance in this respect.

Euroroutes

Euroroutes are the major trans-European trunk roads marked by a white E and number on a green background. A-roads, the other major trunk roads and highways, have one or two-figure numbers and B-roads such as access roads, etc. are numbered in three figures (see also Motoring).

The Euroroutes passing through Denmark are the E 45, E 47, E 55, E 20 and E 39. The E 45 runs from Flensburg on the German border to Frederikshavn in the north of Jutland, largely following the same route as the A 10. The E 20 which joins the E 45 heads west toward Esjberg and east from Kolding via the island of Funen to Zealand and Copenhagen, crossing the Small and Large Belt on bridges and ferries roughly along the line of the A 1. The E 39 runs from Hirtshals to Ålborg.

The E 47 is particularly important for traffic between central and northern Europe, following the shortest road and rail route between central Europe and Scandinavia. Its southern section, from Puttgarden on Fehmarn to Rødbyhavn on Lolland, follows the flight path of birds on migration, hence its nickname of "bird flightline".

It runs from Hamburg to Grossenbrode and then over the Fehmarnsund bridge to the island of Fehmarn. Ferries from Puttgarden over the Fehmarnbelt provide the link to the Danish island of Lolland (Rødbyhavn) then this Euroroute carries on to Falster through a tunnel under the Guldborgsund before crossing the Farø bridge onto Zealand and following the A 2 north to Copenhagen. The final stretch of the E 47 on Danish soil follows the A 3 to Helsingør.

The E 55 branches south from the E 47 on Falster, heading for the ferryport of Gedser.

Events (a selection)

Throughout the year, but particularly in summer, Danish towns and villages stage an enormous number of events, including typically Danish activities such as Viking plays, horse fairs and fish festivals.

Cultural events, such as open-air plays, concerts in halls and churches, and art and sculpture exhibitions are held in many places, and in 1996 Denmark will be the European City of Culture. Golf, horse racing and bicycle tours are included amongst the sporting activities.

A Viking play in Frederikssund

The events usually take place in the same month each year, but the actual dates vary. A small selection of events is given below. For a full list, ask the Danish Tourist Board for their publication "Events in Denmark" (issued twice a year, for summer and winter) or enquire at the local tourist office when you are in Denmark.

Copenhagen: Whitsun Carnival   May
Throughout Denmark: Whitsun fêtes, fairs and markets

Helsingør: round Zealand sailing regatta
Hobro: cattle market
Jelling: Viking play
Køge: junk market
Middelfart: Rock under the Bridge rock festival
Nykøbing Mors: pearl festival
Ringe: Central Funen rock and folk festival
Roskilde: agricultural show
Roskilde: rock and folk festival
Silkeborg: riverboat jazz festival
Skagen: festival (major folk event)
Sønderborg: tilting festival
Throughout Denmark: celebration of midsummer eve (June 23)

Copenhagen: jazz festival   June–July
Frederikssund: Viking festival

Aabrenaa: tilting festival   July
Århus: Viking fair (Moesgard); jazz festival
Copenhagen: international rowing regatta

233

Jazz festival in Copenhagen

	Hasle (Bornholm): herring festival (mid-July) Helsingør: Elsinore jazz festival Rebild: Danish-American Fourth of July celebration Sønderborg: Scandinavia's biggest tilting and town festival
July–August	Copenhagen: summer festival (chamber music) Egeskov: musical matinees (Sun. in the castle) Esbjerg: fish auction for tourists Odense: Hans Christian Andersen festival Vendsyssel: classical music festival
August	Ålborg: Ålborg Days (concerts, etc.) Århus: fair (Tivoli Friheden) Copenhagen: water festival (Copenhagen harbour) Næstved: St Pauli festival (on the canals) Nibe: herring fair Tønder: folk festival Ullerup: junk and horse fair Viborg: jazz festival
September	Århus: Århus festival week (concerts, plays, etc.) Højer (south Jutland): sheep fair

Farm Holidays

Visitors who prefer farm holidays can either stay on a working farm as members of the family, sharing their meals, or they can rent a self-catering holiday flat on a farm, supplying their own bedlinen, etc.

Write to:
Horsens Tourist Office, Søndergade 26, DK-8700;
  Horsens or Landsforeningen for Landboturisme, Låsbyrej 20, DK-8660,
  Skanderborg.

Ferries

Denmark's ferries form an important part of both its foreign and domestic
communications network, and there are regular international ferry services
to Britain, Germany, Poland, Sweden and Norway as well as about 65
internal ferry services between the country's many islands. In most cases
the following list gives the crossing's duration/frequency and the name of
the operator.

Puttgarden–Rødby	1hr/daily	DSB/Scandinavian Seaways	Germany–
Warnemünde–Gedser	1hr 55min./daily	DSB/Scandinavian Seaways	Denmark
Rostock–Gedser	2hr/daily	Europa Linien	
Travemünder–Gedser	3hr 40min.	Europa Linien	
Mukran–Rønne	3hr 30min./ several wkly	Bornholmstraffiken	
Sassnitz–Rønne	3hr 30min./daily	Bornholmstraffiken	
Kiel–Bagenkop	2hr 30min./daily	Langeland-Kiel Linien	
Kiel–Halsskov	5hr 15min./daily	DSB/Scandinavian Seaways	
Gelting–Fåborg	2hr/daily	Fåborg-Gelting Linien	
Sylt–Rømø	55min./daily	Rømø-Sylt Linien	
Travemünde/Lübeck– (Malmö)–Copenhagen	42hr	Silja Line Euroway	

Ferries near Fåborg (Fünen)

Ferries

Norway–Denmark	Oslo–Copenhagen	16hr/daily	Scandinavian Seaways
	Moss–Frederikshavn	7hr/daily	Stena Line
	Oslo–Frederikshavn	10hr/daily	Stena Line
	Oslo Hirtshals	8hr 30min./ several wkly	Color Line
	Larvik–Frederikshavn	6hr/daily	Larvik Line
	Kristiansand–Hirtshals	4hr 30min./daily	Color Line
	Egershund–Hanstholm	6hr 30min./ several wkly	Fjord Line
	Stavanger–Hanstholm	11hr/several wkly	
	Bergen–Hanstholm	16hr 30min./ several wkly	Fjord Line
	Bergen–Esbjerg (via Faroes)	58hr	Smyril Line

Poland–Denmark	Swinoujscie–Copenhagen 10hr		Polferries

Sweden–Denmark	Helsingborg–Helsingør	25min./daily	DSB/Scandinavian Seaways
	Limhamn–Copenhagen	55min./daily	Dragør-Limh. Overfarten
	Landskrona–Copenhagen	1hr 10min./daily	Scarlett Line
	Halmstad–Grenå	4h 15min./daily	Lion Ferry
	Varberg–Grenå	4hr 15min./daily	Lion Ferry
	Göteborg–Frederikshavn	3hr 15min./daily	Stena Line
	Ystad–Rønne	2hr 30min./daily	Bornholmstrafikken

United Kingdom–Denmark	Harwich–Esbjerg	20hr/several wkly	Scandinavian Seaways
	Newcastle–Esbjerg (end March–end Oct.)	19hr/twice wkly	Scandinavian Seaways

Ferry reservations in the UK:

Color Line: tel. (091) 296 1313
Scandinavian Seaways: Harwich, tel. (01255) 240 240; London,
   tel. 0171–409 6060; Newcastle, 0191–293 6262
Stena Line: tel. 01233–615 777

Main internal routes	Halsskov–Knudshoved (Zealand–Funen)	1hr/daily	DSB/Scandinavian Seaways
	Kalundborg–Århus (Zealand–Jutland)	3hr 10min./daily	DSB/Scandinavian Seaways
	Hundested–Grenå (Zealand–Jutland)	2hr 40min./daily	Grenå-Hundested Linien
	Sjællands Odde–Ebeltoft (Zealand–Jutland)	1hr 40min./daily	Mols Linien
	Copenhagen–Rønne (Bornholm)	7hr/daily	Bornholmstraffiken
	Esbjerg–Tórshavn (Jutland–Faroes)	37hr/wkly (April–Sep.)	Smyril Line

The Danish Tourist Board (see Information) publishes a map of Denmark which includes a Car Ferry guide and lists the phone and fax numbers for reservations as well as further details on fares and crossing times. Drivers of cars towing caravans should check with the ferry company or their travel agent on what maximum overall length is permissible.

Fishing

Anglers will find Denmark a country where there is every opportunity to indulge in their favourite pastime. Nowhere is more than 35 miles from the sea and there are plenty of well-stocked lakes and rivers, not to mention the fjord waters around Limfjord. All anglers between the ages of 18 and 67 require a permit irrespective of whether they are intent on freshwater or sea fishing. This permit can be for a year, a week or a day, and is priced accordingly, with the revenue it generates being allocated by the Danish Ministry of Fisheries to benefit fishing throughout the country. Anyone found fishing without a permit will be given just two weeks to pay double the sum charged for the 12-month permit.

Fishing permit

Danish waters are ideal for sea fishing. Throughout the year boats put out from ports such as Helsingør, Esbjerg and Frederikshavn with sea anglers and longshore fishermen on board. Catches include codling, mackerel, flat-fish, gar pike, gurnard, ray and wolf-fish.

Sea angling

Longshore angling is not permitted for 500m either side of river mouths or upstream from estuaries. There is easy access in most places to the sea-shore, but this should be by public roads and footpaths and only during the fishing season. Catches from the beach include salmon, sea trout, codling, eel, mackerel, turbot, plaice, and flounder.

Longshore angling

Most of the fishing rights in inland waters are in private hands but permits for these can usually be obtained from the local tourist offices. Jutland has good trout fishing while some places also have salmon. The lakes are mostly stocked with pike, perch, eel, carp, tench, bream and roach.

Coarse fishing

Information:
Danmarks Sportfiskerforbund, Worsåesgade 1
DK-7100 Vejle; tel. 75 82 06 99

Food and Drink

Hotels and restaurants serve breakfast up to about 11am. This can be either a continental breakfast of jam, rolls, eggs and cheese or a heartier version with plenty of cold cuts.

Mealtimes

Lunch is between noon and 2pm but the main meal of the day is dinner in the evening, served from 6pm onwards.

The great speciality of Denmark is its *smørrebrød*, a wonderful range of tasty open sandwiches on various kinds of bread liberally spread with butter (*smør*). To chose, just tick off the list offered by the waiter, specifying the type of bread (*franskbrød*: white bread; *rugbrød*: rye; *pumpernikkel*: black bread; *knökbrød*: crispbread) as well as what you want on it. *Smørrebrødforetninger* are shops which specialise in *smørrebrød*.

Food

Koldt bord (cold board), another Danish speciality, is a buffet similar to Sweden's *smörgåsbord* which belies its name by including hot as well as cold dishes plus dessert, cheese and coffee.

Other traditional Danish dishes include *frikadeller*, pork and veal meat-balls; *hakkebøf*, beef hamburgers; *flæsketeg med røkal*, roast pork with

Smørrebrod: various open sandwiches

crackling and red cabbage; *medisterpølse*, grilled sausage; *gule ærter*, pea-soup with ham; and *dyreryg*, venison with cranberries.
Popular fish dishes include shrimp, trout and the local version of fried plaice.

Denmark's best-known dessert is *rødgød med fløde*, a delicious jelly of red fruits with whipped cream.

For starters or as a light lunch there are small bowls of delicacies such as eel, salmon, ham, vegetable salad, etc., with cheese often served as the last course of a meal.

Drink

Denmark's light golden beer (*øl*) usually comes in small bottles as well as varying strengths, while Danish lager from the Carlsberg and Tuborg breweries has earned a name for itself throughout the world. Wine is expensive since it has to be imported. *Akvavit*, literally "water of life", is the spirit brandy (38% proof) with a taste of caraway which usually accompanies fish at the start of a meal and cheese at the end.

Food and drink vocabulary

English	Danish
restaurant	restaurant
snack bar	cafetaria
breakfast	morgenmad
lunch	frokost
dinner	aftensmad
eat	spise
drink	drikke
a lot, many	meget, mange
little	lidt
bill, check	regning

English	**Danish**
pay	betale
straightaway	straks
menu	spisekort
soup	suppe
meat	kød
grilled	stegt på grill
roast	steg
beef	bøf, oksekød
ham	skinke
lamb	lam
pork (roast)	flæskesteg
reindeer	ren
sausage	pølse
veal	kalv
fish	fisk
boiled	kogt
fried	stegt
fish balls	fiskeboller
cod	torsk
crayfish	krebs
herring	sild
lobster	hummer
salmon	laks
smoked salmon	røget laks
shrimps	rejer
trout	ørred
vegetables	grøn(t)sager
beans	bønner
cabbage	kål
cauliflower	blomkål
cucumber	agurk
green salad	grøn salat
peas	ærter
potatoes	kartofferl
red cabbage	rødkål
spinach	spinat
tomato	tomat
fruit	frugt
apple	æble
bilberry	blåbær
cherry	kirsebær
cranberry	tyttebær
lemon	citron
orange	appelsin
pear	pære
plum	blomme
raspberry	hindbær
strawberry	jordbær
fruit jelly	rødgrød
ice-cream	is
stewed fruit	kompot
whipped cream	flødeskum

Frontier Crossings

English	Danish
drink	drik
beer	øl
coffee	kaffe
cream	fløde
milk	mælk
mineral water	mineralvand
tea	te
water	vand
wine	vin
red wine	rødvin
white wine	hvidvin
bread	brød
biscuits	kiks
cake	kage
rolls	rundstykke
white bread	franskbrød

Restaurants   See entry

Frontier Crossings

Entry into Denmark has to be through the official frontier crossing points. Those between Germany and Denmark which are open round the clock are at Kupfermühle/Kruså, Ellund/Fröslev (motorway) and Böglum/Sæd. The frontier at Harrislee/Padborg is open from 6am until midnight, while the rest are open between 8am and 10pm. Port customs offices open for the arrival and departure of all shipping.

Getting to Denmark

By air

Most of the international flights to Denmark arrive at Copenhagen's Kastrup International Airport, one of the busiest in Europe. SAS, British Airways and Maersk Air all operate several flights a day from London to Copenhagen (1 hour 45 min.), and there are also regular services from Copenhagen by these and other airlines such as Business Air and New Air UK to other UK destinations, including Manchester (1 hour 45 min.), Birmingham (1 hours 45 min.), Aberdeen (2 hours 35 min.), and Glasgow (1 hour 55 min.), as well as daily Aer Lingus flights to Dublin (3 hours). SAS and a number of other international airlines also operate scheduled flights to Canada and the USA (New York 7 hours 40 min.) and other long-haul destinations. See also Air Transport.

By rail

Denmark has rail links with Sweden and Germany and there are direct through trains to Copenhagen from Hamburg. Another through train which runs from Esbjerg to Copenhagen (5 hours) connects with the ferries into Denmark from the United Kingdom (5 hours). See also Rail and Bus.

By road

Denmark is connected to the rest of the European road network by the Euroroutes (E 45, E 47: see entry) and other main roads through northern Germany. Those who want less motoring can go as far as Hamburg by motorail and drive from there. Drivers planning to use car ferries would be well advised to reserve a space if they intend to travel during the peak holiday season, on public holidays or at weekends.

There is also a long-distance coach service (BB Travel) from London to Århus via the Netherlands (tel. 0171–834 7999), which takes 26 hours.

Ferries are an important means of getting to Denmark as well as playing a major part in the country's internal transport network. See Ferries.

By sea

Golf

The gently undulating landscape typical of large parts of Denmark makes it ideal for golf. Visitors are welcome at its 80 or so golf courses provided they can produce a valid golf club membership card. A leaflet on golf in

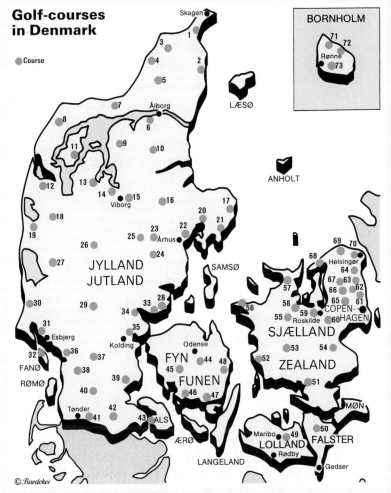

Golf-courses in Denmark

Course

© Baedeker

Golf

Denmark is available from the Danish Tourist Board (see Information), and further information can be obtained from:

Dansk Golf Union
Bredgade 56, DK-1260 Copenhagen K; tel. 42 64 06 66

Golf courses
in Jutland

1 Golf Club Hvide Klit (18), DK-9982 Ålbæk

2 Sæby Golf Club (18), DK-9300 Sæby

3 Hjørring Golf Club (18), DK-9800 Hjørring; tel. 98 90 10 69

4 Løkken Golf Club (18), DK-9480 Løkken; tel. 98 99 26 57

5 Brønderslev Golf Club (18), DK-9700 Brønderslev

6 Ålborg Golf Club (18), DK-9000 Ålborg; tel. 98 34 14 76

7 Han Herreds Golf Club (9), DK-9690 Fjerritslev; tel. 98 21 26 66

8 Nordvestjysk Golf Club , DK-7700 Thisted; tel. 97 97 41 41

9 Himmerland Golf & Country Club (2 x 18), DK-9670 Løgstør; tel. 98 66 16 00

10 Rold Skov Golf Club (18), DK-9520 Skørping; tel. 98 39 26 77

11 Morsø Golf Club (9), DK-7900 Nykøbing M; tel. 97 72 12 66

12 Lemvig Golf Club (18), DK-7620 Lemvig; tel. 97 81 09 20

13 Skive Golf Club (9), DK-7800 Skive; tel. 97 52 16 04

14 Hjarbæk Fjord Golf Center A/S (27), D-8832 Skals; tel. 86 69 62 88

15 Viborg Golf Club (18), DK-8800 Viborg; tel. 86 67 30 10

16 Randers Golf Club (18), DK-8900 Randers

17 Grenå Golf Club (9), DK-8500 Grenå

18 Holstebro Golf Club (18), DK-7570 Vemb; tel. 97 48 51 58

19 Thorsminde Midt-I-Golfbane (9), DK-6990 Ulfborg; tel. 97 49 70 56

20 Kalø Golf Center A/S (18), DK-8410 Rønde

21 Ebeltoft Golf Club (18), DK-8400 Ebeltoft

22 Århus Golf Club (9), DK-8240 Risskov

   Århus Golf Club (18), DK-8270 Højbjerg

23 Tarskov Mølle Golf Club (18), DK-8462 Harlev

24 Skanderborg Golf Club (9), DK-8660 Skanderborg

25 Silkeborg Golf Club (18), DK-8600 Silkeborg

26 Herning Golf Club (18), DK-7400 Herning; tel. 97 21 00 33

27 Dejbjerg Golf Club (18), DK-6900 Skjern; tel. 97 35 09 59

28 Horsens Golf Club (18), DK-8700 Horsens

29 Gyttegård Golf Club (9), DK-7250 Hejnsvig; tel. 75 33 56 49

30 Henne Golf Club (18), DK-6854 Henne; tel. 75 25 56 10

31 Breinholtgård Golf Club (18), DK-6710 Esbjeg V; tel. 75 11 57 00

   Esbjerg Golf Club (18), DK-6710 Esbjerg V; tel. 75 26 92 19

32 Fanø Vesterhavsbads Golf Club (18), DK-6720 Nordby; tel. 75 16 26 00

33 Juelsminde Golf Club (9), DK-7130 Juelsminde

34 Vejle Golf Club (27), DK-7100 Vejle

35 Kolding Golf Club (18), DK-6000 Kolding

36 Kaj Lykke Golf Club (18), DK-6740 Bramming; tel. 75 10 22 46

37 Royal Oak (18), DK-6630 Rødding

38 Ribe Golf Club (9), DK-6760 Ribe; tel. 75 44 12 30

39 Haderslev Golf Club (18), DK-6100 Haderslev

40 Toftlund Golf Club (9), DK-6520 Toftlund

41 Tønder Golf Club (12), DK-6270 Tønder; tel. 74 73 43 13

42 Sønderjyllands Golf Club (18), DK-6360 Tinglev

43 Alssund Golf Club (9), DK-6400 Sønderborg

44 Odense Golf Club (18), DK-5220 Odense S Ø   Funen

45 Vestfyns Golf Club (18 and 9), DK-5620 Glamsberg

46 Fåborg Golf Club (9), DK-5600 Fåborg

47 Svendborg Golf Club (18), DK-5700 Svendborg

48 Skt. Knuds Golf Club (18), DK-5800 Nyborg

49 Golf Club Maribo Sø, DK-4930 Maribo   Lolland

50 Golf Club Storstrømmen (18), DK-4863 Eskilstrup   Falster

51 Sydsjællands Golf Club (18), DK-4700 Næstved   Zealand

52 Korsør Golf Club (18), DK-4220 Korsør; tel. 58 35 01 10

53 Midtsjællands Golf Club (9), DK-4180 Sorø

54 Køge Golf Club (18), DK-4600 Køge

55 Skoldenæsholm Golf Club (18), DK-4174 Jystrup; tel. 53 62 82 93

56 Kalundborg Golf Club (9), DK-4400 Kalundborg

57 Odsherred Golf Club (12), DK-4573 Højby Sj.

58 Holbæk Golf Club (9), DK-4300 Holbæk

59 Roskilde Golf Club (12), DK-4000 Roskilde

60 Golf Club Hedeland (18ú, DK-2640 Hedehusene

  Vallensbæk Golf Club (18), DK-2625 Vallensbæk

61 Københavns Golf Club (18), DK-2800 Lyngby

  Dragør Golf Club (18), DK-2791 Dragør

  Skovlunde Golf Club (9), DK-2750 Ballerup

  Hjortespring Golf Club (9), DK-2730 Herlev

62 Søllerød Golf Club (18), DK-2840 Holte

63 Rungsted Golf Club (18), DK-2960 Rungsted Kyst

64 Kokkedal Golf Club (18), DK-2980 Kokkedal

65 Frederikssund Golf Club (9), DK-3630 Jægerspris

66 Furesø Golf Club (18), DK-3460 Birkerød

  Mølleåens Golf Club (18), DK-3540 Lynge

67 Hillerød Golf Club (18), DK-3400 Hillerød

  Fredensborg Golf Club (18), DK-3480 Fredensborg

68 Asserbo Golf Club (9), DK-3300 Frederiksværk

69 Gilleleje Golf Club (18), DK-3250 Gilleleje

  Passebækgård Golf Center (9), DK-3250 Gilleleje

  Havreholm Slot (9), DK-3100 Hornbæk

70 Helsingør Golf Club (18), DK-3000 Helsingør

Bornholm   71 Nordbornholms Golf Club (18), DK-3760 Gudhjem

72 Nexø Golf Club (18), DK-3720 Nexø

73 Bornholms Golf Club (18), DK-3700 Rønne

Help for the Disabled

Transport

As a country Denmark has a policy of "integration and equality" for the disabled and the Danes themselves do everything they can to help the disabled, visitors included. Disabled passengers flying into Copenhagen's Kastrup airport and travelling on internal flights will find the staff of SAS and the other airlines both helpful and considerate. This also holds good for the staff of Danish State Railways which also operates a policy of disabled access.

Accommodation

A number of Danish hotels, youth hostels, camp sites, etc. are especially equipped for the disabled, with a particular emphasis on wheelchair access. Details about these and other special facilities can be obtained from Danish Tourist Board offices (see Information), together with the leaflet "Access in Denmark – a Travel Guide for the Disabled".

A number of Danish tour operators also arrange tours for the disabled. These can either be booked direct or through a travel agent.

Nine of the chain of holiday centres run by "Dansk folke-ferie" cater for the disabled. The accommodation is particularly well suited for families. For further information contact:

Holiday centres

Dansk folke-ferie
Gammel Kongevej 33
DK-1610 Copenhagen V; tel. 31 31 82 22

Holiday Houses

One inexpensive way of holidaying in Denmark is to stay in a holiday house. Most of these holiday homes are by the sea but there are also many by woods and lakes further inland and on fjords like Limfjord.

They are all well furnished, complete with fridge, crockery, cutlery, etc., but you need to bring your own towels and bedlinen.

Holiday homes of this kind are let by the week during the high season (early July to mid-August) and prices vary according to the time of the year – they are often considerably cheaper off-season – and where they are located. Somewhere on the North Sea, for instance, is more expensive than a place on the Baltic. Holiday houses can be booked through some local tourist offices or through letting agents.

For information contact the Danish Tourist Board.

A thatched holiday house

Hotels and Inns

The level of comfort and service in most Danish hotels is on a par with international standards for the comparable price category. The luxury hotels tend to be in the larger towns and cities but many of the smaller places also have excellent establishments combining comfort with all the typical national features. Denmark has a number of hotel chains as well, including Copenhagen Center Hotels, DanCenter, Scandic Hotels, SAS International Hotels, etc. The Danish Tourist Board publishes "Hotels in Denmark" each year (free of charge).

Prices

Danish hotels are not officially classified into categories so price is usually the best guide to the standard of accommodation on offer. Copenhagen tends to be much more expensive than elsewhere.

Hotel cheques
and discounts

A number of organisations operate a hotel cheque system offering price reductions. These include the Best Western Scandinavia hotel cheque (tel. 0171–930 6666), Scandic hotel cheques (tel. 0171–839 2927), and the Pro-Skandinavia hotel cheque. This covers accommodation with private facilities in 75 hotels all over Denmark and gives savings of up to 50% off the normal price for bed and breakfast (tel. 0171–437 3439).

Discounts are also available with a number of other hotel chains such as the Inter Dan Hotels (tel. 0171–839 2927), with reductions with their Scandinavian Bonus Pass of between 15 and 50%, and the Arp Hansen Hotel Group in Copenhagen which offers special rates and packages at different times of the year (information from Hotel Phønix, Bredgade 37, DK-1260 Copenhagen K; tel. 80 30 30 45).

Mission hotels

The mission hotels found in most towns also play an important role in Denmark's accommodation. These have no religious connotations but many do not sell alcohol. They are solid middle-class hotels, homely and comfortable and moderately priced.

An inn on the island of Fünen

The Danish inn, or *kro*, dates from 1283 when inns were established by royal decree throughout the country. *Kroer* provide comfortable accommodation with a family atmosphere. Dansk Kroferie, an association of 80 inns throughout Denmark, offers discounts of 10–25% off the normal rate for guests paying with Danish Inn Cheques. These should be obtained in advance from travel agents, tourist offices or direct from Dansk Kroferie (Vejlevej 16, DK-8700 Horsens; tel. 75 64 87 00). A list of tour operators booking kro accommodation is also available from the Danish Tourist Board (see Information).

Inns and inn cheques

For the discerning hotel guest there is also the possibility of staying in a stately home which has been converted to accommodate paying guests. Further information from: Danske Slotte og Herregårde, Gammeltoftsgade 14, DK-1355, Copenhagen K.

Stately homes

Denmark's holiday centres combine hotel facilities with self-catering holiday flats. Usually near the beach, they are very popular with families, providing a wide range of activities for children, together with indoor pool, sauna, television room, restaurant, etc. Ask the DTB for their "Holiday Planning Guide" which lists addresses, or write to: Dansk Folke-Ferie, Gammel Kongevej 33, 1610 Copenhagen V. See also Help for the Disabled.

Holiday centres

Bolig-, Motor og Hjælpemiddeludvalget
Landskronagade 66
DK-2100 Copenhagen Ø; tel. 31 18 26 66

Information for wheelchair users

The following list of hotels, inns, guesthouses and motels has been selected from a list produced by the DTB and is in alphabetical order. None of the hotels has been inspected by the AA. Most are in Denmark itself but Greenland and the Faroes are also included. (b=number of beds)

Hotel Europa, H.P. Hanssens Gade 10; tel. 74 62 26 22, 79 b.
Lundsberg Kro, Flensborgsvej 260; tel. 74 61 35 95, 25 b.
Missionshotellet, Klinkbjerg 20; tel. 74 63 00 91, 30 b.
Sølyst Kro, Flensborgvej 164; tel. 74 62 11 63, 31 b.
Sønder Hostrup Kro, Østergade 21, in Sønder Høstrup; tel. 74 61 34 46, 44 b.

Hotels and inns in Åbenrå

Søparken, Søparken 1; tel. 98 24 45 77, 98 b.

Åbybro

Aerohus, Vestergade 38; tel. 62 52 10 03, 56 b.
Det lille Hotel, Smedegade 33; tel. 62 52 23 00, 15 b.

Ærøskøbing

Pension Breidablik, Grammegårdsvej 14; tel. 56 97 40 60, 24 b.
Dams på Bakken, Haregade 14; tel. 56 97 46 66, 58 b.
Rosengården, Bodernevej 28; tel. 56 97 49 50, 54 b.

Åkirkeby

Gammel Kro, Skagensvej 42; tel. 98 48 80 65, 92 b.

Ålbæk

Chagall, Vesterbro 36–38; tel. 98 12 69 33, 131 b.
Helnan Phønix, Vesterbro 77; tel. 96 12 00 11, 370 b.
Hvide Hus, Vesterbro 2; tel. 98 13 84 00, 364 b.
Missionshotellet "Krogen", Skibstedsvej 4; tel. 98 12 17 05, 23 b.
Limfjordshotellet, Ved Stranden 14–16; tel. 98 16 43 33, 440 b. (casino)
Park Hotel, Boulevarden 41; tel. 98 12 31 33, 158 b.
Prinsens Hotel, Prinsensgade 14–16; tel. 98 13 37 33, 86 b.
Scandic Hotel, Hadsundvej 200; tel. 98 15 45 00, 250 b.
Scheelsminde, Scheelsmindevej 35; tel. 98 18 32 33, 164 b.
Slotshotellet, Rendsburggade 5; tel. 98 10 14 00, 272 b.
Sømandshjem, Østerbro 27; tel. 98 12 19 00, 80 b.

Ålborg

Hvide Kro, Jernbanegade 7; tel. 98 64 14 33, 57 b.

Ålestrup

Abildgård, Tejnvej 100, in Sandkås; tel. 56 48 09 55, 250 b.
Allinge, Storegade 5; tel. 56 48 00 25, 38 b.
Boes-Vang, Tejnvej 25; tel. 56 48 07 09, 70 b.
Hammersø, Hammerhusvej, in Sandvig; tel. 56 48 03 64, 87 b.
Nordland, Strandpromenaden 5, in Sandvig; tel. 56 48 03 01, 63 b.

Allinge-Sandvig

Hotels and Inns

Pepita, Langebjergvej 1, in Allinge; tel. 56 48 04 51, 68 b.
Hotel Romantik, Strandvejen 68, in Allinge; tel. 56 48 03 49, 100 b.
Hotel Sandvig, Strandvej 99; tel. 56 48 03 13, 75 b.
Strandhotellet, Strandpromenaden 7, in Sandvig; tel. 56 48 03 14, 74 b.

Ammassalik
Angmagssalik, P.O. Box 117; tel. 182 93, 60 b.

Århus
Angsgar Missionshotel, Bånegardsplads 14; tel. 86 12 41 22, 228 b.
Atlantic, Europaplads 12–14; tel. 86 13 11 11, 189 b.
Eriksens Hotel, Bånegardsgade 6–8; tel. 86 13 62 96, 40 b.
Gammel Vejlby Kro, Vejlbygade 18; tel. 86 21 21 33, 24 b.
Interscan, Skåde Bakker, in Højbjerg; tel. 86 27 32 33, 250 b.
Kong Christian X, Christian X. Vej 70, in Viby; tel. 86 11 61 11, 160 b.
La Tour, Randersvej 139, in Århus N; tel. 86 16 78 88, 250 b.
Marselis, Strandvejen 25; tel. 86 14 44 11, 171 b.
Ritz, Banegårdsplads 12; tel. 86 13 44 44, 110 b.
Royal, Store Torv 4; tel. 86 12 00 11, 185 b. (casino)
Scandic Hotel, Rytoften 3; tel. 86 15 68 44, 325 b.
Windsor, Skolebakken 17; tel. 86 12 23 00, 53 b.

Assens
Marcussens Hotel, Strandgade 22; tel. 64 71 10 89, 68 b.
Stubberup Kro, Middelfartvej 113; tel. 64 79 10 49, 10 b.

Augustenborg
Færgegården, Lillehave 1, in Fynshav; tel. 74 47 43 53, 10 b.
Fjordhotellet, Langdel 2; tel. 74 47 12 22, 16 b.

Auning
Auning Kro, Torvegade 12; tel. 86 48 34 53, 20 b.

Ballen
See Samsø

Billund
Hotel Billund, Vejlevej 10; tel. 75 33 16 55
Billund Kro, Buen 6; tel. 75 33 10 31, 100 b.
Hotel Legoland, Åstvej 10; tel. 75 33 12 44, 472 b.

Bogense
Bogense Hotel, Adelgade 56; ; tel. 64 81 11 08, 120 b.
Bogense Kyst, Grønnevej 8; tel. 64 81 22 79, 216 b.

Brønderslev
Phønix, Bredgade 17–19; tel. 98 82 01 00, 100 b.

Byrum (Læsø)
Nygård, Østerbyvej 4; tel. 98 49 16 66, 56 b.

Christiansfeld
Den Gamle Grænsekro, Koldingsvej 51; tel. 75 57 32 18, 66 b.

Copenhagen/
København
Absalon, Helgolandsgade 15; tel. 31 24 22 11, 467 b.
*Hôtel d'Angleterre, Kongens Nytorv 34; tel. 33 12 00 95, 243 b.
Ascot, Studiestræde 61; tel. 33 12 60 00, 220 b.
Astoria, Banegårdspladsen 4; tel. 33 14 14 19, 208 b.
Avenue, Åboulevarden 29; tel. 35 37 31 11, 128 b.
Centrum, Helgolandsgade 14; tel. 31 31 31 11, 190 b.
City, Peder Skramsgade 24; tel. 33 13 06 66, 145 b.
*Copenhagen Admiral, Toldbodgade 24; tel. 33 11 82 82, 815 b.
Dragør Kro, Strandgade 30, in Dragør; tel. 32 53 01 87, 12 b.
Esplanaden, Bredgade 78; tel. 33 91 32 00, 228 b.
Excelsior, Colbjørnsensgade 4; tel. 31 24 05 85, 174 b.
Grand Hotel, Vesterbrogade 9A; tel. 31 31 36 00, 272 b.
*Kong Frederik, Vester Voldgade 25; tel. 33 12 59 02, 212 b.
Mercur, Vester Farimagsgade 17; tel. 33 12 57 11, 208 b.
Missionshotel Hebron, Helgolandsgade 4; tel. 31 31 69 06, 210 b.
Missionshotel Nebo, Istedgade 6; tel. 31 21 12 17, 146 b.
Opera, Tordenskoldsgade 15; tel. 33 12 15 19, 135 b.

*Palace Hotel, Rådhuspladsen 57; tel. 33 14 40 50, 286 b.
*Park Hotel, Jarmers Plads 3; tel. 33 13 30 00, 102 b.
The Plaza, Bernstorffsgade 4; tel. 33 14 92 62, 165 b.
*Richmond, Vester Farimagsgade 33; tel. 33 12 33 66, 237 b.
*Romantik Hotel 71, Nyhavn, Nyhavn 71; tel. 33 11 85 85, 127 b.
Saga Hotel, Colbjørnsensgade 18; tel. 31 24 49 44, 162 b.
SAS Falconer, Falconer Allé 9, in Frederiksberg; tel. 31 19 80 01, 332 b.
*SAS Royal Hotel, Hammerichsgade 1; tel. 33 14 14 12, 447 b.
SAS Scandinavia Hotel, Amager Boulevard 70; tel. 33 11 23 24, 1066 b.
  (casino)
Savoy, Vesterbrogade 34; tel. 31 31 40 73, 111 b.
Scandic Hotel Bel Air, Løitegårdsvej 99, in Kastrup; tel. 31 51 30 33, 57 b.
Selandia, Helgolandsgade 12; tel. 31 31 46 10, 67 b.
*Sheraton Copenhagen, Vester Søgade 6; tel. 33 14 35 35, 731 b.
*Sophie Amalie, Sankt Annae Plads 21; tel. 33 13 34 00, 258 b.
Triton, Helgolandsgade 7–11; tel. 31 31 32 66, 208 b.
Viking, Bredgade 65; tel. 33 12 45 50, 153 b.
Webers Hotel, Vesterbrogade 11B; tel. 31 31 14 32, 175 b.
West, Westend 11; tel. 31 24 27 61, 50 b.

Ebeltoft, Adelgade 44; tel. 86 34 10 90, 14 b.   **Ebeltoft**
Ebeltoft Strand, Ndr. Strandvej 3; tel. 86 34 33 00, 144 b.
Hvide Hus, Strandgårdshøj 1; tel. 86 34 14 66, 200 b.

Ansgar, Skolegade 36; tel. 75 12 82 44, 101 b.   **Esbjerg**
Bell-Inn, Skolegade 45; tel. 75 12 01 22, 60 b.
Britannia, Torvet; tel. 75 13 01 11, 119 b.
Guldager Kro, Guldager Stationsvej 104; tel. 75 16 70 08, 28 b.
Hermitage Hotel West, Søvej 2; tel. 75 13 50 00, 200 b.
Scandic Hotel Olympic, Strandbygade 3; tel. 75 18 11 88, 196 b.

Interscan Fåborg Fjord, Svendborgvej 175; tel. 62 61 10 10, 272 b.   **Fåborg**
Korinth Kro, Reventlowsvej 10; tel. 62 65 10 23, 57 b.
Strandgade, Strandgade 2; tel. 62 61 20 12, 22 b.

Danland på Fanø, Feriehotel Vesterhavet, in Fanø Bad; tel. 75 16 32 77,   **Fanø**
  860 b.
Fanø Krogård, Langelinie 11, in Nordby; tel. 75 16 20 52, 36 b.
Kromanns Hotel, Sønderland 7, in Sønderho; tel. 75 16 44 45, 15 b.

Samklang, Klintevej 19; tel. 53 71 60 12, 38 b.   **Fakse Ladeplads**

Badehotel Klitrosen, Slettestrandvej 130; tel. 98 21 72 55, 100 b.   **Fjerritslev**
Fjerritslev Kro, Østergade 2; tel. 98 21 11 16, 40 b.

Hotel Store Kro, Slotsgade 1–6; tel. 42 28 00 47, 72 b.   **Fredensborg**

Hybylund, Fælledvej 58; tel. 75 92 98 00, 24 b.   **Fredericia**
Kronprinds Frederik, Vestre Ringvej 96; tel. 75 91 00 00, 160 b.
Landsoldaten, Norgesgade 1; tel. 75 92 15 55, 112 b.

Hoffmans Hotel, Tordenskjoldsgade 3; tel. 98 42 21 66, 141 b.   **Frederikshavn**
Jutlandia, Havnepladsen 1; tel. 98 42 42 00, 196 b.
Motel Lisboa, Søndergade 248; tel. 98 42 21 33, 92 b.
Mariehønen, Skolegade 2; tel. 98 42 01 22, 68 b.
Park Hotel, Jernbanegade 7; tel. 98 42 22 55, 52 b.
Sømandshjem & Hotel, Tordenskjoldsgade 15B; tel. 98 42 09 77, 61 b.
Stena Hotel Frederikshavn, Tordenskjoldksgade 14; tel. 98 43 32 33, 666 b.

Hotels and Inns

Frederikssund	Rådshuskroen, Østergade 1; tel. 42 31 44 66, 19 b.
Frederiksværk	Frederiksværk, Torvet 6; tel. 42 12 22 88, 58 b.
Gedser	Danland i Gedser (Feriehotel), Vestre Strandvej 2; tel. 53 87 99 99, 392 b.
Gilleleje	Gilleleje Feriecenter, Strandvej 8A; tel. 48 30 03 11, 528 b. Strand, Vesterbrogade 4; tel. 48 30 05 12, 39 b.
Gråsten	Axelhus, Borggade 16; tel. 74 65 06 15, 36 b.
Grenå	Grenå Strand, Havneplads 1; tel. 86 32 68 14, 34 b. Sostrup Slot, in Gjerrild; tel. 86 38 41 11, 117 b. Stena Hotel Grenå, Kystvej 32; tel. 86 32 25 00, 300 b.
Gudhjem	Feriegården, Brøddegade 14; tel. 56 48 50 66, 90 b. Gudhjem Hotel & Feriepark, Jernkåsvej 1; tel. 56 48 54 44, 612 b. Mølleparken, Gudhjemvej 111; tel. 56 48 52 48, 80 b.
Haderslev	Motel Haderslev, Damparken; tel. 74 52 60 10, 230 b. Harmonien, Gåskærgade 19; tel. 74 52 37 20, 52 b. Norden, Storegade 55; tel. 74 52 40 30, 101 b.
Hanstholm	Golfhotel Hanstholm, Byvej 2; tel. 97 96 10 44, 162 b. Sømandshjem, Lindbergsgade 71; tel. 97 96 11 45, 61 b.
Havneby	See Rømø
Helsingør	Hamlet, Bramstræde 5; tel. 49 21 05 91, 63 b. Marienlyst, Nordre Strandvej 2; tel. 49 20 33 90, 425 b. Skandia, Bramstræde 1; tel. 49 21 09 02, 85 b.
Henne	Pension Feriegården, Hennebysvej 32; tel. 75 25 51 34, 120 b. Henne Kirkeby Kro, Strandvejen 234; tel. 75 25 54 00, 12 b. Henne Strand (Feriehotel), Klitvej 2; tel. 75 25 50 04, 200 b.
Herning	Eyde, Torvet 1; tel. 97 22 18 00, 174 b. Hammerun, Jernbanegade 8–10; tel. 97 11 88 33, 31 b. Herning, Vardevej 9; tel. 97 22 24 00, 184 b. Østergårds Hotel, Silkeborgvej 94; tel. 97 12 45 55, 146 b.
Hillerød	Hillerød, Milnersvej 41; tel. 48 24 08 00, 244 b.
Hirtshals	Danland i Hirtshals (Feriehotel Fyrklit), Kystvejen 10; tel. 98 94 20 00, 1060 b. Hotel Hirtshals, Havnegade 2; tel. 98 94 20 77, 108 b. Skaga, Willemoesvej 1; tel. 98 94 55 00, 235 b.
Hjørring	Kirkedal, Mårup Kirkevej 30, in Lønstrup; tel. 98 96 02 97, 35 b. Marinella, Strandvejen 94, in Lønstrup; tel. 98 96 07 00, 72 b. Hotel Phønix Aps, Jernbanegade 6; tel. 98 92 54 55, 121 b.
Hobro	Alpina, Hostrupvej 83; tel. 98 52 28 00, 48 b. Motel Hobro, Randersvej 60; tel. 98 52 28 88, 48 b.
Holbæk	Strandparken, Kalundborgvej 58; tel. 53 43 06 16, 62 b.
Holeby	Aktivitetscenter Holeby, Jernbanevej 12; tel. 53 90 72 99, 37 b.

Hotels and Inns

Borbjerg Mølle Kro, Borbjerg Møllevej 3; tel. 97 46 10 10, 50 b.   Holstebro
Krabbes Hotel, Stationsvej 18; tel. 97 42 06 22, 28 b.
Royal Holstebro, Den Røde Plads; tel. 97 40 23 33, 194 b.

Trouville, Kystvej 20; tel. 42 20 22 00, 99 b.   Hornbæk

Dagmar, Smedegade 68; tel. 75 62 57 55, 50 b.   Horsens
Danica, Ove Jensens Allé 28; tel. 75 61 60 22, 70 b.,
Jørgensens Hotel, Søndergade 17; tel. 75 62 16 00, 65 b.
Scandic Hotel Bygholm Park, Schüttesvej 6; tel. 75 62 23 33, 274 b.
Motel Thorsvang, Vejlevej 58; tel. 75 64 25 30, 24b.

Lynæs Kro, Frederiksværkvej 6; tel. 42 33 86 66, 9 b.   Hundested

Arctiv Ilulissat, P.O. Box 501; tel. 441 53, 82 b.   Ilulissat
Hvide Falk, P.O. Box 20; tel. 433 43, 53 b.   (Jakobshavn)
   (Greenland)

Jelling Kro, Gormsgade 16; tel. 75 87 10 06, 9 b.   Jelling
Skovdal Kro, Fårupvej 23; tel. 75 87 17 81, 20 b.

Juelsminde, Odelsgade 22; tel. 75 69 31 50, 24 b.   Juelsminde

Ole Lunds Gård, Kordilgade 1–3; tel. 53 51 01 65, 29 b.   Kalundborg

Hotel Kangerlussuaq, P.O. Box 1006; tel. 111 80, 285 b.   Kangerlussuaq
   (Greenland)

Tornøes Hotel, Strandgade 2; tel. 65 32 16 05, 58 b.   Kerteminde

Sjomansheim, Vikavegur 39; tel. 555 33, 67 b.   Klaksvik
   (Faroes)

See Copenhagen   København

Centralhotellet, Vestergade 3; tel. 53 65 06 96, 38 b.   Køge
Hvide Hus, Strandvejen 111; tel. 53 65 36 90, 227 b.

Kolding, Akseltorv 5; tel. 75 52 50 00, 100 b.   Kolding
Saxildhus, Bånegardspladsen; tel. 75 52 12 00, 151 b.
Scandic Hotel Kolding, Kokholm 2; tel. 75 51 77 00, 296 b.
Hotel Scanticon Kolding, Skovbrynet; tel. 75 50 15 55, 320 b.
Tre Roser, Byparken; tel. 75 53 21 22, 200 b.

Jens Baggesen, Batterivej 3–5; tel. 58 35 10 00, 84 b.   Korsør
Tårnborg Parkhotel, Ørnumvej 6; tel. 558 35 01 10, 230 b.

Fakkelgården, Fjordvejen 44, in Kollund; tel. 74 67 83 00, 21 b.   Kruså

Kværndrup Kro, Bøjdenvej 1; tel. 62 27 10 05, 23 b.   Kværndrup

Industriehotellet, Vasen 11; tel. 97 82 02 00, 34 b.   Lemvig
Nørre Vinkel, Søgårdevejen; tel. 97 82 22 11, 177 b.
Scandinavian Holiday Centre (holiday flat complex), Vinkelhagevej;
   tel. 97 82 27 22, 1036 b.

Lisegården Kursuscenter, Lisegårdsvej 10–12; tel. 42 34 70 50, 49 b.   Liseleje
Liselængen, Liselejevej 62; tel. 42 34 73 06, 48 b.

Hotels and Inns

Løgstør
Hotel du Nord, Havnevej 38; tel. 98 67 21 00, 36 b.
Motel Krogagergård, Lendrupvej 40; tel. 96 67 21 39, 16 b.
Parkhotel, Toftebjerg Allé 6; tel. 98 67 40 00, 150 b.

Løgumkloster
Central Hotel, Markedsgade 15; tel. 74 74 30 50, 13 b.
Løgumkloster Refugium, Refugievej 1; tel. 74 74 33 01, 88 b.

Løkken
Furreby Motel, Løkkensvej 910; tel. 98 99 12 38, 43 b.
Grønhøj Strand (Feriehotel), Ingeborgvej 2, in Ingstrup; tel. 98 88 32 22, 1440 b.
Kallehavegård Badehotel, Søndergade 80; tel. 98 99 10 30, 80 b.
Løkken Badehotel, Torvet 8; tel. 98 99 14 11, 162 b.

Lyngby
Eremitage, Lyngby Storcenter 62; tel. 45 88 77 00, 192 b.
Fortunen, Ved Fortunen 33; tel. 45 87 00 73, 30 b.
Frederiksdal, Frederiksdalvej 360; tel. 42 85 43 33, 117 b.

Mariager
Postgården, Torvet 6; tel. 98 54 10 12, 28 b.

Maribo
Ebsens Hotel, Vestergade 32; tel. 53 88 10 44, 41 b.
Hvide Hus, Vestergade 27–29; tel. 53 88 10 11, 154 b.
Strandbechgård, Maribovej 54; tel. 53 88 33 19, 42 b.

Marstal
Maritim, Kirkestræde; tel. 30 66 24 40, 40 b.
Marstal, Dronningestræde 1A; tel. 62 53 13 52, 10 b.

Middelfart
Byggecentrums Kursuscenter, Hindsgavl Allé 2; tel. 64 41 14 41, 102 b.
Parkhotel, Karensmindevej 3; tel. 64 41 64 74, 268 b.

Millinge
Falsled Kro, Assensvej 513, in Falsled; tel. 62 68 11 11; 26 b.
Steensgaard Herregårdspension, Steensgaard 4; tel. 62 61 94 90, 26 b.

Næstved
Hotel Kirstine, Købmagergade 20; tel. 55 77 47 00, 62 b.
Vinhuset, Skt. Peters Kirkeplads 4; tel. 53 72 08 07, 130 b.

Nakskov
Harmonien, Nybrogade 2; tel. 53 92 21 00, 58 b.
Motel Krukholm, Maribovej 134; tel. 53 92 20 35, 28 b.

Nanortalik
(Greenland)
Kap Farvel, P.O. Box 104; tel. 332 94, 12 b.
Tupilak Bodega, P.O. Box 4; tel. 333 79, 7 b.

Narsaq
(Greenland)
Hotel Perlen, P.O. Box 123; tel. 313 13, 23 b.

Narsarsuaq
(Greenland)
Hotel Narsarsuaq; tel. 352 53, 189 b.

Neksø
Balka Søbad, Vestre Strandvej 25; tel. 56 49 22 25, 314 b.
Balka Strand, Boulevarden 9A; tel. 56 49 21 50, 240 b.
Bornholm, Pilegårdsvejen 1; tel. 56 48 83 83, 150 b.
Sømandshjem, Købmagergade 27; tel. 56 49 24 40, 40 b.

Nordby
See Fanø

Nordby
See Samsø

Nuuk (Godthåb)
(Greenland)
Hans Egede, Aqqusinersuaq 1–5; tel. 242 22, 206 b.
Sømandshjemmet, P.O. Box 1021; tel. 210 29, 53 b.

Nyborg
Hesselet, Christianslundsvej 119; tel. 65 31 29 58, 92 b.
Missionshotellet, Østervoldgade 44; tel. 65 30 11 88
Nyborg Strand, Østerøvej 2; tel. 65 31 31 31, 500 b.

Falster, Skovalleen; tel. 54 85 93 93, 131 b. Nykøbing Falster
Motel Liselund, Lundevej 22, in Sundby; tel. 54 85 15 66, 48 b.
Teaterhotellet, Torvet 3; tel. 54 85 32 77, 39 b.

Parkhuset, Havnen; tel. 97 72 33 00, 36 b. Nykøbing Mors
Sallingsund Færgekro, Sallingsundvej 104; tel. 97 72 00 88, 119 b.

Klintekroen, Klintvej 158, in Klint; tel. 53 42 11 91, 24 b. Nykøbing
Kursuscenter Rørvig, Bystedvej 10; tel. 53 41 11 14, 87 b. Sjælland

The Cottage, Skansevej 19; tel. 53 87 11 25, 60 b. Nysted
Den Gamle Skole, Stubberupvej 9; tel. 53 87 18 90, 10 b.
Hapimag, Stubberupvej 17; tel. 53 87 15 50, 280 b.

Ansgar Missionshotellet, Østre Stationsvej 32; tel. 66 11 96 93, 70 b. Odense
Ansgarhus Motel, Kirkegårds Allé 17–19; tel. 66 12 88 00, 28 b.
Fangel Kro, Fangelvej 55; tel. 65 96 10 11, 65 b.
Frederik VI's Kro, Rugårdsvej 590; tel. 65 94 13 13, 146 b.
Grand Hotel, Jernbanegade 18; tel. 66 11 71 71, 221 b.
Munkeris Hotel, Munkerisvej 161; tel. 66 15 90 41, 134 b.
Odense Plaza Hotel, Østre Stationsvej 24; tel. 66 11 77 45, 105 b.
SAS H. C. Andersen, Claus Bergs Gade 7; tel. 66 14 78 00, 296 b.
Scandic Hotel Odense, Hvidkærvej 25; tel. 66 17 66 66, 223 b.
Windsor, Vindegade 45; tel. 66 12 06 52, 102 b.
Ydes Hotel, Hans Tausensgade 11; tel. 66 12 11 31, 55 b.

Turisthotellet, Torvegade 1; tel. 75 27 10 37, 32 b. Oksbøl

Frederiksminde, Klosternakken 8; tel. 55 99 10 42, 42 b. Præstø

Qaqortoq, P.O. Box 155; tel. 382 82, 42 b. Qaqortoq
Sømanshjemmet, P.O. Box 330; tel. 382 39, 25 b. (Julianehåb)
(Greenland)

Motel Hornbæk, Viborgvej 100; tel. 86 42 67 92, 16 b. Randers
Kronjylland, Vestergade 53; tel. 86 41 43 33, 76 b.
Randers, Torvegade 11; tel. 86 42 34 22, 140 b.
Scandic Hotel Kongens Ege, Gammel Hadsundvej 2; tel. 86 43 03 00, 255 b.

Dagmar, Torvet 1; tel. 75 42 00 33, 100 b. Ribe
Hviding Kro, Rivevej 58, in Hviding; tel. 75 44 52 60, 18 b.
Sønderjylland, Sønderportsgade 22; tel. 75 42 04 66, 15 b.
Weis Stue, Torvet 2; tel. 75 42 07 00. 9 b.

Danland i Søndervig (Feriehotel), in Søndervig; tel. 97 33 92 00, 604 b. Ringkøbing
Fjordgården, Vesterkær 28; tel. 97 32 14 00, 185 b.
Ringkøbing, Torvet 18; tel. 97 32 00 11, 27 b.

Scandic Hotel Ringsted, Nørretorv 57; tel. 53 61 93 00, 170 b. Ringsted
Sørup Herregård, Sørupvej; tel. 53 64 30 02, 219 b.

Danhotel, Havnegade 2, in Rødbyhavn; tel. 54 60 53 66, 100 b. Rødby
Euro-Hotel E 4, Maribo Landevej 4; tel. 54 60 14 85, 120 b.
Lalandia Feriecenter, Lalandiacentret 1; tel. 54 60 42 00, 3200 b.

Færgegården, Vestergade 1–5, in Havneby; tel. 74 75 54 32, 70 b. Rømø
Kommandørgården, Havnebyvej 201, in Mølby; tel. 74 75 51 22, 300 b.
Feriecenter Rim/Rømø, Vestergade 159; tel. 74 75 57 75, 1200 b.
Feriecenter Rømø Strand, Vestergade, in Havneby; tel. 74 75 50 66, 288 b.

Fredensborg, Strandvejen 116; tel. 56 95 44 44, 172 b. Rønne
Hoffmann, Kystvejen; tel. 56 95 03 86, 144 b.
Ryttergården, Stranvejen 79; tel. 56 95 19 13, 330 b.

Hotels and Inns

Roskilde

Prindsen, Algade 13; tel. 42 35 80 10, 72 b.
Scandic Hotel Roskilde, Søndre Ringvej 33; tel. 46 32 46 32, 220 b.
SR Hotel og Kursuscenter, Måglegårdsvej 10; tel. 42 35 66 88, 140 b.
Svogerslev Kro, Hovedgaden 45, in Svogerslev; tel. 46 38 30 05, 37 b.

Rudkøbing

Rudkøbing, Havnegade 2; tel. 62 51 36 18, 18 b.
Skandinavien, Brogade 13; tel. 62 51 14 95, 17 b.

Sæby

Syvsten Kro, Ålborvej 247; tel. 98 46 82 04, 26 b.

Sakskøbing

Saxkjøbing, Torvet 9; tel. 53 89 40 39, 56 b.

Samsø

Ballen Hotel, Avavej 21, in Ballen; tel. 86 59 17 99, 44 b.
Flinchs Hotel, Langgade, in Tranebjerg; tel. 86 59 17 22, 48 b.
Nordby Kro, Hovedgaden 8, in Nordby; tel. 86 59 60 86, 35 b.

Silkeborg

Dania, Torvet 5; tel. 86 82 01 11, 83 b.
Impala, Vestre Ringvej 53; tel. 86 82 03 00, 120 b.
Louisiana, Christian VIII's Vej 7; tel. 86 62 18 99, 48 b.
Scandic Hotel Silkeborg, Udgårdsvej 2; tel. 86 80 35 33, 256 b.
Signesminde Kro, Viborgvej 145; tel. 86 85 54 43, 16 b.

Sisimut
(Holsteinsborg)
(Greenland)

Sisimut, P.O. Box 70; tel. 148 40, 54 b.
Sømandshjemmet, P.O. Box 1015; tel. 141 50, 68 b.

Skælskør

Kobæk Strand, Kobækvej 85; tel. 53 59 45 15, 169 b.

Skagen

Brøndums Hotel, Anchersvej 3; tel. 98 44 15 55, 82 b.
Foldens Hotel, Skt. Laurentiivej 41; tel. 98 44 11 66, 40 b.
Hotel Petit, Holstvej 4; tel. 98 44 11 99, 48 b.
Ruths Hotel, Hans Ruthsvej 1, in Gammel Skagen; tel. 98 44 11 24, 72 b.
Skagen (Feriehotel), Grårisvej 1; tel. 98 44 55 22, 23 holiday flats
Hotel Skagen, Gammel Landevej 39; tel. 98 44 22 33, 200 b.

Skanderborg

Skanderborghus, Dyrehaven 3; tel. 86 52 09 55, 92 b.
Slotskroen, Adelgade 23; tel. 86 52 00 12, 40 b.

Skive

Gammel Skivehus, Søndre Boulevard 1; tel. 97 52 11 44, 120 b.
Hilltop, Søndre Boulevard; tel. 97 52 37 11, 80 b.

Slagelse

Frederik II, Idagårdsvej 1; tel. 53 53 03 22, 158 b.
Slagelse, Bånegardspladsen; tel. 53 52 01 72, 60 b.

Sønderborg

Ansgar, Nørrebro 2; tel. 74 42 24 72, 78 b.
Arnkilhus, Arnkilgade 13; tel. 74 42 23 36, 23 b.
Hotel Garni, Kongevej 96; tel. 74 42 34 33, 27 b.
Interscan Hotel Sønderborg, Ellegårdvej 27; tel. 74 42 26 00, 306 b.
Scandic Hotel Sønderborg, Rosengade 2; tel. 74 42 19 00. 222 b.

Sønherho

See Fanø

Sorø

Krebshuset, Ringstedvej 87; tel. 57 82 01 81, 22 b.
Postgården, Storgade 27; tel. 53 63 22 22, 42 b.

Sørvágur
(Faroes)

Vágar; tel. 329 55, 50 b.

Stege

Præstekilde Kro & Hotel, Klintevej 116, Keldby; tel. 55 81 34 43, 92 b.
Stege Bugt, Langelinie 48; tel. 55 81 54 54, 62 b.

Struer

Grand Hotel, Østergade 24; tel. 97 85 04 00, 132 b.
Humlum Kro, Vesterbrogade 4, in Humlum; tel. 97 86 17 64, 6 b.

Elverkroen, Vestergade 35; tel. 53 84 12 50, 100 b.   **Stubbekøbing**

Siemsens Gård, Havnebryggen 9; tel. 56 49 61, 92 b.   **Svaneke**

Drejø Centret, Broløkken 11, in Drejø; tel. 62 21 39 12, 45 b.   **Svendborg**
Missionshotellet Stella Maris, Kogtvedvænget 3; tel. 62 21 38 91, 38 b.
Royal, Toldbodvej 5; tel. 62 21 21 13, 40 b.
Svendborg, Centrumpladsen 1; tel. 62 21 17 00, 150 b.
Svendborg Amatør Sejlklub, Færgevej 19; tel. 62 22 27 75, 446 b.
Tre Roser, Fåborgvej 90; tel. 62 21 64 26, 256 b.
Troense, Strandgade 5–7, in Troense; tel. 62 22 54 12, 60 b.

Klitmøller Kro Aps, Krovej 15; tel. 97 97 55 22, 40 b.   **Thisted**
Limfjorden, Oddesundvej 39; tel. 97 92 40 11, 112 b.
Thisted, Frederiksgade 16; tel. 97 92 52 00, 39 b.

Kildegård, Hovedgaden 52; tel. 42 30 71 53, 41 b.   **Tisvildeleje**
Tisvildeleje Strandhotel (Højbohus), Hovedgaden 75; tel. 42 30 71 19, 48 b.

Abild, Ribelandevej 66, in Abild; tel. 74 72 58 55, 35 b.   **Tønder**
Hostrups Hotel, Søndergade 30; tel. 74 72 21 29, 46 b.

Føroyar, Oyggjarvegur, P.O. Box 3303; tel. 175 00, 216 b.   **Tórshavn**
Hafnia, Årvegur 4–10, P.O Box 107; tel. 112 70, 103 b.   **(Faroes)**

See Samsø   **Tranebjerg**

Bakkin; tel. 739 61, 18 b.   **Vágur**
                                                                                (Faroes)

Skovbohus, Storegade 56; tel. 75 22 01 40, 22 b.   **Varde**

Gæstgivergård, Frederik VII Gade 15; tel. 75 36 00 45, 20 b.   **Vejen**

Andersens Hotel, Kirketorvet 12; tel. 79 42 79 10, 62 b.   **Vejle**
Bredal Kro og Motel, Horsensvej 581; tel. 75 89 57 99, 88 b.
Motel Hedegården, Valdemar Poulsensvej 4; tel. 75 82 08 33, 135 b.
Munkebjerg Hotel, Munkebjergvej 125; tel. 75 72 35 00, 402 b.
Scandic Hotel Australia, Dæmningen 6; tel. 75 82 43 11, 133 b.

Golfhotel, Randersvej 2; tel. 86 61 02 22, 250 b.   **Viborg**
Kongenshus, Skivevej 142, in Daugbjerg; tel. 97 54 81 25, 19 b.
Palads Hotel, Skt. Mathiasgade 5; tel. 86 62 37 00, 120 b.
Rindsholm Kro, Gl. Århusvej 323, in Rindsholm; tel. 86 63 90 44, 14 b.

Hotel Nord; tel. 510 61, 21 b.   **Vidareidi**
                                                                                (Greenland)
Vinderup, Nørregade 2; tel. 97 44 13 66, 35 b.   **Vinderup**

Kong Valdemar, Algade 101; tel. 53 77 00 95, 125 b.   **Vordingborg**

Information

The Danish Tourist Board produces a wide range of publications in English.   Danish Tourist
"Denmark Holiday Planning Guide" will help those who have never visited   Board
the country to plan their trip. It lists local offices which also publish useful
literature. Zealand, Funen and Jutland also produce regional guides.

Tourist Information
Bernstorffgade 1, DK-1577 Copenhagen V;
tel. 33 11 13 25, fax 33 93 46 69

Information

Information abroad

Australia	Danish Tourist Board 60 Market Street, P.O. Box 4531, Melbourne, Victoria 3001
Canada	Danish Tourist Board P.O. Box 115, Station "N", Toronto, Ontario M8V 3S4
United Kingdom	Danish Tourist Board 55 Sloane Street, London SW1X 9SY; tel. 01891 600109
United States of America	Scandinavian National Tourist Offices 655 Third Avenue, 18th Floor, New York, NY 10017; tel. (212) 949 2333
	Scandinavian Tourist Board (Denmark/Sweden) 150 North Michigan Avenue, Suite 2110, Chicago, IL 60601; tel. (312) 899 1121
	Scandinavian Tourist Board (Denmark/Sweden) 8929 Wilshire Boulevard, Suite 300, Beverly Hills, CA 90211; tel. (213) 854 1549

Information within Denmark

The Danish Tourist Board has branch offices in holiday resorts and the larger towns, some of which close down in the winter months. The staff are extremely helpful and all speak English as well as a number of other languages. If writing for information, simply address the letter: Tourist Bureau, Postcode + Town, Denmark.

Åbenrå	Turistbureau H. P. Hanssens Gade 5 DK-6200 Åbenrå. Tel. 74 62 35 00
Ærø (island)	Turistbureau Torvet, DK-5970 Ærøskøping. Tel. 62 52 13 00
Åkirkeby	See Rønne (Bornholm)
Ålborg	Turistbureau Osterå 8, DK-9000 Ålborg. Tel. 98 12 60 22
Allinge	See Rønne (Bornholm)
Als (island)	See Sønderborg
Århus	Turistbureau Rådhuset DK-8000 Århus C. Tel. 86 12 16 00
Assens	Turistbureau Ladegårdsgade DK-5610 Assens. Tel. 64 71 20 31
Augustenborg	Turistbureau DK-6440 Augustenborg. Tel. 74 47 17 20
Billund	Turistbureau DK-7190 Billund. Tel. 75 33 19 26

Turistbureau
Adelgade 26
DK-5400 Bogense
Tel. 64 81 20 44

Bogense

Turistbureau
Storegade 23
DK-6310 Broager
Tel. 74 44 11 00

Broager

Turistbureau
Bredgade 88
DK-9700 Brønderslev
Tel. 98 80 17 88

Brønderslev

Turistbureau
Kongensgade 5
DK-6070 Christiansfeld
Tel. 74 56 16 30

Christiansfeld

Turistbureau
(Wonderful Copenhagen)
Bernstorffsgade 1
DK-1577 Copenhagen V
Tel. 33 11 13 25
Fax. 33 93 49 69

**Copenhagen/
København**

Turistbureau
Torvet 9–11
DK-8400 Ebeltoft
Tel. 86 34 14 00

Ebeltoft

Turistbureau
Skolegade 33
DK-6700 Esbjørg
Tel. 75 12 55 99

Esbjerg

Turistbureau
Havnegade 2
DK-5600 Fåborg
Tel. 62 61 07 07

Fåborg

Turistbureau
DK-6720 Fanø
Tel. 75 16 26 00

Fanø (island)

See Tórshavn

Faroes

Turistbureau
Østergade 1
DK-9690 Fjerritslev
Tel. 98 21 16 55

Fjerritslev

Turistbureau
Axeltorv
DK-7000 Fredericia
Tel. 75 92 13 77

Fredericia

Turistbureau
Brotorvet 1
DK-9900 Frederikshavn
Tel. 98 42 32 66

Frederikshavn

Information

Frederikssund	Turistbureau Østergade 3 DK-3600 Frederikssund Tel. 42 31 06 85
Frederiksværk	Turistbureau Gjethusgade 5 DK-3300 Frederiksværk Tel. 47 77 06 07
Gedser	Turistbureau Stationsvej 7 DK-4874 Gedser Tel. 53 87 90 41
Gilleleje	Turistbureau Gilleleje Hovedgade 6F DK-3250 Gilleleje Tel. 48 30 01 74
Grenå	Turistbureau Torvet 1 DK-8500 Grenå Tel. 86 32 12 00
Gråsten	Turistbureau Ahlefeldvej 4 DK-6300 Gråsten Tel. 74 65 09 55
Greenland	See Nuuk/Godthåb
Gudhjem	See Rønne (Bornholm)
Haderslev	Turistbureau Sønderbro 3 DK-6100 Haderslev Tel. 74 52 55 50
Hals	Turistbureau Torvet DK-9370 Hals Tel. 98 25 14 33
Hanstholm	Turistbureau Bytorvet DK-7730 Hanstholm Tel. 97 96 12 19
Helsingør	Turistbureau Havnepladsen 3 DK-3000 Helsingør Tel. 49 21 13 33
Herning	Turistbureau Bredgade 2 DK-7400 Herning Tel. 97 12 44 22
Hillerød	Turistbureau Slotsgade 52 DK-3400 Hillerød Tel. 42 26 28 52

Turistbureau
Vestergade 32
DK-9850 Hirtshals
Tel. 98 94 22 20

Hirtshals

Turistbureau
Markedsgade 9
DK-9800 Hjørring
Tel. 98 92 02 32

Hjørring

Turistbureau
Store Torv
DK-9500 Hobro
Tel. 98 52 56 66

Hobro

Turistbureau
Nygade 8
DK-4300 Holbæk
Tel. 53 43 11 31

Holbæk

Turistbureau
Brostræde 2
DK-7500 Holstebro
Tel. 97 42 57 00

Holstebro

Turistbureau
Søndergade 26
DK-8700 Horsens
Tel. 75 62 38 22

Horsens

Turistbureau
Nørregade 22
DK-3390 Hundested
Tel. 42 33 77 88

Hundested

Turistbureau
Gormsgade 19
DK-7300 Jelling
Tel. 75 87 13 01

Jelling

Turistbureau
Odelsgade 17
DK-7130 Juelsminde
Tel. 75 69 33 13

Juelsminde

Turistbureau
Volden 12
DK-4400 Kalundborg
Tel. 53 51 09 15

Kalundborg

Turistbureau
Strandgade 5A
DK-5300 Kerteminde
Tel. 65 32 11 21

Kerteminde

See Copenhagen

København

Turistbureau
Vestergade 1
DK-6400 Køge
Tel. 53 65 58 00

Køge

259

Information

Kolding	Turistbureau Akseltorv 8 DK-6000 Kolding Tel. 75 53 21 00
Korsør	Turistbureau Nygade 7 DK-4220 Korsør Tel. 53 57 08 03
Læsø (island)	Læso Turistbureau Færgeterminalen DK-9950 Vesterø Havn Tel. 98 49 92 42
Lemvig	Turistbureau Toldbodgade 4 DK-7620 Lemvig Tel. 97 82 00 77
Løgstør	Turistbureau Sønderport 2A DK-9670 Løgstør Tel. 98 67 23 99
Løgumkloster	See Tønder
Løkken	Turistbureau Vrenstedvej 6 DK-9480 Løkken Tel. 98 99 10 09
Mariager	Turistbureau Torvet 4B DK-9550 Mariager Tel. 98 54 13 77
Maribo	Turistbureau DK-4930 Maribo Tel. 53 88 04 96
Middelfart	Turistbureau Havnegade 10 DK-5500 Middelfart Tel. 64 41 17 88
Møn (island)	Møns Turistbureau Storegade 5 DK-4780 Stege Tel. 55 81 44 11
Mors (Island)	Morsø Turistforening DK-7900 Nykøbing M Tel. 97 72 04 88
Næstved	Turistbureau Købmagergade 20A DK-4700 Næstved Tel. 53 72 11 22
Nakskov	Turistbureau Axeltorv 6 DK-4900 Nakskov Tel. 53 92 21 72

See Rønne (Bornholm)   **Neksø**

Nuuk Turistkontor   **Nuuk (Godthåb)**
P.O. Box 199
DK-3900 Nuuk
Tel. 29 92 27 00

Turistbureau   **Nyborg**
Torvet 9
DK-5800 Nyborg
Tel. 65 31 02 80

Turistbureau   **Nykøbing F**
Østergade 2
DK-4800 Nykøping F
Tel. 54 85 13 03

See Mors (island)   **Nykøbing M**

Turistbureau   **Odense**
Rådhuset
DK-5000 Odense C
Tel. 66 12 75 20

Turistbureau   **Randers**
Erik Menveds Plads 1
DK-8900 Randers
Tel. 86 42 44 77

Turistbureau   **Ribe**
Torvet 3–5
DK-6760 Ribe
Tel. 75 42 15 00

Turistbureau   **Ringkøbing**
Torvet
DK-6950 Ringkøping
Tel. 97 32 00 31

Turistbureau   **Ringsted**
Sct Bendtsgade 10
DK-4100 Ringsted
Tel. 53 61 34 00

Turistbureau   **Rødby**
Willersgaard, Vestergade 1
Dk-4970 Rødby
Tel. 54 60 21 10

Rømø Turistbureau   **Rømø (island)**
Havnebyvej 30, Tvismark
DK-6792 Rømø
Tel. 74 75 51 30

Bornholms Velkomscenter   **Rønne**
Ndr. Kystvej 3
DK-3700 Rønne
Tel. 56 95 95 00

Roskilde-Egnens Turistbureau   **Roskilde**
Gullandsstræde 15
DK-4000 Roskilde
Tel. 42 35 27 00

Information

Rudkøping

Turistbureau
Torvet 5
DK-5900 Rudkøping. Tel. 62 51 35 05

Samsø (island)

Samsø Turistforenings Bureau
DK-8305 Samsø. Tel. 86 59 14 00

Silkeborg

Turistbureau
Torvet 9
DK-8600 Silkeborg. Tel. 86 82 19 11

Skælskør

Turistbureau
Algade 7
DK-4230 Skælskør. Tel. 53 59 53 74

Skagen

Turistbureau
Sct. Laurentiivej 18
DK-9990 Skagen. Tel. 98 44 13 77

Skanderborg

Turistbureau
Bibliotekstorvet 2
DK-8660 Skanderborg. Tel. 86 52 21 36

Skive

Skive-egnens Turistbureau
Østerbro 7
DK-7800 Skive. Tel. 97 52 32 66

Slagelse

Turistbureau
Løvegade 7
DK-4200 Slagelse. Tel. 53 52 22 06

Sønderborg
(island of Als)

Turistbureau
Rådhustorvet 7
DK-6400 Sønderborg. Tel. 74 42 35 55

Sorø

Turistbureau
Rolighed 5C
DK-4180 Sorø. Tel. 53 63 02 69

Stege

See Mon (island)

Struer

Turistbureau
Rådhuspladsen
DK-7600 Struer. Tel. 97 85 07 95

Svaneke

See Rønne (Bornholm)

Svendborg

Sydfyns Turistbureau
Centrumspladsen. DK-5700 Svendborg
Tel. 62 21 09 80

Thisted

Turistbureau
Det Gamle Rådhus
Store Torv 6
DK-7700 Thisted. Tel. 97 92 19 00

Turistbureau
Torvet 1
DK-6270 Tønder. Tel. 74 72 12 20

Turistbureau
Kunningarstovan
FR-100 Tórshavn (Föroyar). Tel. (002 98) 157 88

Turistbureau
Torvet 5
DK-6800 Varde. Tel. 75 22 32 22

Turistbureau
Bånegardspladsen
DK-6600 Vejen. Tel. 75 36 26 96

Turistbureau
Søndergade 14
DK-7100 Vejle. Tel. 75 82 19 55

Turistbureau
Nytorv 9
DK-8800 Viborg. Tel. 86 61 16 66

Turistbureau
Glambæksvej 3
DK-4760 Vordinborg. Tel. 53 77 02 17

Insurance

Visitors are strongly advised to ensure that they have adequate holiday
insurance including loss or damage to luggage, loss of currency and
jewellery.

Under European Union regulations British and Irish visitors to Denmark are
entitled to medical care under the Danish social insurance scheme on the
same basis as Danish citizens. Before leaving home they should get leaflet
T5 "Travellers Guide to Health", available from public libraries, travel
agents, doctor's surgeries and post offices, which includes form E111 and
advice about completing it. The form must be stamped at a post office in
the UK before setting off to Denmark.
These arrangements may not cover the full cost of medical treatment, and
it is advisable, therefore, even for EU citizens, to take out short-term health
insurance. Visitors from non-EU countries should certainly do so.

Medical
insurance

Visitors travelling by car should ensure that their insurance is comprehensive and covers use of the vehicle in Europe. Although a Green Card is not
compulsory for EU countries it is advisable to have one nevertheless.

Vehicles

See also Travel Documents.

Language

English is very widely spoken in Denmark, making it possible to get by just
about everywhere without knowing any Danish, but it is always useful –
and certainly friendlier – to know some of the main words and phrases.

Along with Swedish and Norwegian, Danish belongs to the northern-
Germanic Scandinavian group of languages. These all tend to use suffixes

and, for example, indicate the definite article by means of an ending. In Danish the vowels æ, ø and å come at the end of the alphabet after z.

Strongly influenced by Low German and Anglo Saxon, until the 10th c. Danish differed very little from the other Scandinavian languages. It is particularly closely related to Norwegian, but its pronunciation is softer and less clipped, with frequent use of the glottal stop and a tendency to "swallow" part of a word.

The pronunciation of some letters differs from English: d after a vowel is softened to the sound of th in "the", or may be mute; g is hard as in "go", but at other times is like the ch in "loch" or mute; j is like y in "yes"; r is a soft sound, not trilled; v before a consonant or at the end of a word becomes a vowel like the French u in "lune"; ej is like the vowel sound in "high"; æ is like a in "take"; ø is like eu in French "deux"; å has the vowel sound of "awe".

Useful words and phrases	**English**	**Danish**
	English	engelsk
	Englishman/woman	englænder
	Englishwoman	engelsk kvinde
	England	England
	Danish	dansk
	Do you speak . . .	taler De . . .
	English	engelsk
	I don't understand	jeg forstår ikke . . .
	yes	ja, jo
	no	nej
	please	værsågod
	thank you	tak
	thank you very much	mange tak
	good morning	god morgen
	hello (good day)	god dag
	good evening	god aften
	good night	got nat
	goodbye	farvel
	man, gents	herre
	woman, ladies	dame, kvinde
	where is . . .?	hvor er . . .?
	the . . . road	gaden
	the road to . . .	gaden vejen til . . .
	the . . . square	. . . pladsen
	the church	kirken
	the museum	museet
	when?	hvornår?
	open	åben
	the town hall	rådhuset
	the post office	posthuset
	a bank	bank
	the station	banegården, stationen
	a hotel	hotel
	overnight accommodation	overnatning
	I would like	jeg vil gerne
	a room	et værelse
	a single room	enkelt værelse
	a double room	dobbelt værelse
	with bath	med bad
	without bath	uden bad
	the key	nøglen

English	Danish	
the toilet	toilettet	
a doctor	læge	
to the right	til højre (til=to the)	
to the left	til venstre	
straight on	lige ud	
above	oppe, ovenpå	
below	nede	
old	gammel	
new	ny	
what does . . . cost?	hvad koster . . .?	
expensive	dyr	
Halt	Stop	Road signs
Customs	Told	
Watch out	Pas på	
Slow	Langsom	
One-way street	Ensrettet	
No entry	Ingen indkørsel	
Road works	Vejarbejde	
mountain	bjerg	Landscape and townscape
hill	høj, bakke	
ridge	ås	
valley	dal	
river	elv	
stream	å	
waterfall	foss	
sound, strait	sund	
water	vand	
beach	strand	
cliff	klint	
island	ø	
forest	skov	
moor	mose	
marsh, bog	sump	
town	by	
church	kirke	
tower	tårn	
castle, manor house	slot	
garden, park	have	
street	gade	
highway, road	landevej	
road	vej	
(market) square	torv, plads	
bridge	bro	
railway	jernbane	
ferry	færge	
See Food and Drink		Eating out

Medical Assistance

All foreign visitors who are in Denmark for a limited period are entitled to free medical or hospital treatment if they are taken ill, a previously diagnosed chronic condition suddenly deteriorates or they are involved in an accident. Most hotels have a doctor they can call on and camp sites, youth hostels and information bureaux can also help with finding a medical practitioner.

The 24-hour emergency number throughout Denmark which can be used to summon an ambulance is 112. There is also always a doctor on call outside surgery hours; for information contact the FALCK organisation (see Emergency Services). Visitors from EU countries should present the doctor with their Form E 111 (see Insurance) but if a charge is made this will be refunded before they leave Denmark. The relevant address can be obtained from the local tourist bureau (see Information).

Chemists' shops in Denmark are essentially dispensaries and are listed in the Danish equivalent of the Yellow Pages under "Apoteker". They have the same opening hours as other shops but in the larger towns and cities there will usually be several which open round the clock.

Motoring

Breakdowns	Breakdown services are operated, for a charge, by the FALCK organisation and DAHU (*Dansk Authjælp*). For telephone numbers see Emergency Services. The Danish Automobile Club, FDM, can also prove helpful but does not operate a breakdown service.
FDM	Forende Danske Motorejere (FDM) Firskovvej 32, DK-2800 Lyngby; tel. 45 93 08 00
Fuel	All petrol stations have unleaded (*blyfry*) petrol (*benzin*), both super and regular. On safety grounds vehicles are not allowed to carry spare cans of gas/fuel. Garages are usually open until 6pm. Those on motorways are open round the clock, and the same applies to many in the main towns. Outside opening hours it is also possible to fill up, using 100 Kroner bills, at the self-service automats.
Speed limits	The speed limit is 50kph/31mph in built-up areas, 80kph/50mph on main roads elsewhere, 110kph/69mph on motorways, and 70kph/44mph for vehicles with trailers. Speeding, even slightly over the limit, is liable to a heavy on-the-spot fine and anyone unable to pay will have their vehicle impounded by the police.
Traffic rules and regulations	Denmark has good motorways (*motorvej*; toll-free) and A roads (*hovedvej*) with relatively little heavy traffic (see also Euroroutes). The rule of the road in Denmark, as in most of Europe, is drive on the right and overtake on the left. Vehicles approaching intersections from the right have priority, but the white broken triangles ("shark's teeth") at junctions mean the crossing traffic has priority. The driver and all passengers, front and back, must wear seat-belts and motor cyclists must wear helmets. Every vehicle is required to carry a red warning triangle. Cars and motorbikes must have their headlights on at all times, dipped or undipped, day and night, and anyone not doing so is liable to a fine. Cars with right-hand drives must have their headlamps covered with an opaque material or beam deflectors, available from motoring organisations and some garages. See also Insurance, Travel Documents.
Drinking and driving	Driving with more than 0.8 millilitres of alcohol in the blood is punishable by a fine, loss of licence or even imprisonment.

Opening Times

Banks	Banks in Copenhagen are open for business Mon. to Wed. and Fri. 9.30am–4pm, and Thurs. 9.30am–6pm. Many bureaux de change are open until 10pm. Opening times in the provinces vary from place to place and some banks close from noon to 2pm.

All shops are open Mon.–Fri. 9am to 5.30pm. On Sat. shops close at noon and department stores at 2pm except on the first Sat. in the month when all shops and stores stay open until 5pm. In addition all shops may open for another ten hours each week either for late-night shopping or between noon and 2pm on Sat. In the smaller places shops close during the lunch-hour.

Department stores and shops

Most museums are open daily; some close on Mon. Opening hours may be longer in summer (Apr.–Oct.) than in winter, when the museum may open only at weekends. Some manor houses open only during Jul. and Aug., while outdoor museums and entertainments (such as Tivoli) open in summer months only. Some sights and parks are open all year, but with shorter hours in winter. Churches in towns and villages are likely to be open every day but have shorter opening hours, and may not welcome sightseers on Sun. It is worth checking with the local tourist office before setting off.

Museums, etc.

See Motoring

Filling stations

See Post, Telephone

Post offices

The Tourist Office in Copenhagen is open from mid-Sept. until end Apr. Mon.–Fri. 9am–5pm and Sat. 9am–2pm; during May, daily, from 9am–6pm and from Jun. to mid-Sept., daily 9am–8pm. In the rest of Denmark they open for longer hours during the summer months, including evenings and weekends.

Tourist Offices

Post

Post offices are generally open from Mon.–Fri. 9am or 10am to 5pm, some open on Saturday mornings until noon. Post boxes are bright red

A Danish letter-box

and, like post offices, are marked by the sign of a bugle and crossed arrows surmounted by a crown. Post offices can also be used for sending telegrams and making telephone calls (see Telephone).

There is a single postal rate for postcards and for letters up to 20 gr. within Denmark, to other Scandinavian countries, Austria, Switzerland and member states of the European Union. Stamps can also be bought at the same time as postcards or from stamp machines.

Public Holidays

New Year's Day: January 1st
Maundy Thursday
Good Friday
Easter Monday
Day of Prayer: 4th Friday after Easter
Ascension Day
Whit Monday
Christmas Day and Boxing Day

On June 5th, Constitution Day, shops and office close at noon and banks are closed all day.
On Christmas Day and New Year's Eve (December 31st) banks and many offices close for the whole day but shops close at noon, 2pm or 4pm.

Greenland also has public holidays on January 6th, June 21st (National Day) and December 24th and 31st.

The Faroes have their National Day as a public holiday on July 29th, Olaf's Day.

Radio and Television

News on
Radio Denmark

The news in English is broadcast on Radio Denmark's Radio One (90.8 MHz VHF) at 8.10am Monday to Friday. It is also possible to pick up BBC programmes on longwave and the World Service, as well as the American networks in Europe.

Television

Danish Television transmits from 7.30am to 11.30pm. Foreign films are shown in their original language with Danish sub-titles.

Rail and Bus

DSB

Denmark has a rail network of about 2600km/1626 miles. Some 2000km/1243 miles are operated by Danish State Railways (DSB) which is also responsible for 210km/130 miles of ferry routes.

The rail network is complemented, mainly in areas with no train service, by bus lines operated either by DSB or the private sector.

Intercity
services

DSB Intercity services link most towns in Denmark, running hourly on the major routes. Copenhagen is also served by ultra-fast trains, or "lyntog".

Reservations

Reservations are required for "lyntog" trains, for all Intercity trains crossing the Great Belt, and for places in sleeping cars and couchettes.

DSB fare
reductions

Fares are based on a zone system and there are cheap day tickets, for example, which offer a discount on 2nd class travel for journeys taken on

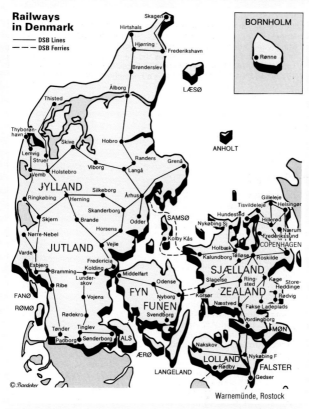

Railways in Denmark
—— DSB Lines
- - - DSB Ferries

BORNHOLM

Rønne

Skagen

Hirtshals

Hjørring

Frederikshavn

Brønderslev

Ålborg

LÆSØ

Thisted

Thyborøn-havn

Skive Hobro

ANHOLT

Lemvig

Struer

Viborg Randers Grenå

Holstebro

Vemb Langå

JYLLAND Silkeborg

Ringkøbing Herning Århus

Skanderborg

Gilleleje

Tisvildeleje Helsingør

Skjern Brande Odder SAMSØ

Hundested Hillerød

Nykøbing Sj Nærum

Nørre-Nebel Horsens Frederikssund

Varde Vejle Kolby Kås COPENHAGEN

JUTLAND Holbæk

Fredericia Kalundborg Tølløse Roskilde

Esbjerg Kolding SJÆLLAND

Bramming Middelfart Odense Slagelse Ringsted Køge Store-Heddinge

Lunder-skov Nyborg ZEALAND

Ribe FYN Korsør Rødvig

FANØ Vojens Næstved Fakse Ladeplads

RØMØ FUNEN

Rødekro Svendborg Vordingborg MØN

Tønder Tinglev Nakskov Nykøbing F

Padborg Sønderborg ALS Rødby FALSTER

ÆRØ LOLLAND Gedser

LANGELAND

© Baedeker

Warnemünde, Rostock

Tuesday, Wednesday or Thursday over at least 13 zones (about 100km/62 miles). Children under 4 years of age travel free; between the ages of 4 and 12 they travel for 50% of the adult fare. There are also special discounts for young people aged between 11 and 25, for people over 65 and groups of three or more adults travelling together. (See Travel Discounts.)

Inter-Rail cards and Eurailpass are valid in Denmark and there is an Inter-Rail Centre at Copenhagen Central Station (see Youth Hostels for Inter Rail Point Centres). The Nordic Tourist Ticket which used to operate throughout Scandinavia has been replaced by the ScanRail Ticket. There is also a national railcard, the "Danmarkskort", which covers travel for a month on all DSB trains and ferries within Denmark.
For further information contact the Danish Tourist Board (see Information) or, in Britain, Scandinavian Seaways who act as the DSB's representatives (see Ferries).

Railcards

Restaurants

Denmark has a good choice of restaurants in addition to those found in the big hotels. They cover the whole spectrum of eating out, from simple

Restaurants

traditional local fare to sophisticated gourmet cuisine in elegant surroundings. Many of them were once inns, hence the name *kro* (see Food and Drink).

For anyone in search of a quick snack or a really inexpensive meal there are milk bars and cafeterias as well as the Danish version of pubs and the special smørrebrød shops. Restaurant prices include a service charge of 15% and 22% VAT. The list below is a selection.

Restaurants in Åbenrå
Landbohjem, Søndertorv 3
Sølyst Kro, Flensborgvej 164
Viking, H.P. Hanssens Gade 43

Ærøskøbing
Landbogården, Vestergade 54
Mumm, Søndergade 12
Pilebækken, Vestergade 55

Åkirkeby
Christianshøy Kroen, Segenvej 48

Ålborg
Bondestuen, Vingårdgade 5
Brigaderen, Vesterbro 77
Duus Vinkjælder (in Jens Bangs Stenhus), Østerågade 9
Ellen Marsvin (wine bar), Østergade 25
Faklen, Jomfru Anegade 21
Fyrtøjet, Jomfru Anegade 17
Kniv og Gaffel, Maren Tureis Gade 10
Penny Lane (fish restaurant), Sankelmarksgade 9
Rio Bravo, Østerågade 27

Århus
Europa, Europaplads 6
De fire Årstider, Vestergade 39
Gammel Åbyhøj, Bakke Allé 1
Greven & Baronen, Åboulevarden 60
Guldhornet, Banegårdsplads 10
Kroen-i-Krogen, Banegårdsplads 4
Munkestuen, Klostertorv 5
René, Frue Kirkeplads 1
Windsor Pub, Skolebakken 17

Assens
Aborghus Kro, Middelfartvej 55

Augustenborg
Augustenborghus, Østergade 6
Skipperkroen, by the marina

Ballen
Dokken, Strandvejen 83

Bronderslev
Borgerstuen Brunderhus, Nørrengade 30–36

Christiansfeld
Den Gamle Grænsekro, Koldingvej 51

Copenhagen
Alsace (French), Ny Østergade 9
Bernstorff, Bernstorffsgade 7
Den Grønne Kælder (vegetarian), Klarboderne 10
Det Lille Apotek, Store Kannikestræde 15
Havfruen, Nyhavn 39
Kong Hans, Vingårdsstræde 6
Krogs Fiske-Restaurant, Gammelstrand 38
Leonora Christine, Nyhavn 9
Lumskebugten, Esplanaden 21
Napoli (Italian), Købmagergade 63
Nouvelle, Gammelstrand 34
Skipperkroen, Nyhavn 27
Sorte Ravn, Nyhavn 14

Gasten, Jernbanegade 26 Hvimde Kok, Enggyden 2 Rådhuskronen, Adelgade 28	**Ebeltoft**
Den Røde Okse, Tarphagevej 9 Korskroen, Skads Hovedvej 116 Kunstpavillonen, Havnegade 20 Palads Restaurant, Skolegade 14 Parken, Søvej 9	**Esbjerg**
Det Lille Apotek, Torvet 17 Mosegård, Nabyden 31 Ved Brønden, Torvet/Tårngade 5	**Fåborg**
Gefion, Hovedgaden 35	**Fakse Ladeplads**
Fjerritslev Kro, Østergade 2	**Ferritslev**
Den Lille Hornblæser, Jyllandsgade 53 Håndværkeren, Vendersgade 61 Hvilested Kro, Fredericiavej 462	**Fredericia**
Det Gule Pakhus, Tordenskjoldsgade 14 Færgekroen, Lodsgade 8 La Bagatelle, Havnegade 7 Gastronomen, Jernbanegade 7 Møllehuset, Skovalleen 45 Vægteren og Vinkiælderen (music), Havengade 8	**Frederikshavn**
Færgekroen Bi-Lidt, Strandvejen 2 Kalvø, Kalvøen	**Frederikssund**
Færgegården, Færgevej 1	**Fynshav**
Mariknakroen, at the marina	**Gedser**
Gilleleje Havn, Havnevej 14 Karen og Marie, Nørdre Havnevej	**Gilleleje**
Harresø Kro, Hærvejen 147	**Givskud**
Den Gamle Kro, Slotsgade 6	**Gråsten**
Det Gyldne Krus, Lillegade 18 Drop-inn, Havnevejen 10	**Grenå**
Bokulhus, Bokulvej 4 Tagskægget, Jernkåsvej	**Gudhjem**
Hotel Harmonien, Gåskærgade 19 Hotel Norden, Storegade 55	**Haderslev**
Hotel Hanstholm, Byvej 2	**Hanstholm**
Kommandørgården, in Mølby	**Havneby**
Færgegården, Stengade 81B Hos Anker, Bramstræde 1 Klostercafeen, Skt. Annægade 35	**Helsingør**
Hotel Hammerum, Jernbanegade 8–10	**Herning**
Slotsherrens Kro, Frederiksborg Slot 5 Slotskroen, Slotsgade 67	**Hillerød**

Restaurants

Hirtshals Fyrklit, Kystvejen 10
Hirtshals Kro, by the harbour

Hjørring Messing Jens, Jernbanegade 19
Skammekrogen, Østergade 38

Hobro Teaterrestauranten, Vestergade 4

Holbæk Linden, Markedspladsen 9

Holstebro Den lille Havfrue, Nørregade 26
Jensen's Bøfhus, Brotorvet
Rådhuskælderen, Rådhusstræde
Tinghuset, Store Torv

Horsens Eydes Kælder, Søndergade 17–19
Kronborg, Åboulevarden 4–6
Lille Heimdal, Rædesgade 8–10
Los Chicos, Smedetorvet 8–10

Jelling Hos Thyra, Vejlevej 24
Skovdal Kro, Fårupvej 23

Juelsminde Likniepavillionen, Færgehavnen

Kalundborg Fjorden, Banegårdspladsen
Slotskælderen, Kordilgade 40

Kastrup Allékroen, Alléen 54
SAS Royal Restaurant, at the airport

Kerteminde Rusen, Strandgade 2
Varmestuen, Dosseringen

Klampenborg Peter Lieps Hus, Dyrehaven 8

København See Copenhagen

Køge Richters Gård, Vestergade 16
Rio Bravo, Skt. Gertrudsstræde 2

Kolding Bacchus Bistro, Akseltorv 5
Kryb-i-ly Kro, Landevej 160

Korsør Skovhuset, Skovvej 120
Sølyst, Havnepladsen 13

Lemvig Marina, Vinkelhagevej

Løkken Peter Bådsmand, Sdr. Strandvej

Lyngby Duetten, Lyngby Storcenter 62
Oasen, Likørstræde 4

Mariager Landgangen, Oxendalen 1

Marstal Den Gamle Vingård, Kirkestræde

Middelfart Det Gyldne Marsvin, Østergade 36
Kongebrogården, Kongebrovej 63

Næstved Det Røde Pakhus, Riddergade 1
Trolden, Jernbanegade 21

Vinkælderen, Axeltorv 9   **Nakskov**

Krogården, Langelinie 11   **Nordby** (Fanø)

Danehofkroen, Slotspladsen   **Nyborg**

Stegepanden, Torvet 19   **Nykøbing Falster**
Taghaven, Torvet 3

Apoteker-Hjørnet, Algade 33   **Nykøbing**
Lyngkroen, Rørvigvej 217   **Sjælland**

Den Gamle Kro, Overgade 23   **Odense**
Den Grimme Ælling, Hans Jensens Stræde 1
Det Gyldne Får, Elmegårdsvej 3A
Knudsens Gård, Hunderupgade 2
Målet, Jernbanegade 17
Næsbyhoved Skov, Kanalvej 52
Odense Congress Center, Ørbækvej 350
Sortebro Kro, Sejerskovvej 20
Under Lindetræet, Ramsherred 2

Turisthotel, Torvegade 1   **Oksbøl**

Skipperkroen, by the harbour   **Præstø**

Mundskænken, Slotsventret   **Randers**
Munken, Brødregade 23
Storkereden, Kirketorvet 2
Tronborg, Grenåvej 2

Hvidding Kro, Ribevej 58   **Ribe**
Weis Stue, Torvet 2

Røgind Kro, Røgind   **Ringkøping**

Apotekergården, Nørregade 12   **Ringsted**

Rådhuskroen, Nørregade 2   **Rønne**
Skovly, Nyker Strandvej 40

Club 42, Skomagergade 42   **Roskilde**
Gastronetten, Karen Olsdatterstræde 9
Palæcafeen, Stænertorvet 8

Æventyrmølen, Spodsbjergvej 247   **Rudkøping**
Degnehaven, Spodsbjergvej 277

Henrik Ibsen, Vestergade 23   **Sæby**

Forsamlingsbygningen, Vestergade 26   **Silkeborg**
La Strada, Torvet 1
Underhuset, Torvet 7

Hesteskoen, Algade 15C   **Skælskør**

Skagen Fish Restaurant, Fiskehuskajen   **Skagen**
Trekosten, Højensvej 4, in Gamle Skagen

Eldorado, Nordbanevej 23   **Skive**

Arnehavehus, Slagelse Lystskov   **Slagelse**
Sixpence Pub, Jernbanegade 10

Sønderborg	Bella Italia, Lille Rådhusgade 33
	Byens Smørrebrød, Perlegade
Sorø	Skovperlen, Slagelsevej 105
Stege	The Laughing Duck, Møllebrøndsstræde 2
Struer	City, Østergade 36
Svendborg	Spisehus, Korsgade 1
	Stella Maris, Kogtvedvænget 3
Tisvildeleje	Bakkefrydgård Bodega, Godhavensvej 13
Tønder	Hotel Tønderhus, Jomfrustien 1
Vejle	Banketten, Kirkegade 3
	Paladskroen, Ved Anlægget 14
	Rådhuskroen, Rådhustorvet
Viborg	Palæ, Skt. Mathiasgade 78
	Salonen, Radersvej
Vinderup	Sevel Kro, Sevel
Vordingborg	Snekken, by the harbour
	Pizzeria Roma, Algade

Riding

There are riding stables throughout Denmark where horses can be hired or arrangements can be made for horse-drawn wagon rides. Some riding schools, especially those in Jutland and Zealand, also offer holiday accommodation and others cater specifically for children and young people. Anyone planning to go horseback riding across country should check on the route beforehand since certain areas may be closed to them.

Sailing

Danish waters offer plenty of opportunities for sailing. There are some 600 large and small harbours around the islands, including Bornholm, and the boating fraternity can chose between a variety of courses, whether in open water on the Kattegat and the Baltic or in the more sheltered waters of the South Funen Sea between Zealand and Lolland/Falster, or the Limfjord in North Jutland.

Sailing boats and cruisers fitted out with all the requisite safety equipment, navigational aids, crockery, cutlery, etc., are available to rent in many places. Rental is by the week and prices are much cheaper off-season. Under Danish law all rented boats must be licensed by the appropriate authorities, and it is advisable to check that this has been done before signing the rental agreement.

Regattas — The two big regattas in which many foreign vessels take part in May/June every year are those round Funen (information from: Odense Sejlklub, Heltzengade 4, DK-5000 Odense; tel. 66 14 88 07) and round Zealand (information from: Helsingør Amatör Sejlklub, Standpromenaden 6, DK-3000 Helsingør; tel. 49 21 15 67).

"Round Zealand" sailing regatta

An elegant shop in Copenhagen

Shopping

Souvenirs   The Danes have elevated design to a fine art and the beautifully crafted objects they produce combine the timeless appeal of quality with clearcut modern line. Copenhagen stores such as Illums Bolighus, Magasin du Nord, Bing & Grøndal and Royal Copenhagen Porcelain are all good showcases for the great range of fine wares that Denmark has to offer. Silver jewellery and tableware, porcelain, Homegård glass, and other less expensive craft items such as amber, ceramics and candles are all particularly popular souvenirs of a trip to Denmark.

Sport

See separate headings for Bathing Beaches, Cycling, Diving, Fishing, Golf, Riding, Sailing, Windsurfing

Telephone

Telephone calls can be made from public telephone booths and post offices (see Post) using 1, 5 and 10 Dkr. coins, with an international call requiring at least 5 Dkr. There are also plenty of telephones which take phonecards.

Dialling codes   To call Denmark from abroad dial your own international code followed by 45; Greenland is 299 and the Faroe Islands 298.
To call abroad from Denmark dial 00 followed by your own country code (Australia 61, Canada 1, Eire 353, New Zealand 64, South Africa 27, United Kingdom 44, United States 1).

Time

Denmark observes Central European Time, one hour ahead of Greenwich Mean Time and six hours ahead of New York. Summer time (two hours ahead of GMT) is in force from the end of March/beginning of April until the end of September. The Faroes observe Western European summer time which is the same as Greenwich Mean Time. In Greenland the time is three hours ahead of Greenwich Mean Time.

Travel Discounts

Four towns in Denmark offer special reductions for visitors. The period of validity (eg perhaps only during school holidays), the number of days the pass is valid and the number of sights included, may vary each year.
Further information is available from the Danish Tourist Board in your home country or in the towns below.

The Copenhagen Card: valid for one, two or three days, gives the user unlimited travel by public transport, not only in the city but also in much of North Zealand, including Koge and Roskilde, and free admission to over 50 museums.
Alborg: a 3-day pass gives visitors free city transport, free entrance to some sights and activities, and reductions for food and drinks in some restaurants.
Arhus: a 7-day bus pass gives visitors free city transport and free entrance to 7 sights.
Odense: 1- or 2-day Adventure pass gives free transport in Odense and its suburbs, free admission to over a dozen museums and 6 swimming pools, a free tour of the town hall and reduced admission to other sights and activities.

Travel Documents

Provided their stay is for no longer than three months visitors to Denmark from other European Union countries, the United States, Canada, etc. simply require a valid passport.

Personal papers

As well as the vehicle registration papers, drivers of motor vehicles must carry their national driving licence and this must clearly indicate that it applies to a vehicle of the type being driven.

Motor vehicles

When to Go

Due to its maritime setting and temperate winds, Denmark enjoys relatively milder temperatures than the rest of continental Europe. This makes it a possible holiday destination, provided the main aim is not swimming and sunbathing, from early May until late October when the weather is often very pleasant. However the busiest month, which also coincides with the Danish school holidays, is July.

Westerly winds along the North Sea coast of Jutland bring higher rainfall than in the east of the country which gets dry sunny weather in summer, particularly when there is an east wind. Daytime temperatures from June to August are between 15 and 17°C/59 and 63°F but can get as high as 25°C/77°F. The North Sea warms up faster than the Baltic in the spring and early summer, thanks to the Gulf Stream and the effect of the tides, but does not reach the same high temperatures in the height of the summer. The light summer nights in the north of the country are at their longest in June. Unlike the rest of Scandinavia, Denmark does not have a skiing season in winter, so this is precisely the time of year when the cultural season in Copenhagen is in full swing.

Windsurfing

Windsurfing

Denmark's coastal waters are good for surfing, and the country has over 30 windsurfing schools, usually open from May to September. The courses include theory, navigation and safety components as well as windsurfing instruction:

Information about Danish operators, courses and hire of equipment is available from local tourist offices and the Danish Tourist Board (see Information).

Youth Hostels

Danish youth hostels take both young people and adults, and often also have family rooms. Bedlinen can be hired at the hostel; quilted sleeping bags are not permitted. To qualify for an overnight stay it is necessary to have an internationl youth hostel card issued by an affiliate of the International Youth Hostel Association. Guest cards can also be obtained locally.

The Danish Tourist Board publishes a free list of youth and family hostels in Denmark (see Information). Another, more detailed, listing is also available from:

Danmark Vandrerhjem (Denmark's Youth Hostels)
Vesterbrogade 39
DK-1620 Copenhagen V; tel. 31 31 36 12

Inter Rail
Point Centres

The YMCA AND YWCA also run two Inter Rail Point Centres with overnight accommodation in Copenhagen (for information: tel. 33 11 30 31).

Index

Index

Notes

Notes